Sports Law
and Legislation

Recent Titles in
Bibliographies and Indexes in Law and Political Science

Human Rights: An International and Comparative Law Bibliography
Julian R. Friedman and Marc I. Sherman, compilers and editors

Latin American Society and Legal Culture
Frederick E. Snyder, compiler

Congressional Committees, 1789-1982: A Checklist
Walter Stubbs, compiler

Criminal Justice Documents: A Selective, Annotated Bibliography of
U.S. Government Publications Since 1975
John F. Berens, compiler

Terrorism, 1980-1987: A Selectively Annotated Bibliography
Edward F. Mickolus, compiler, with Peter A. Flemming

Guide to the *Archiv für Sozialwissenschaft und Sozialpolitik* Group,
1904-1933
Regis A. Factor

Contemporary Canadian Politics: An Annotated Bibliography, 1970-1987
Gregory Mahler, compiler

The Executive Branch of the U.S. Government: A Bibliography
Robert Goehlert and Hugh Reynolds, compilers

Access to U.S. Government Information: Guide to Executive and
Legislative Authors and Authority
Jerrold Zwirn

Niccolò Machiavelli: An Annotated Bibliography of Modern Criticism
and Scholarship
Silvia Ruffo Fiore, compiler

From Erasmus to Tolstoy: The Peace Literature of Four Centuries; Jacob
ter Meulen's Bibliographies of the Peace Movement before 1899
Peter van den Dungen, compiler

Ocean Politics and Law: An Annotated Bibliography
James C. F. Wang

SPORTS LAW AND LEGISLATION

An Annotated Bibliography

Compiled by
JOHN HLADCZUK, SHARON HLADCZUK,
CRAIG SLATER, and ADAM EPSTEIN

Foreword by Glenn M. Wong

BIBLIOGRAPHIES AND INDEXES IN LAW
AND POLITICAL SCIENCE, NUMBER 15

GREENWOOD PRESS
New York • Westport, Connecticut • London

Library of Congress Cataloging-in-Publication Data

Sports law and legislation : an annotated bibliography / compiled by
  John Hladczuk . . . [et al.].
    p. cm.—(Bibliographies and indexes in law and political
  science, ISSN 0742-6909 ; no. 15)
  Includes indexes.
  ISBN 0-313-26499-6 (alk. paper)
  1. Sports—Law and legislation—United States—Bibliography.
  2. Sports—Law and legislation—Bibliography. I. Hladczuk, John.
  II. Series.
  KF3989.A1S66 1991
  016.34473'099—dc20   91-30204
  [016.34730499]

British Library Cataloguing in Publication Data is available.

Library of Congress Catalog Card Number: 91-30204
ISBN: 0-313-26499-6
ISSN: 0742-6909

First published in 1991

Greenwood Press, 88 Post Road West, Westport, CT 06881
An imprint of Greenwood Publishing Group, Inc.

Printed in the United States of America

The paper used in this book complies with the
Permanent Paper Standard issued by the National
Information Standards Organization (Z39.48-1984).

10 9 8 7 6 5 4 3 2 1

This book is dedicated to athletes—
of all ages—throughout the world.

CONTENTS

Foreword by Glenn M. Wong ix

Acknowledgements xi

Introduction xiii

Abbreviations xv

1. Agents 1
2. Amateur Athletics and Sports 11
3. Antitrust 19
4. Baseball 27
5. Basketball 49
6. Boxing 53
7. Chemical Substances 57
8. Civil Rights/Discrimination in Sports 65
9. Eligibility Rules 67
10. Football 69
11. Golf 79
12. Hockey 81
13. Injuries 85
14. Intercollegiate Athletics 101
15. International Sports Law 115
16. Liability 125
17. Medical Care 139

18. National Collegiate Athletic Association (NCAA)   143
19. Negligence   157
20. Olympics   161
21. Other Indoor Sports   165
22. Other Outdoor Sports   167
23. Professional Sports   181
24. Property   209
25. Recreation and Recreational Sports   215
26. Rights   219
27. Sex Discrimination   223
28. Spectators   231
29. Sport   237
30. Sports and the Law   251
31. Sports Broadcasting and Programming   265
32. Swimming   275
33. Taxation   277
34. Violence and Sports   291
35. Women in Sports   299

    Author Index   305
    Subject Index   319

FOREWORD

In the 1980's, the cigarette company Virginia Slims promoted the women's tennis tournament with the slogan "We've come a long way baby." This same phrase could be applied to the study of Sports Law. Back in the early 1970's when Sports Law courses were first being offered, there was very little in the way of research and publications relating to Sports Law. In 1970, according to John Hladczuk's bibliography, there were only 12 Sports Law related law review articles written that year (and 298 for the entire decade). The tremendous increase in the publication of articles began in the 1980's and has continued into the 1990's, with 50-60 articles being written in some years.

In some instances, topics or issues have had volumes written about them. For example, the important 1984 United States Supreme Court decision of _NCAA_ v. Board of Regents of The University of Oklahoma and University of Georgia Athletic Association produced 25 articles on the subject. At the other end of the spectrum are more obscure and/or less popular topics for research such as the Aerobic Fitness Industry, and "torts on the Courts" (tennis injuries), bowling alley tort liability, and wheelchair participation in road racing. This book investigates this wide range of topics in addition to presenting a section on International Sports Law, which presents articles regarding international athletic federation issues, international sport rules and sanctions, and regulations involving the international athlete. These law review articles also include sport law issues encountered in other countries.

Sports Law and Legislation: An Annotated Bibliography also contains law review articles on more recent sport law issues, such as drug testing and sex discrimination. These issues, as well as others, have contributed to the increase in the past 20 years in the amount of research performed and number of publications produced. One should not conclude, though, that Sports Law throughout the early 20th century. There were union-management issues in baseball, antitrust issues, formation of rival leagues and litigation which reached the U.S. Supreme Court in the seminal case of Federal Baseball Club of Baltimore, Inc. v. National League of Professional Baseball Clubs, which was decided in 1922. Ever since the start of baseball, foul balls and home runs have gone into the stands and have injured spectators. The oldest case involving this scenario was Edling v. Kansas City Baseball and Exhibition Company with the first law review article on the subject written in 1915. And while cases still go to court today regarding these same arguments, most decisions follow the precedents which were established in the early 1900's.

In the early 1980's, I advised people interested in Sports Law to read everything about Sports Law, including every law review article and book about sports law. With the proliferation of books and law review articles, this is no longer practical advice. Both the person interested in learning about Sport Law and the experienced practitioner will benefit from *Sports Law and Legislation: An Annotated Bibliography*. The novice can get an overview of sports law and read articles which are current and of interest to the reader. The experienced practitioner can keep up with developments in the field. This bibliography should be the starting point for every sports lawyer and sports law researcher.

Glenn M. Wong

ACKNOWLEDGEMENTS

We would like to thank our editor, Ms. Mildred Vasan, Dr. Jan Sadlak of Toronto, Ontario; Dr. Francisco Gomes de Matos of Recife, Brazil; Professor Glenn Wong, of the University of Massachusetts in Amherst; Flavia Laviosa of Columbus, Ohio; the French Graduate Association at the State University of New York at Buffalo; Trevor Smith of Buffalo, New York; Dr. Sibry Tapsoba in Burkina Faso; Mr. Jason Epstein of Knoxville, Tennessee; Ms. Elizabeth Wixon of Williamsville, New York; Mr. Junko Kanamura, of Buffalo, New York; Ms. Pat Glinski of the State University of New York at Buffalo; Ms. Hanna Fryer of Williamsville, New York; Mr. Pavel Reinberger of Buffalo, New York; Ms. Kathy Curtis of Buffalo, New York; Ms. Karen Nemeth of Buffalo, New York and Ms. M. C. Josine DeWolde of Buffalo, New York.

Finally, we would also like to thank Amy Epstein and A. J. Hladczuk for their help on this project.

INTRODUCTION

SPORTS LAW AND LEGISLATION: AN ANNOTATED BIBLIOGRAPHY presents national and international legal issues and questions which have arisen due to the nature of sports. The volume provides comprehensive coverage of the field of sports law.

This bibliography covers the literature from books, domestic and international law journals, and bar publications. While it may seem that the bibliography emphasizes recent articles and books, this is not really the case. Only recently have a considerable number of articles on sports law been published.

Every effort has been made to make the bibliography and its 1,367 entries and the annotations easily accessible to the reader and researcher. The volume is divided into thirty-five chapters on the various sports, topics of major importance, and key issues in sports law and legislation. Topics such as agents, amateur athletics, baseball, chemical substances, discrimination, medical care, spectators, sports broadcasting, violence, and women in sports are among the chapter headings.

Each chapter is then subdivided into sections so that the user of the bibliography can examine a series of works on different subtopics. Author and subject indexes provide further access to information given in the entries and in their annotations. Nonetheless, it is important for the user to recognize that as efficient as the book appears, the need remains to cross-check parts of the bibliography in order to maximize one's research. For example, when examining the subject of antitrust from a comparative perspective, note the antitrust sections in a number of other sections of chapters, as well as in the chapter on antitrust.

In many ways sports mirrors society, reflecting social, economic, political, and legal developments. For instance, although activities such as hunting and fishing were once required for survival, now they and other activities have become sports, a form of leisure activity rather than a necessity.

The importance of sports has increased over the years. Also, sports have evolved and endured because they involve not only the participants but, with the help of mass medial coverage, increasingly include nonparticipants as well. It can be said that there is a direct relationship between the growth of leisure time and the growth of sports.

From the early game laws to collective bargaining agreements, the rules of sport became codified and institutionalized. Sports have gone beyond the beginnings of Abner Doubleday's and James Naismith's classification of sports as amusement and entertainment. Instead sports make up an industry that is complex and multifaceted.

Sports as an industry encompasses many different matters, from school records to the pay-per-view broadcasting of sports. It covers sports from the elementary school to the college or university level and amateur and professional competitions. Sports law deals with the resolution of issues that the industry faces concerning academics, discrimination, gender, and women's participation in sports, negligence, liability, health and medical care, players and agents rights, substance abuse, antitrust and trade restrictions, broadcasting rights and so forth.

Once simply a local concern, sport has gone beyond local, state and national boundaries. Decreased travel time and increased global communications have changed sports law dramatically. Questions arise which involve such issues such as immigration, taxation, broadcast rights, violence, and property which need to be resolved on international terms. The resolution of such questions is how amateur and professional sports can be said to contribute to the cultural fabric of countries and the world as we increasingly become a global society.

ABBREVIATIONS

AAU -   Amateur Athletic Union
AFL -   American Football League
AIAW -   Association for Intercollegiate Athletics for Women
ARPA -   Association of Representative of Professional Athletes
CFA -   College Football Association
CFL -   Canadian Football League
ERA -   Equal Rights Amendment
FCC -   Federal Communications Commission
HEW -   Health, Education and Welfare
INS -   Immigration and Naturalization Service
IOC -   International Olympic Committee
IRS -   Internal Revenue Service
MCC -   Model University Coach Contract
MLBPA -   Major League Baseball Players' Association
NAIA -   National Association of Intercollegiate Athletics
NASL -   North American Soccer League
NBA -   National Basketball Association
NCAA -   National Collegiate Athletic Association
NFL -   National Football League
NFLMC -   National Football League Management Council
NFLPA -   National Football League Players' Association
NFSHA -   National Federation of State High School Associations
NHL -   National Hockey League
NLRA -   National Labor Relations Act
NLRB -   National Labor Relations Board
PAT -   Prescription Athletic Turf
SFAA -   San Francisco Arts & Athletics, Inc.
TEFRA -   Tax Equity and Fiscal Responsibility Act of 1982
TRA -   Tax Reform Act

UCC -   Uniform Commercial Code
USFL -   United States Football League
USOC -   United States Olympic Committee
WHA -   World Hockey Association

Sports Law
and Legislation

1

AGENTS

General

0001.　　　Jenkins, John A.　"Knuckleball Law:　Washington's Hard-Hitting Sports Lawyers." 6 <u>District Lawyer</u> 28-35. (November-December 1981).

　　　　　　　Insights into the Washington D.C. sports law practices of Donald Dell, Richard Berthelsen, Richard Bennett and James F. Fitzpatrick.

0002.　　　Jennings, Marianne and Zioiko, Lynn.　"Student-Athletes, Athlete Agents and Five Year Eligibility:　An Environment of Contractual Interference, Trade Restraint and High-Stake Payments." 66 <u>University of Detroit Law Review</u> 179-220. (Winter 1989).

　　　　　　　Examines at what time an athlete can be legally recruited, whether student-athlete has a contractual relationship with his institution (and whether an agent is interfering with this contract if athlete is recruited before eligibility expires) and whether NCAA is achieving its goal of protecting amateur sports with its present rules.

0003.　　　Kaplan, David A.　"Springtime of His Disconsent."　9 <u>The National Law Journal</u> 1. (May 4, 1987).

0004.　　　Kohn, Alan.　"U.S. Judge Dismisses Claim by Agents Against NFL Player:　Declines Role as 'Referee Between Thieves'." 198 <u>New York Law Journal</u> 1. (December 18, 1987).

0005.　　　Korn, Peter L.　"Never be a Sports Lawyer." 11 <u>Barrister</u> 12(8). (Winter 1984).

Points out the nature, rewards and hazards of being a sports lawyer.

0006.   McLeese, Don. "A Whole New Ball Game for Lawyers." 9 Student Lawyer 40(6). (October 1980).
Provides insights into the business of legally representing professional athletes. Discusses the nature of the business with a sports lawyer.

0007.   Newman, Pamela J. "Managing Risk and Insurance in the Entertainment and Sports Industries." 5 Entertainment and Sports Lawyer 11(3). (Spring 1987).

0008.   Pate, Steve. "Double Agents: Hendricks Brothers Thrive by Dealing in Fairness." 50 Texas Bar Journal 1108(3). (November 1987).
Explores the sports agent business of Alan and Randy Hendricks.

0009.   Waugh, Katherine. "Shake 'em Hard in the Sports Side." 11 The National Law Journal 8. (April 3, 1989).

Agent-Athlete Relationship

0010.   Crandell, Jeffrey P. "Agent-Athlete Relationship in Professional Sports: The Inherent Potential for Abuse and the Need for Regulation." 30 Buffalo Law Review 815-849. (Fall 1981).
Examines athlete's practical necessity of having an agent. Reviews recurrent problems and abuses in the relationship and how problems arose. Provides potential solutions to agent-athlete dilemma. Compares lawyer and non-lawyer agents and professional and amateur sports.

0011.   Ehrhardt, Charles W. and Rodgers, J. Mark. "Tightening the Defense Against Offensive Sports Agents." 16 Florida State University Law Review 633-674. (Fall 1988).
Focuses on the agent-athlete relationship. Explores the need for agents, the agent's role, the phenomenon of the bad agent and legislative measures that some states are taking to regulate the agent, specifically Florida, Georgia, Indiana, Minnesota, Ohio and Tennessee.

0012.   Elmore, Len. "The Agent's Role in Professional Sports: An Athlete's Perspective." 31 Boston Bar Journal 6(3). (July-August 1987).

Discusses what to look for in an agent, financial planning, good reputation, client contact, and the roles of the coach and parents.

0013.   Garvey, Ed. The Agent Game. Washington, D.C.: Federation of Professional Athletes AFL-CIO, 1984.
Explores relationship between athletes and agents. Stresses perils athlete faces in negotiating own contract and need for an agent. Discusses how sports agent operates. Points out what standards to apply in selecting an advisor, what athlete or agent will negotiate, whether athlete can sort out fair fees for services, and how to settle disputes. Provides appendices.

0014.   Giulietti, James J. "Agents of Professional Athletes." 15 New England Law Review 545-572. (1979-1980).
Note examining the relationship between agents and professional athletes. Discusses relevant law in the agent-athlete relationship. Provides a general overview and the applicable principles of agency and contract law. Reviews current rules of the NCAA, ABA and the Association of Representatives of Professional Athletes (ARPA) pertaining to the governing of agent practices. Surveys existing case law and the need for regulatory measures to protect the rights of athletes.

0015.   Remick, Lloyd Zane and Eisen, David Spencer. "The Personal Manager in the Entertainment and Sports Industries." 3 Entertainment & Sports Law Journal 57-86. (Spring 1986).
Reviews the nature and role of a personal manager. Explores the aspects that should be considered in a personal management agreement. Offers suggestions for governmental regulation of such a relationship.

0016.   Williams, Weldon C., III. "Gladiator Traps: A Primer on the Representation of Black Athletes." 9 Black Law Journal 263-279. (Winter 1986).
Stresses the tremendous influence an agent has over the athlete and how the sports career is determined by the quality of the representative. Advises the athlete how to select the best agent. Offers current legal protections which athletes should recognize. Uses case examples.

Certification and Regulation

0017.   Benitez, Miriam. "Of Sports, Agents, and Regulations--The Need for a Different Approach." 3 Entertainment and Sports Law Journal 199-221. (Fall 1986).

Focuses on the issue of regulating the sports agent. Reviews the options for regulation, possible roadblocks and the issues of enforcement and registration.

0018.   Dow, T. Andrew. "Out of Bounds: Time to Revamp Texas Sports Agent Legislation." 43 Southwestern Law Journal 1091-1118. (May 1990).
Presents background on the evolution of sports agents, services provided, types of misconduct, attempts at regulation, aspects of the Texas regulatory scheme and the alternative of federal regulation.

0019.   Dunn, David Lawrence. "Regulation of Sports Agents: Since at First It Hasn't Succeeded, Try Federal Legislation." 39 Hastings Law Journal 1031-1078. (July 1988).
Discusses the extent to which agents abuse the agent/athlete relationship. Reviews legislative and nonlegislative attempts to regulate agents. Considers need for federal legislation and the proposed Professional Sports Agency Act of 1985. Suggests what would be the most appropriate federal legislative response.

0020.   Fox, Dana Alden. "Regulating the Professional Sports Agent: Is California in the Right Ball Park?" 15 Pacific Law Journal 1231-1259. (July 1984).
Examines athlete/agent relationship. Discusses differences between being represented by an attorney and non-attorney. Explores effectiveness of present methods of regulating agents. Concludes with suggestions for improving regulation of agents.

0021.   Hawkins, Deborah H. "Regulating Personal Managers." 134 New Jersey Lawyer 524. (May-June 1990).
Reviews the licensing environment in New Jersey, California and New York State.

0022.   Johnson, David V. "Athlete Agents: Regulate." 5 Georgia State University Law Review 451-457. (Fall 1987).
Discusses the creation of the Georgia Athlete Agent Regulatory Commission (1988) which is an attempt to regulate sports agents.

0023.   Lefferts, Lori J. "The NFL Players Association's Agent Certification Plan: Is it Exempt from Antitrust Review?" 26 Arizona Law Review 699-714. (1984).
Discusses models of labor management relations, development of the labor exemption from antitrust scrutiny and the application of labor exemption to NFLPA regulations, particularly the agent certification plan.

0024.   Massey, Craig. "The Crystal Cruise Cut Short: A Survey of the
            Increasing Regulatory Influences Over the Athlete-Agent in
            the National Football League." 1 Entertainment and Sports
            Law Journal 53-78. (Spring 1984).
                Reviews the regulation of athlete-agents in the NFL.
            Includes aspects of the NFL Collective Bargaining Agreement
            of 1982, state statutes plus remedies and means of enforcement.
            Discusses the licensed attorney and the non-licensed agent.

0025.   Paragano, Vincent D. "To Catch a Rising Star." 134 New Jersey
            Lawyer 46-48. (May-June 1990).
                Discusses the representation of entertainers and
            professional athletes. Examines entertainment law
            agreements.

0026.   Ring, Bart Ivan. "An Analysis of Athlete Agent Certification
            and Regulation: New Incentives with Old Problems." 7 Loyola
            Entertainment Law Journal 321-335. (1987).
                Presents the attempt by players associations and the
            California State Legislature to ensure that sports agents are
            qualified and certified before they may represent clients. This
            has arisen due to flagrant abuses in the field.

0027.   Rodgers, J. Mark. "Update: 19 States Target Sports Agents." 8
            The Sports Lawyer 1-4. (Spring 1990).
                Review of the action of Nevada and Arkansas. Lists
            requirements of 19 states.

0028.   Ruschmann, Paul A. "Are Sports Agents Facing a Regulatory
            Blitz?" 65 Michigan Bar Journal 1124-1127. (November 1986).
                Analyzes the nature, role, responsibility and regulation of
            sports agents. Discusses regulation by unions and through
            state and federal legislation.

0029.   Shropshire, K. L. "Athlete Agent Regulation: Proposed
            Legislative Revisions and the Need for Reforms Beyond
            Legislation." 8 Cardozo Arts & Entertainment Law Journal 85-
            112. (1989).

0030.   Smith, Frederick F., Jr. "Sports Attorneys: Scoring Form the
            Sidelines." 1 California Lawyer 40-43+. (December 1981).
                Focuses on California sports law. Reviews relationship
            between football attorneys and NFLPA.

0031.   Sobel, Lionel S. "The Regulation of Sports Agents: An
            Analytical Primer." 39 Baylor Law Review 701-786. (Summer
            1987).

Supports regulation between players and agents. Demonstrates some problems exist if each state enacts its own legislation. Provides historical perspectives of player-agent relationship, function which agents serve and criticisms over malicious agent practices. Overviews current agent regulations among states, professional sports leagues and NCAA.

Ethics and Abuses

0032.   Fraley, Robert E. and Harwell, F. Russell. "The Sports Lawyer's Duty to Avoid Differing Interests: A Practical Guide to Responsible Representation." 11 Comm/Ent 165-217. (Winter 1989).
Discusses ethical issue of conflict of interest for the sports lawyer. Offers guidelines to avoid conflicts of interest including self-enforcement suggestions.

0033.   Fraley, Robert E. and Harwell, F. Russell. "Ethics and the Sports Lawyer: A Comprehensive Approach." 13 Journal of the Legal Profession 9-95. (1988).
Comprehensive overview which examines ethical rules, solicitation, competence, conflict of interest, reasonable fee and the use of the media for self-promotion. Appendix contains the Code of Ethics of the Association of Representatives of Professional Athletes.

0034.   Goodman, Mark C. "The Federal Mail Fraud Statute: The Government's Colt 45 Renders Norby Walters and Lloyd Bloom Agents of Misfortune." 10 Loyola Entertainment Law Journal 315-333. (1990).
Provides a statement of the case, the court's decision, background on the federal mail fraud statute, an analysis of the application of the statute, errors of the Walters court and implications of the case.

0035.   Hainline, Jon S. "Matchpoint: Agents, Antitrust, and Tennis." 64 University of Detroit Law Review 481-503. (Spring 1987).
Comments on the antitrust violation of agents' practice of using "World-Class" tennis players to guarantee success of tennis tournaments. Reviews requirements of monopoly and cites casework.

0036.   Kohn, Gary P. "Sports Agents Representing Professional Athletes: Being Certified Means Never Having to Say You're Qualified." 6 Entertainment and Sports Lawyer 1(15). (Winter 1988).
Surveys representation abuses by sports agents. Lists various players' association requirements for being an agent.

Reviews NCAA requirements and state legislation. Points out questions of ethics and offers solutions.

0037.   Ruxin, Robert H. "Unsportsmanlike Conduct: The Student-Athlete, The NCAA, and Agents." 8 Journal of College and University Law 347-367. (1981-1982).
Reviews and discusses what the NCAA rules forbid and allow in the relationship between student-athletes and agents. Provides suggestions to correct the current situation including educating the athlete and reevaluation of the NCAA's rules and enforcement procedures.

0038.   Sullivan, Michael J. "Remedying Athlete-Agent Abuse: A Securities Law Approach." 2 Entertainment and Sports Law Journal 53-77. (Fall 1984).
Analyzes the causes of agent-athlete abuses and possible solutions including a securities law approach. Includes the Athlete-Agent Disclosure Act.

Litigation

0039.   Chambers, Marcia. "Firm's Advice Was Focus of Agents' Trial." 11 The National Law Journal 13. (May 8, 1989).

0040.   "Joint Trial Ordered for Sports Agents." 135 Chicago Daily Law Bulletin 1. (March 1, 1989).

0041.   Mills, Michael R. and Woods, Richard P. "Tortious Inference with an Athletic Scholarship: A University's Remedy for the Unscrupulous Sports Agent." 40 Alabama Law Review 141-186. (Fall 1988).

0042.   "7th Circuit Sends Sports Agent Case to Trial Court." 134 Chicago Daily Law Bulletin 3. (November 17, 1988).

0043.   "Sports Agents' Trial Wraps Up." 135 Chicago Daily Law Bulletin 1. (April 4, 1989).

0044.   Woods, Richard P. and Mills, Michael R. "Tortious Interference with an Athletic Scholarship: A University's Remedy for the Unscrupulous Sports Agent." 40 Alabama Law Review 141-186. (Fall 1988).
Examines the use of the tortious interference with contractual and business relations as a remedy against sports agents whose actions get a student-athlete declared ineligible.

Representational Contracts

0045.   Kiersh, Edward. "The Puck Stops Here: Kaminsky Wraps Up Hockey Olympians." 2 The National Law Journal 1. (March 24, 1980).

0046.   Manisco, Joseph Michael. "Offer Sheet: An Attempt to Circumvent NCAA Prohibition of Representational Contracts." 14 Loyola of Los Angeles Law Review 187-211. (December 1980).

            Focuses on agent's offer sheet. Surveys role that the agent, athlete and the NCAA play in representational contracts. Examines whether a contract formed in violation of NCAA rules is enforceable. Reviews the unclean hands defense, illegality of the contract as a defense and the potential for tort liability of the agent.

Role of Lawyer and Sports

0047.   Etter, William F. "Representing the Professional Athlete." 37 Washington State Bar News 12-16. (October 1983).

            Presents considerations regarding the representational needs of the professional athlete. Offers background on the world of professional sports, why an athlete needs representation, an analysis of the lawyer/agent dichotomy and the services provided, and the importance of contract negotiations.

0048.   Nimoy, Adam B. and Hamilton, Jackson D. "Attorneys and the California Athlete Agencies Act: The Toll of the Bill." 7 Communications and Entertainment Law Journal 551-574. (Summer 1985).

            Discusses the role of agents, player associations and the NCAA. Explores provisions of the Act which was designed to protect athletes from abusive agents. Points out flaws in its enforcement and suggests the player associations need to take the lead in regulating agents.

0049.   Safian, Robert. "Leigh Steinberg: Most Valuable Player; Steinberg has been Setting Standards in the NFL Negotiations Since His First Deal, at Age 26, For Steve Bartkowski, the Top Player of the 1975 College Draft." 11 American Lawyer 156(3). (July-August 1989).

0050.   Shulruff, Lawrence. "The Football Lawyers." 71 American Bar Association Journal 45-49. (September 1985).

Discusses the unique life of the sports agent. Provides popular agents as examples. Mentions the vital importance of the player contract.

0051.   Winter, Bill. "Is the Sports Lawyer Getting Dunked?" 66 American Bar Association Journal 701. (June 1980).
Brief discussion on the discrepancies, advantages and disadvantages in the practices of sports agents and sports lawyers.

Solicitation

0052.   Fraley, Robert E. and Harwell, F. Russell. "Sports Law and the Evils of Solicitation." 9 Loyola Entertainment Law Journal 21-42. (1989).
Reviews issue of solicitation in sports law. Examines Shapiro v. Kentucky Bar Ass'n. and its relevance to sports law. Provides arguments on solicitation as it involves the sports attorney.

2

AMATEUR ATHLETICS
AND SPORTS

General

0053.   Ashman, Allan. "Courts...Saturday Afternoon Fever." 68
         American Bar Association Journal 484-485. (April 1982).
              Brief discussion of Georgia High School Association v.
         Waddell where the Supreme Court of Georgia ruled that courts
         do not have the authority to review the referee's decisions in a
         football game.

0054.   Barnes, John. "Myers v. Peel County Board of Education." 17
         Canadian Cases On The Law of Torts (Canada) 285-290. (1979).

0055.   Burkow, Steven H. and Slaughter, Fred L. "Should Amateur
         Athletes Resist The Draft?" 7 Black Law Journal 314-346.
         (Winter 1981).
              Provides overview of amateur player draft rules. Analyzes
         antitrust attack against amateur player draft systems. Discusses
         legality of player drafts. Proposes draft systems for football and
         basketball.

0056.   Carrafiello, Vincent A. "Jocks Are People Too: The
         Constitution Comes To The Locker Room." 13 Creighton Law
         Review 843-862. (Spring 1980).
              Highlights some of the issues raised in the litigation of
         athletes, the schools and coaches for whom they play and the
         national and regional associations which administer their
         competitive activities. Discusses the state action requirement,
         foreign student athletes and the Constitution, and judicial
         approbation of NCAA regulations.

0057.   DeGiorgi, Maria Vita. "Liberta e Organizzazione Nell 'Attivita Sportiva" (in Italian). 127 Giurisprudenza Italiana (Italy) 122-127. (1975).

Explores whether sporting activities should be organized or not concerning amateur and professional athletes and sports.

0058.   Jarriel, Judith E. "Possibility of Skin Problems Not Sufficient to Invalidate School's Clean Shaven Policy." 14 Stetson Law Review 780-781. (Summer 1985).

Brief discussion of Davenport v. Randolph County Board of Education, 730 F.2d. 1395 (11th Cir. 1984) where the Court of Appeals affirmed the lower court's decision and thus the constitutionality of high school grooming policies.

0059.   Joiner, W. Joseph. "Should Kentucky Student Athletes Be Covered By The Workers' Compensation Statutes?" 50 Kentucky Bench and Bar 16(3). (Spring 1986).

0060.   Koch, James V. "The Economic Realities of Amateur Sports Organization." 61 Indiana Law Journal 8-29. (Winter 1985).

Shows how NCAA has acted as a cartel and how economic motives have effected its decision.

0061.   "Lawsuit Fears Spur School Program Changes." 135 Chicago Daily Law Bulletin 1. (August 29, 1989).

0062.   Lowell, Cym H. "Judicial Review of Rule-Making In Amateur Athletics." 5 Journal of College and University Law 11-42. (Fall 1977).

Judicial review of the nature, extent and implications of the rule-making process in amateur athletics. Reviews administrative structure of amateur athletics, the legal status of amateur athletic organizations and institutions, judicial review of public institutional rule-making and the nature of rule-making by private institutions.

0063.   Mellowitz, Jim. "Feuding at Pan Am Games Moves To Courtroom: Three Separate Suites Are Filed." 9 The National Journal 8. (September 7, 1987).

0064.   Mullins, Charles E. "Family Law Issues In High School Athletic Eligibility: Equal Protection v. The Transfer Rule." 20 Journal of Family Law 293-322. (January 1982).

Focuses on family law issues, transfer rule and questions of protection and violation of equal protection under the fourteenth amendment. Examines problems of divorce, change of custody and interstate movement, and athletic eligibility. Analyzes cases typifying the state of the law. Reports on Kentucky High School Athletic Association v.

Hopkins County Board of Education and Jackson v. Kentucky High School Athletic Association. Discusses related issues and provides a suggested transfer rule.

0065.   Nafziger, James A. R. "The Amateur Sports Act of 1978." 1983 Brigham Young University Law Review 47-99. (1983).

Analyzes structure of Act, its definitions, objects and purposes, national goals, working relationships with other sports organizations, areas of exclusive jurisdiction, representation, promotion of competition, public participation, development of amateur athletic programs, conflict resolution and athlete's rights, development of facilities, informational dissemination, and encouragement of women, the handicapped, and minorities.

0066.   "Open Membership Sports Organization Is A Qualified Amateur Sports Organization." 27 Tax Management Memorandum 317-318. (November 24, 1986).

0067.   Ostroff, Ron. "No Right To Play In Varsity Schools, Appeal Court Says." 99 The Los Angeles Daily Journal 1. (January 17, 1986).

0068.   Plouvin, J.-Y. "Libre circulation des sportifs professionnels a l'interieur de la communaute" (in French). 21 Revue du Marche Commun (France) 516-526. (November 1978).

Examines the free movement of athletes within the European community. Defines the distinction between professional and nonprofessional players. Discusses guidelines involved in the movement of professional and nonprofessional players. Presents examples of national policies relating to the use of "foreign" professional athletes. Reviews limited casework relating to the athletic rules and regulations of the European community.

0069.   Schuck, Donald L., Jr. "Administration of Amateur Athletics: The Time For An Amateur Athlete's Bill of Rights Has Arrived." 48 Fordham Law Review 53-82. (October 1979).

Examines situations in which athletic participation is impaired by governing bodies (the AAU, the NCAA and the National Federation of State High School Associations [NFSHSA]). Explore the remedies when amateur's interest in participation is jeopardized. Discusses the Amateur Sports Act of 1978. Analyzes the appropriateness of judicial intervention in arbitrating amateur disputes and proposes an Athletes Bill of Rights.

0070.   Silas, Faye A. "Not Something To Squawk About." 11 Bar Leader 29. (March-April 1986).

0071. Steinbach, Sheldon Elliot. "Workman's Compensation and The Scholarship Athlete." 19 Cleveland State Law Review 521-527. (September 1970).

Deals with the question: Should a scholarship athlete, whose scholarship is solely dependent upon active participation on an athletic team, and who is injured in practice of a game, be able to qualify for workman's compensation. Looks to Ohio law for statutory guidance on employee-employer requirements that are amenable to the Workman's Compensation Act. Reviews two cases where scholarship players were found to be employees for the purpose of the Act (in Colorado and California). Suggests how the terms of a scholarship would be worded.

0072. Stern, Ralph D. "Legal Issues in Extracurricular Education." 9 NOLPE School Law Journal 142-163. (Winter 1981).

Explores the legal issues of liability, obligation, eligibility, financing, marital discrimination, sex discrimination, and handicapped students.

0073. Wong, Glenn M. Essentials of Amateur Sports Law. Dover, Massachusetts: Auburn House Publishing Company, 1988.

Discusses new legal concepts and issues plus basic tort law, contract law, trademark law and constitutional law. Describes the major intercollegiate and interscholastic amateur sports organizations in detail. Presents a glossary of legal and sports terms, samples of contracts and legal forms, tables, lists, and flow charts. Presents each chapter as a self-contained unit which can be used as a quick reference. Includes case citations and brief summaries of cases, law review articles, names and addresses of relevant organizations, and other information intended to lead to additional sources of information.

0074. Wong, Glenn M. and Ensor, Richard J. "Recent Developments In Amateur Athletics: The Organization's Responsibility To The Public." 2 Entertainment and Sports Law Journal 123-165. (Fall 1985).

Areas examined are access to public records, public access to televised college football games, public funding of athletic facilities and matters relating to the delegation of a public responsibility.

A.A.U.

0075. "Government of Amateur Athletics: The NCAA-AAU Dispute." 41 Southern California Law Review 464-490. (Winter 1968).

Reviews the international and national structure of amateur athletics, the nature of the NCAA-AAU dispute, the role and responsibility of national federations, and the validity of the national federations' domestic regulation. Explores solutions to the dispute including voluntary agreement, arbitration, judicial intervention and legislation.

Academics and the Student Athlete

0076. Adams, Frank. "Montana Court Oks 'No Pass, No Play'; Rule Adopted By Two Schools." 9 The National Law Journal 33. (October 20, 1986).

0077. Koester, Anne Y. "No Pass, No Play Rules: An Incentive Or An Infringement?" 19 University of Toledo Law Review 87-133. (Fall 1987).

0078. Shannon, David J. "No Pass, No Play: Equal Protection Analysis Under The Federal and State Constitutions." 63 Indiana Law Journal 161-179. (Winter 1988).
Reviews the state and federal constitutional challenges to the "no pass, no play" rule in interscholastic sports.

Antitrust

0079. Kirby, Wendy T. and Weymouth T. Clark. "Antitrust and Amateur Sports: The Role of Noneconomic Values." 61 Indiana Law Journal 31-51. (Winter 1985).
Discusses rule of reason analysis determination in television regulation case. Explores the extent courts should look to noneconomic values in considering antitrust violations. Offers historical perspective in NCAA decision and provides case examples.

0080. Scanlan, John A., Jr. "Introduction: Antitrust - The Emerging Legal Issue." 61 Indiana Law Journal 1-7. (Winter 1985).
Introduction to a series of articles on the Antitrust Issues In Amateur Sports Symposium.

Coaching

0081. Clark, Alan W. "Workers' Compensation - Compensation Rate Determined By Aggregating Salaries From Three Positions Worked For A Single Employer." 16 Seton Hall Law Review 285-287. (Winter 1986).

Reports on the case of <u>Stack v. Boonton Board of Education</u> where it was ruled that compensation should be determined by the aggregate value of the total number of contracts signed with the same employer.

0082.   Davis, Melonie L. "Sports Liability of Coaches and School Districts." 39 <u>Federation of Insurance & Corporate Counsel Quarterly</u> 307-319. (Spring 1989).

Examines relationship between coach school district, and athlete. Reviews duties of coach and school district. Surveys liability defenses including assumption of risk, contributory negligence, and governmental immunity.

0083.   Graves, Judson. "Coaches In The Courtroom: Recovery In Actions For Breach of Employment Contracts." 12 <u>Journal of College and University Law</u> 545-559. (Spring 1986).

Discusses the coaching contract as an employment contract with recoverable damages due to a breach. Analyzes <u>Rodgers v. Georgia Tech Athletic Association</u> as a prime example.

0084.   Poskanzer, Steven G. "Spotlight On The Coaching Box: The Role of The Athletic Coach Within The Academic Institution." 16 <u>Journal of College and University Law</u> 1-42. (Summer 1989).

Examines role of college coach. Reviews recent developments concerning conventional and alternative perceptions of role of the coach.

0085.   Stoner, Edward N., II and Nogay, Arlie R. "The Model University Coaching Contract ("MCC"): A Better Starting Point For Your Next Negotiation." 16 <u>Journal of College and University Law</u> 43-92. (Summer 1989).

Discusses issue and aspects of intercollegiate coaching contracts. Presents Model University Coaching Contract to serve as guide for drafting of coach's contract.

Federal Intervention

0086.   Lowell, Cym H. "Federal Administrative Intervention In Amateur Athletics." 43 <u>George Washington Law Review</u> 729-790. (March 1975).

Analyzes legislative proposals which would involve the U.S. government in the administration of amateur athletics. Focuses on the Amateur Athletic Act of 1974 (passed by the Senate in the 93rd Congress) and whether or not, and in what way, the U.S. government should become involved in the regulation of amateur athletes. Evaluates the Act, its impact on the developing principles of amateur athletics, and the extent of protection provided for athletes.

0087.   McGahey, Robert L., Jr.   "A Comment On The First
           Amendment and The Scholar-Athlete." 6 Human Rights 155-
           167. (Winter 1977).
               Argues that first amendment rights should be enjoyed by all
           students whether they are athletes or not.   Presents an
           overview of students' first amendment rights and discusses
           the status of scholar-athletes.

Interscholastic Sports

0088.   Conway, Ellen Sue.   "Protection of Public High-School
           Athletics Under The California Constitution: Steffes v.
           California Interscholastic Federation." 22 University of San
           Francisco Law Review 587-598. (Spring 1988).
               Discusses instant case which held that the California
           Constitution did not guarantee students the right to engage in
           interscholastic athletics.   Reviews and analyzes the question of
           athletic participation as a privilege and as a right within the
           context of education.   Concludes with discussion of the
           constitutionality of rule 214 of the California Interscholastic
           Federation.

0089.   Cypher, Elspeth B.   "School Committees May Agree To
           Implement Rules of Interscholastic Athletic Associations." 19
           Suffolk University Law Review 453-457. (Summer 1985).
               Reports on Herbert v. Ventetuolo, 480 A.2d 403 (R.I. 1984),
           where the Supreme Court of Rhode Island rules that a school
           committee could implement the rules of an interscholastic
           athletic league if the rules relate to the school committee's
           goals.

0090.   Goodman, Stephen S., IV.   "The University Interscholastic
           League of Texas: Who Are These Guys and What Can They
           Do?" 16 St. Mary's Law Journal 979-1014. (1985).
               Discusses history of the League, its current status, and the
           nature and extent of judicial intervention in the functioning of
           the League.

Sex Discrimination

0091.   Riffer, Jeffrey K.   "An Overview of Sex Discrimination In
           Amateur Athletics."   6 Comm/Ent Law Journal 621-651.
           (Spring 1984).
               Identifies four areas of sex discrimination and the bases for
           challenging them: federal constitution's equal protection

clause, state constitutions, Title IX, and various state statutes and regulations.

0092.   Rivera, Rhonda R. and Frank, Janice R. "Othen v. Ann Arbor School District: A Weakening of Title IX Protection Against Sex Discrimination." 26 St. Louis University Law Journal 857-874. (June 1982).
Reviews case. Court ruled that only programs that receive direct federal assistance are protected by Title IX. Examines the fact and the scope of Title IX protection. Argues that said decision weakened the protective intent of Title IX.

3

ANTITRUST

General

0093.   Blecher, Maxwell M. and Daniels, Howard F. "Professional Sports and the "Single Entity" Defense Under Section One of The Sherman Act." 4 <u>Whittier Law Review</u> 217-238. (1982).
        Reviews doctrines pertaining to development of Section I of Sherman Antitrust Act as it applies to "single entity" defense of separate corporate defendants. Examines standards of separate incorporation and necessity to cooperate.

0094.   Campbell, Dana Mark. "Antitrust Analysis In Professional Sports Management Cases: The Public Cries 'Foul'!" 25 <u>Arizona Law Review</u> 995-1021. (1983).
        Reviews antitrust issues and implications involved in management of professional sport franchises. Offers model for antitrust analysis. Discusses three major restrictions involved in the movement, ownership, and awarding of franchises.

0095.   Cummings, William Leamon. "Cross-Ownership Ban." 4 <u>Loyola Entertainment Law Journal</u> 203-209. (1984).
        Reports on <u>North American Soccer League v. N.F.L.</u> where decision found cross-ownership ban to be in violation of the antitrust laws.

0096.   Goldman, Lee. "Sports, Antitrust, and The Single Entity Theory." 63 <u>Tulane Law Review</u> 751-797. (March 1989).
        Offers comprehensive analysis of application of section 1 of Sherman Act to operations of professional sports leagues from player draft to franchise relocations. Reviews casework regarding single entity theory. Provides comments by three

legal scholars.   Argues sports leagues should be judicially supervised.

0097.   Johnson, Frederic A.   "The Law of Sports: The Unique Performer's Contract and The Antitrust Laws." 2 Antitrust Bulletin 251-266. (January 1957).

Examines nature of athletic performers contract-particularly the reserve clause-from perspective of management and athlete.   Reviews organizational, competitive and legal history of organized baseball.   Reports on role of Judge Kenesaw Mountain Landis in the development of organized baseball and includes his handling of player's contracts.

0098.   Keating, Kenneth B.   "The Antitrust Threat to Professional Team Sports." 1959 Antitrust Law Symposium 23-30. (1959).

Discusses the Senate Bill S. 616 proposed by Senators Hennings, Dirkson and Keating designed to deal with the antitrust status of professional team sports and which would promote the public interest in honest and competitive team play.   The legislation is to be a middle-of-the-road approach between complete exemption and complete subjection of those sports to the antitrust laws.   Describes the Bill, deals with the problem of the regulation of telecasting major league games into minor league areas, and dispells some misconceptions voiced about the legislation.   Gives examples of the exemptions to the antitrust laws and argues that the same kind of exemptions be accorded to team sports.

0099.   Kempf, Donald G., Jr.   "The Misapplication of Antitrust Law To Professional Sports Leagues." 32 DePaul Law Review 625-633. (Spring 1983).

Argues that the trial level decision (wherein it was ruled that the NFL's franchise relocation restriction was in violation of section 1 of the Sherman Act) was misapplication of antitrust law to professional sports.

0100.   Lazaroff, Daniel E.   "Antitrust Analysis and Sports Leagues: Re-examining The Threshold Questions."   20 Arizona State Law Journal 953-988. (Winter 1988).

Examines threshold single entity and market question in professional sports.   Explores a rejection of the single entity status for sports leagues.   Analyzes market definition in relation to rule of reason cases.   Raises questions regarding application of antitrust laws to the operation of professional sports leagues.

0101.   Lazaroff, Daniel E.   "The Antitrust Implications of Franchise Relocation Restrictions in Professional Sports." 53 Fordham Law Review 157-220. (November 1984).

Examines antitrust ramifications of professional sports' franchise relocation restriction. Discusses single entity defense and whether per se illegality or rule of reason analysis should apply. Reviews alternatives of exemption and/or regulation for relocation restriction.

0102.   McClelland, Robert W.   "Flood In The Land of Antitrust: Another Look At Professional Athletes, The Antitrust Laws and The Labor Exemption." 7 Indiana Law Review 541-578. (1974).

A note which deals with the reserve systems and players' contracts. Reports the dissatisfaction in professional sports as expressed in contract disputes including Flood v. Kuhn (1972). Discusses U.S. baseball, football, basketball and hockey players associations. Reviews antitrust laws and the labor exemption, suits brought by individual players and competitors, and concludes that antitrust exemption for professional sports is for Congress, and not the courts, to decide.

0103.   Nelson, Paul L.   "Professional Sports and The Non-Statutory Labor Exemption To Federal Antitrust Law. McCourt v. California Sports, Inc." 11 University of Toledo Law Review 633-653. (Spring 1980).

Consists of the origin of the labor exemption to the antitrust laws and the relationship between professional sports and the antitrust laws. Reviews McCourt within the context of the antitrust laws and the labor exemption.

0104.   Neville, John W.   "Who's On First?" 36 Michigan State Bar Journal 13. (Spring 1957).

Questions the different antitrust treatments of professional baseball and football. Analyzes how this came to be beginning with Federal Baseball Club of Baltimore v. National League of Professional Baseball, 259 U.S. 200 (1922) (giving professional baseball immunity from the antitrust laws). Reviews Gardella v. Chandler, Toolson v. New York Yankees, United States v. Southeastern Underwriters Association, United States v . International Boxing and Radovich v. National Football League. Concludes that baseball has a special antitrust status which discriminates against other professional sports and all other businesses which are subject to the antitrust laws.

0105.   "Panel Presentation: Developments In Sports and The Law and The Interplay of Antitrust and Labor Law." 125 West's Federal Rules Decisions 293-317. (June 1989).

0106.   Pierce, Samuel R., Jr.   "Organized Professional Team Sports and The Antitrust Laws." 43 Cornell Law Quarterly 566-616. (1958).

Detailed examination of the extent which professional sports should be exempt from the antitrust laws. Surveys history of the problem beginning with 1922 Federal Baseball case. Reviews the organization and the operating practices of baseball, hockey, football and basketball, and their relationship to the antitrust laws. Presents policy and Congressional alternatives to deal with the nature of the relationship between professional sports and the antitrust laws. Concludes with the proposal that professional sports should fall under the antitrust laws of the United States but with specific exemptions. Enumerates the specific exemptions and provides a detailed outline of the proposed legislation.

0107.   Professional Sports Antitrust Bill - 1965. Hearing Before The Subcommittee On Antitrust and Monopoly of The Committee On The Judiciary. United States Senate. Washington, D.C.: Government Printing Office, 1965.
Hearing on bill S. 950. Contains statements by various representatives of the media, Congress, amateur and professional sports. Includes exhibits.

0108.   "Professional Sports: Has Antitrust Killed The Goose That Laid The Golden Egg?" 45 Antitrust Law Journal 290-314. (1976).
Panel discussion on the nature of the relationship between the antitrust laws and professional sports.

0109.   Roberts, Barry S. and Powers, Brian A.   "Defining The Relationship Between Antitrust Law and Labor Law; Professional Sports and The Current Legal Battlegrounds." 19 William and Mary Law Review 395-467. (Spring 1978).
Comprehensive overview of the relation and applicability of antitrust laws and professional sports. Discusses evolution of labor exemptions in professional and non-professional sports cases. Reviews the NFL-NFLPA Collective Bargaining Agreement, the labor exemption and Agreement.

0110.   Roberts, Gary R.   "Sports League Restraints On The Labor Market: The Failure of Stare Decisis." 47 University of Pittsburgh Law Review 337-405. (Winter 1986).
Criticizes courts for lack of consistency in applying antitrust law and insufficiently clarifying their policy.   Examines Supreme Court and lower court cases and decisions involving player restraint, allocation and exemption issues.

0111.   Tagliabue, Paul J.   "Antitrust Developments In Sports and Entertainment." 56 Antitrust Law Journal 341-359. (1987).
Reviews recent changes in the entertainment industry which will affect antitrust interpretation.   Presents

developments in antitrust principles and labor exemptions in professional sports.

0112.   Weistart, John C. "League Control of Market Opportunities: A Perspective On Competition and Cooperation In The Sports Industry." 1984 Duke Law Journal 1013-1070. (December 1984).
Examines governance of NFL and its relationship to antitrust law and public policy issues. Focuses on Los Angeles Memorial Coliseum Commission v. National Football League (Ninth Circuit Court). Presents case background and basic themes of Court's decision. Overviews alternative antitrust theories. Reassesses the majority's rule of reason and single entity analyses. Asks which antitrust theory would be most appropriate for professional sports leagues.

PreSeason/Season Tickets

0113.   "Antitrust: Preseason Football Tickets and Tie-Ins."   1975 Washington University Law Quarterly 495-506. (1975).
Examines Coniglio v. Highwood Services, Inc. (1974) (the Court of Appeals held there was no violation of the Sherman Antitrust Act where the requirement of purchasers of regular season tickets to purchase exhibition game tickets was not an illegal tying arrangement). Analyzes the decision in light of Supreme Court decisions. Suggests that restriction of this decision should be make considering sound antitrust policy and the increasing recognition of consumers' rights.

0114.   "IRS Cracks Down On Season Tickets."   10 Taxation for Lawyers 140-141. (November-December 1981).

0115.   Levick, Marsha. "Tying Arrangements In The Sale of Season Tickets." 47 Temple Law Quarterly 761-770. (Summer 1974).
Note discussing five suits involving the sale of season tickets. Examines the law of tying relationships, as it exists under the Sherman Act, and its applicability. Reports on disposition of suits in question.

0116.   Symington, James W. "Symington Urges Deductibility of Sports Tickets." 27 Tax Notes 648. (May 6, 1985).

Restraint of Trade

0117.   Heydon, J. D. "Recent Developments In Restraint of Trade." 21 McGill Law Journal (Canada) 325-360. (Fall 1975).
Examines court decisions since Esso Petroleum Co., Ltd. v. Harpers Garage (Stourport) (1968) affecting the doctrine of

restraint of trade and which have widened the scope of the doctrine that, in certain respects, overcomes some of the deficiencies of antitrust legislation. Defines what is "trade" and what is "restraint" and attempts to predict the immediate future of the law.

0118.   Ward, Brian. "Professional Sport and Restraint of Trade." 59 Law Institute Journal (Australia) 545-551. (June 1985).
Focuses on relationship between the issue of restraint of trade and professional sports. Examines areas of restraint of trade, generally, and the right to work. Discusses Trade Practices Act of 1974. Offers guidelines for a safe system.

Sherman Act

0119.   Ashman, Allan. "Antitrust Law...Cross-Ownership Ban." 68 American Bar Association Journal 852. (July 1982).
Brief overview of the N.F.L.'s policy of banning the cross-ownership of professional teams in competing leagues. Discusses the decision in North American Soccer League v. National Football League where it was decided that said ban was in violation of Section 1 of the Sherman Act.

0120.   Brock, James L., Jr. "A Substantive Test For Sherman Act Plurality: Applications For Professional Sports Leagues." 52 University of Chicago Law Review 999-1031. (Fall 1985).
Argues that certain operations of leagues should be exempt from section 1 violations. Uses Copperweld decision as proper standard and offers analysis of the case. Discusses unique nature of sports leagues. Offers courts' handling of single and plural entity and potential economic competition tests. Reports new approach which courts have taken regarding plurality issues.

0121.   Graver, Myron C. "The Use and Misuse of The Term 'Consumer Welfare': Once More To The Mat On The Issue of Single Entity Status For Sports Leagues Under Section 1 of The Sherman Act." 64 Tulane Law Review 71-116. (November 1989).
Response to Professor Lee Goldman's article (63 Tulane Law Review 751 (1989)). Examines the concepts of consumer welfare and consumer wealth maximization as the goals of antitrust. Examines these concepts within the context of single entity theory as it applies to professional sports leagues.

0122.   Moynihan, David S. "North American Soccer League v. National Football League: Applying "Rule of Reason" Analysis Under The Sherman Act To Private Bans On Cross-

Ownership." 15 New England Law Review 697-764. (Summer 1979-1980).

Explores the application of the rule of reason to both the ownership and cross-ownership of professional sports franchises. Reviews professional soccer as a business, this case, the N.F.L.'s ban on cross-ownership and an antitrust analysis of the ban.

0123. "Professional Football Immune From Sherman Act As A Team Sport Not Consulting Interstate Commerce." 105 University of Pennsylvania Law Review 110. (November 1956).

Reviews Court of Appeals in Radovich v. National Football League that football was not interstate commerce as meant by antitrust laws. Questions court's rationale. Discusses Court's result as possibly having some economic justification. Compares 1922 Federal Baseball case, 1953 Toolson case and 1955 United States v. International Boxing Club. Concludes that if a practice used by team sports cannot survive the rule of reason (and is still defended as necessary), the courts would not decide the exemption-Congress should.

0124. Roberts, Gary R. "The Antitrust Status of Sports Leagues Revisited." 64 Tulane Law Review 117-145. (November 1989).

Response to Professor Lee Goldman's article (63 Tulane Law Review 751 (1989)). Analyzes and counters Goldman's position. Reviews the single entity issue regarding professional teams and professional sports leagues.

0125. Roberts, Gary R. "The Single Entity Status of Sports Leagues Under Section 1 of The Sherman Act: An Alternative View." 60 Tulane Law Review 562-595. (January 1986).

Denounces Professor Daniel Lazaroff's argument [53 Fordham Law Review 157-220 (November 1984)] regarding legality of franchise relocation in professional sports leagues. Points out that entire league should be treated under section 1 analyses rather than independent teams battling as horizontal competitors.

0126. Roberts, Gary R. "Sports Leagues and The Sherman Act: The Use and Abuse of Section 1 to Regulate Restraints on Interleague Rivalry." 32 UCLA Law Review 219-301. (December 1984).

Argues restraint should prevail when applying antitrust rules and laws to a professional sports league. Posits that a sports league is a different kind of business and that the league itself should be conceptualized as a single firm. Proposes framework for application of Section 1 to sports leagues.

4

BASEBALL

General

0127.   Allen, Richard B. "Lawyers, Law, and Baseball." 64 <u>American</u>
             <u>Bar Association Journal</u> 1530-1535. (October 1978).
                 Points out the evolving relationship between lawyers, law
             and professional baseball. Focuses on roles of Judge Kenesaw
             Mountain Landis, Albert "Happy" Chandler and Bowie Kuhn.
             Discusses the baseball commissioner's exercise of dictatorial
             power.

0128.   "Baseball and The Law-Yesterday and Today." 32 <u>Virginia Law</u>
             <u>Review</u> 1164-1177. (November 1946).
                 Surveys early origins of baseball from a strictly amateur
             sport to a professional sport. Discusses the formation of the
             National League, attempts to form the American Association,
             Union Association, Players' League, Players' Brotherhood,
             American League, Baseball Players' Fraternity and the Federal
             League. Examines the issue of baseball contracts particularly
             the reserve and release clauses. Reviews significant cases.
             Briefly reviews the question of whether baseball is a monopoly
             and the relationship between labor and baseball.

0129.   "Baseball Law." 17 <u>Law Notes</u> 207-208. (February 1914).
                 A note concerning the validity of the reserve clause in
             baseball contracts which would restrain a player who violates
             his contract from playing with another club. Reviews six cases.
             Reports it would seem the courts look with disfavor upon the
             true reserve clause in that it is so wanting in mutuality that no
             court of equity would compel compliance with it.

0130.   "Baseball Not A 'Game' But A National Recreation."   68
            Central Law Journal 341-342. (May 7, 1909).
                Examines the judicial recognition of baseball. Discusses
            State v. Prather (100 Pac. 57) wherein the Supreme Court of
            Kansas differentiated baseball from being categorized as a game,
            as intended and conveyed by statute, and saw baseball as a
            national recreation. Briefly traces the origination of baseball
            from 1839 in Cooperstown, New York. Concludes that the
            statute in question was directed at a class of activities- games-
            which were, as far as the popular mind perceived them,
            associated with gambling.

0131.   Chelius, James R. and Dworkin, James B. "Free Agency and
            Salary Determination In Baseball." 33 Labor Law Journal 539-
            545. (August 1982).
                Reviews relationship between baseball free agency and
            salary determination. Presents historical overview of player
            movement and managerial response. Provides empirical
            analysis of impact of free agency on salaries.

0132.   "Common Law Origins of The Infield Fly Rule."   123
            University of Pennsylvania Law Review 1474-1481. (June 1975).
                An aside which examines whether the same type of forces
            that fashioned the development of common law also
            generated the baseball Infield Fly Rule. Concludes the
            dynamics of common law and the development of this
            technical rule of baseball share significant elements.

0133.   Curle, David. "On Higher Ground: Baseball and The Rule of
            Flood v. Kuhn." 8 Legal Reference Services Quarterly 29-62.
            (1988).
                Provides overview and analysis of the rule from Flood v.
            Kuhn. Explores the foundation and origin of the rule and how
            it has been applied by courts. Reviews relationship of the rule
            to Sunday baseball, the concept of democracy, franchise
            relocation and spectator injury cases. Examines and comments
            on the dynamism of baseball jurisprudence.

0134.   Dworkin, James B. "Collective Bargaining In Baseball: Key
            Current Issues." 39 Labor Law Journal 480-486. (August 1988).
                Reviews collective bargaining in professional baseball,
            salary arbitration, free agency and drug testing. Provides
            statistics on salaries and arbitration.

0135.   Eisen, Jeffrey M.   "Franchise Relocation In Major League
            Baseball." 4 Entertainment and Sports Law Journal 19-56.
            (Spring 1987).
                Discusses major league baseball's rules for franchise
            relocation. Reviews circumstances of the franchises which

relocated. Reports on the role of Congress and the judiciary in franchise relocation. Surveys the case of Los Angeles Memorial Coliseum Commission v. National Football League. Offers suggests on what the league should examine when a request for relocation is made.

0136.   Elie, Steven J. "Joy In Wrigleyville? The Mighty Cubs Strike Out In Court." 8 Journal of Communications and Entertainment Law 289-300. (Winter 1986).

Examines the issues and controlling statute and ordinance in The Chicago National League Ball Club v. Thompson which prohibited the installation of lights for the playing of night baseball in Wrigley Field. Discusses legal arguments, separation of powers, equal protection and special legislation. Concludes with analysis of decision.

0137.   Halligan, T. F. "Organized Baseball and The Law." 19 Notre Dame Lawyer 262-272. (March 1944).

A note which briefly discusses the history of baseball. Reports on cases which involve the liabilities of baseball clubs to spectators, contractual obligations, altercations, the suspension of players, insurance, and the construction of ball parks and the role of the Commissioner of Baseball.

0138.   Hazelwood, Mark F. "Constitutional Law: Cubs Lose On Justice Ward's Error." 7 Loyola Entertainment Law Journal 371-384. (1987).

Presentation and analysis of the decision which prevented the Chicago Cubs from play "under the lights" at Wrigley Field.

0139.   Hill, James Richard and Spellman, William. "Pay Discrimination In Baseball: Data From The Seventies." 23 Industrial Relations 103-112. (Winter 1984).

Study examining pay discrimination in professional baseball in the 1970s. Analyzes racial barriers to entry into baseball. Concludes that the study found neither barriers to entry nor wage discrimination.

0140.   Holahan, William L. "Long-Run Effects of Abolishing The Baseball Players Reserve System." 7 Journal of Legal Studies 129-137. (January 1978).

Reviews the Rottenberg-Demsetz position on the reserve clause. Explores the financial impact upon professional baseball teams if the reserve system were to be abolished, including the training of new players.

0141.   Jacobson, Charles. "The Supreme Court of Baseball." 23 Case and Comment 665-667. (January 1917).

Reports on the origin, organization, purpose, scope and processes of major league baseball's National Commission. Focuses on a number of cases, relating to the reserve clause, which have been heard in the courts.

0142.   Johnson, Frederic A.   "Baseball Law."   73 <u>United States Law Review</u> 252-270. (May 1939).
Examines the development of equitable protection of contract rights in baseball. Discusses player attempts in the late 1880's to organize-a Brotherhood-and play in their own league. Shows the conflict between this attempt and the concept of the reserve clause.   Reviews at length a number of the cases, during 1889-1990, relating to the reserve clause. Overviews the origins of the American League, and a number of cases particularly <u>Philadelphia Ball Club, Ltd. v. Lajoie</u> (202 Pa. 210; 51 Atl. 973).   Briefly discusses attempts to establish a third major league organization, the Federal League, and the litigation surrounding such an attempt. Concludes by saying that the circumstances and outcome of the George Sisler issue ultimately led to the selection of Judge Kenesaw Mountain Landis as the Commissioner of Baseball.

0143.   "Judicial Criticism of Baseball Playing."   50 <u>National Corporation Reporter</u> 554. (May 6, 1915).
Brief discussion of <u>Edling v. Kansas City Baseball & Exhibition Company</u>, 168 S.W. 908, wherein plaintiff was injured by a foul-ball which entered a defective portion of screening behind home plate. Kansas City Court of Appeals affirmed the lower court stating that despite the assumption of risk by the plaintiff, the defendant had the duty to keep the screen free from various defects. Failure to exercise such reasonable care resulted in defendant being guilty of negligence.

0144.   "Judicial Criticism of Baseball Playing." 47 <u>Chicago Legal News</u> 227. (April 3, 1915).
Brief note on <u>Edling v. Kansas City Base-ball and Exhibition Company</u>, 168 SW. 908, wherein Kansas City Court of Appeals affirmed judgment in favor of the plaintiff. Court decision argues that it was the duty of the defendant to exercise reasonable care to keep the screen, in the screened portion of the grandstand, free from defects. When such a duty is not exercised, the defendant is guilty of negligence.

0145.   "Jurisprudence of Pine Tar, The." 5 <u>Cardozo Law Review</u> 409-410. (Winter 1984).
Brief editorial on the pervasive jurisprudential debate that the George Brett "...pine tar incident..." created throughout America.

0146.   Kirby, James. "The Year They Fixed The World Series." 74 <u>American Bar Association Journal</u> 65-69. (February 1988).

    Examines the gambling controversy involving the 1919 World Series between the Chicago White Sox and the Cincinnati Reds.

0147.   Kosin, Phil. "Diamond Classics: Baseball Lawyers Make Mark." 71 <u>American Bar Association Journal</u> 34-35. (October 1985).

    Reports on nine baseball-related lawyers who have had an impact on the game. Those discussed are: James O'Rourke, John Montgomery Ward, Hughie Jennings, Kenesaw Mountain Landis, Miller Huggins, Branch Rickey, Happy Chandler, Bowie Kuhn and Tony LaRussa.

0148.   Meltzer, Bernard. "A Baseball Buff's Brief Memoir." 27 <u>University of Chicago Law School Record</u> 37. (Fall 1981).

    Author shares his baseball dreams of boyhood and the baseball reality of adulthood. Muses on his desires to play and/or manage and his experiences as a baseball salary arbitrator.

0149.   "More Baseball Law." 18 <u>Law Notes</u> 22-23. (May 1914).

    Reports by Chancellor J. P. Henderson at Hot Springs, Arkansas (baseball training camp) who holds that a baseball contract is property and entitled to consideration as such where no person has a right to induce a breach of contract. Even though the contracts lack mutuality and were voidable at the instance of the players, third parties could not interfere with the fulfillment of the contracts of the parties involved. Reports ruling of United States District Judge Sessions at Grand Rapids, Michigan which holds the option or reserve clause of the Philadelphia club contract invalid. Mentions changes in the new contract which is believed will stand the legal test.

0150.   Rapson, Donald J. "A "Home Run" Application of Established Principles of Statutory Construction: U.C.C. Analogies." 5 <u>Cardozo Law Review</u> 441-453. (Winter 1984).

    Review of reasoning process in George Brett pine tar case, application of the principles of statutory construction and analogies to the Uniform Commercial Code.

0151.   Roseberg, Normal L. "Here Comes The Judge!" The Origin of Baseball's Commissioner System and American Legal Culture." 20 <u>Journal of Pop Culture</u> 129-146. (Spring 1987).

    Provides analysis and comparison of development of professional baseball's commissioner system with the traditional legal system. Examines role of the press in development of the Commissioner System with particular focus on Chicago White Sox and 1919 World Series.

0152.   Seymour, Harold. "Ball, Bat and Bar." 6 Cleveland-Marshall Law Review 534. (September 1957).

Discusses the economics and practices of professional baseball, which are under baseball's complicated body of private law. Reveals the cash nexus in numerous auxiliary enterprises and businesses related to baseball. Examines position of courts to organized baseball, analyzes Radovich v. National Football League (1957) with respect to baseball. Considers possible actions of Congress to rectify position the Court placed itself in by invoking antitrust laws on football but by exempting baseball. Presents arguments for and against invoking antitrust laws on professional baseball. Predicts baseball will be given limited exemption and antitrust laws will be applied except for practices and restrictions deemed necessary to successful operation of the baseball business.

0153.   Shapiro, Paul W. "Monopsony Means Never Having To Say You're Sorry-A Look At Baseball's Minor Leagues." 4 Journal of Contemporary Law 191-209. (Spring 1978).

Includes discussions on the history and development of minor league baseball, the organization of minor league baseball, and a number of restrictive practices in relation to the antitrust laws.

0154.   Sobel, Lionel S. "Santiago Fernandez: The L.A. Dodgers' Clubhouse Lawyer." 8 Los Angeles Lawyer 16-24. (October 1985).

Surveys the activities of the general counsel to the Los Angeles Dodgers.

0155.   Steinberg, David. "Application of The Antitrust and Labor Exemptions To Collective Bargaining of The Reserve System In Professional Baseball." 28 Wayne Law Review 1301-1346.

Surveys relationship between antitrust laws, labor exemption, and reserve system in professional baseball. Examines player/owner conflict, reserve system in baseball, and applicability of antitrust laws, recent Congressional response to baseball's antitrust exemption, and the labor exemption.

0156   "Take Me Out To The Ball Game." 25 Fordham Law Review 793-794. (Winter 1956-1957).

Reports on baseball's pervasive influence in American society. Cites casework which supports baseball's apparent pre-eminent position among sports in the United States.

0157.   Tanick, Marshall H. and Munic, Martin D. "Baseball Law In
         Minnesota: From Foul Balls To Family Court." 45 Bench and
         Bar of Minnesota 16-22. (April 1988).

0158.   Wilder, L. A. "Baseball and The Law." 19 Case and Comment
         151-162. (August 1912).
              Compares the sport of baseball to the law using definitions
         from Black's Law Dictionary and several legal doctrines to
         illustrate the concepts they have in common. Includes three
         photographs of famous baseball players and much discussion
         of baseball incidents and comments of some players, coaches,
         managers and judges in connection with legal principles and
         practice. States that with few exceptions court decisions pertain
         to either a contract relation of club and players or the
         application of nuisance or Sunday laws to baseball. Reviews
         cases and the principles pertaining to baseball from 1882 on.

Antitrust

0159.   "Applicability of Federal and State Antitrust Laws To The Sport
         of Baseball, The--Flood v. Kuhn 443 F. 2d 264 (2d Cir. 1971)."
         1971 University of Toledo Law Review 594-610. (Spring 1971).
              Examines the case where it was ruled by the Second Circuit
         Court of Appeals, that professional baseball was not under the
         authority of either state or federal antitrust laws. Discusses
         other baseball cases which have come before the U.S. Supreme
         Court. Presents Floods' argument vis a vis these and other
         cases.

0160.   "Baseball Players and The Antitrust Laws." 53 Columbia Law
         Review 242-258. (February 1953).
              Provides the structure of organized baseball, a discussion of
         the minor and major leagues and their agreements, and the
         self-regulation of their business. Discusses the player's right to
         sue, the obstacle of the Federal Baseball case of 1922, and the
         validity of that case in the light of modern conditions, and
         with respect to antitrust violations concerning restraining the
         potential competitions of persons outside and within
         organized baseball. Reviews remedies provided under
         antitrust laws and the possibility of and reasons for inability to
         recover.

0161.   Berger, Robert G. "After The Strikes: A Reexamination of
         Professional Baseball's Exemption From The Antitrust Laws."
         45 University of Pittsburgh Law Review 209-226. (Fall 1983).
              Examines professional baseball's antitrust exemption, its
         history and development.

0162.   Classen, H. Ward. "Three Strikes and You're Out: An Investigation of Baseball's Antitrust Exemption." 21 Akron Law Review 369-390. (Spring 1988).

Examines the economics of professional sports, baseball antitrust exemption and its implications in relation to other professional sports. Cites casework with focus on Federal Baseball Club v. National League. Argues that continuation of the exemption is both economically inefficient and a constitutional infringement upon players.

0163.   Coleman, Edward G. "Constitutional Law-Baseball and the Antitrust Laws-A Game or a Conspiracy." 24 Notre Dame Lawyer 372-383. (Spring 1949).

Presents brief history of baseball and the player's contract, the history and interpretation of the commerce clause, and the validity of the reserve clause of players' contracts. Presents cases and comments calling the 1944 Supreme Court decision in United States v. South-Eastern Underwriters Association et al. (declaring insurance to be interstate commerce) to be probably one of the most far-reaching decisions of the decade. Reports Judge Learned Hand's decision to rule mainly on the lucrative radio and television contracts as interstate commerce. Analyzes that after the Supreme Court rules that baseball is an activity within interstate commerce, Congress will probably act to exempt baseball (as to players' contracts) from the antitrust laws analogous to that done with insurance.

0164.   Cromley, Charles. "Baseball and The Anti-Trust Laws." 34 Nebraska Law Review 597-612. (May 1955).

Presents the structure of organized baseball and its self-imposed body of rules regulating its activity, judicial attacks upon baseball and case analyses concerning baseball activities, Congressional investigations and recommendations, Supreme Court's determination of baseball's status under antitrust laws, the effect of 1953 Toolson decision on other sports, and policy considerations of peculiarities of baseball which preclude easy solution. Speculates on possible solutions Congress could legislate defining permissive limits of antitrust exemption or establish a Baseball Commission and identify its responsibilities.

0165.   Dunn, Scott A. "The Effect of Collective Bargaining On The Baseball Antitrust Exemption." 12 Fordham Urban Law Journal 807-839. (1983/1984).

Reviews antitrust exemption in baseball and other professional sports. Examines historical background of labor exemption to antitrust laws, application of exemption to professional sports, and limitations of exemption in professional sports.

0166.   Eppel, J. P. "Professional Sports." 33 <u>American Bar Association Antitrust Law Journal</u> 69-75. (1967).

Examines the exemption from federal antitrust laws which professional baseball enjoys. Reviews the casework regarding the history and the nature of the exemption. Concludes with a discussion of the present status and future prospects of the exemption.

0167.   Hoffman, Scott Lee. "Pooling of Local Broadcasting Income In The American Baseball League-Antitrust and Constitutional Issues." 32 <u>Syracuse Law Review</u> 841-878. (Summer 1981).

Analyzes antitrust and constitutional issues involved in pooling of local broadcast income in professional baseball.

0168.   Johnson, Frederic A. "Baseball, Professional Sports and The Antitrust Acts." 2 <u>Antitrust Bulletin</u> 678-701. (September-December 1957).

Argues that exemption of professional sports from antitrust laws is unconstitutional. Explores relationship between Sherman Act and 14th amendment and issues of national sovereignty, 14th amendment and slavery. States reserve clause is involuntary servitude and in violation of 13th amendment, that continued exemption of baseball from antitrust laws places organized baseball in the position of being "...a government within the governments..." and thus abnegates sovereignty of United States.

0169.   Kessler, Remy. "Baseball Remains Exempt From Antitrust Laws." 4 <u>Loyola Entertainment Law Journal</u> 197-203. (1984).

Reports on <u>Henderson Broadcasting Corp. v. Houston Sports Ass'n</u>, 541 F.Supp. 263 (S. D. Tex. 1982), which failed to make the radio broadcasting of sports exempt from the antitrust laws.

0170.   Lewis, Frank B. "Antitrust Laws and Professional Baseball." 19 <u>New York University Intramural Law Review</u> 235-251. (1963-1964).

Discusses legislative and judicial processes which have led to the present state of the law being that baseball is the only professional sport not within antitrust laws. Presents an argument which might persuade a court to hold <u>Federal Baseball</u> (1922) and <u>Toolson v. New York Yankees</u> (1953) no longer controlling because of current circumstances of operation in organized baseball.

0171.   Markham, Jesse W. and Teplitz, Paul V. "Siegried At Bat: Mudville Revisited." 28 <u>Antitrust Bulletin</u> 783-790. (Fall 1983).

Discussion of their book, Baseball Economics and Public Policy. Defends their suggestion of ending baseball's antitrust exemption. Discusses ways in which baseball is different from conventional business.

0172.   Martin, Philip L. "The Aftermath of Flood v. Kuhn: Professional Baseball's Exemption From Antitrust Regulation." 3 Western State University Law Review 262-283. (Spring 1976).
Discusses the Flood case in perspective beginning with Federal Baseball Club v. National League. Examines the response of the judiciary as it involves implementation and interpretation of the Flood decision. Reports on legislative and player reactions to Flood.

0173.   Martin, Philip L. "Labor Controversy In Professional Baseball: The Flood Case." 23 Labor Law Journal 567-571. (September 1972).
Reviews the nature of professional baseball's reserve clause, professional baseball's antitrust exemption, Congressional intent as regards baseball and the antitrust laws including the results and effects of the decisions.

0174.   McKenney, Samuel S. "Baseball-An Exception To The Anti-Trust Laws." 18 University of Pittsburgh Law Review 131. (Fall 1956).
Reports monopolistic structure of organized baseball as being an illegal monopoly under antitrust laws. Discusses judicial decision on organized baseball (1922 Federal Baseball 1949 Gardella and others). Includes legislative decisions, present legal status and legal doubts raised by judicial decisions. Concludes Congress, through legislation, would enable courts to resolve conflict between logical legal analysis and practical demands of the public and the sport itself.

0175.   Menitove, Barton J. "Baseball's Antitrust Exemption: The Limits of Stare Decisis." 12 Boston College Industrial and Commercial Law Review 737-746. (March 1971).
Determines the impact of Salerno v. American League of Professional Baseball Clubs (1970) and Flood v. Kuhn (1970) and earlier baseball decisions on the law-making processes. Examines the rationale used to exempt baseball from antitrust laws and considers the propriety of the Supreme Court's reinterpretation of previously passed statutes.

0176.   "Monopsony In Manpower: Organized Baseball Meets The Anti-trust Laws." 62 Yale Law Journal 576-639. (March 1953).
Presents history of organized baseball's dominion and its challenge in court system with three lines of defense used to

preserve its existing hegemony. Examines the monopsony in the player market, farm system and its vertical integration, the division of consumer markets ("territorial rights") and the exclusion of competitors. Analyzes organized baseball and the Sherman Act, judicial issues and merits of cases which violate the Sherman Act. Presents consequences of Act enforcement, exemption from antitrust laws, and alternative statutory solutions.

0177.   Neville, John W.   "Baseball and The Antitrust Laws."   16 Fordham Law Review 208-230. (November 1947).
          Gives examples of organized baseball's self-government in its operation explaining some agreements and rules. Reviews National League of Professional Baseball Clubs v. Federal Baseball Club of Baltimore, Inc. (1922) which exempts baseball from antitrust laws. Discusses the application of a legal formula and several cases including United States v. South-Eastern Underwriters Association (1944) which declares insurance to be commerce and therefore subject to the antitrust laws. Argues the evolution of law is such that baseball should no longer enjoy exemption.

0178.   Paonessa, Joseph P. "Antitrust Law- Baseball Reserve System- Concerted Conspiracy- Stare Decisis- Congressional Inaction- Professional Baseball Remains Exempt From State and Federal Antitrust Statutes." 48 Notre Dame Lawyer 460-474. (December 1972).
          In-depth comment on Flood v. Kuhn and the Supreme Court's treatment of whether professional baseball is subject to the federal antitrust laws. Presents comprehensive treatment of the issues of interstate commerce, broadcasting, exemption theory, and the Flood decision.

0179.   Prescott, Allie J., III. "Applicability of The Antitrust Laws To Baseball." 2 Memphis State University Law Review 299-312. (Spring 1972).
          Reviews the rationale of the premise, and the changes through which professional baseball has gone, wherein professional baseball was deemed not to be interstate commerce. Presents brief historical overview of the Sherman and Clayton Acts. Discusses the history of professional baseball within the context of the two Acts up to Flood v. Kuhn.

0180.   Rogers, C. Paul, III. "Judicial Reinterpretation of Statutes: The Example of Baseball and The Antitrust Law." 14 Houston Law Review 611-634. (March 1977).
          Discusses questions dealt with and raised, solutions arrived at, and the ramifications of those solutions as it pertains to judicial reinterpretation of statutes relating to baseball.

Examines early history of organized baseball, later challenges to the Federal Baseball decision, implications of the Federal Baseball and Flood decisions, and role of Congress, the doctrine of stare decisis, and nonjudicial decisions.

0181.   Thorpe, James A. "Constitutional Law- Preemption- Baseball's Immunity From State Antitrust Law." 13 Wayne Law Review 417-425. (Winter 1967).
          Note discussing an action to enforce a state antitrust law. Action was against the owners of the team and the league, a consequence of defendants decision to move the team (Milwaukee Braves) from the state (Wisconsin). Action held that defendants were engaged in a monopoly and that the decision to leave was unreasonable. Lower court held. Appeals court held, reversed. Since there are no federal antitrust laws applicable to baseball, it is also free from state antitrust laws as a function of the commerce and supremacy clauses of the U.S. Constitution. Reviews the applicability of the Sherman Antitrust Act to baseball in Federal Baseball Club of Baltimore v. National League. Discusses supremacy clause, preemption and Congressional intent.

0182.   Topkis, Jay H. "Monopoly In Professional Sports." 58 Yale Law Journal 691-712. (April 1949).
          Discusses Gardella v. Chandler and events leading to it (a professional baseball player who formerly played on the New York Giants team "jumped" to the Mexican League for the 1946 season) and opinions cited in the decision. Describes the organization of baseball, ice hockey and football including contracts, salaries and some historical references and draws comparisons. Responds to predictions of ruin by presenting arguments of keeping the status quo and those of free competition and speculates on the outcomes with regard to salaries and the number of and distribution of teams.

Arbitration

0183.   Dworkin, James B. "Salary Arbitration in Baseball: an Impractical Assessment After Ten Years." 41 Arbitration Journal 63-69. (March 1986).
          Article which presents historical perspective of salary arbitration. Discusses the crucial role that final-offer arbitration has on negotiations.

0184.   Fischman, Joel and Potter, Dirk D. "Pinch-Hitting For Baseball's Present System- Impartial Arbitration As A Method of Dispute Resolution." 14 UC Davis Law Review 691-709. (Spring 1981).

Advocates baseball's adoption of impartial arbitration to settle disputes. Reviews current system of dispute resolution, powers of the commissioner, the ease of obtaining judicial review, and the nature and extent of judicial scrutiny of Commissioner's Acts under Major League Agreement and the Basic Agreement. Provides defenses and criticisms of the current system of dispute resolution.

0185.　Goldstein, Mark L. "Arbitration of Grievance and Salary Disputes In Professional Baseball: Evolution of A System of Private Law." 60 Cornell Law Review 1049-1074. (August 1975).

Traces the maturation of labor relations in professional baseball. Assesses the protection which labor arbitration offers for the interests of the players, club owners, and fans of professional sports. Concludes that professional baseball shows the flexibility of the labor arbitration process. A system of private law can be designed which protects the interests of those concerned with improving the employment relationship.

0186.　Grebey, C. Raymond, Jr. "Another Look At Baseball's Salary Arbitration." 38 Arbitration Journal 24-30. (December 1983).

Argues free agency system has significantly altered process of salary arbitration in professional baseball. Reviews Article V, Section F relating to arbitration and free agency. Discusses arbitration and salary developments over last ten years and pressures on management.

0187.　Lock, Ethan and DeSerpa, Allan. "Salary Increases Under Major League Baseball's System of Final Offer Salary Arbitration." 2 The Labor Lawyer 801-817. (Fall 1986).

Discusses the role of salary arbitration in major league baseball. Presents analysis of the market forces which affect a player's worth and the effect of the dramatic increase in television revenues on salaries. Offers appendix which outlines arbitrated player salaries and their decisions from 1974-1985.

0188.　Miller, Marvin J. "Arbitration of Baseball Salaries: Impartial Adjudication In Place of Management Fiat." 38 Arbitration Journal 31-35. (December 1983).

Refutes Raymond C. Grebey, Jr.'s (38 Arbitration Journal 24-30, [December 1983]) argument of free agency's effect on salary arbitration. Offers suggestions for improvement of salary arbitration process. Outlines position of the owners.

0189.　Nicolau, G. "Wait 'Til Next Year: Musings of Baseball's Arbitrator." 42 New York University Conference on Labor 13.1-.17. (1989).

0190.   Reaves, Lynne. "Baseball Bucks: Arbitrator Shares His
             Stories." 70 American Bar Association Journal 45. (April 1984).
                  Reports on the comments of an arbitrator in professional
             baseball.

0191.   Rings, Kevin A.   "Baseball Free Agency and Salary
             Arbitration." 3 Ohio State Journal on Dispute Resolution 243-
             262. (1987).
                  Reviews process by which baseball disputes are settled.
             Discusses history of baseball, various legal challenges and
             salary arbitration.   Provides specific examples of dispute
             resolution.

0192.   Seitz, Peter. "Transplanting of Industrial Relations Tissues and
             Organs; or, Is The Baseball Salary Arbitration System
             Compatible With Interest Arbitration In The Private Sector,
             Generally." 28 NYU Conference on Labor 347-358. (1975).
                  Discusses the system of salary arbitration in professional
             baseball. Examine the feasibility of applying this system to
             private industry.

0193.   Seitz, Peter. "Footnotes To Baseball Salary Arbitration." 29
             Arbitration Journal 98-103. (June 1974).
                  Comments of an arbitrator-participant in a recent round of
             arbitration of salaries of major league baseball players. Presents
             the use of High-Low arbitration and its administration in this
             case and compliments those involved for using imagination
             and innovative courage worthy of employers' and unions'
             emulation.

0194.   Wong, Glenn M.   "Major League Baseball's Grievance
             Arbitration System: A Comparison With Nonsport Industry."
             38 Labor Law Journal 84-99. (Fall 1987).
                  Reviews the workings of the grievance arbitration system
             in major league baseball. Examines the interplay between
             individual and collective interests which has resulted from
             special convenants in athletic contracts. Discusses the issues of
             termination, determination of salary, benefits, discipline and
             grievance arbitration.

0195.   Wong, Glenn M.   "Major League Baseball's Grievance
             Arbitration System: A Comparison with Nonsports Industry."
             12 Employee Relations Law Journal 464-490. (Winter
             1986/1987).
                  Presents overview of recent decisions under professional
             baseball's arbitration system. Examines special convenants,
             free agency, option clause, strike payment clauses, termination,

termination pay, salary amounts, benefits, discipline and grievance procedure.

0196.   Wong, Glenn M. "A Survey of Grievance Arbitration Cases In Major League Baseball." 41 Arbitration Journal 42-62. (March 1986).

Overviews impact which grievance arbitration has had on the game. Discusses grievance procedure, free agency, salaries, termination and other important issues which have been handled through arbitration. Uses case examples.

Collective Bargaining

0197.   McCormick, Robert A. "Baseball's Third Strike: The Triumph of Collective Bargaining in Professional Baseball." 35 Vanderbilt Law Review 1131-1169. (October 1982).

Presents historical review of professional baseball players' attempts to achieve contractual freedom. Argues that labor law has afforded the only opportunity to gain contractual freedoms. Concludes labor exemption to antitrust laws will govern future player-owner disputes.

0198.   Staudohar, Paul D. "Players Salary Issues In Major League Baseball." 33 Arbitration Journal 17-21. (December 1978).

Survey of the development of collective bargaining in professional baseball and its effects on player salaries, team loyalty, and the cost of tickets. Discusses the question of freedom. Presents statistics on baseball salaries.

Contracts

0199.   "Baseball Contracts." 50 National Corporation Reporter 402. (April 8, 1915).

Discusses Weeghman v. Killefer, 215 Federal Reporter 168, and American League Baseball Club of Chicago v. Chase, 149 New York Supplement 6. Both cases deal with aspects of a professional baseball player's contract. The cases, specifically, involved, a breaking of the contract. Each court of record applied the equitable maxim, "He who comes into equity must come with clean hands."

0200.   "Landis Case." 7 American Bar Association Journal 87-89. (February 1921).

Discusses the circumstances of and presents a brief chronology of United States Judge Kenesay M. Landis' entering into a contract to act as a salaried arbitrator for organized baseball. Concludes with quoted statements from Judge Landis and U.S. Attorney General A. Mitchell Palmer.

0201.   "Negative Convenant In Baseball Contracts." 18 Law Notes 83. (August 1914).
Brief report on Cincinnati Exhibition Co. v. Johnson wherein the ten-day notice in the release clause of baseball contracts and injunctive relief of the negative convenant (preventing a player from playing for any other team while still under contract) were sustained. Quotes excerpts from Court's decision.

0202.   Sloane, Arthur A.   "Collective Bargaining In Major League Baseball: A New Ball Game and Its Genesis." 28 Labor Law Journal 200-210. (April 1977).
Discusses the extent of player gains, failed past attempts of player organizations, reasons behind the recent successes from the players and owners perspectives and plus brief discussions on the philosophical differences regarding employee relations and the financial resources of the industry.

Federal Control

0203.   Beavers, Timothy P.   "Labor Law-Professional Baseball Not Exempt From Federal Labor Laws." 5 Florida State University Law Review 137-144. (Winter 1977).
Comment on Kansas City Royals Baseball Corp. v. Major League Baseball Players Association, 532 F2d 615 (8th Cir. 1976), ruled that the issue between the Leagues of Professional Baseball and the Baseball Players Association [MLBPA] was within the scope of grievance and arbitration provision of article X of the 1973 Basic Agreement.   Despite baseball's antitrust exemption, baseball was subject to other federal laws which, in this case, were federal labor laws.

0204.   Hoffman, Robert B.   "Is The NLRB Going To Play The Ball Game?" 20 Labor Law Journal 239-246. (April 1969).
Examines the NLRB's reluctance to assert jurisdiction in and over the game of baseball. Reviews history of the U.S. Supreme Court's involvement in antitrust cases in professional sports. Explores recent cases. Discusses the jurisdiction of the NLRB, its reluctance to become involved in baseball and its assertion over other, albeit lesser, sports.

Interstate Commerce

0205.   "Constitutional Law-Commerce and Supremacy Clause
                   Exempt Professional Baseball From State Antitrust Statute." 35
                   Fordham Law Review 350-355. (December 1966).
                      Note on State v. Milwaukee Braves, Inc. (1966) wherein the
                   Supreme Court of Wisconsin rules that removal of a
                   professional baseball team was in violation of a state antitrust
                   statute but that the state statute could not be applied because it
                   would be in violation of the commerce and supremacy clauses
                   of the U.S. Constitution.   Reviews casework regarding the
                   extent to which a state might legislate in the area of interstate
                   commerce and the intent of Congress as to the legislative
                   regulation of baseball.

0206.   Eckler, John. "Baseball-Sport or Commerce?" 17 University of
                   Chicago Law Review 56-78. (Autumn 1949).
                      Reviews the questions of whether baseball is an illegal
                   monopoly. Examines relevant cases including Federal Baseball
                   Club of Baltimore v. National League of Professional Baseball
                   Clubs, and its impact on organized baseball. Discusses Gardella,
                   Fred Martin and Max Lanier cases against organized baseball.
                   Describes the organization of baseball and offers a review of the
                   agreements which comprise "baseball law." Focuses on the
                   "reserve clause" and the power to trade features of the
                   Uniform Player's Contract. Concludes that the questions raised
                   are not peculiar to baseball: all professional sports have
                   adopted similar operating systems.

0207.   Lockman, John S. "Baseball As Interstate Commerce Within
                   The Meaning of the Antitrust Laws."   5 Intramural Law
                   Review of New York University 206-220. (March 1950).
                      Discusses questions raised by Gardella v. Chandler.
                   Discusses 1922 U.S. Supreme Court "Federal Baseball" case
                   which held that baseball was not interstate commerce. Presents
                   formula (of essential commerce contrasted with incidental
                   commerce) used for determination. Presents history of baseball
                   and several other entertainment and business cases, their
                   application of the formula and developments which would
                   seem to have overruled the authority of the old formula by
                   implication.   Concludes baseball is engaged in interstate
                   commerce within the meaning of anti-trust laws.

0208.   "What Constitutes Interstate Commerce." 34 Harvard Law
                   Review 559. (March 1921).
                      Briefly discusses the ruling (Federal Baseball Club v.
                   National League) that professional baseball leagues are not

considered as "interstate trade" within the meaning of the Sherman Antitrust Act.   Reviews case history of the conceptualization and regulation of interstate commerce.

Negligence

0209.   "Negligence-Landowners-Duty of Baseball Club To Protect Invitees From Injurious Acts of Third Parties." 12 Vanderbilt Law Review 299-301. (December 1958).

Brief discussion of Lee v. National League Baseball Club of Milwaukee 4 Wis.2d. 1968, 89 N.W.2d 811 (1958), wherein plaintiff received judgment as the result of being injured by other spectators scrambling to recover a foul ball. Landowner, manager, and operator of a place of amusement must exercise reasonable care to protect invitees, and former party has a duty to control third parties on premises and to protect other invitees from the misconduct of third parties. Questions the inconsistency between the generally accepted assumption of risk at places of amusement and this case.

Release Clauses

0210.   Hill, James Richard and Spellman, William. "Professional Baseball: The Reserve Clause and Salary Structure." 22 Industrial Relations 1-19. (Winter 1983).

Analysis of changes in the compensation structure which resulted from the 1976 Basic Agreement in professional baseball. Examines the period 1976-1977. Discusses historical background and total compensation levels and length of player contracts. Provides compensation models by which to examine changes in the reserve system.

0211.   "Release Clause In Baseball Contracts." 18 Law Notes 82-83. (August 1914).

Brief note on the ten-day release clause in organized baseball. Reviews litigation, directly and indirectly related to organized baseball, involving release from contracts.

Reserve Clause

0212.   Blackwell, Richard B. "Baseball's Antitrust Exemption and The Reserve System: Reappraisal of An Anachronism." 12 William and Mary Law Review 859-877. (Summer 1971).

Examines the antitrust exemption including its legal basis and affect on player controls, specifically the reserve rule, the legality of such controls without the exemption, and possible alternative means of player control if the exemption were abolished. Comments on the pending appeal of Flood v. Kuhn (1970) which should present the opportunity to review the viability of the exemption.

0213. Boswell, Thomas M. and McKeown, Richard B. "Baseball-From Trial By Law to Trial By Auction." 4 Journal of Contemporary Law 171-189. (Spring 1978).

Discusses the reserve clause and collective bargaining in professional baseball. Presents history of the reserve clause. Offers an overview of the merits of the reserve clause including balanced competition, integrity and public confidence, the issue of player development and economic stability.

0214. Enten, Harold N. "Baseball and The Reserve Clause." 1 New York Law School Student Law Review 159-164. (Summer 1952).

Defines and explains the reserve clause in the contract between professional baseball players and the first club that signs them. Illustrates the conflicts that stem from this clause. Touches on Gardella v. Chandler, Toolson v. New York Yankees and other cases which raise the question of the legality of the clause. Considers areas of violation of the Sherman Act where a court may have to rule in the future.

0215. McQuaide, John J. "Curt Flood At Bat Against Baseball's 'Reserve Clause'." 8 San Diego Law Review 92-109. (1971).

Reviews the facts of Flood v. Kuhn (1970) and examines baseball's exemption from the antitrust laws. Presents the implications of Toolson v. New York Yankees, Inc.. (1953) and the possibility of the Supreme Court overruling Toolson. Discusses the labor antitrust exemption. Reports the National Labor Relations Board is a forum where the Player's Association cap now brings unfair practice of grievance charges with bargaining parity with the owners."

0216. Meissner, Nancy Jean. "Nearly A Century In Reserve: Organized Baseball: Collective Bargaining and The Antitrust Exemption Enter The 80's." 8 Pepperdine Law Review 313-366. (January 1981).

Provides brief history of the reserve system in professional baseball. Discusses judicial doctrine as it related to baseball's antitrust exemption and the reserve clause. Reviews the casework pertaining to the birth and growth of the antitrust exemption, the creation of the exemption, the Flood case, and the role of the Congress and the courts. Reports on the collective bargaining process as it operates in baseball. Examines the development and role of antitrust applications and the labor exemption in baseball's past, present and future.

0217.   "Messersmith Decision and The 1976 Basic Agreement: Baseball's Emancipation Proclamation." 46 UMKC Law Review 239-281. (Winter 1977).

Analyzes the decision, and the Agreement between the American and National major leagues and the Major League Baseball Players Association (MLBPA). Examines the history of the reserve clause and explores the future of it. Reviews major cases involving professional baseball plus the advent of collective bargaining.

0218.   "Organized Baseball and The Law." 46 Yale Law Journal 1386-1390. (1937).

Examines the origin and nature of the "reserve clause." Questions legality of the reserve clause and the possibility of a baseball player to be truly a free agent. Examines briefly the possibility of changing the "reserve clause" situation including attempts to do so.

Torts

0219.   Dragonetti, Gerald C. "Torts-Assumption of Risk-Matters of Common Knowledge." 32 Temple Law Quarterly 127-129. (Fall 1958).

Discusses Lee v. National League Baseball Club of Milwaukee, 4 Wis.2d 168, 89 N.W.2d 811 (1958), wherein plaintiff was injured by third parties attempting to retrieve a foul ball. Reviews the general rule of assumption of risk, and states the rule is inconsistent with the case. Argues in favor of the assumption of risk stating that the spectator brings certain realizations, regarding both the game and the fans, to a baseball game. Cites cases involving unusual circumstances upholding the assumption of risk. Concludes with an analysis of the courts' argument stating that it is unrealistic and unsound.

0220.   Lempinen, Edward W. "When It Goes Foul: Duck?" 18 Student Lawyer 6-7. (April 1990).

0221.   St. John, Mary C. "Strike One, and You're Out: Should Ballparks Be Strictly Liable To Baseball Fans Injured By Foul Balls?" 19 Loyola Of Los Angeles Law Review 589-621. (December 1985).

Proposes strict liability for stadiums where spectator is injured. Presents analysis of landmark decisions and assumption of risk defense. Examines judges' opinions of a recent case.

Trade Regulations

0222.   "Trade Regulation-Sherman Act-Amenability of Organized
             Baseball." 34 Iowa Law Review 545-551. (March 1949).
                 Presents summary of Gardella v. Chandler, that the basis for
             the authority to suspend Gardella was a contract conforming to
             agreements which constitute a conspiracy in restraint of trade
             and a means of fostering monopolies which action was
             brought under the Sherman and Clayton Antitrust Acts. The
             case on appeal, held, reversed and remanded. Reports the
             three opinions written and their contrasting tests for further
             application. Discusses history of the court's concept of
             interstate commerce and the conceptions of baseball as a
             business including the development of doctrine which does
             not bar the amenability of the baseball business to the antitrust
             laws.

5

BASKETBALL

General

0223.   McCormick, Robert E. and Tollison, Robert D. "Crime and
           Income Distribution In A Basketball Economy." 6
           International Review of Law and Economics 115-124. (June
           1986).
                Finds that basketball violations generally parallel criminal
           activity and that a greater number of fouls (crime) in basketball
           is associated with a more equal distribution in scoring
           (income).

Antitrust

0224.   Daspin, D. Albert. "Of Hoops, Labor Dupes and The Antitrust
           Ally-Oops: Fouling Out The Salary Cap." 62 Indiana Law
           Journal 95-125. (Winter 1986).
                Discusses 1983 salary cap policy of NBA. Argues it
           constitutes market restraint on top draft choices. Relates
           Mackey v. NFL regarding labor-management agreements.
           Shows salary cap violates section 1 of Sherman Act.

0225.   Foraker, Scott J. "The National Basketball Association Salary
           Cap: An Antitrust Violation?" 59 Southern California Law
           Review 157-181. (November 1985).
                Shows how the salary cap violates antitrust law. Applies
           the Sherman Act to sports, discusses the Major League Baseball
           statutory labor and nonstatutory labor exemptions. Argues in
           favor of the Rule of Reason analysis.

0226.   Garland, Jeffrey.   "Antitrust Law: Procedural Safeguard
               Requirements In Concerted Refusals To Deal: An Application
               To   Professional   Sports-<u>Denver   Rockets   v.   All-Pro
               Management, Inc.</u> (C.D. Cal. 1971). 10 <u>San Diego Law Review</u>
               413-424. (February 1973).
                    Presents the court's reasoning where the court found an
               established National Basketball Association rule to be in
               violation of the antitrust laws and declared the rule to be
               illegal. Describes the court's analysis and its significance which
               should have a tremendous impact on the entire professional
               sport industry if followed. (The players draft and other
               established procedures may also be declared illegal).

0227.   Haray, Richard J. "Balancing Antitrust and Labor Policies On
               The Court: <u>Wood v. National Basketball Association</u>" 61 <u>St.
               John's Law Review</u> 326-341. (Winter 1987).
                    Discussion of the case where an athlete argued that the
               NBA-NBPA collective bargaining agreement was in violation
               of antitrust laws. Challenge was ruled invalid.

Collective Bargaining

0228.   Newton, Jon P.   "Suggestion For The New Collective-
               Bargaining-Agreement In Professional Basketball: The Legacy
               of The <u>Albert King</u> Case." 19 <u>Connecticut Law Review</u> 1001-
               1020. (Summer 1987).
                    Discusses free-agency and collective-bargaining agreement
               issues in the NBA. Focuses on salary cap and concerns over
               the nature of modifications of salary contracts. Offers case
               examples.

National Basketball Association

0229.   Burger, John Edward. "NBA's Four Year Rule: A Technical
               Foul?" 1972 <u>Law and The Social Order</u> 489-506. (1972).
                    Discusses <u>Denver Rockets v. All-Pro Management, Inc.</u>, in
               relation to <u>Silver v. New York Stock Exchange</u> and a number
               of other antitrust cases.   Reviews what amounts to
               justifications for the four-year rule. Examines whether the
               hardship exemption to the NBA four-year rule can satisfy
               <u>Silver</u>.

0230.   Simon, Richard K. "The First Great Leap: Some Reflections
               On The Spencer Haywood Case." 48 <u>Los Angeles Bar Bulletin</u>
               149-154. (March 1973).
                    Reviews <u>Denver Rockets, et al. v. All-Pro Management,
               Inc., et al.</u> Explores Spencer Haywood's "jumping" from the

ABA to the NBA, the player draft, the reserve clause and the NBA's four-year rule.

6
BOXING

General

0231.   Ensor, Richard J. "Fist-To-Fist Reform." 134 <u>New Jersey Lawyer</u> 35-39. (May/June 1990).
         Reviews sports regulatory practices in New Jersey regarding boxing. Discusses the 1983 inquiry, the SCI Interim Report of 1984, legislative action and future trends.

0232.   "Homicide and Boxing?" 14 <u>Criminal Justice Newsletter</u> 6. (August 29, 1983).
         Analyzes the increase in the national homicide rate immediately after a heavyweight championship fight. Found a 12.46% increase.

0233.   New York Joint Legislative Committee on Sports and Physical Fitness. <u>Report on Professional Boxing</u>. N.P.: State of New York, 1963.
         Examines the history and administration of professional boxing in New York State. Discusses safety rules and equipment, the morality, medical and financial aspects, and role of the underworld in boxing. Presents conclusions and recommendations. Appendices include revenue and expense comparisons, and a sample of the financial questionnaire.

0234.   Philippart, M. "Urgence de l'assainissement des combats du ring" (in French). 75 <u>Journal des Tribunaux</u> (Belgium) 37. (January 1960).
         Involves the urgency of making boxing more sane and less violent. Reviews history of an attempt to legislatively prohibit boxing and wrestling. Examines injuries incurred in boxing. Includes opinions of the medical community as it involves the

nature of boxing. Concludes that protection of the athlete in boxing is of primary importance.

0235.   "Pugilist and The Law, The." 20 Law Notes 182-184. (January 1917).
             Brief note questioning what seems to be a double-standard in a prize fighting case. Plaintiff (prize fighter) brought suit against defendant, the fight promoting club, for refusing to pay the prize fighter after he had lost as the result of a foul. Court denied recovery arguing that plaintiff violated the rules of his contract thus causing termination of the fight.

0236.   "Save Boxing From Barbarism." 97 The Los Angeles Daily Journal 4. (December 17, 1984).

Betting

0237.   "Crimes-Games-Wagering On A Prize Fight." 23 New York University Law Quarterly Review 195-197. (January 1948).
             A short discussion of Sections 1710 and 1712, and the "Walker Law" of the New York Penal Law as they relate to prize fighting and wagering on prize fights. Cites a recent decision that reiterates that distinction between casual betting or gambling, and betting or gambling as a business or a profession. The courts have treated casual betting and gambling more leniently than gambling as a business or profession.

Liability

0238.   Laufer, Laurence. "Uniform Health and Safety Standards For Professional Boxing: A Problem In Search of A Federal Solution?" 15 Columbia Human Rights Law Review 259-294. (Spring 1984).
             Reviews physical risks in professional boxing, failure of boxing industry to regulate itself, state regulation, the possibility of federal regulation, alternatives to federal regulation and the abolition of boxing as a sport.

0239.   Miller, Michael J. "Aftermath of A Tragedy-Liability of The New York State Athletic Commission For Injuries Suffered In A Prizefight." 14 Syracuse Law Review 79-84. (Fall 1962).
             Note exploring the possible liability of the New York State Athletic Commission which sanctioned a prizefight that resulted in the death of one of the fighters. Presents a brief history and purpose of the New York State Athletic Commission. Reviews Rosensweig v. State 5 NY2d 404, 158

N.E.2d 229, 185 NYS2d 521 (1959), (decided that the state was
not liable for the death of a fighter when the death was shown
to be caused by the negligence of the examining physician).
Reports that, because the fighter relied on the evaluation of the
examining physician, the rule of assumption of risk does not
apply. Cites changes in the law which makes the examining
physician one who is compensated by the state. Explores the
question of what elements must be present in order to prove
the state's liability.

Motion Pictures

0240.   "Motion Pictures of Prize Fights."   31 <u>Law Notes</u> 144-145.
              (November 1927).
              Note regarding 1912 Act of Congress which prohibited
              interstate transportation of films on prize fighting. Discusses
              purpose of the Act, what it expressly forbade, and the fact that
              the Act served a specific purpose at a specific time. Relates how
              evading the Act has been accomplished.

7

CHEMICAL SUBSTANCES

General

0241.   Arkfield, JoAnn M. "Crimes; Controlled Substances-Athletic
             Ability." 19 Pacific Law Journal 535. (January 1988).
                 Brief review of California's Health and Safety Code 11153.5
             regarding the use of a controlled substance and it being used to
             increase athletic ability.

0242.   Brower, Edith S. "High Anxiety." 134 New Jersey Lawyer 21-
             26. (May/June 1990).
                 Discusses drug use, student searches, right of privacy, due
             process issues and federally based claims regarding student use
             of drugs.

0243.   Fonti, Joseph F. "Does The National Collegiate Athletic
             Association's Drug Testing Program Test Positive If It Is
             Subjected To Constitutional Scrutiny?" 37 Drake Law Review
             83-102. (1987/1988).
                 Examines whether NCAA is a state actor, whether it is
             subject to fourth and fourteenth amendments of U.S.
             Constitution and whether the drug testing program is
             constitutional. Questions whether drug testing program is in
             violation of the fifth amendment.

0244.   Leeson, Todd A. "The Drug Testing of College Athletes." 16
             Journal of College and University Law 325-341. (Fall 1989).
                 Reviews NCAA's drug testing program as well as state and
             federal litigation. Surveys other issues related to drug testing.

0245.   Roth, Norma. "Sports Policies Toward The Use of Drugs By
             Players." 31 Boston Bar Journal 28. (July-August 1987).

0246.   Wolff, Maria Tai. "Play By The Rules? A Legal Analysis of
               The United States Olympic Committee-Soviet Olympic
               Committee Doping Control Agreement." 25 Stanford Journal
               of International Law 611-646. (Spring 1989).
                    Examination of the doping control agreement between the
               USOC and the Soviet OC. Reviews said Agreement from
               Olympic ideal and rights of athletes perspectives.

Drug Testing

0247.   Ayers, Deanne L.   "Random Urinalysis: Violating The
               Athlete's Individual Rights." 30 Howard Law Journal 93-142.
               (1987).
                    Discusses drug testing agreements of participants in
               professional tennis (MIPTC), NBA, NFL and major league
               baseball (MLBPA). Raises constitutional questions of testing.
               Argues against random testing for professional sports.

0248.   Brock, Stephen F. and McKenna, Kevin M. "Drug Testing In
               Sports." 92 Dickinson Law Review 505-570. (Spring 1988).
                    Outlines drug testing programs in horse and harness racing,
               professional baseball, football, basketball, hockey, the NCAA
               and other amateur sports. Presents cases which challenge
               under privacy and nonprivacy constitutional and contractual
               violations. Finds general permissibility of voluntary and
               reasonable cause testing.

0249.   Cochran, J. Otis. "Drug Testing of Athletes and The United
               States Constitution." 92 Dickinson Law Review 571-607.
               (Spring 1988).
                    Argues that mandatory drug testing is a violation of
               athlete's rights.   Examines professional and amateur drug
               testing programs in a constitutional setting.   Questions
               effectiveness of drug testing as a means of combatting use of
               drugs. Offers alternative plan.

0250.   Covell, Kerrie S. and Gibbs, Annette. "Drug Testing and The
               College Athlete." 23 Creighton Law Review 1-18. (1989/1990).
                    Reviews current drug testing programs for college athletes,
               how they work, why test for drugs, the student response and
               court decisions.

0251.   Dobberstein, Eric. "Drug Testing: The Toughest Competition
               An Athlete Ever Faces." 13 Thurgood Marshall Law Review
               143-160. (Fall/Spring 1987/1988).
                    Presents history of drug testing. Reviews drug testing
               within context of issues of state action, equal protection,

procedural due process, reasonable search and seizure, the fifth amendment, and the right to privacy and civil rights.

0252. Ford, James B. "Drugs, Athletes, and The NCAA: A Proposed Rule For Mandatory Drug Testing In College Athletics." 18 John Marshall Law Review 205-236. (Fall 1984).

Discusses need for drug testing rule in college athletics. Addresses necessity of conforming to the Constitution. Treats relationship between courts' determination that NCAA is a state actor, and subsequent scrutiny of NCAA in relation to due process and equal protection clauses. Proposes drug testing rule to balance NCAA goals and student-athlete rights.

0253. Greenblatt, David J. "Urine Drug Testing: What Does It Test?" 23 New England Law Review 651-666. (Winter-Spring 1989).

Analyzes the accuracy and interpretation of urine testing for drug abuse. Cocaine and marijuana are examined separate from anabolic steroids.

0254. Keenan, Robert M., III. "Shoemaker v. Handel and Urinanalysis Drug Testing: Looking For An American Standard." 21 Georgia Law Review 467-504. (Fall 1986).

Discusses decision of Third Circuit Court of Appeals which upheld reasonableness of urinanalysis testing for jockeys. Explores fourth amendment law and battle between government interest and individual liberty. Notes most courts hold this decision as anomalous, and argues Court's analysis in case was erroneous.

0255. Lock, Ethan. "The Legality Under The National Labor Relations Act of Attempts By National Football League Owners To Unilaterally Implement Drug Testing Programs." 39 University of Florida Law Review 1-54. (Winter 1987).

Explores historical influence of drugs and drug programs on NFL. Shows how unclear the courts, management, and the players association approach the issue of unilateral drug testing. Provides different analyses of drug testing from existing case law. Discusses role of drug issue in terms of collective bargaining agreement.

0256. Lock, Ethan. "Drug Testing In The NFL and The Obligation To Bargain Under The NLRA." 3 The Labor Lawyer 239-266. (Spring 1987).

Abridgement of an article by same author published in 39 University of Florida Law Review (Winter 1987). Points out the role that the drug testing issue would play in the collective bargaining agreement between the NFLMC and NFLPA. Shows the uncertainty over the legality of a unilateral mandatory drug testing program.

0257.   Lock, Ethan and Jennings, Marianne. "The Constitutionality of
           Mandatory Student-Athlete Drug Testing Programs: The
           Bounds of Privacy." 38 University of Florida Law Review 581-
           613. (Fall 1986).
                Analyzes various questions according the constitutionality
           of drug testing programs of the NCAA and member schools.
           Focuses on fourth amendment privacy rights and protections
           to student-athletes. Discusses reasonableness of mandatory
           drug testing.

0258.   Martin, Gordon A., Jr. "Why Not Understand Drug Testing?"
           23 New England Law Review 645-649. (Winter-Spring 1989).
                Calls for a greater understanding of the basis for the drug
           testing of urine.

0259.   McBride, Deborah Holmes. "The NCAA Drug-Testing
           Program and The California Constitution: Has California
           Expanded The Right of Privacy?" 23 University of San
           Francisco Law Review 253-290. (Winter 1989).
                Examines NCAA drug-testing program and its
           constitutionality in relation to the California Constitution,
           including privacy, the drug-testing program itself, and the
           outcome on appeal of Hill v. NCAA.

0260.   Meloch, Sally L. "An Analysis of Public College Athlete Drug
           Testing Programs Through The Unconstitutional Condition
           Doctrine and The Fourth Amendment." 60 Southern
           California Law Review 815-850. (March 1987).
                Considers whether drug testing programs in public
           collegiate athletics invades right of privacy of student-athletes.
           Considers Fourth Amendment rights and reasonableness of
           mandatory drug testing as a search. Outlines justifications for
           these programs. Concludes these drug testing programs are
           unconstitutional and that bodily privacy outweighs interests of
           colleges.

0261.   Meredith, Robert J. "The NCAA Declares War: Student-
           Athletes Battle The Mandatory Drug Test." 16 Capital
           University Law Review 673-700. (Summer 1987).
                Focuses on NCAA drug testing policy and presents program
           at The Ohio State University. Weighs pros and cons of
           mandatory testing including the constitutionality of such
           activities. Offers case examples. Supports testing program as a
           battle against drugs and as a matter of public policy.

0262.   Pernell, LeRoy. "Drug Testing of Student Athletes: Some
           Contract and Tort Implications." 67 Denver University Law
           Review 279-300. (1990).

Focuses on the contractual link between the athlete and the university, and some common tort implications of drug testing. Appendices include sample consent and release forms for drug testing.

0263.   Rose, Allison. "Mandatory Drug Testing of College Athletes: Are Athletes Being Denied Their Constitutional Rights?" 16 Pepperdine Law Review 45-75. (December 1988).

Examines constitutionality of NCAA's mandatory drug testing program and its relationship of fourth amendment protections. Reviews state action requirement and whether there is state action in drug testing program. Discusses questions of search and seizure, and privacy rights. Provides appendix of NCAA banned substances.

0264.   Rose, Laurence H. and Girard, Timothy H. "Drug Testing In Professional and College Sports." 36 Kansas Law Review 787-821. (Summer 1988).

Examines issues involved in drug testing in college and professional sports. Discusses types and extent of drug use, why athletes use drugs, and drug testing programs in college athletics and in professional football, basketball, baseball and other professional sports. Speculates on the future of drug testing in sports.

0265.   Scanlan, John A., Jr. "Playing The Drug-Testing Game: College Athletes, Regulatory Institutions, and The Structures of Constitutional Argument." 62 Indiana Law Journal 863-983. (1986/1987).

Overviews present state of drug testing in college sports in light of relationship between law and society. Views process as a series of games between counselors, litigators and judges. Presents NCAA and Indiana University plans to test for drug use. Offers thorough constitutional analysis of process with case examples. Emphasizes role which social values and judicial doctrine play when considering such matters.

0266.   Scott, Mary L. "Is Innocence Forever Gone? Drug Testing High School Athletes." 54 Missouri Law Review 425-442. (Spring 1989).

Examines Schaill v. Tippecanoe County School Corp. including the proposed drug testing program, the logistics and enforcement. Focuses on relationship between program and fourth amendment rights. Analyzes decision in relation to other casework.

0267.   "Search and Seizure-Suspicionless Drug Testing-Seventh Circuit Upholds Drug Testing of Student Athletes In The

Public Schools." 103 Harvard Law Review 591-597. (December 1989).

Review facts, decision and reasoning in Schaill v. Tippecanoe County School Corp., 864 F.2d 1309 (7th Cir. 1988). Seventh Circuit decided that random drug testing did not violate a student's fourth amendment rights.

0268.   Spicer, Robert E., Jr. "Drug Testing, Student Athletes, and The Constitution." 13 Virginia Bar Association Journal 11(8). (Winter 1987).

0269.   Tapp, Mara. "Olympic Dispute Leads To International Legal Maze." 130 Chicago Daily Law Bulletin 1. (October 16, 1984).

0270.   Thaler, Craig H.   "The National Collegiate Athletic Association, Random Drug-Testing, and The Applicability of The Administrative Search Exception." 17 Hofstra Law Review 641-688. (Spring 1989).

Explores the question of search and seizure reasonability of the NCAA drug testing program under the fourth amendment.

0271.   Trossman, Jeff. "Mandatory Drug Testing in Sports: The Law in Canada." 47 University of Toronto Faculty of Law Review (Canada) 191-219. (Fall 1988).

Discusses drug abuse and mandatory drug testing in sports in North America. Examines mandatory drug testing programs within context of Canadian law. Reviews issues of search and seizure, their reasonability and the nature of consent in relation to mandatory drug testing programs.

Substance Abuse

0272.   Constant, Jean. "Belgian Legislation Against Drug-Taking In Sport." 19 Northern Ireland Legal Quarterly (U.K.) 160-181. (June 1968).

Points out that sport is a social phenomenon which involves both the spectators and the participants. Thus, as such, one will find in sport not only social phenomenon but legal action, reaction and response to said phenomenon. Reports on the 1965 Belgian law on drug taking. Briefly discusses the attraction that sport holds, the origin of drug-taking, the danger of drug-taking. Examines at length the Belgian legislative response to drug-taking.

0273.   Constant, Jean. "La Repression de la Pratique de Doping a l'occasion des Competitions Sportives." 47 Revue de Droit Penal et de Criminologie (Belgium) 207-242. (December 1966).

Surveys the phenomenon of "doping" in sports activities. Discusses the anti-doping law of 2 April 1965.

0274.   Doll, P.-J. "Repression de l'usage des stimulants a l'occasion des competitions sportives" (in French).   39 La Semaine Juridique, Juris-Classeur Periodique (France) 1927. (July 1965).

Overview of the use of stimulants in athletic competition. Reviews historic aspects of drug use in ancient Greece. Examines the circumstances under which sanctions can be applied to athletes when they are found to be using stimulants.

0275.   Freundenberger, Tim.   "Eliminating Drug Use In Sports-Utilizing Contractual Remedies." 6 Entertainment and Sports Lawyer 1(18). (Summer 1967).

Explores drug use by professional athletes, the options that a professional team may exercise when a player is found to be using drugs and how such drugs use affects the athlete's contract. Provides examples.

0276.   Wong, Glenn M. and Ensor, Richard J. "Major League Baseball and Drugs: Fight The Problem or The Players?" 11 Nova Law Review 779-813. (Winter 1987).

Reviews past and current drug testing issues and policies in Major League Baseball.   Examines changes which new Commissioner Ueberroth promoted regarding drug use in baseball.

8
CIVIL RIGHTS/ DISCRIMINATION IN SPORTS

0277.   Allen, William B. "Rhodes Handicapping Or Slowing The Pace of Integration." 19 New Perspectives 19-24. (Winter 1988).

0278.   Brennan, Mary Lynn. "Civil Rights In The Locker Room." 2 Journal of Communications and Entertainment Law 645-669. (Summer 1980).
          Discusses Ludtke v. Kuhn wherein plaintiff, a female sports writer, charged that the barring of her from a baseball locker room was in violation of her civil rights. Presents facts and circumstances of the case, a review of the state action issue, the argument of sex discrimination, and the applicability of equal protection and due process.

0279.   Forlati Picchio, Laura. "Discriminationi Nel Settore Sportivo e Comunita Europee" (in Italian). 59 Rivista di Diritto Internazionale (Italy) 745-760. (1976).
          Discussion of discrimination in the area of sports in the European Economic Community.

0280.   Lapchick, Richard E. "The Student Athlete." 19 New Perspectives 34-45. (Winter 1988).

0281.   McCormick, Robert E. and Meiners, Roger E. "Sacred Cows, Competition, and Racial Discrimination." 19 New Perspectives 46-52. (Winter 1988).

0282.   McKenna, Kevin M. "Age Limitations and The National Collegiate Athletic Association: Discrimination Or Equating Competition?" 31 Saint Louis University Law Journal 379-407. (March 1987).
          Discusses Butts v. NCAA regarding NCAA Bylaw 5-1-(d)-(3) and the age/experience limitation. Reviews the promulgation

of the Bylaw, its constitutional limitations, judicial interpretation and its application to <u>Butts</u>. Provides statistics on average age by race and per conference of Division I basketball players. Examines the Bylaw in the foreign student athlete context.

0283.   "Need an Author? "Civil Rights Law: State Action-National Collegiate Athletic Association v. Tarkanian." 12 <u>Harvard Journal of Law and Public Policy</u> 1106-1120. (Summer 1989).

0284.   Oliver, Eugene, Jr. "Constitutional Rights of Black People." 197 <u>New York Law Journal</u> 36. (May 1, 1987).

0285.   Parker, Johnny Clyde. "Civil Rights Legislation: Getting Black Executives Off First Base In Professional Team-Sports." 1986 <u>Columbia Business Law Review</u> 219-231. (1986).

   Explores presence of black executives in professional sports and differential application of Title VII standards across employment case continuum. Focuses on football, baseball and basketball. Reviews professional sports industry and the Title VII framework.

0286.   Petr, Todd A. "Bylaw 5-1-(j): A Historical Perspective." 19 <u>New Perspectives</u> 15-18. (Winter 1988).

9

ELIGIBILITY RULES

0287.   Anderson, Mark F. "Sherman Act and Professional Sports Associations' Use of Eligibility Rules." 47 <u>Nebraska Law Review</u> 82-90. (January 1968).

          Consists of an analysis of the use of eligibility rules of one professional sports association against another competing professional sports association. Argues that the use of eligibility rules are intended to suppress competition, and are used as a secondary or group boycott in per se violation of the Sherman Act.

0288.   Chamblis, Samuel M., III. "Professional Football's Four-Or-Five Year Eligibility Rule: High Time To Punt." 14 <u>Memphis State University Law Review</u> 517-548. (Summer 1984).

          Discusses possible antitrust violation of rule which establishes professional eligibility. Provides historical perspective of applications of antitrust laws to professional sports. Compares the per se and rule of reason analyses. Offers similar eligibility rules in other professional sports leagues. Presents possible defenses to violations and justifications for these rules. Concludes the rule violates section 1 of Sherman Act.

0289.   Demoff, Marvin A. "Eligibility Requirements For Young Athletes." 4 <u>Los Angeles Lawyer</u> 34(7). (June 1981).

          Discusses N.F.L. rules 14.2 and 12.1 pertaining to the eligibility of athletes, and whether such an unwillingness to deal with the athletes in question is in violation of antitrust laws.

0290.   Petrie, John T. "Interscholastic Sports Eligibility-The Transfer Rule." 37 <u>Washington State Bar News</u> 17-20. (October 1983).

Examination of Washington Interscholastic Activities Association's (W.I.A.A.) transfer rule and its effect on interscholastic sports eligibility. Offers case law analysis pertaining to the rule.

0291.   Rothenberg, Alan I. and Tellem, Arn, H.   "Restraints On Professional Athletes." 4 Los Angeles Lawyer 35(7). (June 1981).

Focuses on the restraints on the mobility of professional athletes and its relationship to the antitrust laws, the four-or-five year rule, per se illegality of refusal to deal, professional hockey's 20-year-old rule and the N.F.L.'s eligibility rules.

0292.   Tarone, Gregory J. "Amateur Athletes and Eligibility." 93 Case and Comment 3(4). (May-June 1988).

0293.   Tarone, Gregory J.   "Advising The Amateur Athlete To Preserve Eligibility." 62 Florida Bar Journal 23-25. (February 1988).

Suggests ways and reasons for athletes to maintain their amateur status. Discusses athletics from both an Olympic and an intercollegiate perspective.

0294.   Uerling, Donald F. "High School Athletics and Due Process: Notice of Eligibility Rules." 57 Nebraska Law Review 877-892. (1978).

Reports on Teare v. Board of Education, and Compagno v. Nebraska School Activities Association (whether high school athletic participation is protected by the due process clause of the fourteenth amendment and whether the notice of eligibility rules for participation satisfied the requirements of the amendment. Discusses matters of fact and due process.

10

FOOTBALL

General

0295.   Brown, Fred R.   "Torts-Master-Servant-Respondeat Superior-
"Free Time" As Within The Scope of Employment."   13
Duquesne Law Review 349-358. (Winter 1974).
         Examines Nauk v. Wright, 367 F.Supp. 961 (M.D. Pa. 1973),
wherein defendant's motion for summary judgment was
denied.   Court's denial was based on the finding that
defendant, a professional football player in summer camp, was
still within the scope of employment even thought the
accident in question occurred during "free time."   Includes
discussion of two admiralty cases upon which the court based
its decision.

Antitrust

0296.   Abrams, Bobby. "Take Me Out To The Ballgame." 16 Journal
of The Beverly Hills Bar Association 163-170. (Summer 1980).
         Examination of the NFL draft, its relationship to the
antitrust laws, public policy, labor policy, its deficiencies and
alternative to it.

0297.   Bartolini, Anthony L. "Sherman Anti-Trust Act-Exemption of
Professional Football." 2 Villanova Law Review 120-122.
(November 1956).
         Reviews court of appeals in Radovich v. National Football
(9th Cir. 1956) that football is not within scope of antitrust laws.
Points out 1953 Toolson case and 1955 United States v.
International Boxing Club and their relationship to case.
Concludes it is difficult to perceive decision being upheld

because the baseball exemption would then extend to football and other professional team sports (basketball and hockey): the the International Boxing Club decision has given fair warning that judicial immunity awarded to baseball (Toolson case) is to be narrowly construed.

0298.   Barton, B. J.   "Anti-Trust Law-Interstate Commerce-Professional Football." 11 Southwestern Law Journal 516. (Fall 1957).
Reports Radovich v. National Football League places organized football within provision of antitrust acts due to volume of interstate business involved. Presents background of cases, interpretations of "trade or commerce," and 1922 Federal Baseball case and others (including Gardella and Toolson) which attempted to apply anti-trust laws to entertainment.   Argues for legislation to end arbitrary discrimination which favors baseball but not other professional sports.

0299.   Brown, Charles C. "Professional Football and The Antitrust Laws: Impact of United States Football League v. National Football League and A Proposal for Change." 31 Saint Louis University Law Journal 1057-1081. (October 1987).
Discusses Sherman Antitrust Act and its relation to sports. Points out relevant product and geographic market determinations. Analyzes case and rejects the per se doctrine approach for determining monopolizations (particularly the television market) by the NFL. Proposes to amend Sports Broadcasting Act of 1961 to break off Commissioner's power over the television market and to allow for greater competition.

0300.   Brumbaugh, John C.   "Trade Regulation-Antitrust Acts-Unlawful Conspiracy-Non-Coverage of Professional Football." 25 University of Cincinnati Law Review 519-521. (Fall 1956).
Comments on the Radovich v. National Football League (held and affirmed that professional football is immune from the antitrust laws). Explains 1922 Federal Baseball, 1953 Toolson, 1955 United States Boxing and that (according to the courts) baseball is not a business but boxing is; football is not a business, based on the baseball exemption. Suggests that likely opinion of Supreme Court is that it won't exempt football from federal antitrust laws but will leave exemption a matter for Congress.

0301.   Bryce, Philip R. "Sherman Act and Professional Team Sports: The NFL Rozelle Rule Invalid Under The Rule of Reason." 9 Connecticut Law Review 336-345. (Winter 1977).

Discusses <u>Mackey v. National Football League</u> (the United States Court of Appeals for the Eighth Circuit found that the "Rozelle Rule" was in violation of the Sherman Act). "Roselle Rule" was deemed to be an unreasonable restraint of trade. Discusses court's rejection of the per se doctrine in favor of the rule of reason.

0302.   Clendenon, Donn A. "Antitrust-Restraint of Trade-Group Boycott-NFL College Draft." 15 <u>Duquesne Law Review</u> 747-756. (Summer 1977).

Reviews <u>Smith v. Pro-Football</u>, 420 F. Supp. 738 (D.D.C. 1976), wherein plaintiff initiated an antitrust action. He argued that the college football draft was a concerted refusal to deal, constituting a group boycott, and that the boycott prevented the plaintiff from being able to market himself in a free market which resulted in the plaintiff unable to secure a contract which would have economically protected him.

0303.   Eglinski, Georgann Hansen. "Antitrust-Professional Football-The Rozelle Rule As An Unreasonable Restraint of Trade." 26 <u>Kansas Law Review</u> 121-132. (Fall 1977).

Note examining the Rozelle Rule in the context of <u>Mackey v. National Football League</u>. Reviews the progress of <u>Mackey</u> through the district and circuit court. Considers the revised version of the rule resulting from the collective bargaining agreement.

0304.   Elliott, Jeffrey M. "NFL Draft and The Antitrust Laws-The Player Draft of The National Football League Held To Violate The Federal Antitrust Laws." 41 <u>Albany Law Review</u> 154-161. (1977).

Discusses <u>Smith v. Pro-Football</u>, 421 F. Supp. 738 (D.D.C. 1976), wherein the professional football draft of college players constituted a per se violation of the antitrust laws. Due to the absence of a collective bargaining agreement, the labor law exemption to the antitrust laws was not applicable. Provides a review and analysis of the nonstatutory labor law exemption, the per se rule, and the rule of reason as they relate to the draft.

0305.   Grauer, Myron C. "Recognition of the National Football League As A Single Entity Under Section 1 of the Sherman Act: Implications of The Consumer Welfare Model." 63 <u>Michigan Law Review</u> 1-59. (October 1983).

Analyzes relationship and interplay between Sherman Act enforcement and consumer wealth maximization as regards the efficient function of the NFL. Cites <u>Los Angeles Memorial Coliseum Commission v. NFL</u> and <u>North American Soccer League v. NFL</u> among other cases.

0306.   Holford, Elizabeth J. "Punt, Impasse or Kick: The 1987 NFLPA
                 Antitrust Action." 22 Akron Law Review 61-79. (Summer
                 1988).
                    Reviews NFLPA's antitrust action against NFL following
                 1987 strike. Provides brief historical overview of the NFL,
                 NFLPA, collective bargaining history between the two and the
                 nature and extent of antitrust litigation in professional football
                 including current suit which includes analysis of district
                 court's opinion.

0307.   Kornmehl, Bernard B. "National Football League Restrictions
                 On The Competitive Bidding For Players' Services." 24 Buffalo
                 Law Review 613-641. (Spring 1975).
                    Reviews the NFL's restrictions pertaining to competitive
                 bidding for a player's athletic services. Reports on Kapp v.
                 National Football League. Provides historical overview of
                 professional sports and the antitrust laws. Reports the ruling
                 in Kapp that the NFL was in per se violation of the antitrust
                 laws. Discusses the issues of group boycott, price fixing and tie-
                 in contract. Presents a discussion on the rationale and the
                 impact of the decision.

0308.   Kurlantzick, Lewis S. "Thoughts On Professional Sports and
                 The Antitrust Laws: Los Angeles Memorial Coliseum
                 Commission v. National Football League." 15 Connecticut
                 Law Review 183-208. (Winter 1983).
                    Provides case background, discusses issues of franchise
                 relocation and territorial allocation, reviews NFL's practices
                 and restraints, and antitrust questions.

0309.   McCormick, Robert A. and McKinnon, Matthew C.
                 "Professional Football's Draft Eligibility Rule: The Labor
                 Exemption and The Antitrust Laws." 33 Emory Law Journal
                 375-440. (Spring 1984).
                    Analysis of the relationship between professional football's
                 draft eligibility rules and antitrust laws. Discusses draft
                 eligibility rule as part of football's collective bargaining
                 agreement and whether labor exemption provides immunity
                 to the draft rules from antitrust scrutiny. Concludes that draft
                 eligibility rules are in violation of antitrust laws.

0310.   "Professional Football Held Within Purview of Sherman Act."
                 57 Columbia Law Review 725-728. (May 1957).
                    Reviews Radovich v. National Football League 77 Sup. Ct.
                 390 (1957) (professional football subjected to Sherman Act).
                 Surveys and reviews Federal Baseball Club v. National League,
                 Toolson v. New York Yankees, United States v. International
                 Boxing Club and their relation to Sherman Act and to
                 professional football.

0311. Riga, Peter J. "Professional Sports and The Public Interest: A Kick In The Grass." 7 Whittier Law Review 551-589. (1985).

Argues the public interest must be given greater difference in antitrust litigation. Promotes Congressional legislation, and provides the bills in Appendix. Discusses important antitrust cases relation to NFL. Overviews nonstatutory labor exemption.

0312. Roman, Neil K. "Illegal Procedure: The National Football League Players Union's Improper Use of Antitrust Litigation For Purposes of Collective Bargaining." 67 Denver University Law Review 111-134. (1990).

Summarizes Powell v. National Football League, collective bargaining, antitrust litigation and the scope of the nonstatutory labor exemption to the antitrust laws.

0313. Shea, Michael Charles. "The Sherman Act: Football's Player Controls-Are They Reasonable?" 6 California Western Law Review 133-146. (Fall 1969).

Comment examining the use of the player draft and the option clause as means of controlling players in professional football. Explores how these means may be in violation of antitrust laws. Provides methods and suggestions for alleviations and alternative courses for professional football to follow.

0314. Stanley, James R. "Federal Antitrust Laws-Monopolies-Professional Football." 62 Dickinson Law Review 96. (October 1957).

Discusses Supreme Court in Radovich v. National Football League, 352 U.S. 447 (1957). Reviews relationship of professional sports and antitrust laws. Examines Federal Baseball Club v. National League, Toolson v. New York Yankees, and United States v. International Boxing Club. Discusses situation confronting lower courts in Radovich. Reports Boxing case is law while baseball cases are exception. Concludes that problems which Radovich raises must be handled by Congress to regulate interests of all parties involved.

0315. Strauss, Steven M. "Sport In Court: The Legality of Professional Football's System of Reserve and Compensation." 28 UCLA Law Review 252-290. (December 1980).

Argues the 1977 collective bargaining agreement between National Football League Players' Association (NFLPA) and the National Football League Management Council (NFL) is in violation of antitrust laws. Argues that agreement does not qualify for the labor exemption. Provides historical overview of sports in court prior to 1977 Agreement. Discusses 1977 Agreement in relation to antitrust laws, labor exemption as it applies to professional sports, and the applicability of non-statutory labor exemption to Agreement.

0316.   Underhill, David S.   "The National Football League Draft Eligibility Rule, The Labor Exemption, and Antitrust Law: It is Time To Put Amateurism Back Into College Athletics."   3 Cooley Law Review 567-608. (1985).

Argues against the Rule as unreasonable restrain to trade. Determines the Rule fails Mackey test. Finds Rule a violation of Sherman Act. Concludes that elimination of Rule would reinstate amateurism in college sports.

0317.   "The USFL Suit, Antitrust, and Sports: Interview With Howard Cosell." 1 Antitrust 22-26. (Winter 1987).

0318.   Weiss, Allan J.   "Touchdown Or Bring The Ball Back For A 15 Yard Penalty: Ramifications of Hold That The National Football League Is A Monopoly In Professional Football." 1987 Detroit College of Law Review 1151-1180. (Winter 1987).

Provides analysis of the case, verdict and damages awarded in United States Football League v. National Football League. Reviews the role of television, the antitrust exemption allowed facilitating the AFL/NFL merger and the case of Mid-South Grizzlies v. National Football League.

0319.   Whiting, John T.   "Illegal Procedure-The Rozell Rule Violates The Sherman Antitrust Act." 59 Marquette Law Review 632-654. (1976).

Comprehensive examination of John Mackey v. National Football League. Case centered on plaintiffs contention that the Rozelle Rule was a violation of antitrust laws. Court rules in favor of the plaintiffs, that the Rozelle Rule was a violation. Contains the Rozelle Rule. Cites related casework and provides quotes from cases.

Canada

0320.   Sopinka, J.   "Extra-Contractual Aspects of Canadian Professional Football." 16 Faculty of Law Review (University of Toronto) (Canada) 38-52. (April 1958).

Examines contractual aspects of professional football in Canada raising questions to validity. Reviews Detroit Football Co. v. Dublinski ([1956] O.R. 744; 4 D.L.R.(2d) 688 [Ont. High Ct.]). Discusses processes of negotiation list and draft. Explains role of Canadian Rugby Union card (C.R.U. card) and control that agreement and teams have over individual player.

Questions whether such agreement is a conspiracy, restraint of trade, a conspiracy to inure, proscribed by statute, or against public policy. Explores whether player has remedy. Calls for individualization of professional sports through legislation.

Contracts

0321.   Hogrogian, John. "Professional Football-Are Three One-Year Agreements Signed At One Sitting Actually One Contract? Are Players Public Figures?: Chuy v. Philadelphia Eagles Football Club, 431 F. Supp. 254 (E.D. Pa. 1977)." 10 Connecticut Law Review 350-364. (Winter 1978).

Reviews case where plaintiff sued for breach of contract and defamation. Discusses the ambiguity involved in the drafting and signing of three single-season contracts.

National Football League

0322.   Ahern, Terrance. "N.F.L.'s Final Victory Over Smith v. Pro-Football, Inc.: Single Entity-Interleague Economic Analysis." 27 Cleveland State Law Review 541-564. (1978).

Examines the relationship between the restrictive process processes of the NFL and the Sherman Antitrust Act. Discusses the player draft, the signing of the Standard Player Contract, the tampering rule, the Rozelle Rule, and the option clause. Explores the validity of restrictive processes in light of the decision. Includes an economic analysis which the author identifies as being cooperative more than it is competitive.

0323.   Brody, Burton F. "NFL Free Agency: A Modest Proposal." 67 Denver University Law Review 155-164. (1990).

Reviews the current situation and the author's proposal for a free agency system.

0324.   Demoff, Marvin A. "Eligibility Requirements For Young Athletes." 4 Los Angeles Lawyer 34(7). (June 1981).

Discusses N.F.L. rules 14.2 and 12.1 pertaining to the eligibility of athletes, and whether such an unwillingness to deal with the athletes in question is in violation of antitrust laws.

0325.   Farnsworth, A. Randall. "Herschel Walker v. National Football League: A Hypothetical Lawsuit Challenging The Propriety of The National Football League's Four-or-Five Year Rule Under The Sherman Act." 9 Pepperdine Law Review 603-640. (1982).

Examines antitrust laws, underpinnings and history of Sherman Act, rule of reason, per se illegality and group boycotts, and antitrust laws in professional sports. Analyzes the hypothetical lawsuit, the NFL's defenses, standing to sue under Sherman Act, application of rule of reason, of per se, and a number of NFL policies justifying the rule.

0326. Garvey, Ed. "Foreword To The Scope of The Labor Exemption In Professional Sports: A Perspective On Collective Bargaining In The NFL." 1989 Duke Law Journal 328-338. (April 1989).

Discusses the current stalemate between the NFLPA and the NFLMC and calls for a settlement in bargaining. Suggests the unions should concentrate more on an agreement over a fixed percentage of gross revenues than on free agency.

0327. Gray, John A. and Walters, Stephen J. K. "Is The NFL An Illegal Monopoly?" 66 University of Detroit Law Review 5-32. (Fall 1988).

Discusses Section 2 of Sherman Act in relation to professional football. Provides brief background of the NFL. Reviews the AFL case against the NFL including the antitrust exemption allowing the two leagues to merge. Reviews the USFL case in depth, the focuses, claims, theories, evidence and the relief involved.

0328. Kovach, K. A. "Labor Relations In The National Football League: Illegal Procedure, Delay of Game, and Unsportsmanlike Conduct." 41 Labor Law Journal 249-256. (April 1990).

0329. Lock, Ethan. "Powell v. National Football League: The Eighth Circuit Sacks The National Football League Players Association." 67 Denver University Law Review 135-154. (1990).

Examines employment relationship in the NFL, current dispute between the NFLPA and NFL and the decision in the case.

0330. Lock, Ethan. "Employer Unfair Labor Practices During The 1982 National Football League Strike: Help On The Way." 6 University of Bridgeport Law Review 189-226. (1985).

Discusses NLRA and its relation to 1982 NFL player strike. Offers cost-benefit analysis of unfair labor practices and overviews charges filed against NFL. Provides eventual costs and benefits to league. Stresses that employers have incentives for unfair labor practices since the Act does not provide for punitive damages.

0331.   Marencik, Karen A. "The National Football League Eligibility Rule and Antitrust Law: Illegal Procedure." 19 Valparaiso University Law Review 729-763. (Spring 1985).

Explores traditional antitrust analysis of businesses to the environment of the NFL. Points out the unavoidable conflict when applying both labor and antitrust law. Criticizes courts applications and interpretations of nonstatutory labor exemptions and offers solution.

0332.   "National Football League v. Beachland Ventures, Inc. 6 University of Miami Entertainment & Sports Law Review 139-153. (Spring 1989).

0333.   Novick, Donald. "Legality of The Rozelle Rule and Related Practices In The National Football League." 4 Fordham Urban Law Journal 581-596. (Spring 1976).

Analyzes Kapp v. NFL, and Mackey v. NFL. Reviews these cases, their relation to various NFL rules and the NFL rules' violation of antitrust laws. Surveys the per se doctrine and the rule of reason aspects of antitrust law. Explores the reasonableness of the challenged rules. Examines the challenged rules in terms of their purpose, effects and alternatives to them. Discusses collective bargaining and its relationship to the cases.

0334.   Prettyman, Keith A. "True Story of What Happens When The Big Kid Says, "It's My Football, and You'll Either Play By My Rules Or You Won't Play At All"." 55 Nebraska Law Review 335-361. (1976).

Note examining restrictive rules on player acquisition and player movement in professional football. Examines Kapp v. National Football League. Provides antitrust and labor law analysis on restrictive rules. Concludes with suggests for the NFL and the players.

0335.   Rothernberg, Alan I. and Tellem, Arn H. "Restraints On Professional Athletes." 4 Los Angeles Lawyer 35(7). (June 1981).

Focuses on the restraints on the mobility of professional athletes and its relationship to the antitrust laws, the four-or-five year rule, per se illegality of refusal to deal, professional hockey's 20-year-old-rule and the N.F.L.'s eligibility rules.

0336.   Singman, Bruce H. "Free Agency and The National Football League." 8 Loyola Entertainment Law Journal 259-274. (1988).

Focuses on feasibility of the total free agency plan proposed by NFL Players Association. Discusses issues of right of first refusal and compensation. Offers modifications of NFLPA "Game Plan '87" to please owners and players.

0337.　　　　Thornley, Arthur and Kruger, Daniel H. "The Crisis of Player Mobility: The NFL Strike of 1982." 38 <u>Labor Law Journal</u> 48-62. (January 1987).

Analyzes 1982 NFL players' strike. Provides history of player/owner confrontations. Surveys conflicting issues such as the Rozelle Rule, option clauses, the draft, trades and waivers and discipline and fines. Traces the development of the NFLPA. Discusses player demands, owner responses, nature of the pressures of the strike and the agreement.

0338.　　　　Zollers, Frances E. "From Gridiron To Courtroom To Bargaining Table: The New National Football League Agreement." 17 <u>American Business Law Journal</u> 133-153. (Summer 1979).

Explores the impact of antitrust laws and labor laws on those laws and on the future of professional football. Discusses NLRB certification of NFL Players' association, the collective bargaining agreement between the NFL and the NFL Players' Association, and the resulting labor law exemption.

11

GOLF

General

0339.   Enrenberg, Ronald G. and Bognanno, Michael L. "The Incentive Effects of Tournaments Revisited: Evidence From The European PGA Tour." 43 <u>Industrial and Labor Relations Reviews</u> 574-588. (February 1990).

0340.   "Legal Questions Relating to Golfing and Golf Courses." 31 <u>Scottish Law Review</u> (Scotland) 194-199. (September 1915).
Explains position of the Courts concerning the rights, privileges and duties of playing golf. Covers topics such as the taxing of golf clubs, the licensing of golf clubs, the issue of trespass, on private and cultivated lands, in pursuit of errant golf balls, the duty and responsibility of the management of golf clubs to prevent trespass; the rights of golfers, and the question of and possibility for liability between and among golfers who are struck during the course of play.

0341.   Watson, John H. "Three That Was Four." 54 <u>American Bar Association Journal</u> 777-780. (August 1968).
Holmesianian humor and analysis on golf and the controversy surrounding the 1968 Masters Tournament in Augusta, Georgia. In the tournament playing partner Tommy Aaron mistakenly wrote "4" instead of "3" as Roberto de Vicenzo's score for the seventeenth hole which resulted in de Vicenzo's losing by one stroke.

Negligence

0342.   Abrams, Robert.   "The Negligent Golfer."   18 New York University Intramural Law Review 167-178. (March 1963).

        Examines the American golfer's liability and the legal duties which American courts have imposed on the sporting golfer.   Outlines the limits of player liability.   Describes the essential elements of a cause of action against a golfer.   Gives the issues most often given to a jury to decide a case. Concludes that the golfer has been treated fairly and intelligently by the courts and has generally not been liable for the bad or unskillful shot and can generally play the game without fear or future legal liability if the legal duties have been performed.

0343.   Kelly, G. M.   "The Errant Golf Ball: A Legal Hazard."   1968 New Zealand Law Journal (New Zealand) 301+. (July 23-August 20, 1968).

        Reviews the relationship of golf to other branches of the law.   Reports on golf ball cases particularly those from the United States.   Discusses precedents and relevant legal principles.   Analyzes tort liability of other players, caddies and club employees, spectators and other lawful visitors, and trespassers.

0344.   Lambert, Thomas F., Jr.   "Sports Promoters' Liability: Golf."   29 ATLA Law Reporter 9-10. (February 1986).

        Discusses case of Baker v. Mid-Maine Medical Center, 499 A.2d 464 (Me. 1985) regarding the responsibilities incumbent on the sponsors of a golf exhibition to protect spectators from golfballs.

0345.   "Negligence-Infants-Standard of Care-11 Year-Old Boy Who Had Taken Golf Lessons and Had Played Golf Regularly Held to Adult Standard of Care While On The Golf Course."   33 Albany Law Review 434-437. (Winter 1969).

        Analyzes Neumann v. Shlansky, 58 Misc.2d, 128, 294 N.Y.S. 2d 628 (Westchester County Ct. 1968).   Contains supporting casework for discussion of standard of care, contributory negligence, and the holding of infants to higher standards of care.

0346.   O'Kane, H. J. and Schaller, W. L.   "Injuries From Errant Golf Balls: Liability Theories and Defenses."   37 Federation of Insurance and Corporate Counsel Quarterly 247-272. (Spring 1987).

        Analyzes cases of injured persons or damaged property due to golf balls traveling beyond and within golf course boundaries.

12

HOCKEY

General

0347.   Brent, Audrey S. "Hockey Violence - <u>Regina v. Langton</u> - Case Note." 32 <u>Criminal Reports</u> (N.S.) (Canada) 121-125. (1976).

Focuses on the case which was the first time that a Canadian appellate court considered questions of criminal law as they apply to the participants of organized sport. Points of law raised and examined in this case where consent, self-defense, and <u>ex turpi causa non oritur actio</u>. Cities appropriate criminal code, and casework relating to said point of law, as well as the parameters for each defense. Concludes by stating that the Court of Appeals did not render a written decision in said case.

Antitrust

0348.   Miller, Mark S. "National Hockey League's Faceoff with Antitrust: <u>McCourt v. California Sports, Inc.</u>" 42 <u>Ohio State Law Journal</u> 603-626. (1981).

Reviews development of statutory and non-statutory labor exemption from antitrust laws. Examines the purpose and problems of equalization provisions. Discusses relationship of antitrust laws to baseball, football and hockey. Explores and responds to arguments presented by <u>McCourt</u> dissent.

Compensation

0349.   Jones, J. C. H. and Walsh, William D. "Salary Determination In The National Hockey League: The Effects of Skills,

Franchise Characteristics, and Discrimination." 41 Industrial and Labor Relations Review 592-604. (July 1988).

Empirically examines the relationship between salary and factors of skill, monopoly, monopsony and discrimination in the N.H.L. Found that skill is the most dominant determinant of salary.

0350. Macdonald, J. Ross. "Stemkowski and Hanna v. Commissioner: The Canadian Hockey Players' Lament Turns To A (Partial) Paean." 31 Canadian Tax Journal (Canada) 475-477. (May-June 1983).

Discussion of the case regarding the method of allocation of total compensation to U.S. sources paid to Canadian hockey players.

Contracts

0351. Kyer, Clifford Ian. "A Case Study In Party Stipulation of Remedy: The NHL Standard Player's Contract." 39 University of Toronto Faculty of Law Review (Canada) 1-29. (Spring 1981).

Examines the issue of party stipulation of remedy (as found in Clause six of the standard player's contract-1977 Form - of the National Hockey League), and the court's traditional approach to the issue. Examines the business of professional hockey, development of the standard player's contract, and reasons for Clause six. Concludes with an argument of why the courts should give effect to the Clause.

Reserve System

0352. Econn, Douglass Andrew. "Antitrust-Servitude in Professional Sport. McCourt v. California Sports, Inc." 2 Whittier Law Review 559-574. (Spring 1980).

Reviews the case particularly plaintiff's contention that the reserve system of the N.H.L. is in violation of Section 1 of the Sherman Act. Reviews prior antitrust litigation in professional sports, the per se rule, rule of reason, labor exemption and alternative approaches.

0353. Steinberg, David L. "National Hockey League Reserve System: A Restraint of Trade?" 56 University of Detroit Journal of Urban Law 467-523. (Winter 1979).

A comment which analyzes the reserve system in professional hockey (vis a vis reserve systems in other professional sports), labor case law establishing grounds for antitrust liability exemption, and judicial decisions in various major sports. Analyzes whether the 1974 National Hockey

League reserve rule pertaining to free agents constitutes a violation of the Sherman Antitrust Act.

0354.   Wulsin, Richard. "Hockey's Reserve System and The Labor Exemption: McCourt v. California Sports, Inc." 15 New England Law Review 765-779. (Summer 1979-1980).

Examines the reserve system in the N.H.L. at the time of the W.H.A. (1972) and McCourt (1978, 1979) cases. Reviews the McCourt case from the district and appeals court perspective particularly regarding the nonstatutory labor exemption.

13

INJURIES

General

0355.   Amador, M. Dennis. "Judicial Scrutiny of Tortious Conduct In Professional Sports: Do Professional Athletes Assume The Risk of Injuries Resulting From Rule Violations?" 17 California Western Law Review 149-168. (Fall 1980).

Note which presents a broad overview of the theories of negligence and assault and battery as applied to professional and nonprofessional sports litigation. Addresses whether or not a professional athlete in a contact sport should be subject to liability for reckless violation of a safety rule. Should the doctrine of assumption of the risk be available to limit or bar recovery?

0356.   Briggs, William B. "Injury Grievance In the National Football League." 63 Law Institute Journal (Australia) 164-167. (March 1989).

Discusses the background and filing procedures for injury grievance in the NFL. Reviews special defenses that the team may use in response to injury grievance. Outlines hearing procedure and standards for determining a "physical inability to perform." Remarks on current status of the issue.

0357.   Burmeister, Joachim.   "Aufopferungsrechtliche Entschadigungsanspruce Staatlich Geforderter Hochleistungssportler."   36 Neue Juristische Wochenschrift (West Germany) 2617-2623. (November 1983).

Speaks to the issue of obligatory compensation for injured state-sponsored athletes.

0358.   Carlesen, Chris J.   "Sports Injuries; Obstacles To Recovery." 25 American Trial Lawyers Association 76-81+. (August 1989).

Discusses plaintiff's causes of action and four obstacles to recovering for sports injury. Tort causes of action are: intentional, generally, battery, recklessness negligence. Obstacles include reluctance of the court's consent and assumption of risk; plaintiff's reluctance to proceed via civil suit; and problems of multiple jurisdictions and tort doctrines.

0359.   Champion, Walter T., Jr. and Swygert, H. Patrick. "Non-professional Sport-Related Injuries and Assumption of Risk In Pennsylvania: Is There Life After Rutter?" 54 Pennsylvania Bar Association Quarterly 43-52. (January 1983).

Presents historical overview of use of assumption of risk doctrine in nonprofessional sports-related injuries in Pennsylvania. Examines cases from early 1900's including Schentzel, Jones and Rutter.

0360.   "Civil or Criminal Liability for Injuries In Field Sports." 46 Irish Law Times and Solicitor's Journal (Ireland) 308-309. (November 30, 1912).

Excerpts from an article in Case and Comment pertaining to loss of life resulting from football injuries. Compares prosecution for homicide resulting from prize fighting and football and the application of the law. Reviews two cases (1878 and 1898) of prosecution for manslaughter resulting from violence on the football field, the instructions of the justices to the juries and the verdicts returned.

0361.   Colapietro, Bruno.   "The Promoters' Liability For Sports Spectator Injuries."   46 Cornell Law Quarterly 140-158. (Fall 1960).

Extensive comment examining the injuries which were received by spectators only as a direct result of the game.   Provides a table listing the number of spectator liability cases from 1890 to 1959. Sports surveyed were: baseball, golf, auto racing, hockey, horse racing, wrestling and "others."   Discusses the duty of reasonable care, assumption of risk and contributory negligence. Points out that the courts have different rules for different sports. Argues for the adoption of a single set of general rules of liability for sports.

0362.   "Duty To Prevent Injuries By Third Persons."   13 Texas
           Law Review 146-147. (December 1934).
                Points out that a place of amusement must exercise
           reasonable care for the safety of its guests. A patron can
           recover against a place of amusement for injuries
           sustained as the result of actions by third persons.

0363.   Epstein, Robert K. "The Case Against Artificial Turf."   13
           Trial 42-45. (January 1977).
                Consists of an examination of the financial and
           physical costs involved in playing professional football on
           artificial turf. Discusses efforts made by various groups
           and organizations to address turf safety. Concludes with
           an introduction of Prescription Athletic Turf (PAT) as a
           reasonable alternative to artificial turf.

0364.   Girginov, A. and Dokovska D. "Sportnite   Travmi   i
           Nakazatelnata   Otfovornost" (in Bulgarian).   34
           Sotsialistichesko Pravo (Bulgaria) 54-59. (1985).
                Discusses sports injuries and the liability for these
           injuries.

0365.   Gorla, Gino. "A Decision of The Rota Fiorentina of 1780
           On Liability For Damages Caused By The 'Ball Game'."   49
           Tulane Law Review 346-357. (January 1975).
                Presents a decision of the Rota Fiorentina (one of the
           highest courts in the Granducy of Tuscany) and comments
           on its historical value and contemporary interest
           concerning immunity from liability in tort, a limitation of
           freedom of action for owners of sports establishments, and
           the burden, for those owners of suffering the
           inconvenience or minor damages incurred during
           ordinary play or "natural" course of the game.

0366.   Grayson, Edward. "Breaking New Ground In Schools."
           138 New Law Journal (U.K.) 532-533. (July 29, 1988).
                Discusses Van Oppen v. The Clerk To The Trustees of
           The Bedford Charity (Harper Trust). High Court decided
           that schools are not legally required to insure students
           against injuries incurred during sporting activities.

0367.   Grayson, Edward. "Re-visiting The Field of Play."   135
           New Law Journal (U.K.) 629-630. (June 28, 1985).
                Focuses on the application of duty of care principles to
           contact between players in sports.   Discusses said
           principles from their jurisprudential, practical and social
           standpoints as well as their application to the cases of
           Lewis v. Brookshaw, and Condon v. Basi.

0368.   Honorat, J.   "Repression des atteines a l'integrite corporelle consecutives a l'exercise des sports" (in French). Recuil Dalloz Sirey (France) 207. (October 1969).

Discusses injury in sports. Analyzes the role and responsibilities of the referee. Reviews circumstances and judicial outcomes in a number of sports.

0369.   Horvitz, David. S.   "Tort Law-Reckless Misconduct In Sports." 19 Duquesne Law Review 191-198. (Fall 1980).

In-depth analysis of Hackbart v. Cincinnati Bengals, Inc. and its relationship to tort law.

0370.   Joyal-Poupart, Renee.   "L'accident sportif; fondement du recours de la victime" (in French). 5 Themis (Canada) 143-150. (1970).

Discusses accidents in sports and the basis for the victim's appeal. Examines the extent and nature of contractual obligations and responsibilities in matters of sport.

0371.   Kirkwood, Genevieve and Purdue, Michael. "Amusement Arcades-Planning Permission Granted Contrary To Known Policy-Traders Not Consulted." Journal of Planning and Environmental Law (U.K.) 18-24. (January 1988).

0372.   Langerman, Samuel and Fidel, Noel.   "Responsibility Is Also Part of The Game." 13 Trial 22-25. (January 1977).

Discussion of sports injuries and the relationship to responsibility. Provides suggestions to plaintiff's attorney in a sports injury action. Examines and enumerates the responsibilities incumbent upon coaches and athletic programs. Stresses counsel's need to be familiar with the sports literature in question and the theory of assumed risk as a defense.

0373.   Marcus, Richard M.   "Sport Safety: On The Offensive." 8 Trial 12-13. (July-August 1972).

Lists statistics regarding sport injuries. Identifies four areas for recreational safety: safe premises, safe equipment, safe training, and safe supervision. Reviews the lawyer's role in sport safety, public remedies (legislation) and private remedies (litigation). Briefly cites examples of legislation and litigation pertaining to safety.

0374.   Martha, Paul J. and Cavrich, Joseph W.   "Keeping Your Head Down At The Ballpark: Running A Stadium Is a Risky Litigation Game." 17 Brief 22(12). (Winter 1988).

0375.   Moore, Charles C.   "Civil or Criminal Liability For Injuries In Field Sports." 19 Case and Comment 163-166. (August 1912).

Discusses Req. v. Bradshaw (1878), 14 Cox. C.C. 83 and Req. v. Moore, 14 Times L. R. 229, at the Leicester Assizes in 1898. Deals with question of whether playing within the rules of the strenuous game of football is immaterial or not in the decision concerning football fatalities and whether usual and ordinary caution was in use. Includes tests used to determine whether the defendant's action was lawful or not. Reports the jury in the first case returned a verdict of not guilty: the verdict in the second case was guilty.

0376.   Peterson, Terri L. and Smith, Scott A.   "Role of The Lawyer On The Playing Field." 7 Barrister 10-13. (Summer 1980).

Survey of the number, percentage and costs of athletic injuries. Reviews role of lawyer, doctors and courts in sports injuries and sports injuries litigation. Discusses the role of intent in sports injuries and the impact of rising insurance costs on certain sports and litigation.

0377.   Postel, Theodore.   "Student Sues For Sport Injury."   136 Chicago Daily Law Bulletin 1. (January 12, 1990).

0378.   Postell, Claudia J.   "Workers' Comp: More Athletes Seek Benefits." 24 Trial 87-89. (June 1988).

0379.   Prusak, J.   "Urazy a Poskodenia Zdravia Pri Sporte a Problem Sportoveho a Pravneho Deliktu" (in Slovak). 124 Pravnik (Czechoslovakia) 791-804. (1985).

Discusses accidents and injuries occuring in physical training in Czechoslovakia. Identifies football, ice hockey, handball, basketball and skiing as the most dangerous sports in the country. Reviews the legal responsibility inherent in hard versus brutal play.

0380.   Rathie, D. S.   "Sporting Injuries and The Law."   18 Queensland Law Society Journal (Australia) 101-106. (April 1988).

0381.   "Res Ipsa Loquitur Sufficiency of Pleadings." 3 Louisiana Law Review 246-248. (November 1940).

A brief note discussing the application of res ipsa loquitur in a suit where plaintiff fell and was injured while walking up stairs in defendant's theater (Bentz v. Saenger-Ehrlich Enterprises, Inc., 197 So. 659 [La App.

1940]). Concludes that the application of <u>res ipsa loquitur</u> was justifiable in that owner has a duty to provide a frequent and comprehensive inspection of his premises.

0382.   Rueter, Dieter. "Probleme der Transferentschadigung Im Fussballsport." 36 <u>Neue Juristische Wochenschrift</u> (West Germany) 649-656. (March 1983).

Reports that according to a DFB statute, the club that receives a player in trade is responsible for paying for injury compensation. Since 1980, a club may not put a player into "cold storage" until negotiations are complete.

0383.   Samuels, Alec. "Sport Injury and The Law." 24 <u>Medicine, Science and The Law</u> (U.K.) 254-260. (October 1984).

Reviews legal claims arising out of participating in sports. Examines defenses, liability and responsibility in a number of sports.

0384.   Spevacek, Charles E.   "Injuries Resulting From Nonintentional Acts In Organized Contact Sports: The Theories of Recovery Available To The Injured Athlete." 12 <u>Indiana Law Review</u> 687-711. (April 1979).

A note which examines a new chapter in sports litigation in the light of relative historical and legal perspectives surrounding the law and organized athletics (where an Illinois appellate court held that a participant in a contact sport may be found liable in tort for injuries inflicted nonintentionally upon another player). Analyzes this rule in the context of cases which have sought to interpret it and explores future application of the rule.

0385.   Steele, Robert T. "Sports Injuries and Sick Play." 124 <u>Solicitor's Journal</u> (U.K.) 354-355. (May 23, 1980).

Treats the issues of whether an injured athlete is entitled to sick pay while injured and whether that injury could result in the employee's termination.

0386.   Todaro, Gerald J. "Allocation of Risk Based On The Mechanics of Injury In Sports: A Proposed Presumption of Non-Fault." 10 <u>Communications and Entertainment Law Journal</u> 33-60. (Fall 1987).

Explores the influence of sports medicine on the reduction of sports injuries. Discusses the judicial attempts to differentiate the concepts of inherent risk, assumption of risk and risk due to negligence. Suggests presumption of non-fault.

0387. Torbert, Dixie; Spurgin, Gerald; and Snider, Jim. "Workmen's Compensation: Intentional Torts As Exceptions To The Exclusiveness of The Workmen's Compensation Acts-Injury Sustained On Employers' Softball Team Held Not Compensable-Common Law Action For Defamation Is Not Precluded By Exclusivity Provision, Workmen's Compensation Act." 6 American Journal of Trial Advocacy 529-534. (Spring 1983).

Discusses, in part, the Kemp case, 386 Mass. 730, 473 N.E.2d 526 (1982) where it was ruled that an employee's injury which result from the voluntary participation on an employer's softball team did not result from employment and was not compensable.

0388. Troy, F. E. "In Defense of Synthetic Turf." 13 Trial 46-48. (January 1977).

Brief report reviewing and safety record of artificial turf. Cites statistics and references.

0389. Wacke, Andreas. "Accidents In Sport and Game In Roman and Modern German Law." 42 Tydskrif Vir Hedendaagse Romeins-Hollandse Reg. (South Africa) 273-287. (August 1979).

Examines Roman law texts which pertain to accidents in sport and game. Discusses modern German law as it relates and applies to the accident under discussion. Includes injuries inflicted on passer-by and spectators by sportsmen, injuries of team-mates, duels between combatant athletes, the hiring of gladiators, and an accident caused by tossing someone in a blanket.

0390. Zuckman, Harvey L. "Throw Them To The Lions (or Bengals): The Decline and Fall of Sports Civilization As Seen Through The Eyes of A United States District Court." 5 Journal of College and University Law 55-63. (Fall 1977).

Overview of the application of tort law to sports. Discusses implications and relevance of Hackbart v. Cincinnati Bengals, Inc. and Nabozny v. Barnhill to and for colleges and universities. Demonstrates the distinguishing between actionable and non-actionable violations of the rules.

Civil Liability

0391. Leduc, Benoit. "La responsabilite de l'ecole en matiere d'education sportive" (in French). 33 Revue du Barreau (Canada) 454-473. (1973).

Focuses on the civil responsibility of the school in matters of sports education. Reports on the relationship between the parents and the schools from historical and current perspective. Presents incidents under discussion, including matters pertaining to the responsibility of the school, the nature of the offence, evidence related to the offence, and the standard and special means through which the school can achieve exoneration.

0392.   Nadel, Peter.   "On Finding Civil Liability Between Professional Football Players: Hackbart v. Cincinnati Bengals, Inc." 15 New England Law Review 741-764. (Summer 1979-1980).

Reviews the case. Includes facts of the case, an analysis of the holdings, remedies available and a discussion on civil liability and legislative action.

Criminal Liability

0393.   Chorlton, M. D.   "Consent In Games."   47 Journal of Criminal Law (U.K.) 75. (May 1983).

Review of the case of R. v. Taylor regarding injurious contact-and the consent to such contact - in a rugby football match.

0394.   Kligman, R. D.   "Tort Liability For Sports Injuries."   1 Canadian Insurance Law Review (Canada) 153-178. (1989).

0395.   Love, John J.   "Criminal Law: Consent As A Defense To Battery-The Problem of Athletic Contests."   28 Oklahoma Law Review 840-845. (Fall 1975).

A note which explores the defense of consent as that applies to criminal battery and relates to the question of one player inflicting injury against another player during an athletic contest.   Presents three stages where the legal system may proceed against the athlete.

Participants

0396.   Barklage, Daniel K.   "Torts-Participant In Athletic Competition States Cause of Action For Injuries Against Another Participant."   42 Missouri Law Review 347-354. (Spring 1977).

Discusses Nabozny v. Barnhill 33 Ill. App. 3d 212, 334 N.E. 2d 258 (1975) where plaintiffs, a goal keeper, who was injured during play while being in possession of the ball in the penalty area, sued for injuries sustained because soccer rules prohibit opposing players from making contact with the goal tender under the mentioned conditions. Examines theories upon which actions to recover for injuries caused by another player can be based.

0397.   Capetta, John. "The "Booby" Trap: Does The Violent Nature of Professional Football Vitiate The Doctrine of Due Care In Participant Tort Litigation?: Hackbart v. Cincinnati Bengals, Inc., 435 F. Supp. 352 (D. Colo. 1977)." 10 Connecticut Law Review 365-376. (Winter 1978).

Note examining the interplay of the principles of duty of care, recklessness and assumption of risk in a professional football game. Analyzes the court's rationale in allowing the defendant to escape civil liability for inflicting a serious injury on the plaintiff. Discusses the legal and social implications of this decision.

0398.   Capper, James E. "Torts: Athlete States Cause of Action For Injury During A Professional Football Game." 19 Washburn Law Journal 646-651. (Spring 1980).

Stresses the concept that willful or wanton disregard of the rules during a professional athletic contest which results in an injury to a player may give rise to tort liability.

0399.   Dolling, D. "Die Behandlung der Korperverletzung In Sport Im System Der Strafrechtlichen Sozialkontrolle" (in German). 96 Zeitschrift Fur Die Gesamte Strafrechtswissenschaft (West Germany) 36-65. (1984).

Discussion of sports injuries and their relation to the law. Considers injuries as they occur to participants and spectators in an athletic contest. Differentiates and reviews three types of sporting activities as they apply to the participants.

0400.   Grunsky, Wolfgang. "Zur Haftung Bei Sportunfallen." 30 Juristenzeitung (West Germany) 109-112. (February 1975).

Discusses a 1974 ruling which dismisses the suit of a player injured by a member of the opposing team unless a rule violation could be proved.

0401.   Hayes, Jacquelyn K. "Professional Sports and Tort Liability: A Victory for The Intentionally Injured Player." 1980 Detroit College of Law Review 687-709. (Summer 1980).

Review of Hackbart v. Cincinnati Bengals, Inc. Provides background and context of cases and relates case to previous casework. Examines court of appeals decision in Hackbart, reviews applicable theories of liability, explores reckless misconduct as the appropriate standard, discusses theory of respondeat superior and focuses on use of videotapes in future cases.   Concludes with a consideration of the precedent set, its value, and its possible influence on future cases.

0402.   Helal, Basil.   "Physical Risks In Modern Sport."   24 Medicine, Science and The Law (U.K.) 247-248. (October 1984).
Surveys occurrence of medical problems in boxing, fencing, running, rugby, football and swimming.

0403.   Hudson, A. H.   "Care In Sports."   102 Law Quarterly Review (U.K.) 11-13. (January 1986).
Raises questions regarding the issue of standard of care by players involved in contact sports. Reviews Condon v. Basi [1985], Wooldridge v. Summer [1963] and others.

0404.   Jacobs, Donald P.   "Federal Jurisdiction-Torts-Federal District Court In Diversity Suit May Not Refuse Jurisdiction Over Professional Football Player's Claim For Damages Resulting From Blow Intentionally Inflicted-Applicable Tort Standard For Recovery Is Reckless Misconduct."   11 Rutgers Camden Law Journal 497-506. (Spring 1980).
Comment examining Hackbart v. Cincinnati Bengals, Inc., wherein the court of appeals reversed the trail court's decision that claims which are the result of injuries incurred while playing professional football should not be adjudicated. The court of appeals applied the tort standard of reckless misconduct to the actions of the defendant.

0405.   Joseph, Kenneth.   "Tort Law-Negligence-Assumption of Risk-sports Injuries-the Pennsylvania Supreme Court Has Held That Except In Certain Instances, The Doctrine of Assumption of Risk Is Abolished In Pennsylvania."   21 Duquesne Law Review 815-833. (Spring 1983).
Discusses decision in Rutter v. Northeastern Beaver County School District which resulted in doctrine of assumption of risk being essentially abolished in Pennsylvania.

0406.   Lambert, Dale J.   "Tort Law and Participant Sports: The Line Between Vigor and Violence."   4 Journal of Contemporary Law 211-217. (Spring 1978).
Presents an overview and summary of tort law as it relates to the participants in athletic contests.   Offers discussion of appropriate casework.

0407.   Lindgren, Penny P. and Ream, Davidson. "Participants In Hazardous Recreational Activities." 27 For The Defense 5-9. (December 1985).

0408.   McKinney-Browning, Mabel C. "Playing With Pain: What Can You Do About A Sport Where Everyone Gets Injured?' 7 Update 26(9). (Fall 1983).
Round-table discussion on the issue of playing with an injury. Participants included three professional players and two lawyers.

0409.   Morris, Timothy P. "Sports and The Law." 5 Oklahoma City Law Review 659-682. (Fall 1980).
Analysis of Hackbart v. Cincinnati Bengals, Inc. Reviews the reasoning of the district and appellate courts. Juxtaposes the reasoning with tort tradition and the applicability of standards of criminal liability. Presents the facts, the criminal sanctions and defenses, and an analysis of tort concepts and defenses.

0410.   Narol, Mel. "Courts Defined Standard of Care In Player vs. Player Litigation." 12 The National Law Journal 23. (November 20, 1989).

0411.   Parmanand, Suryia K. "The Ambit of The Consent Defence In Sport Injury Litigation: The American Judicial Attitude." 19 Comparative and International Law Journal of Southern Africa (South Africa) 304-310. (1986).
Brief overview of the consent defence as it applies to sport injuries. Examines various tests and theories of sport injuries. Cites supporting casework for the majority and minority viewpoints. Analyzes what risks are assumed by those who participate in sports.

0412.   Quinn, Terence R. "Litigating Youth Sports Injuries." 22 Trial 76-79+. (March 1986).
Presents discussion of plaintiff's attorney's role and options available in youth sports injuries cases. Examines assumption of risk defense and ways of overcoming it, including analysis of factors involved with consent such as youth and inexperience, rules, equipment and waiver and releases. Provides suggestions for trial strategy.

0413.   Rochefort, Lawrence P. "A Course of Action For Florida Courts To Follow When Injured Sports Participants Assert Causes of Action." 4 Entertainment and Sports Law Journal 257-282. (Fall 1987).
Explores remedies available to a sports participant, defenses, the doctrine of assumption of risk in Florida and

problems with express assumption of risk.   Offers
suggestions for the Florida courts on how to deal with
contract sport cases.

0414.   Seki, James H.   "A Professional Football Player Owes A
Duty To All Participants To Refrain From Reckless
Misconduct   In The Course of a Professional Football
Game." 15 Gonzaga Law Review 867-879. (1980).
    Note on the Hackbart decision.   The Tenth Circuit
Court of Appeals held that recovery for injuries received
from reckless misconduct of a participant during a
professional football game is possible. Examines the tort
theories of ordinary negligence, recklessness, assault and
battery, and their applicability between sports participants.
Presents defenses of assumption of risk and contributory
negligence in the same context.

0415.   Sosniak, Mieczyslaw.   "On The Legal Problems of
Damages Caused During Games" (in Polish). 16 Palestra
(Poland) 22-33. (February 1972).
    Focuses on sports injuries for participants. Examines
the international aspects and solutions of the problem of
sports injuries.   Reports that this phenomenon has
experienced very little research in Poland.   Discusses
attempts to devise a single formula to handle the problem
of sports injuries.

0416.   "Sport and The Law-Supreme Court Blows The Whistle."
10 Queensland Law Society Journal (Australia) 295-296.
(October 1980).
    Reports on the case of McNamara v. Duncan (1971)
regarding a blow that the plaintiff received during the
court of a rugby game. Discusses the case, the ruling for
the plaintiff and the defenses of consent and "volenti non
fit injuria."

0417.   "Torts-Civil Liability of Athletes-Professional Football
Players May Have Had Tort Claim For Injuries
Intentionally Inflicted During Football Game."   84
Dickinson Law Review 753-768. (Summer 1980).
    Overviews the possibility of civil liability for injuries
received during a sporting event. Points out three tort
theories for bases of recovery.

0418.   Tucker, Neil R.   "Assumption of Risk and Vicarious
Liability In Personal Injury Actions Brought By
Professional Athletes." 1980 Duke Law Journal 742-765.
(September 1980).

Examines <u>Hackbart v. Cincinnati Bengals, Inc</u>. and <u>Tomjanovich v. California Sports, Inc.</u>, which allow recovery for personal injuries. Analyzes the history of the assumption of risk defense and tort litigation in sports. Discusses whether a team should be held liable for the tortious conduct of its employees. Concludes that for some actions the players should be personally liable rather than the team.

Spectators

0419. "Baseball Game; Injury To Spectator." 41 <u>Washington Law Reporter</u> 658-659. (n.d.).

Discusses the length to which management must go in their warning and safeguarding of spectators at a baseball game. The fact that the management post, in large letters and conspicuously in the grandstands, that the management will not be responsible for injuries incurred as the result of batted or thrown balls, was enough to prove that management took precautions. Further, that when management provided the spectator a choice between a seat protected by a screen (assuming that the screen is reasonable and sufficient) and an open seat, the management is exercising precaution and care.

0420. Bluver, Howard C. "Owner Liability For International Torts Committed By Professional Athletes Against Spectators." 30 <u>Buffalo Law Review</u> 565-586. (Summer 1981).

Examines extent of owner liability for injuries sustained by spectator and committed by member of a professional team. Provides background on intentional tort by players against spectators. Considers whether respondeat superior and negligent hiring and supervision are grounds by which to hold owner liable.

0421. Dworkin, Gerald. "Injuries To Spectators In The Course of Sporting Activities." 25 <u>Modern Law Review</u> (U.K.) 738. (November 1962).

Notes on <u>Woolridge v. Sumner</u> ([1962] 3 W.L.R. 616; [1962] 2 All E.R. 973 (C.A.)), wherein the plaintiff was injured by a horse ridden by the defendant's employee. Explores the principles and nuances of assumption of risk and negligence. Examines the relationship between them within the context of a sporting event.

0422. Pooler, Sanford; Lubinsky, Theodore A.; and Psarakis, Emanual N. "Survey of The Law On Injuries To

Spectators."   39 <u>Boston University Law Review</u> 53-61. (1959).

Survey of development of law relating to the injury of spectators in New England and the rest of the United States.   Reviews general rules regarding the duty of the owner/proprietor to provide reasonable care for the protection of spectators.   Examines the law and the casework in the sports of baseball, ice hockey, wrestling, auto racing and marksmanship exhibitions.

0423.   Postel, Theodore.   "Crowd Control Injury."   132 <u>Chicago Daily Law Bulletin</u> 1. (March 6, 1986).

0424.   Scutti, Thomas A.   "Tort Law: McEnroe Tries A Different Court: No Injury From A Big Mac Attack."   7 <u>Loyola Entertainment Law Journal</u> 465-471. (1987).

Presents case where spectator sued John McEnroe for infliction of emotional stress, assault and battery, but lost on all three theories.   Differentiates the standard business pursuits of an athlete as opposed to other individuals.

0425.   Siskind, Gary E.   "Liability for Injuries To Spectators."   6 <u>Osgoode Hall Law Journal</u> (Canada) 305-315. (October 1968).

Reports on the present position of <u>volenti non fit injuria</u>.   Discusses this doctrine and significant casework for England, Canada, and the United States.   Examines both the implied and expressed assumptions of risk. Presents brief statistics on injuries.   Explores methods of attack when a spectator is injured.

0426.   "Sports: Risks of Non-Participants."   4 <u>Australian Lawyer</u> (Australia) 59. (May 1963).

Considers cases where spectators are injured during the course of a sports event.   Examines the English doctrine of the "reasonable man" and the phenomenon of non-participant injuries.   Cites <u>Bolton v. Stone</u>, <u>Douglas v. Stevenson</u>, <u>Hilder v. Associated Portland Cement Manufacturers Limited</u>, <u>Woolridge v. Sumner</u>, and <u>Castle v. St. Augustine's Links Limited</u>.   Discusses negligence, assumption of risk, and liability.

0427.   Zollmann, C.   "Injuries From Flying Baseballs To Spectators At Ball Games."   24 <u>Marquette Law Review</u> 198-204. (June 1940).

Overviews duty of owner of a baseball club to take reasonable care to protect spectators from baseballs, including location of the baseball diamond and providing a properly and adequately maintained screened section.

Surveys assumption of risk which applies to inexperienced and experienced spectators. States the assumption of risk requires only one ball being in motion at any one time. Thus, batting practice is limited to one batter at a time.

14

INTERCOLLEGIATE ATHLETICS

General

0428.   Cozzillio, M. J.   "the Athletic Scholarship and The College National Letter of Intent: A Contract By Any Other Name."   35 Wayne Law Review 1275-1380. (Summer 1989).

0429.   Horn, Stephen.   "Intercollegiate Athletics: Waning Amateurism and Rising Professionalism."   5 Journal of College and University Law 97-105. (1978-1979).
         Discusses a perceived sense of increasing professionalism in college sports and the role of the NCAA.   Reviews influences which impinge upon the student-athlete.   Surveys reform and the NCAA.   Provides a bill of rights for the student-athlete. Points out future directions which the issue may take.

0430.   Intercollegiate Athletics.   Denver Co: Legislative Council. Report To The Colorado General Assembly.   Research Publication 163, December 1970.
         Reports role of intercollegiate athletics in eight of Colorado's four-year state colleges and universities.   Examines athletic program funding, budgeting and accounting practices, control of athletic expenditures, and athletic policies of other states.

0431.   Kaplan, Richard L.   "Intercollegiate Athletics and The Unrelated Business Income Tax."   80 Columbia Law Review 1430-1473. (November 1980).
         Analyzes the developing contours of the unrelated business income tax and the nature of college sports to assess the validity of the de facto exemption created by the Internal Revenue Service in 1978 and the implications for the tax itself.

Presents background of the levy and the tacit exemption of college athletics, and thirty-year development of the tax law, the application of the concepts to intercollegiate programs, and the statute's explicit exceptions as they may relate to these programs. Includes policy considerations. Summarizes tax issues and some nontax aspects concerning the question.

0432.   Safian, Robert.   "Collegiate Sports Law: A Whole New Ballgame." 9 American Lawyer 11(1). (January-February 1987).

0433.   Staton, Richard.   "Recent Cases Concerning The Rights of Student Athletes."   10 Journal of College and University Law 209-224. (Fall 1983/1984).

Examines issues of dismissal of athletes for disruptive behavior, freedom of speech and due process, the liability of university officials for tortious conduct, confidentiality of financial aid information.

0434.   Yasser, Ray. "Are Scholarship Athletes At Big-Time Programs Really University Employees?-You Bet They Are!" 9 Black Law Journal 65-78. (Spring 1984).

Explores the court's treatment of a student on athletic scholarship being considered an employee of the university when attempting to recover under applicable workers' compensation laws.   Presents discussion on worker's compensation. Cites appropriate casework including Nemeth, Dennison, Van Horn, and Rensing. Discusses the question of athletes as employees.

Academic Standards

0435.   DiNardo, Annemarie. "The New NCAA Academic Standards: Are They Constitutional?   Are They Effective?"   4 Entertainment and Sports Law Journal 411-426. (Fall 1987).

Reviews the constitutionality of the new NCAA academic standards.   Examines current eligibility rules, grounds for potential challenge and alternative approaches to eligibility guidelines.

0436.   Dixon, Thomas M.   "Achieving Educational Opportunity Through Freshman Ineligibility and Coaching Selection: Key Elements In The NCAA Battle for Academic Integrity of Intercollegiate Athletics." 14 Journal of College and University Law 383-398. (Fall 1987).

Defines what university owe their student-athletes. Criticizes graduation rates as the most significant measure of success.   Examines Proposition 48 and offers other reforms which would place greater emphasis on academics.

0437.   Howard, James J.   "Incentives Are Needed To Increase
          Graduation Rates of Scholarship Athletes."   10 Seton Hall
          Legislative Journal 201-212. (1987).
              Criticizes the failure of some educational institutions to
          show sincere interest in academic welfare of their athletes.
          Proposes possible solutions, including federal legislation (the
          College Athlete Education and Protection Act).

0438.   Smith, Rodney K.   "An Academic Game Plan For Reforming
          Big-Time Intercollegiate Athletics."   67 Denver University Law
          Review 213-278. (1990).
              Reviews the values under which the NCAA says it
          operates, the values that intercollegiate athletics should
          operate and the structural reform of intercollegiate athletics by
          focusing on academic values.

0439.   Stokes, Jerome W.D.   "The Jan Kemp Case: No Penalty For
          Pass Interference."   16 Journal of Law and Education 257-270.
          (Summer 1987).
              Analyzes the case involving the University of Georgia
          student-athletes, teachers and administrators.   Discusses
          implications of the working relationship between an
          institution, its employees and its students.

0440.   Waicukauski, Ron.   "The Regulation of Academic Standards In
          Intercollegiate Athletics."   1982 Arizona State Law Journal 79-
          108. (1982).
              Reviews NCAA's scheme to regulate intercollegiate
          academic standards.   Examines regulation of admissions and
          academic standards.   Discusses legal actions relating to
          academic standards and acquisition of an education.   Presents
          suggestions to reform regulatory scheme.

0441.   Yasser, Ray.   "The Black Athletes' Equal Protection Case
          Against The NCAA's New Academic Standards."   16 Gonzaga
          Law Review 83-103. (1983/1984).
              Discusses possibility of an equal protection challenge by
          black collegiate athletes to the academic standards adopted in
          January of 1983 and scheduled to take effect on August 1, 1986.
          Analyzes the equal protection challenge in terms of meeting
          state action requirement and by attacking the classification
          scheme of the new academic standards.

Antitrust

0442.　　　Austin, Arthur D. "Legality of Ticket Tie-Ins In Intercollegiate Athletics." 15 University of Richmond Law Review 1-37. (Fall 1980).

Explores the phenomenon of ticket tie-ins as being in violation of antitrust laws. Discusses applicability of state action exemption. Examines the jurisdiction of the antitrust laws over intercollegiate athletics. Identifies elements of an illegal tying arrangement. Surveys the football ticket tie-in cases.

0443.　　　Klein, Deborah E. and Briggs, William Buckley. "Proposition 48 and the Business of Intercollegiate Athletics: Potential Antitrust Ramifications Under The Sherman Act." 67 Denver University Law Review 301-340. (1990).

Reviews the NCAA's amenability to a suit, the standards of judicial review and the possibility of Proposition 48 being attacked as a group boycott.

0444.　　　"Tackling Intercollegiate Athletes: An Antitrust Analysis." 87 Yale Law Journal 655-679. (January 1978).

A note analyzing antitrust liability of the National Collegiate Athletic Association (NCAA), a self-regulatory organization. Suggests a model with which the application of the Sherman Act to similar organizations ought to be effected.

0445.　　　Weistart, John C. "Antitrust Issues In The Regulation of College Sports." 5 Journal of College and University Law 77-96. (1978-1979).

Examines antitrust issues as they relate to the regulation of intercollegiate athletics. Discusses the antitrust issue concerns of the NCAA, regional athletic conferences and the liability of individual schools.

Bibliography

0446.　　　Edmonds, Edmund P. "Postsecondary Athletics and The Law: A Selected Bibliography." 5 Journal of College and University Law 65-76. (Fall 1977).

Brief annotated bibliography covering general materials (books and articles), sex discrimination and Title IX, the NCAA and the regulation of collegiate sports, broadcasting, transnational sports, sports violence, sports, law and medicine, and miscellaneous topics. Also provides a list of publications generated by various sports organizations.

College Athletes

0447.   Atkinson, Mark Alan. "Workers' Compensation and College
           Athletics: Should Universities Be Responsible For Athletes
           Who Incur Serious Injuries?"   10 Journal of College and
           University Law 197-208. (Fall 1983/1984).
               Examines the application of workman's compensation to
           scholarship athletes. Analyzes appropriate case law, discusses
           public policy ramifications and presents alternative solution.

0448.   Cross, Harry M. "The College Athlete and The Institution." 38
           Law and Contemporary Problems 151-171. (Winter-Spring
           1973).
               Deals with the problem of making college athletic programs
           more supportive of educational goals. Explains the admission
           process including recruiting and eligibility restrictions. Locates
           the athlete's status within the student body, athletes as
           employees and the controls on the conduct of student-athletes.
           Explains the issue of disqualification of the athlete.

0449.   Duckworth, Roy D., III. "Student-Athlete and The National
           Collegiate Athletic Association: The Need For A Prima Facie
           Tort Doctrine." 9 Suffolk University Law Review 1340-1371.
           (Summer 1975).
               Examines whether courts have the jurisdiction to hear the
           grievances of student-athletes.   Rejects the position that the
           activities of the NCAA are under the color of state law. Argues
           that any student-athlete declared ineligible by the NCAA
           should have recourse of remedy in a prima facie tort action.

0450.   Pauly, Judith Anne. "Williams v. Hamilton: Constitutional
           Protection of The Student-Athlete." 8 Journal of College and
           University Law 339-408. (1981/1982).
               Review of case pertaining to the NAIA's transfer rule.
           Presents facts of the case, a review of prior casework and an
           analysis of the case. Analysis includes discussion of the issues
           of state action, due process and equal protection.

0451.   Ross. C. Thomas.   "Is Student Athlete A Contradiction In
           Terms?   How Universities Deny Student Athletes An
           Education." 7 Update 6(5). (Spring 1983).
               Questions the concept of the student-athlete. Reviews the
           difference between educational exploitation and educational
           malpractice. Examines the casework on the duty to educate the
           student-athlete as well as NCAA standards.

0452.   Rush, Sharon Elizabeth. "Touchdowns, Toddlers, and Taboos:
           On Paying College Athletes and Surrogate Contract Mothers."
           31 Arizona Law Review 549-614. (1989).

Article comparing college athletics to the institution of motherhood. Recognizes the problems, myths and stereotypes which society perpetuates and reinforces. Discusses the vital role that money plays in both institutions.

0453.   Shulman, Leonard M. "Compensation For Collegiate Athletes: A Run For More Than The Roses." 22 San Diego Law Review 701-723. (May/June 1985).

Argues that student athletes are employees of their respective school and should be compensated financially. Offers hypothetical example. Suggests that the NCAA has not approached the status quo of athletics realistically and that it has violated the athlete's constitutional and statutory rights.

0454.   Springer, Felix J. "A Student-Athlete's Interest In Eligibility: Its Context and Constitutional Dimensions." 10 Connecticut Law Review 318-349. (Winter 1978).

Focuses on whether the student-athlete who is participating in intercollegiate athletics has a property or liberty right which is protected by the fourteenth amendment. Examines issue in the context of Board of Regents v. Roth. Surveys institutional and individual interests in intercollegiate athletics. Discusses the NCAA, its regulations, enforcement procedures and their relationship to the student-athlete. Analyzes the relationship between the NCAA and the Constitution in terms of state action and equal protection.

Higher Education

0455.   Alessandro, Christopher J. "The Student-Athlete Right-To-Know Act: Legislation Would Require Colleges To Make Public Graduation Rates of Student Athletes." 16 Journal of College and University Law 287-324. (Fall 1989).

Provides an overview of the Student-Athlete Right-To-Know Act and problem the Act is attempting to deal with. Concludes with discussion on possible impact and modifications of, and for, the Act.

0456.   Faccenda, Philip J. "Introduction To The Symposium On Athletics In Higher Education." 8 Journal of College and University Law 291-293. (Summer 1981).

Brief overview of the importance of the symposium, and the articles and comments presented and discussed.

Minority Athletes

0457.   Greene, Linda S.   "The New NCAA Rules Of The Game:
           Academic Integrity or Racism?" 28 St. Louis Law Journal 101-
           151. (February 1984).
                Examines academic standards adopted by NCAA January
           1983.   Questions whether the standards reflect academic
           integrity or racism.   Reviews constitutional issues involved
           with the new rules.

Post-Secondary Athletes and The Law

0458.   Ashman, Allan. "Hut One, Hut Two, No Comp For You." 69
           American Bar Association Journal 828-829. (June 1983).
                Brief discussion of Rensing v. Indiana State University
           Board of Trustees, 444 N.E.2d 1170 (1983) where it was ruled
           that a college football player injured during practice was not an
           employee of the university within the context of Indiana's
           workers' compensation statute.

0459.   Buoniconti, Nicholas A. "Are Athletes Covered By Workers'
           Compensation?" 13 Brief 4(6). (November 1983).
                Raises the question of the working relationship between
           college and professional athletes and their universities and
           their employers.

0460.   De Santis, Kathleen. "The Disabled Student Athlete: Gaining
           A Place On The Playing Field." 5 Comm/Ent Law Journal 517-
           548. (Spring 1983).
                Reviews law as it relates to disabled student-athlete.
           Examines Constitutional and other means for challenging
           athletic rules and disqualification decisions.   Includes
           discussion of challenging decision under section 504 of
           Rehabilitation Act.

0461.   Hermann, Anne Marie Canali. "Sports and The Handicapped:
           Section 504 of The Rehabilitation Act of 1973 and Curricular,
           Intramural, Club and Intercollegiate Athletic Programs In
           Postsecondary Educational Institutions." 5 Journal of College
           and University Law 143-159. (1978-1979).
                Discusses the compliance regulations which postsecondary
           institutions must follow when providing either physical
           education courses or an athletic program.   Provides two
           situation scenarios regarding handicapped students. Reviews
           means of enforcing Section 504 rights.

0462.   Johnson, Derek Quinn. "Educating Misguided Students
           Athletes: An Application of Contract Theory." 85 <u>Columbia</u>
           <u>Law Review</u> 96-129. (January 1985).
              Examines the possibility of recourse to contract action by
           student-athletes where universities are failing to educate them.
           Discusses problem of uneducated student-athletes and the
           movement toward accountability. Examines possibility that a
           contract exists and the bases for recovery under contract.
           Includes appendices of matters relating to National Letter of
           Intent.

0463.   Kaplin, William A. "An Overview of Legal Principles and
           Issues Affecting Postsecondary Athletics." 5 <u>Journal of College</u>
           <u>and University Law</u> 1-9. (Fall 1977).
              Survey of legal principles and issues relating to
           postsecondary athletics: procedural due process, first
           amendment rights, tort law, sex discrimination and
           discrimination on the basis of handicap. Discusses legal
           principles regarding athletic associations and conferences.

0464.   Norton, Clark. "Not Time For Classes." 4 <u>California Lawyer</u>
           44-48. (July 1984).
              Focuses on the relationship between academics,
           amateurism, and responsibility in intercollegiate sports.
           Questions who is responsible for educational malpractice of
           student-athlete. Discusses Amateur Sports Act of 1978 and the
           reform of college sports.

0465.   Rafferty, Robert C. "<u>Rensing v. Indiana State University Board</u>
           <u>of Trustees</u>: The Status of The College Scholarship Athlete -
           Employee or Student?" 13 <u>Capitol University Law Review</u> 87-
           103. (Fall 1983).
              Focuses on the context of college athletics as a business, the
           student-athlete as an employee, the existence of a contract
           between the athlete and the institution, and the NCAA
           constitution and bylaws. Considers the impact of instant case
           on intercollegiate athletics.

0466.   Weistart, John C. "Rule-Making In Interscholastic Sports: The
           Bases of Judicial Review." 11 <u>Journal of Law and Education</u>
           291-336. (July 1982).
              Reports on bases for judicial review in interscholastic
           sports. Focuses on transfer rules. Discusses traditional
           standard for judicial review. Considers implications for the
           future.

Title IX

0467.   Caliendo, Nat S. "Title IX Policy Interpretation." 6 Journal of College and University Law 78-79. (Winter 1980).
          Outline of presentation on Title IX consisting of a discussion on the pre capita standard and comparability in non-financially measurable items.

0468.   Cox, Thomas A. "Intercollegiate Athletics and Title IX." 46 George Washington Law Review 34-64. (November 1977).
          Analyzes the effect of Title IX and HEW's implementing regulation on intercollegiate sports. Discusses Title IX within the context of the constitutional issue of the equal protection doctrine and within the context of the proposed equal rights amendment.

0469.   deCrow, Karen. "Hardlining Title IX: Who's Off-Side Now?" 12 Perspectives 16-23. (Summer 1980).
          Response and position statement to critics of Title IX.

0470.   DeVine, Stephen W. "Judicial Deference To Legislative Reality: The Interpretation of Title IX In The Context of Collegiate Athletics." 14 North Carolina Central Law Journal 601-627. (Spring 1984).
          Reviews three different judicial interpretations of the triggering language of Title IX. Argues the direct funding interpretation of Title IX should be the one that courts adopt. Presents supporting and other appropriate casework.

0471.   Gaal, John and DiLorenzo, Louis P. "The Legality and Requirements of HEW's Proposed "Policy Interpretation" of Title IX and Intercollegiate Athletics." 6 Journal of College and University Law 161-194. (1979-1980).
          Explores the legality of HEW's proposed policy interpretation statement of Title IX. Presents an overview of Title IX, its regulations, and its applicability to intercollegiate athletics. Reviews HEW's interpretation of Title IX. Discusses the demands of HEW's proposed policy interpretation of Title IX.

0472.   Gaal, John; DiLorenzo, Louis P.; and Evans, Thomas S. "HEW's Final 'Policy Interpretation' of Title IX and Intercollegiate Athletics." 6 Journal of College and University Law 345-361. (1979-1980).
          Reviews jurisdiction, athletic financial aid and other athletic benefits provisions of the final interpretation. Offers observations on the final policy interpretation pertaining to jurisdictional extension, procedural change, and substantive changes such as financial aid, recruitment, coaching

compensation and assignments, and the accommodation of student interests and abilities.

0473.   Graf, Richard M. "Title IX and Intercollegiate Athletics: Adducing Congressional Intent." 24 Boston College Law Review 1243-1282. (September 1983).

Analysis of Congressional intent regarding the application of Title IX to intercollegiate athletics. Specifically examines the impact of the Richmond, Haffer, and North Haven, cases. Reviews the history of Title IX, its regulations and the relationship between indirect funding and the scope of Title IX.

0474.   Guthrie, R. Claire; McDonald, Eugene J.; and Caliendo, Nat S. "Title IX Athletics." 6 Journal of College and University Law 73-77. (Winter 1980).

Outline of conference presentation which consists of the background of Title IX, the requirements of proposed guidelines, controversial policy elements of the guidelines; and, the current status of the proposed guidelines.

0475.   "Implementing Title IX: The HEW Regulations." 124 University of Pennsylvania Law Review 806-842. (January 1976).

Comments on Title IX of the 1972 Education Amendments. Analyzes the statute concerning overt discrimination, facially neutral regulations which have a discriminatory effect, regulations concerning unique physical characteristics, and the separate but equal doctrine. Deals with four subparts of the HEW regulations: Introduction and coverage (A and B), admission and recruitment (C), and especially with programs and activities (D). Concludes that Title IX should be construed broadly in the general prohibition of sex discrimination in education but narrowly in the limited living facilities, and other areas where disrobing occurs) and that the HEW regulations adhere fairly closely to this but, in areas such as athletics, a middle course has been attempted resulting in ambiguous requirements which could make enforcement difficult.

0476.   Jensen, June E. "Title IX and Intercollegiate Athletics: HEW Gets Serious About Equality In Sports?" 15 New England Law Review 573-596. (Summer 1979-1980).

Overview of Title IX. Includes statutory history, interpretation and the goal of equality in sports. Concentrates on the 11 December 1979 policy interpretation issued by HEW. Reviews its intent, focus and effectiveness.

0477.   Johnson, Christina. "The Evolution of Title IX: Prospects For
            Equality In Intercollegiate Athletics."   11 Golden Gate
            University Law Review 759-800. (Summer 1981).
                Review of Title IX.   Considers its legislative history,
            proposed regulations and its final policy interpretation of
            December 1979. Reviews Title IX in relation to public policy
            goals. Suggests remedies which may help ensure equal athletic
            opportunity.

0478.   Kadzielski, Mark A. "Title IX of The Education Amendments
            of 1972:   Change of Continuity?"   6 Journal of Law and
            Education 183-203. (April 1977).
                Examines provisions of Title IX in-depth to illuminate their
            approach to ending sex discrimination in education. Provides
            relevant case law.   Advances some conclusions for the
            prospects of ending sex discrimination in American education
            with the hope that it extends to all aspects of American society
            as well.

0479.   Koch, James V. "Title IX and The NCAA." 3 Western State
            University Law Review 250-261. (Spring 1976).
                Examines the relationship between Title IX and the NCAA.
            Focuses on aspects of implementation of Title IX.   Presents
            arguments for and against the implementation guidelines.

0480.   Krakora. Joseph E. "The Application of Title IX To School
            Athletic Programs." 68 Cornell Law Review 222-235. (January
            1983).
                Analyzes scope of Title IX. Presents legislative history of
            Title IX and case law under Title IX. Concludes with structure
            to resolve issue of the scope of Title IX.

0481.   Kuhn, Janet Lammersen.   "Title IX: Employment and
            Athletics Are Outside HEW's Jurisdiction." 65 Georgetown
            Law Journal 49-77. (October 1976).
                Argues that Title IX neither extends to employment
            practices nor to the beneficiaries of programs which are not
            federally funded. Provides legislative history of Title VI of the
            Civil Rights Act of 1964 and application of Title VI to
            educational agencies; legislative history of Title IX, Title IX and
            athletic information, the Pinpoint Termination Provision and
            its legislative history, and other information in support of her
            argument.

0482.   Martin, James P.   "Title IX and Intercollegiate Athletics:
            Scoring Points For Women." 8 Ohio Northern Law Review
            481-497. (July 1981).
                Examination of sexual discrimination in intercollegiate
            athletics. Reviews myth of needing to protect health and safety

of women in athletics.   Discusses psychological impact of discrimination.   Analyzes use of equal protection argument against discrimination, ramifications of Title IX, and impact of Title IX on revenue producing sports.

0483.   Oliphant, Judith Lee.   "Title IX's Promise of Equality of Opportunity In Athletics: Does It Cover The Bases?"   64 Kentucky Law Journal 432-464. (1975-1976).
             Reviews the equality of opportunity doctrine and the intent of Title IX and the implementing regulations of the HEW with regard to physical education and athletics.   Examines the slow development of judicial application of the equal protection clause to invalidate sex discrimination.   Analyzes athletic discrimination suits in cases in which teams are not provided for women and one case in which teams are provided for women.   Provides history and development of Title IX and the regulations.   Concludes that so many questions remain as to what equality of opportunity for women in athletics requires.   While the schools now have to put into effect their conception of equal opportunity and women need to demand that which the regulations make possible, funds are needed to effectuate the changes.   States that the necessary changes concerning financing and improved training, facilities and publicity should result in more women athletes with more careers for women in sports in the long run.

0484.   Podgers, James. "New Title IX Game Plan: Lawyers To Get The Ball." 66 American Bar Association Journal 28-29. (January 1980).
             Reviews and discusses factors which may lead to an increase in Title IX related litigation as a greater number of colleges may challenge HEW Title guidelines.   Offers HEW response to the colleges' criticisms of the compliance guidelines.

0485.   Pogge-Strubing, Marianne.   "Has Title IX Done Its Jobs In Fighting...The Sexist Underground In Sports?" 7 Update 16(5). (Spring 1983).
             Examines the impact that Title IX has had on interscholastic and intercollegiate sports.

0486.   Quinn, Thomas F.   "Sex Discrimination -Title IX of The Education Amendments of 1972 Prohibits All-Female Teams In Sports Previously Dominated By Males."   14 Suffolk University Law Review 1471-1485. (Fall 1980).
             Comment on Gomes v. Rhode Island Interscholastic League, 469 F. Supp. 659 (D.R.I. 1979), wherein plaintiff argued that rule prohibiting him from competing on an all-female volleyball team, on the basis of sex, was in violation of the

fourteenth amendment and Title IX. Explores Supreme Court decisions involving classifications based on sex. Argues the language of the HEW regulations was given inadequate attention.

0487.   Ross, Gail. "Termination of Federal Funding To School Athletic Programs Under Title IX of The Education Amendments of 1972." 5 University of San Fernando Valley Law Review 417-431. (Fall 1977).
              Reviews athletic programs in post secondary education, the athletic provisions within HEW regulations and the enforcement provision of Title IX. Explains the "pinpoint provision" and the Taylor County v. Finch case.

0488.   Simmons, Sheryl L. "Grove City College v. Bell: The Controversy Applied To Athletics." 22 Houston Law Review 869-907. (May 1985).
              Reviews the differences between a restrictive and broad interpretation of Title IX. Reports on Grove City and its effect on Title IX. Describes the application of Title IX to athletic programs and legislative attempts to override Grove City.

0489.   Smith, Walt. "Enforcing Title IX Cutting College Sports?" 12 Perspectives 22-23. (Summer 1980).
              Brief review of the impact that Title IX has on intercollegiate sports.

0490.   Tashjian-Brown, Eva S. "Title IX: Progress Toward Program Specific Regulation of Private Academia." 10 Journal of College and University Law 1-62. (Summer 1983).
              Discussion of the impact of Title IX on private institutions of higher education. Reviews this issue within the context of University of Richmond v. Bell 543 F.Supp. 321, 323 (E.D. Va. 1982). Examines the regulations, the government's approach and recent case law. Includes plaintiff's approach and recent case law. Includes plaintiff's motion for summary judgment and plaintiff's reply to cross-motion for summary judgment.

15

INTERNATIONAL
SPORTS LAW

General

0491.   Carter, P. B. "International Amateur Athletic Federation-Membership Open To Any 'Country' - Whether 'Country' Equivalent To 'State' - Expulsion of Taiwan Invalid." 1979 British Year Book of International Law (U.K.) 217-256. (1981).

0492.   Dobray, Debra. "A Survey of Legal Issues Facing The Foreign Athlete." 4 Entertainment and Sports Law Journal 1-17. (Spring 1987).
         Examines the constitutional rights and limitations to those rights of the foreign athlete. Reviews questions of immigration, naturalization and taxation of resident and nonresident athletes.

0493.   "Holt v. Verbruggen." 20 Canadian Cases On The Law of Torts (Canada) 29-41. (1982).
         Examination of the case involving a retaliatory attack in an hockey game. Reviews and discusses the traditional Canadian rule and casework from Australia, England and Canada

0494.   Jacobs, Francis G. "Tourism, Sports and Other Forms of Leisure From The Point of View of International Law." 42-43 Annuaire de L'A.A.A. (Netherlands) 52-61. (1972-1973).
         Briefly discussion of the relationship between sport and a society which is becoming transnational. Revies impact of sports on international law beginning with the ancient Greeks. The rules of games provided a form of an independent legal order. Carries the example of sports into the other legal activities including cultural, archaeological, radio and

television programming, tourism and other phenomena related to the freedom of movement across national frontiers.

0495.   Leyendecker, R. Socini. "Federations sportives internationales dans le domaine des organisations" (in French).   42-43 Annuaire de L'A.A.A. (Netherlands) 41-51. (1972-1973).

Discusses international sports federations.   Specifically examines non-governmental sports federations, their operations, functioning, and their role from a national and international perspective.

0496.   Moriarty,   Dick.   "Comparing   Canadian-American Sport/Athletic Policy and The Law." 6 Crime and/et Justice (Canada) 22-30. (1978).

Examines and compares aspects of sports/athletics in Canada and the United States. Discusses the organization of amateur, college, and professional sports/athletics. Explores the differences in the Canadian and American legal systems, and their ramifications for sport/athletics.

0497.   Nafziger, James A. R. International Sports Law. Dobbs Ferry, New York: Transnational Publishers, Inc., 1988.

Presents an overview history institutional and legal framework of the field.   Reviews national politics, international legal regulation, boycotts and social issues involved in international sports. Examines the U.S. Amateur Sports Act of 1978.   Provides appendices relating to international sports.

0498.   Nafziger, James A. R.   "Nonaggressive Sanctions In the International Sports Arena." 15 Case Western Reserve Journal of International Law 329-342. (Spring 1983).

Discusses use of sport as a nonaggressive international sanction. Reviews international sports rules, sanctions used, and recommendation for protecting Olympic Games.

0499.   Nafziger, James A. R. "The Regulation of Transnational Sports Competition: Down From Mount Olympus." 5 Vanderbilt Journal of Transnational Law 180-212. (Winter 1971).

Explores the regulation of transnational sports and the effect of the world order. Examines the characteristics and goals of sports competition and the structure and characteristics of Olympic decision making. Presents evaluative case studies in the areas of creeping professionalism, the nation-state politicalization of competition, ping-pong diplomacy, and the protection of human rights.

0500.   Pocar, Fausto. "Problemi di diritto Internazionale Privato In Tema   di   Infortuni   Sciatori   e   Prospettive   di   Una

Regolamentazione Internazionale" (in Italian).   12 Revista di Diritto Internazionale Privato e Processuale (Italy) 491-506. (July-September 1976).

Review of the problems of international private law regarding injured skiers and the possibility and potential of uniform international regulation.

0501.   Ramphal, Shridath S.   "Apartheid Sport."   New Zealand Law Journal (New Zealand) 1-3. (January 1985).

Excerpts from a speech calling for unity in the international sports boycott of South Africa.

0502.   Saunders, O. O. R.   "A Question of Sport For The Treaty of Rome."   132 Solicitor's Journal (U.K.) 1450-1452. (October 21, 1988).

Provides analysis of the question of free movement of sportpersons within European community.   Examines right of free movement in relation to rules and restrictions of sports governing bodies.   Reviews free movement and Treaty of Rome and discusses issues of contract of, and for, services.

Australia

0503.   Bieker, Neal and von Nessen, Paul.   "Sports and Restraint of Trade: Playing The Game The Court's Way."   13 Australian Business Law Review (Australia) 180-197. (August 1985).

0504.   Nanscawen, Peter.   "In Re Adamson; Ex Parte W.A. National Football League."   12 Melbourne University Law Review (Australia) 567-574. (December 1980).

Review the case which, inter alia, deals with the restraint of trade, restriction of the supply of services and the lessening of competition regarding the playing status of an Australian footballer.

0505.   Uren, Tom.   "Environmental Decision Making."   4 University of New South Wales Law Journal (Australia) 5-9. (June 1981).

Pertains to alleged improprieties in the New South Wales State Government's decision to build a sports stadium in Sydney.

Austria

0506.   Schambeck, H.   "Osterreichs Sportforderung im Liche des Rechts-und Bundesstaates" (in German).   23 Ostereichische Juristen-Zeitung (Austria) 113-124. (May 1968).

Involves an examination of the promotion of sports in Austria. Focuses on the promotion of sport within the context of Austrian law. Discusses the relationship between modern man, the growth of sports, and the state.

Brazil

0507. Lyra Filho, J. "Autonomia e tipicidade do contrato desportivo" (in Portuguese). 237 Revista Forense (Brazil) 34-38. (January-March 1972).

Explores the nature and relationship of the contract between soccer clubs and their professional players. Reviews Brazilian legislation, customary law and international rules.

Canada

0508. Barnes, John. "Canadian Sports Torts: A Bibliographic Survey." 8 Canadian Cases On the Law of Torts (Canada) 198-206. (1979).

Note categorizing Canadian sports torts. Includes a general discussion of liability of players to other players, of players to spectators, of facility operators to spectators, of facility operators to players, to persons outside sports facilities, of clubs and teams, of sports governing bodies, of coaches and teachers, and alternatives to compensation in tort.

0509. Jones, J. C. H. and Davies, D. K. "Not Even Semitough: Professional Sport and Canadian Antitrust." 23 Antitrust Bulletin 713-742. (Winter 1978).

Reviews the 1976 revision to the Canadian Combines Investigation Act which will allow professional sports leagues to adopt restrictive agreements. Analyzes the rationale for preserving a "reasonable balance" of competition. Focuses on the unique features and alternative behavioral models of professional league sports and the derivation and testing of alternative predictions. Concludes with a discussion on labor market restrictions, league sports and Canadian trust.

0510. Letourneau, Gilles. "Sports, Violence and Criminal Law In Canada." 22 Criminal Reports (Canada) 103-106. (October 15, 1981).

Overview of sport violence in Canada.

0511. Trossman, J. "Mandatory Drug Testing In Sports: The Law In Canada." 47 University of Toronto Faculty of Law Review (Canada) 191-219. (1988).

0512.   White, Diane.   "Sports Violence as Criminal Assault:
             Development of the Doctrine By Canadian Courts." 1986 Duke
             Law Journal 1030-1054. (December 1986).
             Compares Canadian to United States means of controlling
             violent behavior in professional sports.   Presents historical
             background of Canadian criminal prosecutions in sports.
             Provides analysis of the consent defense.   Mentions Canadian
             courts 3 bright-line tests when considering sports violence
             lawsuits.   Determines that the U.S. courts would adopt similar
             doctrines regarding sport violence without unnecessary
             legislation.

Czechoslovakia

0513.   Prusak, J. "Urazy a Poskodenia Zdravia Pri Sporte a Problem
             Sportoveho a Pravneho Diliktu" (in Slovak).   124 Pravnik
             (Czechoslavakia) 791-804. (1985).
             Discusses accidents and injuries occurring in physical
             training in Czechoslovakia.   Identifies football, ice hockey,
             handball, basketball and skiing as the most dangerous sports in
             the country.   Reviews the legal responsibility inherent in hard
             versus brutal play.

France

0514.   Jedruch, Stanislaw. "Legal Regulation of Sport In France" (in
             Polish). 31 Panstwo i Pravo (Poland) 96-103. (October 1976).
             Reports on the effects and dangers of sport on youth and
             society in France. Points out the chemical and mechanical aids
             utilized in sports, their danger to the participants, and the legal
             lengths which must be achieved to protect the participants.

Ireland

0515.   Power, Vincent J. G. "Injunctions and Rugby Tours: The Irish
             Experience." 1985 New Zealand Law Journal (New Zealand)
             200. (October 1985).
             Brief discussion of John Lennon v. Robert Ganley, Robert
             Fitzgerald in Ireland where an injunction was sought to
             restrain the Irish Rugby Football Union from going to South
             Africa. Presents excerpted portions of the opinion as well as
             brief discussion of the stumbling blocks in obtaining an
             injunction.

Japan

0516.   Shimoyama, E. "Professional Baseball and Bribery: Various Problems Arising From The Baseball Contract" (in Japanese). 453 Jurisuto (Japan) 41-47. (July 1, 1970).

Discusses bribery, termination of player contracts, the power of the Commissioner concerning player contract termination, the problem of recruiters writing in money amounts after player has signed the contract, and the problem of players not being allowed to play professional baseball without a contract. Elaborates further on the highly organized business of baseball concerning the draft system, keeping players when players want to play on other teams, trading privileges, and the relation of organized baseball to the law which prohibits monopoly or restraint in trade (Dokusen Kinshi Ho).

0517.   Tanaka, Y. "Public Sports and Prevention of Illegalities" (in Japanese). 453 Jurisuto (Japan) 56-61. (July 1, 1970).

Presents a general overview of public sports and mentions illegal activities, problems, and policies concerning public sports. Discusses legal and illegal betting activities on the legal betting sports of horse racing, bicycle racing, boat racing and small automobile race. Focuses on the illegal activities of unofficial betting inside and outside the sports arena or stadium, bribery, the illegal business of purchasing tickets of others and being paid to do so, and the illegality of underage (18) people, players or workers at the stadium with regard to betting.

New Zealand

0518.   Baragwanath, David. "The Tour." 1985 New Zealand Law Journal (New Zealand) 221-227. (1985).

In-depth review of the New Zealand High Court's decision which postponed the All Black rugby tour to South Africa. Presents the background, opposition and rules of the New Zealand Rugby Football Union.

0519.   Brookfield, F. M. "Springboks and Visas." 1982 New Zealand Law Journal (New Zealand) 142-145. (April 1982).

Surveys Ashby v. Minister of Immigration, raising issue of discretionary powers provided the Minister of Education under s14 of the New Zealand and Immigration Act. Case involves South African Springbok rugby team.

0520.   Eagles, Ian. "Public Law and Private Corporations." 45 Cambridge Law Journal (U.K.) 406-413. (November 1986).

Analyzes Finnigan v. New Zealand Rugby Union. Mentions how the New Zealand Court of Appeal used public law concepts of standing and reasonableness and related them to private law.

Poland

0521.   Bojarski, Marek. "Wylaczenie Odpowiedzialnosci Karnej Za Wypadki w Sporcie" (in Polish).   26 Nowe Prawo (Poland) 1443-1451. (October 1970).
Reviews the issue of limitations of liability in sports accidents in Poland.

0522.   Szwarc, A. J.   "Strafrechtliche Beurteilung Von Sportverletzungen In Polen" (In German).   22 Jahrbuch fur Ostrecht (West Germany) 363-372. (1981).
Discussion of legal decisions pertaining to sports accidents in Poland. Examines the extent of cases of sports accidents in Poland.

Spain

0523.   Coma, M. Bassols. "Administracion Deportiva: Evolucion y Posible Configuracion" (in Spanish).   85 Revista de Administracion Publica (Spain) 375-390. (January-April 1978).
Review of the evolution, structure and administration of sports in Spain.

0524.   Gonzales, Grimaldo, Mariano-Carmelo. "Las Vias de Garantia y la Exclusion Jurisdiccional en el Ordenamiento Juridico-Deportivo" (in Spanish). 71 Revista de Administracion Publica (Spain) 181-201. (May-August 1973).
Reviews the development, organization and administration of sports and sports law in Spain.

0525.   Vera, Jose Bermejo. "El Marco Juridico Del Deporte en Espana" (in Spanish). 110 Revista de Administracion Publica (Spain) 7-30. (1986).
General discussion of jurisprudential aspects and their relationship to the sports movement and sports law in Spain.

United Kingdom

0526.   "Control of Public Entertainment." 103 Justice of The Peace (U.K.) 783-784. (December 9, 1939).

Overview of the application of the Defence Regulations controlling the assemblage of people for public entertainment in Great Britain. Reviews a number of subsequent Restriction Orders and how they applied to assemblage for public entertainment.

0527.   Cullum, Philip R. A. "The Missed Match: The SRU, South Africa and The Law." Scots Law Times (U.K.) 25(4). (January 26, 1990).

0528.   Evans, A. "Freedom of Trade Under The Common Law and European Community Law: The Case of the Football Bans." 102 Law Quarterly Review (U.K.) 510-548. (October 1986).

Raises British legal questions regarding the 1985 F.I.F.A. banning of all football matches between English clubs and any other national association.

United States, Foreign Sports Policy

0529.   Busto, Mercedes C. "Executive's Foreign Relations Power and the New York Courts-A Case of Unwarranted Difference." 18 Columbia Journal of Transnational Law 557-578. (1980).

Casenote discussing the federal government's claim of a foreign relations interest in Liang Ren-Guey v. Lake Placid 1980 Olympic Games, Inc. and the deference that the courts in question gave to the executive branch of the federal government. Case dealt with issues pertaining to the manner in which Taiwan was to be represented at the 1980 Winter Olympic Games in Lake Placid.

0530.   Nafziger, James A. R. "Legal Aspects of A United States Foreign Sports Policy." 8 Vanderbilt Journal of Transnational Law 837-855. (Fall 1975).

Deals with special problems related to the possibility of U.S. involvement in the diplomatic exploitation of sports in the external affairs of the government. Presents current U.S. government involvement in sports, preliminary legal aspects of a U.S. foreign sports policy, and information toward an authoritative process to shape such policy. Concludes that the U.S. should develop a foreign sports policy rooted in the Olympic movement, values and norms.

0531.   Shropshire, Kenneth L. "Thoughts On International Professional Sports Leagues and The Application of United States Antitrust Laws." 67 Denver University Law Review 193-212. (1990).

Examines the antitrust issues involved in an international sports league. Reviews jurisdictional, league formation and post formation issues.

West Germany

0532.   Herrmann, H.   "Erteilung Von Bundesliga-Vereinslizenzen und Diskriminierungsverbot" (in German). 29 Wirtschaft und Wettbewerb (West Germany) 149-161. (March 1979).

Discusses the process of granting- or denying-licenses to participate as a soccer team. Explores the guidelines for qualification including an economic examination of various soccer teams in Germany.

0533.   Weiland, Bernd H.   "Keine Lizenzen Fur Bilanzschwache Fussballvereine?" 31 Neue Juristische Wochenschrift (West Germany) 737-741. (April 1978).

Discusses the renewal of practicing licenses for various football leagues and teams in West Germany.

0534.   Wessels, Hubert.   "Developpment du droit aerien et spatial en allemagne depuis le 1er auot 1963" (in French).   28 Revue Generale de l'air et de L'Escape (France) 133-143. (1965).

Discusses the development of air and space law in Germany since 1 August 1963. Reviews appropriate and applicable casework.

16

LIABILITY

General

0535.   "Assault and Battery-Defences-Blows Struck In Course of Lawful Sport-Whether Privileged.   Martin et al. v. Diagle, [1969] 6 D.L.R. (3d) 634." 15 McGill Law Journal (Canada) 504-505. (1969).
          Brief discussion of case where plaintiff sought to recover damages incurred during the course of a hockey game. Trial judge found for plaintiff. Appeal Division commented that immunity from liability in lawful sport has limits and the blow struck in this case is actionable.

0536.   Bojarski, Marek.   "In Search of A Formula Excluding Responsibility For Accidents In Sports" (in Polish). 15 Palestra (Poland) 33-37. (December 1971).
          Discusses the search for a formula to limit liability in sports accidents.

0537.   David, Ernest L.   "Liability To Patron For Negligence of Concessionary." 21 Case and Comment 728-730. (February 1915).
          Focuses on the duty of those who lease their land to concessionaries and the duty of the lessor to supervise and inspect the land to prevent negligence. Cites cases supporting the position that the owner of the land, in these cases fair boards and an agricultural society, is liable for injuries sustained by a patron as a result of concessionary negligence. Asks to what extent the owner must inspect the various amusement rides which the concessionary provided for the patron.

0538.   Eves, Roderick D.   "The Classification of Athletes and Entertainers As Plaintiffs In Defamation Suits."   4 Entertainment and Sports Law Journal 333-356. (Fall 1987).
         Analyzes classification includes athletes as pervasive public figures, vortex public figures and public personalities. Includes a brief historical perspective.

0539.   Grant, David and Wilson, Stephen R.   "Nuisance Rules OK?- I." 129 Solictor's Journal (U.K.) 139-141. (March 1, 1985).
         Examines the degree to which a football club is liable for acts committed by spectators who come to its contests.   Reviews casework on the questions and issues of the consequence of the defendant's acts, the application of nuisance rules to football crowds, locality and the notion of coming to a nuisance.

0540.   Jedruch, Stanislaw. "Some Legal Aspects of The Responsibility For Damages Caused During Practising Sports" (in Polish). 15 Palestra (Poland) 14-28. (January 1971).
         Discusses the issue of responsibility as it regards insurance claims relating to sport injuries of athletes. Examines the issue as it relates to a number of sports. Explores the legal definition of responsibility.

0541.   Khan, A. N. and Wolfgarten, A. "Liability For Foul Play." 129 Solicitor's Journal (U.K.) 859-860. (1985).
         Discusses the duty of care which sport spectators and competitors assume at a sporting event. Offers case examples.

0542.   MacDonald, Alistair. "The Bradford Football Fire." 137 New Law Journal (U.K.) 481-484. (May 22, 1987).
         Analyzes decision in case; the cause of the fire, Bradford City Football Club's liability, role of Health and Safety Executive, pertinent legislation, grounds inspection and the substance of case against the Executive.

0543.   Musuals, Kevin G. "Liability for Injured Baseball Spectators Under Rudnick v. Golden West Broadcasters: Still Playing The Same Old Game?" 12 Western State University Law Review 345-358. (Fall 1984).
         Review of California tort law as it relates to contributory negligence, assumption of risk, and premises liability. Presents an historical background on the traditional defenses to negligence. Specifically analyzes the assignment of liability for a spectator injured by a foul ball through an examination of Quinn v. Recreation Park Ass'n and Rudnick v. Golden West. Also cites other appropriate casework.

0544.   Philo, Harry M. and Stine, Gregory. "The Liability Path To Safe Helmets." 13 Trial 38-40. (January 1977).

Argues that despite improvements in design of football helmets much more can be done, but it will only occur as a result of liability. Surveys the annual number of deaths and head and neck injuries in football. Provides suggestions on how to reduce these numbers from a technical/design and a citizen/activist approach.

0545.   Wilkinson, Allen P. "Sports Products Liability: It's All Part of The Game-Or Is It?" 17 Trial 58-62. (November 1981).

Discusses basis upon which sports product liability case may be developed. Lists defenses and the availability, role and significance of evidence.

Coaches

0546.   Blodgett, Nancy. "Good Samaritan: Bill Shields Unpaid Coaches." 72 American Bar Association Journal 34. (February 1986).

Brief discussion of legislation introduced in New Jersey and Pennsylvania limiting the liability of volunteer coaches.

0547.   Clear, Delbert K. and Bagley, Martha. "Coaching Athletics: A Tort Just Waiting For A Judgement?" 10 NOLPE School Law Journal 184-192. (Spring 1982).

Reviews the tort possibilities facing interscholastic coaches. Suggests means by which to lessen the problem.

0548.   "Coaches' Liability In Gymnastics Injuries Explored In Article." 93 The Los Angeles Daily Journal 4. (August 26, 1980).

Manufacturer

0549.   Coben, Larry E. "Sports Helmets: More Harm Than Protection." 25 Trial 74-82. (March 1989).

Focuses on components of helmet construction, potentially liable parties and responsibilities of manufacturers of components. Reviews adequacy of warnings associated with helmets. Suggestions to attorneys involve procedure, patents, related literature, applicable theories, discovery, testing of helmet and procedure at trial.

0550.   Houser, Douglas G.; Ashworth, John P.; and Clark, Ronald J. "Product Liability In The Sports Industry." 23 Tort & Insurance Law Journal 44-69. (Fall 1987).

Examines issue of lawsuits arising from injuries caused by recreational equipment. Discusses product liability in general and its specific application to sports industry. Reviews defenses available, trends in the field, and practice tips. Provides listing of cases in sixteen different sports.

0551.   Merritt, William C.   "The Football Helmet vs. Products Liability." 39 <u>Federation of Insurance & Corporate Counsel Quarterly</u> 393-407. (Summer 1989).
Presents history of the football helmet, theories used in liability suits against helmet manufacturers and medical data on the helmet-neck injury relationship.

0552.   Pichler, J. "Haftungsfragen Rund Um Die Schibindung (II)." 31 <u>Osterreichische Juristen-Zeitung</u> (Austria) 458-466. (September 1976).
Reviews the liability associated with ski bindings.

0553.   Pichler, J. "Haftungsfragen Rund Um Die Schibindung (I)." 31 <u>Osterreichische Juristen-Zeitung</u> (Austria) 421-426. (August 1976).
Examines the questions of the legal liability pertaining to and involving ski bindings.

0554.   Quade, Vicki. "Sports Injuries; Suits Threaten Manufacturers." 71 <u>American Bar Association Journal</u> 34. (May 1985).
Brief discussion on the increase of lawsuits directed at the manufacturers of sports equipment.

Owner Liability

0555.   "Assumption of Risk-Landowner's Liability In Oregon."   1 <u>Williamette Law Journal</u> 405. (Fall 1960).
A note examining <u>Hunt v. Portland Baseball Club</u> 207 Ore. 337, 296, P.2d. 495 (1956) (plaintiff sued due to injury receive at a baseball park).   Court bared recovery ruling the plaintiff assumed the risk.   Reviews history of consideration of the doctrine of assumption of risk in Oregon beginning in 1904. Reports the application of assumption of risk was limited to master and servant.   All other cases had the doctrine of assumption of risk applied as contributory negligence.   <u>Hunt v. Portland Baseball Club</u> was the first case in Oregon to which the doctrine of assumption of risk was applied.   Cites recent cases that support the decision in <u>Hunt</u>.

0556.   Barrett, John C. "Good Sports and Bad Lands: The Application of Washington's Recreational Use Statute Limiting Landowner Liability." 53 <u>Washington Law Review</u> 1-29. (December 1977).
Examines Washington's statutes which limit a landowner's liability when landowner's land is used for recreational purposes.   Discusses the general impact of recreational use

legislation on the common law, liability limitations and residual duties under the Washington statute, and the limits on the applicability of the recreational use statute.

0557.   Buskus, Michael L.   "Tort Liability and Recreational Use of Land." 28 Buffalo Law Review 767-794. (Fall 1979).
Discusses recreational liability statutes and risks landowners take by offering private land for public use.

0558.   Chamberlain, John D. "Liability of Proprietor of Place of Public Amusement For Injury to Patron." 21 Case and Comment 718-727. (February 1915).
Presents discussion of decisions in cases involving horse racing, the use of firearms, the collapse of seats or grandstands, falling objects, a bathing resort, assault (action of an employee on a patron) and other miscellaneous holdings.

0559.   Donnelly, Joseph C. "Torts-Liability of Owners or Proprietors of Places of Amusement or Entertainment." 12 University of Detroit Law Review 169-170. (May 1949).
Describes very briefly several court decisions from some other states relating to "ordinary" and "reasonable" care owed to patrons of wrestling matches, baseball and hockey games and other amusements.   Concludes that in those situations such court holdings are logical in that requiring a higher standard of care or "strict liability" could result in higher operational costs leading to increased costs of admission which, together with patrons' perceived cautious attitudes, could discourage people from attending sports and recreational events.

0560.   "Injury From Fall of Seats Or Grand Stands." 23 Law Student's Helper 28. (March 1915).
Brief comment on the liability for injury incurred as a result of persons falling from seats or grandstands, due to the seats or grandstands being negligently constructed, maintained or inspected. Reports instances where such liability resulted.

0561.   "Liability For Personal Injuries To Patrons." 16 Tennessee Law Review 887-889. (April 1941).
Discusses liability of dance hall owner concerning the shooting of one patron by another. The duty of the owner to protect his patron against the risk created by another patron was not breached by the owner in that the locking of the door after the bouncer removed the patron from the premises was suficient as ordinary prudence and indicative of reasonable care. There was no evidence that the owner should have anticipated the two criminal acts of breaking the door of a locked building and committing a felonious assault.

0562.   "Liability of Management For Injury To Spectator Under
                 Implied Contract As To Safety." 38 The National Corporation
                 Reporter 347. (April 22, 1909).
                 Briefly discusses that spectator safety is a duty of
                 managers/proprietors as the result of an implied contract. The
                 implied contract is that the stands be reasonably fit and proper
                 for the use being put to them and that the
                 managers/proprietors exhibit a relatively high degree of care in
                 order to prevent disaster.

0563.   "Liability Of Public Amusement Company for Injury Sustained
                 By Person While Passing Through Turnstile." 18 Law Notes
                 73. (July 1914).
                 A short note presenting the facts of the case and describes
                 the issue. Includes a portion of what the Court said concerning
                 employees' actions whether being negligent and willful (Marx
                 v. Ontario Beach Hotel & Amusement Co., (N.Y.) 105 N.E. 97).

0564.   Rosenblatt, Albert M.   "After The Fall." 5 Trial 44-45.
                 (February-March 1969).
                 Reviews the liability of ski areas for injuries sustained by
                 skiers. Discusses the extent to which assumption of risk,
                 misrepresentation of skiing conditions and negligence would
                 apply. Examines the questions of liability as it applies to the
                 hit-and-run skier.

Participant

0565.   Beumler, Candyce. "Liability In Professional Sports: An
                 Alternative To Violence? 22 Arizona Law Review 919-938.
                 (1980).
                 Note which examines the liability of athletes who injure
                 another participant during sport. Stresses the increase in
                 violence in professional sports due to the increased salaries,
                 drugs, coaching techniques, revenge factors and gate receipt
                 concerns. Differentiates the negligence standard in amateur
                 athletics with the reckless misconduct standard in professional
                 sports. Proposes that the legal system can help reduce violence
                 through criminal sanctions and civil liability.

0566.   Friedrich, Paul M. "Haftung Des Sportlers aus s823 Abs. 1
                 BGB." 19 Neue Juristische Wochenschrift (West Germany)
                 755. (April 1966).
                 Reviews the liability of athletes during competition.
                 Argues that an athlete who injures another athlete while
                 observing the rules of play has not acted illegally.

0567.   Goldstein, Lynn A. "Participant's Liability For Injury To A
           Fellow Participant In An Organized Athletic Event."   53
           Chicago-Kent Law Review 97-108. (1976).
               Comment on Nabozny v. Barnhill, 31 Ill. App. 3d 212, 334
           N.E.2d 258 (1975), (plaintiff's action contended that injuries
           sustained by the plaintiff were due to the defendant's
           negligence). Provides a brief overview of the facts of the case.
           Reviews cases in other jurisdictions.   Discusses the
           Nabozny opinion.

0568.   Hastings, Leslie. "Playing With Liability: The Risk Release In
           High Risk Sports." 24 California Western Law Review 127-159.
           (1987/1988).
               Analyzes risk releases in high school sports. Reviews the
           history of risk releases in California and relation between the
           risk release and assumption of risk. Also raises a number of
           related points.

0569.   Jahn, Gary Norman.   "Civil Liability: An Alternative To
           Violence In Sporting Events." 15 Ohio Northern Law Review
           243-261. (1989).
               Comment which explores tests and proposals which have
           attempted to impose liability on an athlete during a sporting
           event. Examines reasons for the failure of the system to deter
           violent conduct in sports. Recommends changes and offers a
           four-part test to impose liability.

0570.   Krzywicki, Clausen J. "The Racers' Assumption of Risk: What
           Is It?" 9 George Mason University Law Review 159-183.
           (Winter 1986).
               Suggests objective test to determine liability for injured
           participants in an automobile race. This foreseeability of
           events standard would replace the current subjective standard
           and set minimum safety measures.

0571.   "Liability of Polo Players To Spectator Injured While Watching
           Game." 19 Law Notes 73. (July 1915).
               Brief discussion of Douglas v. Converse (Pa.), 93 Atl. 955,
           wherein plaintiff's son, while a spectator at a polo game, was
           injured when a polo pony trampled him. Court stated that
           players and bystanders assumed the chance of risk involved in
           the game of polo. The spectator, however, does not assume
           said risk when the nature of the play becomes reckless.

0572.   Opie, Hayden. "Condon v. Basi-Negligence-Duty of Care-Sport
           Involving Physical Contact-Existence of Duty-Breach-Foul
           Tackle." 15 Melbourne University Law Review (Australia) 756-
           762. (December 1986).

Reviews the rational and arguments at both the trail and appellate levels in Condon v. Basi wherein plaintiff sued defendant for injury sustained during soccer game. Plaintiff recovered at trial level. Defendant's appeal was dismissed.

0573.   Partin, Matt. "Tort Liability For Players In Contact Sports." 45 UMKC Law Review 119-129. (Fall 1976).

A note which discusses Nabozny v. Barnhill 31 Ill. App. 3d 212, 334 N.E.2d 258 (1975) decided by an Illinois Appellate Court concerning the legal duty of care and liability for negligence of players of contact sports. (The case pertains to soccer). Presents Missouri law corresponding to Nabozny rule with discussion of the shortcomings of an assumption of risk defense. Concludes that "conduct that is willful or reckless and in violation of a safety rule of the sport" should be applied to other contact sports, at the professional level as well.

0574.   Sandefer, Larry.   "College Athletic Injuries: Does The Buoniconti Case Create A Duty of An Athlete Not To Play?" 63 Florida Bar Journal 34-36. (February 1989).

Analysis of the Buoniconti case, assumption of risk defense and the argument that an athlete has an ultimate duty not to play regardless of what team physicians and/or coaches may say.

0575.   Schuett, Patricia K.   "Tort Liability In Professional Sports: Battle In The Sports Arena." 57 Nebraska Law Review 1128-1139. (1978).

A note presenting the facts, historical background and decision in Hackbart v. Cincinnati Bengals, Inc. 435 F. Supp. 352 (D. Colo. 1977)., appeal docketed, No. 77-1812 (10th Cir. august 25, 1977). (Where a football players received a blow to the head during game play).   Discusses whether the courts should become involved in the playing field acting in professional football.   States that legal intervention is difficult because "violence is an inherent factor in many sports" and that legal orders are perceived to damage the unique institution of sport. Argues for a solution which give injured professional athletes recourse rather than emphasize the idea of sports as an institution.

0576.   "Sportsman's Charter." 78 Law Quarterly Review (U.K.) 490-496. (October 1962).

Examines the duty of care owed to spectators of sporting events by the participants. Specifically examines Woolridge v. Sumner, where a spectator was injured by a horse at a horse show. Lower court found the defendant negligent in his riding and management of the horse. Court of appeal reversed the judgment: that an error or errors of judgment do not constitute a breach of duty of reasonable care that participants in a sporting event owe the spectator. Discusses the concept of the "inherent risk" involved with sporting events.

0577.   "Torts-Assumption of Risk-A Professional Football Player Assumes The Risk of Receiving a Blow, Delivered Out of Anger and Frustration But Without Specific Intent To Injure During A Game." 12 Georgia Law Review 380-392. (Winter 1978).

Discussion of Hackbart v. Cincinnati Bengals, Inc. 435 F. Supp. 352 (D. Colo. 1977), appeal docketed, No. 77-1812 (10th Cir. August 25, 1977). States the court's decision does more than prevent injured athletes from recovering for their injuries, it, in effect, gives professional athletes license to engage in violent behavior. To "allow no recovery at all would render professional contact sports an unfortunate abberation in American tort law."

Referee

0578.   Davis, Victoria J. "Sports Liability: Blowing The Whistle On The Referees." 12 Pacific Law Journal 937-964. (July 1981).

Discusses the possibility of an athlete recovering from a negligent referee. Provides a background on torts, sports and the courts. Examines the liability of the participants, employer, school district and the referee. Surveys elements of legal liability of the negligent referee. Analyzes the refutation of the sports defense of assumption of risk.

0579.   Lewis, Darryll M. and Forbes, Frank S. "A Proposal For A Uniform Statute Regulating The Liability of Sports Officials For Errors Committed In Sports Contests." 39 DePaul Law Review 673-708. (Spring 1990).

Reviews the personal liability of sports officials, attempts to limit such liability, casework attempting to overturn the decisions of referees and the authors' proposal for a "Uniform Sports Official Immunity Law."

School Liability

0580.   Harty, James D. "School Liability for Athletic Injuries: Duty, Causation and Defense." 21 Washburn Law Journal 315-341. (Winter 1982).

Discusses liability that school districts and their personnel face in relation to athletic injuries. Reviews elements of duty and causation of tort liability. Contains defenses which may be used by school; sovereign immunity, failure to prove actionable negligence, contributory negligence, assumption of risk, and technical defenses.

0581.   McBroom, Douglas D.   "Sports Torts & School Athletics."   37 Washington State Bar News 21-23. (October 1983).

Reviews issue of standard of care as it applies to interscholastic athletics. Points out the duty of school district to anticipate hazards, warn the athletes of hazards and to develop a well-designed interscholastic sports program. Includes section on determining liability for sports injury.

Skiing

0582.   Antonioli, Pierre.   "Quelques cas recents de responsabilite penale en matiere d'accidents de ski" (in French).   99 Schweizerische Zeitschrift fur Strafrecht (Switzerland) 129-158. (1982).

Examines cases involving skiing accidents and legal responsibility and liability. Discusses homicidal negligence, skiing accidents and care of injured skiers. Cites specific casework involving the legal liability of skiers.

0583.   Blaxland, Michael. "The Assessment of Liability In Ski Injury Actions-Recent British Columbia Decisions." 46 Advocate (Canada) 25-35. (1988).

Reviews British Columbia decisions involving ski accidents. Examines seven factors or combinations of factors (causation, duty of care, forseeability, volenti, contractural waiver, Occupier's Liability Act, and contributory negligence) to determine if the skier's negligence action against the ski resort was successful.

0584.   Chalat, James H. and Kroll, Lea. "The Development of The Standard of Care In Colorado Ski Cases." 15 Colorado Lawyer 373-380. (March 1986).

Focuses on the development of standard of care in Colorado ski law. Provides history of ski law in Colorado. Discusses the inherent danger rule, Tramway Safety Board Act, Colorado Ski Safety Act of 1979, and Pizza v. Wolf Creek Development Corp. Examines existing casework in collision and equipment cases and offers tips for lawyers.

0585.   Faber, Wendy A.   "Utah's Inherent Risk of Skiing Act: Avalanche From Capitol Hill." 1980 Utah Law Review 355-368. (1980).

Examines Utah's statute passed in the wake of Sunday v. Stratton Corp. where the court held the ski resort liable for a skiers's injuries. Argues the new statute is one-sided at best and that it abrogates traditional tort principles in favor of a group that the legislature found to contribute to the economy of the state of Utah. Concludes the statute should be amended to reflect traditional balancing of interests which would be consistent with long-established tort principles.

0586.   Fagen, John E. "Ski Area Liability For Downhill Injuries." 49 Insurance Counsel Journal 36-49. (January 1982).
Reviews the historical development of ski area liability for downhill skiers, assumption of risk doctrine and attacks which can be used against the assumption of risk defense. Discusses Sunday v. Stratton Corporation. Presents method for determining responsibility for ski injuries.

0587.   Farrow, Michael J. "Ski Operators and Skiers-Responsibility and Liability." 14 New England Law Review 260-287. (Fall 1978).
Surveys case law on ski injuries to ascertain whether the responsibility for injuries rests on the ski operator or the skier. Reviews the historical adherence to the doctrine of assumption of risk. Includes criticism of the application of the assumption of risk doctrine and an exploration of the legal relationship between skiers and ski area operators. Discusses the Massachusetts Ski Act of 1978, the advantages and inadequacies of the statute and suggested changes to the statute.

0588.   Faverhelm, Kent; Lund, John; Chalat, James H.; and Kunz, Marco B. "From Wright to Sunday and Beyond: Is The Law Keeping Up With The Skiers?" 1985 Utah Law Review 885-918. (1985).
Presents historical perspective on development of ski tort law. Proceeds from the perspective of the defendant and the ski resort. Cites appropriate casework from Wright v. Mt. Mansfield Lift, Inc. to Sunday v. Stratton. Includes a discussion of the liability of the ski patrol.

0589.   "Haftung Bei Skiunfallen Scholten." 13 Neue Juristische Wochenschrift (West Germany) 558. (March 1960).
Examines the circumstances under which a skier is liable for a ski accident.

0590.   Hagglund, Clarence E. "Ski Liability." 32 Federation of Insurance Counsel Quarterly 223-233. (Spring 1982).
Overviews development of ski liability. Analyzes developments in legislature and the courts and examines categories of activities which result in liability actions including faulty ski rental equipment, particularly bindings; failure of gondolas, chair lifts, rope tows and the like; and

maintenance of ski hill. Discusses law of waiver and overcrowding on ski slopes.

0591.   Hames, Eugene S. "Liability For Ski Injuries Caused By Defective Bindings." 27 <u>Federation of Insurance Counsel Quarterly</u> 311-316. (1977).

Focuses on the liability of those who provide ski bindings to public skiers. Presents an overview of the history and development of ski bindings. Discusses problems with bindings and anti-friction devices. Provides recommendations to reduce both injuries to skiers and the claims which result from such injuries.

0592.   Hepp, Camill. "Verkehrssicherungspflicht Des Bergbahnunternehmers Fur Skiabfahrtsstrecken." 26 <u>Neue Juristische Wochenschrift</u> (West Germany) 2085-2089. (November 1973).

Examines the assignment of liability for the safety and conditions of ski runs.

0593.   Kleppe, Peter. "Rechtspflichten Der Skilehrer, Des Skifuhrer Und Der Skischulen." 64 <u>Schweizerische Juristen-Zeitung, Revue Suisse de Jurisprudence</u> (Switzerland) 329. November 1968).

Discusses the legal responsibility of ski instructors, skiers and ski schools.

0594.   Lisman, Carol H. "Ski Injury Liability." 43 <u>University of Colorado Law Review</u> 307-320. (March 1972).

Discusses and analyzes the traditional tort duties and defenses which have been established in ski injury litigation. Examines lift and tow injuries and injuries in downhill skiing.

0595.   Marilla, G.-D. "La responsabilite des communes et des autres collectivities publiques en matiere de ski: les 20 ans de l'arret lafont" (in French). 61 <u>La Semaine Juridique, Juris-Classeur Periodique</u> (France) 3285. (1987).

Examines the extent and responsibility of the <u>communes,</u> and other public groups regarding skiing accidents. Discusses and differentiates differences in types of skiing. Reviews the development of jurisprudential rules and their application to skiing.

0596.   Muller, P. "Verkehssicherungspflicht fur Skipisten." 27 <u>Neue Juristische Wochenschrift</u> (West Germany) 170-173. (January 1974).

Discusses the handling and assignment of liability on ski runs.

0597.   Nachin, G. "Responsabilite civile du skieur" (in French). 71 Revue Trimestrielle de Droit Civil (France) 701-721. (October-December 1973).

Discusses the civil responsibility of the skier. Including examinations of the responsibility inherent in contractual mistakes and the self-control of the skier. Examines the interplay between fault, assumption of risk, and the conditions that the injured skier encounters.

0598.   Nirk, Rudolf. "Haftung Bei Skiunfallen." 17 Neue Juristische Wochenschrift (West Germany) 1829. (October 1964).

Comments on the uncertainty that caselaw has created regarding the liability of skiers.

0599.   Pichler, J. "Skiunfall und Haftung. [II]" (in German). 21 Osterreichische Juristen-Zeitung (Austria) 144-152. (March 1966).

Reviews injuries in sports specifically skiing. Discusses ski accidents and the legal consequences of skier involvement. Focuses on the possibilities of remedies and recovery as a result of sport injuries.

0600.   Pichler, J. "Skiunfall und Haftung. [I]" (in German). 21 Osterreichische Juristen-Zeitung (Austria) 113-119. (March 1966).

Review of ski accidents and liability for those accidents. Focuses on skiing, kinds of skiing accidents and related liabilities. Also cites appropriate casework.

0601.   Rosenblatt, Albert M. "Ski Area Liability: What The Courts Say." 18 Harvard Law School Bulletin 12-15, 29-30. (January 1967).

Comments on the law concerning ski liability fashioned over the last decade. Categorizes two types of lawsuits: Those involving injuries skiers sustained while skiing and those resulting from the use of lifts or tows. Discusses assumption of risk and several court decisions. Mentions New York State legislation that a ski lift cannot be a common carrier and the ramifications of the statute.

0602.   Sinischalchi, Vincenzo M. "Scontro Fra Sciatori" (in Italian). 22 Diritto e Giurisprudenza (Italy) 715-718. (November-December 1966).

Discusses the regulation of and the legal liabilities of accidents between skiers.

0603.   Stiffler, Hans-Kaspar. "Verkehrssicherungspflicht Fur Skipisten II." 67 Schweizerische Juristen-Zeitung, Revue Suisse de Jurisprudence (Switzerland) 121. (April 1971).

Reports that the various agencies held responsible for the safety of the skislopes and surrounding area are determined by each individual case.

Spectator

0604.   Gregory, I. Francis, II and Goldsmith, Arthur H.   "The Sports Spectator As Plaintiff." 16 Trial 26-29. (March 1980).
Overview on issues of legal liability of spectators and stadium owners. Specifically examines ways to reduce legal liability. Areas of legal liability discussed are promotion, premises, products, patron, and participatory risks.

0605.   "Liability of Baseball Management For Injury To Person Attending Game." 17 Law Notes 134. (October 1983).
Considers the rule applied in two cases comparing the court instructions to the jury. Concludes the question of liability should be a question for the jury to decide as to what precaution the ordinary prudent person who furnishes public amusement of this kind should take to warn and protect spectators who may be ignorant of the attendant dangers.

0606.   Siskind, Gary E.   "Liability For Injuries To Spectators."   6 Osgood Hall Law Journal 305-315. (December 1968).
Examines the doctrine of volenti no fit injuria in the jurisdictions of England, Canada and the United States. Reviews implied and expressed assumptions of risk. Briefly reviews specific injury cases and presents injury statistics for hockey and baseball. Concludes with recommendations for change.

17

MEDICAL CARE

General

0607.   Gignoux, C. and Ribette, J. "Problemes medico-sociaux de l'air
         et de l'escape" (in French). 28 <u>Revue Generale de l'Escape</u>
         (France) 99-105. (1965).
             Discusses the medical and social problems involved with
         and relating to the personnel who are responsible for the
         functioning of an aircraft.

0608.   Kelly, G. M. "Prospective Liabilities of Sports Supervisors." 63
         <u>Australian Law Journal</u> (Australia) 669-685. (October 1989).

0609.   King, Joseph H., Jr. "Duty and Standard of Care For Team
         Physicians." 18 <u>Houston Law Review</u> 657-705. (May 1981).
             Examines the question of duty of the physician of a
         professional sports team to the person receiving the
         physician's services. Analyzes the duty question and the issue
         of standard of care.

0610.   Macfarlane, Neil. "Editorial." 24 <u>Medicine, Science and the
         Law</u> (U.K.) 157-159. (July 1984).

0611.   Preston, F. S. "Travel and Performance." 24 <u>Medicine, Science
         and The Law</u> (U.K.) 249-253. (October 1984).
             Reviews the relationship between travel and the mental
         and physical performance of an athlete. Offers
         recommendations.

0612.   Russell, Charles V. "Legal and Ethical Conflicts Arising From
         The Team's Physician's Dual Obligations To the Athlete and

Management."   10 <u>Seton Hall Legislative Journal</u> 299-325. (1987).

Explores difficulties team physicians may encounter due to their obligations to both the athlete and management. Discusses the dramatic increase in the field of sports medicine in recent years. Illustrates the higher standard of care which is demanded of the sports physician, and advises change in the dual role of the team doctor.

0613.   Ryan, Allan J. "Medical Practices in Sports." 38 <u>Law and Contemporary Problems</u> 99-111. (Winter-Spring 1973).

Discusses current educational programs in sports medicine and the proliferation of sports medicine publications in the U.S. and Europe. Elaborates on the organization of medical services for the athletes with regard to the physician, health care, and the athletic trainer. Explains sports safety citing common injuries and preventive measures. Presents the economics of medical supervision of sports.

0614.   Sanbar, S. S. et al. "Some Medicolegal Aspects of Sports Medicine." 9 <u>Legal Aspects of Medical Practice</u> 5-8. (July 1981).

0615.   Shafer, Nathaniel. "Sports Medicine." 9 <u>Lawyer's Medical Journal</u> (Second Series) 31-109. (May 1980).

Overview of sports medicine and the problems and injuries which an athlete may incur. Includes a lengthy editor's comment on the virtues and effects of physical activity, sports medicine, programs, the loci or sports injuries, injury therapies and a discussion of common misperceptions related to athletic participation.

Medical Malpractice

0616.   Balbi, Lonny. "The Liability of Professional Team Sports Physicians." 22 <u>Alberta Law Review</u> (Canada) 247-269. (1984).

Compares and contrasts standards of care in sports suits which may be similar to standards used in non-athletic suits. Provides background on role of team physician and the possibility of negligence. Discusses issues of negligence and liability from perspective of athlete and physician. Reviews medical malpractice, the principle of duty of care, and the question of standard of care. Presents theories relating to how the standard of care can be varied to better serve all interested parties.

0617.   Balbi, Lonny L. "The Liability of Professional Team Sports Physicians (Part 2)." 5 <u>Health Law In Canada</u> (Canada) 41-46. (Fall 1984).

Overview of the athlete/team physician relationship. Discusses theories on standard of care, and pressures on the athlete and team physician.

0618.   Balbi, Lonny L. "The Liability of Professional Team Sports Physicians (Part 1)." 5 Health Law In Canada (Canada) 20-27. (Summer 1984).

Explores the importance of the area of medical liability in professional sports. Provides a background review of the subject, a discussion of medical malpractice, generally, and the concept of duty of care.

0619.   Davis, James H. "Fixing" The Standard of Care: Motivated Athletes and Medical Malpractice." 12 American Journal of Trial Advocacy 215-237. (Fall 1988).

Explores application of standard malpractice legal principles to sports and sports medicine. Argues the standard of care within a sports context must be different, thus distinguishing professional and other high caliber amateur athletes from recreational athletes. Reports context in which sports medicine is practiced. Reviews application of consent and assumption of risk in sports and concludes these concepts should be the basis for dealing with medical malpractice claims in sports.

0620.   Lubell, Adele. "Questioning The Athlete's Right To Sue." 17 The Physician and Sports Medicine 240. (March 1989).

0621.   Pitt, Morley Ben. "Malpractice On The Sidelines: Developing A Standard of Care For Team Sports Physicians." 2 Journal of Communications and Entertainment Law 579-599. (Spring 1980).

Explores the role of the physician on the professional sports team. Analyzes the legal standard of care, the pressures involved and the uniqueness of the physician-patient relationship. Distinguishes pressure from responsibility. Presents pertinent case law regarding the establishing and development of a standard of care.

0622.   Todaro, Gerald J. "Sports Medicine Malpractice." 21 Trial 34-38. (May 1985).

Discussion of the doctrine of informed consent and its relationship to recreational athletes. Explores the basis for proving a claim of lack of informed consent as well as suggesting a procedure for investigating such claim.

18

NATIONAL COLLEGIATE ATHLETIC ASSOCIATION (NCAA)

General

0623.   Brody, Burton F. "NCAA Rules and Their Enforcement: Not Spare The Rod and Spoil the Child-Rather Switch The Values and Spare The Sport." 1982 Arizona State Law Journal 109-131. (1982).

Discusses NCAA enforcement and due process, the organizational structure, and enforcement as it pertains to coaches and students. Examines legislative structure of NCAA and its enforcement process, structure of NCAA enforcement, the issues of cooperation and confidentiality, and the standards of sanction.

0624.   Dickerson, Jaffe D. and Chapman, Mayer. "Contract Law, Due Process, and The NCAA." 5 Journal of College and University Law 107-121. (1978-1979.

Argues the NCAA performs a governmental function, and therefore becomes subject to the due process rules of the Constitution. Examines the relationship between the NCAA and its member institutions. Surveys the nature, functions and responsibilities of the NCAA. Explores the issue of the due process requirements and the student-athlete.

0625.   Fletcher, Shirley. "NCAA Eligibility Regulations and The Fourteenth Amendment-Where Is The State Action?" 13 Ohio Northern Law Review 433-446. (1986).

Proposes changes in status quo of role of education for NCAA Division I student-athletes. Discusses effects of tougher academic standards on black athletes. Treats case examples of several issues involving NCAA and argues NCAA actions do not fulfill state action requirement. Recognizes problem as stemming from emphasis which society places on athletics and a potential professional athletic career.

0626. Gaona, David F. "National Collegiate Athletic Association: Fundamental Fairness and The Enforcement Program." 23 Arizona Law Review 1065-1102. (1981).

Overviews Enforcement Program and its procedures. Discusses judicial scrutiny of NCAA procedures, the relationship between NCAA and state action, and NCAA are due process. Includes suggested increased procedural safeguards for NCAA.

0627. Keyes, G. Preston. "The NCAA, Amateurism, and The Student-Athlete's Constitutional Right Upon Ineligibility." 15 New England Law Review 597-625. (1979-1980).

Note exploring constitutional problems raised by the NCAA's determining the eligibility of a student-athlete. Examines whether the eligibility/ineligibility determination of the NCAA meets the state action prerequisite. Discusses the possibility of the student-athlete being protected by the equal protection clause of the fourteenth amendment. Examines the due process clause and its suitability as a constitutional protection. Concludes with a critique and analysis of the NCAA's position on what currently constitutes amateurism and what must be done in order to legally safeguard the student-athlete.

0628. Koch, James V. "A Troubled Cartel: The NCAA." 38 Law and Contemporary Problems 135-150. (Winter-Spring 1973).

Examines the National Collegiate Athletic Association (and the recent move to a three-division structure) in terms of economic theory in the area of cartelization. Describes the NCAA as a cartel and its structure as a source of trouble. Presents recent legal challenges as a function of heterogeneous membership, the internal adjustments made by the NCAA, and predicted future behavior.

0629. McKenna, Kevin M. "A Proposition With a Power Punch: The Legality and Constitutionality of NCAA Proposition 48." 26 Duquesne Law Review 43-77. (Fall 1987).

Analyzes controversial Bylaw of 1983 and presents pros and cons. Discusses contention that Prop 48 discriminate against minorities. Mentions that no athlete challenged constitutionality of the rule. Presents Conference Report Card which lists ineligible recruits of 1986-1987 season in both football and basketball for each team in Division I and I-AA schools.

0630.   McKenzie, Richard B. and Sullivan, E. Thomas. "Does The
             NCAA Exploit College Athletes?   An Economics and Legal
             Reinterpretation."   32 Antitrust Bulletin 373-399. (Summer
             1987).
                 Economic analysis of the NCAA as a joint venture rather
             than a cartel. Argues against popular belief that college athletes
             are underpaid or exploited.

0631.   Miller, David K. "The Enforcement Procedure of The National
             Collegiate Athletic Association: An Abuse of The Student-
             Athlete Right To Reasonable Discover."   1982 Arizona State
             Law Journal 133-149. (1982).
                 Discusses NCAA Enforcement Program, issue of student-
             athlete as a representative of the institution, the private
             association/state action argument, interests of student-athlete,
             and student-athlete's due process right to reasonable discovery.

0632.   "National Collegiate Athletic Association v. Tarkanian:
             Supreme Court Upholds NCAA's Private Status Under The
             Fourteenth   Amendment,   Repelling   Shark's   Attack   on
             NCAA's Disciplinary Powers."   17 Pepperdine Law Review 217-
             252. (December 1989).

0633.   "The NCAA and State Action: The Supreme Court Dunks
             Jerry Tarkanian."   40 Syracuse Law Review 1123-1144. (1989).

0634.   Pemstein, Jason Michael. "Constitutional Law: Is The NCAA
             Eligible For A New Interpretation of State Action?"   7 Loyola
             Entertainment Law Journal 337-351. (1987).
                 Discusses effects Arlosoroff v. NCAA have on the NCAA's
             ability to control the lives of its students-athletes. Criticizes the
             Court's decision and analysis for determining whether the
             NCAA was a state actor.

0635.   Remington, Frank J.   "NCAA Enforcement Procedures
             Including The Role of The Committee on Infractions."   10
             Journal of College and University Law 181-196. (Fall 1983/1984).
                 Overviews role of NCAA Infractions Committee, the
             enforcement process, the kind and nature of violations
             occurring, issues involved and overall evaluation for
             improvement of enforcement process.

0636.   Richard, Andrea Leah. "Constitutional Law-Enforcement of
             NCAA Sanctions By A Public Institution-Is There State Action
             By The NCAA?"   National Collegiate Athletic Association v.
             Tarkanian. 25 Land & Water Law Review 281-293. (1990).
                 Analyzes Supreme Court's decision in case. Reviews
             background and Court's determination that the NCAA was a
             private actor.

0637.   Sahl, J. P. "College Athletics and Due Process Protection: What's Left After National Collegiate Athletic Association v. Tarkanian." 21 Arizona State Law Journal 621-661. (Fall 1989).

0638.   Smith, Rodney K. "Reforming Intercollegiate Athletics: A Critique of The Presidents Commission's Role In The NCAA's Sixth Special Convention." 6 North Dakota Law Review 423-462. (1988).
         Provides history of the Commission. Discusses Commissions' attempts at reforming intercollegiate athletics at the NCAA's Sixth Special Convention.

0639.   Smith, Rodney K. "The National Collegiate Athletic Associations Death Penalty: How Educators Punish Themselves and Others." 62 Indiana Law Journal 985-1059. (1986/1987).
         Provides historical perspective of intercollegiate athletics and NCAA. Discusses influential role of the Presidents Commission. Explore death penalty legislation, provisions and implementation. Lists important steps taken to ensure integrity in college sports. Concludes that interests of student-athlete should become a greater priority.

0640.   Wilson, Ryan S. "Statutory Law: The Oklahoma Open Records Act: Are NCAA Investigation Records Accessible?" 42 Oklahoma Law Review 145-159. (Spring 1989).
         Discusses whether the Act should allow individuals or members of the media to gain access to information involving alleged NCAA violations by state supported universities. Supports exempting investigative records from disclosure. Outlines provisions of the Act. Provides exemptions to the Act.

0641.   Wright, Charles Alan. "Responding To an NCAA Investigation Or, What To Do When An Official Inquiry Comes." 1 Entertainment and Sports Law Journal 19-35. (Spring 1984).
         Offers suggestions, with the use of an hypothetical set of allegations, on how a university should proceed to handle an NCAA inquiry.

Accountability

0642.   Weistart, John C. "Legal Accountability and the NCAA." 10 Journal of College and University Law 167-180. (Fall 1983/1984).
         Foreward to a special issue on athletics in higher education. Explores need for accountability in the functioning of NCAA.

Survey's NCAA's structural problems, monolithic control and its multiple objectives.

0643.   Wong, Glenn M. and Ensor, Richard J.   "The NCAA's Enforcement Procedure-Erosion of Confidentiality."   4 Entertainment and Sports Lawyer 1(7). (Summer 1985).
Review of the NCAA's enforcement procedures, the issue of whether the NCAA is a public or private organization, the question of confidentiality and its impact on amateur athletic organizations.

Antitrust

0644.   Arico, James S. "NCAA v. Board of Regents of The University of Oklahoma: Has The Supreme Court Abrogated The Per Se Rule of Antitrust Analysis?" 19 Loyola of Los Angeles Law Review 437-472. (December 1985).
Presents background information to Sherman Act, the Court's per se and rule of reason analyses, and the facts of case. Suggests the rejection of the per se doctrine may lead to confusion.

0645.   Ashman, Allan. "No NCAA Kickoff On Television?" 69 American Bar Association Journal 1310-1311. (September 1983).
Brief discussion of the case of Board of Regents of The University of Oklahoma v. National Collegiate Athletic Association.

0646.   Bashinsky, Major.   "Anti-trust Law-National Collegiate Athletic Association Held Subject To The Rule of Reason Test of The Sherman Anti-Trust Act." 7 Cumberland Law Review 505-515. (Winter 1977).
Discusses Hennessey & Hudson v. NCAA wherein plaintiffs brought suit against the NCAA on the basis of several theories include one which argued that the NCAA bylaw in question was a group boycott in violation of the Sherman Anti-Trust Act. Court applied rule of reason test and found the bylaw in question did not violate anti-trust laws.

0647.   Bellas, Peter W. NCAA v. Board of Regents [104 S.Ct. 2948]: Supreme Court Intercepts Per Se Rule and Rule of Reason." 39 University of Miami Law Review 529-547. (May 1985).
Reviews Supreme Court case which determined that NCAA television plan violated antitrust standards of Sherman Act.   States Court will determine potential "competitive qualities of restraint" before it applies either Per se Rule or Rule of Reason antitrust standards (more realistic economic factors will be considered to promote competition).

0648. Bhirdo, Kelly W.; Haviland, Linda A.; and Warth, Thomas J.
"McCormick v. National Collegiate Athletic Association:
College Athletics Sanctions From An Antitrust and Civil
Rights Perspective." 15 Journal of College and University Law
459-476. (Spring 1989).

Discusses questions of the antitrust issue, standing, and
violations as they pertain to the NCAA and concern
McCormack.

0649. Bourque, Stephen. "Antitrust Law-NCAA Rules That Limit
The Number of Televised Intercollegiate Football Games
Violates Section 1 of The Sherman Act." 10 Thurgood
Marshall Law Review 632-644. (Spring 1985).

0650. Daniels, Eric D. "Did The Supreme Court Fumble?: The
Supreme Court's Failure To Endorse A Market Power
Threshold To The Application of The Rule of Reason for Cases
Under Section 1 of The Sherman Act in NCAA v. Board of
Regents." 27 Boston College Law Review 579-607. (May 1986).

Discusses Supreme Court rule of reason analysis which
declared that the NCAA television plan violates section 1 of
the Sherman Act. Criticizes the Court for abandoning the
alternate market power threshold analysis. Presents historical
case precedent regarding rule of reason, per se and market
power threshold analyses under section 1 claims.

0651. DiLisi, Richard A. "NCAA v. Tarkanian: A Delegation of
Unfettered Discretion." 39 Case Western Reserver Law Review
1423-1434. (1988/1989).

Provides history, opinions and analysis of the case.

0652. "The Effect of NCAA v. Board of Regents On the Power of The
NCAA To Impose Television Sanctions." 18 Indiana Law
Review 937-958. (Fall 1985).

Examines decision and its effects. Agrees NCAA's attempt
to control television appearances violated Sherman Act but
argues that television sanctions also violate Act. Shows show
NCAA's justification to promote a competitive balance was
not accepted by courts.

0653. Fabian, David M. "Antitrust-Price Fixing-NCAA May Not
Establish Price and Output Level of Televised College Football
Games-NCAA v. Board of Regents, 104 S.Ct. 2948 (1984)." 16
Seton Hall Law Review 170-191. (1986).

Historical perspective of the case and the per se and rule of
reason analyses adopted by the Supreme Court. Offers case
precedents. Notes the importance which television revenues
play in an extremely competitive market.

0654.   Greenspan, David. "College Football's Biggest Fumble: The Economic Impact of The Supreme Court's Decision In National Collegiate Athletic Association v. Board of Regents of The University of Oklahoma." 33 Antitrust Bulletin 1-65. (Spring 1988).

Reviews NCAA's television policy, the formation of the CFA and the Supreme Court decision in the case. Reviews decisions economic impact upon colleges and universities, television broadcasters, and advertising. Discusses litigation resulting from Supreme Court decision. Cites statistics.

0655.   Gulland, Eugene D.; Byrne, J. Peter; and Steinback, Sheldon E. "Intercollegiate Athletics and Television Contracts: Beyond Economic Justifications In Antitrust Analysis of Agreements Among Colleges." 52 Fordham Law Review 717-731. (April 1984).

Reviews NCAA v. Board of Regents. Argues that the rule of reason (not the per se rule) was most appropriate analysis considering the circumstances of this particular case.

0656.   Hickman, William. "The NCAA and Televised College Football: Does Economic Efficiency Score Points?" 11 Oklahoma City University Law Review 323-355. (Summer 1986).

Examines problems in applying Sherman Act to NCAA, a non-profit, self-regulating body. Shows courts inconsistencies. Spotlights lawsuit of which Universities of Oklahoma and Georgia against NCAA for unreasonable restraint of trade regarding televised college football. Reviews Supreme Court decision which upheld lower court's injunction against NCAA's limited television appearance plan.

0657.   Huff, Michele Iris. "Antitrust-Breaking Away From The NCAA: The Deregulation of College Football Television." 1984 Arizona State Law Journal 581-600. (1984).

Examines Board of Regents v. National Collegiate Athletic Association wherein it was held that the NCAA's television plan was in violation of section 1 of Sherman Act. Reviews the case facts, legal background, history of Regents decision, analysis of the legal issues and implications of the decision.

0658.   Jackstadt, Robert L. "Board of Regents of The University of Oklahoma v. National Collegiate Athletic Association: Antitrust Violations In College Football." 29 St. Louis University Law Journal 207-228. (December 1984).

Includes facts of case, application of antitrust doctrines, rule of reason and per se rule, and analyses of the opinions of the district court, Tenth Circuit and Supreme Court.

0659.   Jennings, Marianne M.   "Tarkanian: The Demise of Legal
          Accountability For The NCAA; Clarification of State Action
          and A Shift In The Litigation Burden To Academic
          Administrators." 11 Whittier Law Review 77-109. (1989).
          Analyzes the nature and impact of the Supreme Courts
          decision in the case.

0660.   Kemp, Deborah A.   "National Collegiate Athletic Association
          v. Tarkanian. 23 University of San Francisco Law Review 521-
          539. (Summer 1989).
          Argues that the Supreme Court decision in case was in
          error and that the NCAA was indeed a state actor.

0661.   Kirby, Robert J.   "Antitrust Law-NCAA Thrown For A Loss by
          Court's Traditional Antitrust Blitz-NCAA v. Board of Regents
          of The University of Oklahoma, 104 S.Ct. 2948 (1984).   18
          Creighton Law Review 917-952. (1984/1985).
          Reviews facts and holdings of case.   Provides background
          on the roots of the NCAA, its purposes, NCAA case law, the
          goals and purposes of antitrust law, and reviews the per se rule
          and the rule of reason.   Contends the NCAA does not fall
          under traditional antitrust analysis, and that because the Court
          shifted between the per se and rule of reason tests the NCAA
          found itself in a no-win predicament.

0662.   Klammer, Steven R.   "Constitutional Law-Due Process-
          National Collegiate Athletic Association Is Not Considered A
          State Actor Under The Fourteenth Amendment.   National
          Collegiate Athletic Association v. Tarkanian, 109 S.Ct. 454." 21
          Rutgers Law Journal 519-536. (Winter 1990).
          Provides history and analysis of the case including majority
          and minority opinions.

0663.   Kozik, Susan Marie.   "National Collegiate Athletic Association
          v. Board of Regents of The University of Oklahoma and
          University of Georgia Athletic Association." 61 Chicago-Kent
          Law Review 593-609. (Summer 1985).
          Reviews the case.   Includes facts of the case, the Court's
          decision, majority and dissenting reasoning and use of the per
          se rule.

0664.   McLain, William T.   "NCAA Actions Do Not Constitute State
          Action For Federal Constitutional Purposes: NCAA v.
          Tarkanian." 20 Texas Tech Law Review 1345-1380.
          Reviews case. Examines the nature of the law before case
          and analyzes the case.

0665.   McManus, Bill. "NCAA v. Tarkanian: May A Student-Athlete
            Receive Constitutional Protection From The NCAA's Action
            Or Has The Final Door Been Closed?" 57 UMKC Law Review
            949-962. (Summer 1989).
                Overview, analysis and evaluation of the case. Discusses
            state action and prior cases.

0666.   "National Collegiate Athletic Association's Certification
            Requirement: A Section 1 Violation of The Sherman
            Antitrust Act." 9 Valparaiso University Law Review 193-219.
            (Fall 1974).
                Contends that the certification requirements of the
            National Collegiate Athletic Association are in violation of the
            Sherman Antitrust Act. Locates five aspects of violation. State
            that while the requirement of certification violates the Act, the
            requirement should not be abolished in its entirety.

0667.   O'Connor, Christine. "Final Score: Board of Regents 3, NCAA
            O-Supreme Court Affirms Tenth Circuit's Finding That NCAA
            Television Plan Constituted Restraint of Trade." 62 Denver
            University Law Review 377-388. (Winter 1985).
                Analyzes the case of National Collegiate Athletic
            Association v. Board of Regents of The University of
            Oklahoma. Explores the background; the District, Court of
            Appeals and Supreme Court majority and dissenting opinions;
            and the consequences of the decision.

0668.   Patino, Jose Luis. "Constitutional Carte Blanche For Quasi-
            Public Institutions?" 24 Harvard Civil Rights-Civil Liberties
            Law Review 543-560. (Spring 1989).
                Presents factual background of National Collegiate Athletic
            Association v. Tarkanian, the legal setting, the lower court
            decision and Supreme Court opinion and implications of the
            decision wherein NCAA was viewed as a private and not a
            state actor.

0669.   Pfeifer, Robert M.   "Board of Regents of University of
            Oklahoma v. National Collegiate Athletic Association,
            Application of The Per Se Rule To Price Fixing Agreements."
            18 University of Richmond Law Review 185-202.
                Analyzes Tenth Circuit Court's decision under the per se
            rule and rule of reason. Briefly hypothesizes on Supreme
            Court's treatment of case.

0670.   Rand, Suzanne E.   "The Commercialization of College
            Football: The Universities of Oklahoma and Georgia Learn An
            Antitrust Lesson in NCAA v. Board of Regents." 12
            Pepperdine Law Review 515-534. (January 1985).

Presents background on antitrust law, facts of case, decisions in case and the application of the rule of reason. Discusses the practical impact on NCAA, universities and broadcasting companies. Also examines legal impact of the decision.

0671.   Randolph, Robert D., Jr. "NCAA v. Board of Regents: Is the Rule of Reason Unreasonable?" 1985 Detroit College of Law Review 201-214. (Spring 1985).

Argues that Supreme Court's application of the rule of reason was inadequate to the issues under consideration. Presents history of rule of reason. Provides analysis/ramifications of case.

0672.   Riguera, Jose R. "The State Action Doctrine Faces a Half-Court Press." 44 University of Miami Law Review 197-232. (September 1989).

Analyzes the Supreme Court decision in Tarkanian regarding the NCAA not being a state actor. Offers casework perspective on state action.

0673.   Rowe, Karol K. "NCAA v. Board of Regents: A Broadening of the Rule of Reason." 11 Journal of College and University Law 377-397. (Winter 1984).

Examines the history and facts of instant case, prior law and development of per se rule and rule of reason. Concludes with analysis of case.

0674.   Schwartz, J. M. "NCAA v. Tarkanian: State Action In Collegiate Athletics." 63 Tulane Law Review 1703-1710. (June 1989).

Reviews instant case and its relation to due process violation, state actor determination and liability for damages under 42 U.S.C. Section 1983. Examines majority and dissenting opinions of Supreme Court.

0675.   Scully, Thomas. "NCAA v. Board of Regent of The University of Oklahoma: The NCAA's Television Plan Is Sacked by the Sherman Act." 34 Catholic University Law Review 857-887. (Spring 1985).

Presents Supreme Court analysis using the Rule of Reason test for possible antitrust violations. Provides the Court's decision. Suggests the holding was proper and that the NCAA will strengthen and become more competitive.

0676.   Seib, Jonathan E. "Antitrust and Nonmarket Goods: The Supreme Court Fumbles Again-National Collegiate Athletic Association v. Board of Regents, 104 S.Ct. 2948 (1984)." 60 Washington Law Review 721-737. (June 1985).

Offers background information regarding antitrust analysis. Examines the reasoning of the Court. Notes the unique characteristics of the NCAA relating to antitrust law and suggests that the Court's analysis was flawed.

0677.   Sims, William. "NCAA v. Board of Regents and Truncated Rule of Reason: Retaining Flexibility Without Sacrificing Efficiency." 27 Arizona Law Review 193-210. (1985).
Provides historical perspective of the per se rule and rule of reason regarding antitrust analysis. Analyzes the Court's decision. Notes significance of the holding as progressive for antitrust analysis by creating a hybrid test.

0678.   Turow, Stuart. "Oklahoma Routs NCAA 7-2 In The 'Television Bowl': National Collegiate Athletic Association v. Board of Regents of The University of Oklahoma." 6 University of Bridgeport Law Review 335-358. (Spring 1985).
Argues the ruling will have negative effects. Discusses Sherman Act and provides antitrust analysis. Reviews the case, decision and judicial opinions.

0679.   VanCamp, Stephen R. "National Collegiate Athletic Association v. Tarkanian: Viewing State Action Through The Analytical Looking Glass." 92 West Virginia Law Review 761-793. (Spring 1990).
Overview of the case including prior law, majority and minority opinions.

0680.   Westover, Susan. "National Collegiate Athletic Association v. Tarkanian: If NCAA Action Is Not State Action Can Its Members Meaningfully Air Their Dissatisfaction?" 26 San Diego Law Review 953-976. (September/October 1989).
Reviews the structure of the NCAA, facts of the case, history of the state action doctrine, the majority and minority opinions and alternatives for member schools.

0681.   Wong, Glenn M. and Ensor, Richard J. "The Impact of The U.S. Supreme Court's Antitrust Ruling On College Football." 3 Entertainment and Sports Lawyer 3-6. (Winter 1985).
Discussion of the impact of the Supreme Court's decision in NCAA v. Board of Regents of the University of Oklahoma.

0682.   Young, Rowland L. "NCAA's TV Pact Violates The Sherman Act." 70 American Bar Association Journal 128(2). (September 1984).
Brief review of the Supreme Court decision in National Collegiate Athletic Association v. Board of Regents involving the televising of collegiate football.

Judicial Review

0683.   "Judicial Review of The NCAA's Bylaw 12-1." 29 Alabama
                Law Review 547-562. (Spring 1978).
                    Judicial review of the NCAA bylaw which put a limit on
                the number of assistant basketball and football coaches that
                Division I member school could employ. Surveys judicial
                scrutiny of the NCAA. Discusses exemptions from the bylaw
                an application of the fourteenth amendment to the NCAA and
                the relationship between the bylaw and the fourteenth
                amendment.

0684.   Martin, Gordon A., Jr. "Due Process and Its Future Within The
                NCAA." 10 Connecticut Law Review 290-317. (Winter 1978).
                    Analysis of four cases which have generated a public
                interest in the internal mechanisms and workings of the
                NCAA (Colorado Seminary (University of Denver) v. NCAA,
                Regents of The University of Minnesota v. NCAA, Hunt v.
                National Collegiate Athletic Association, Tarkanian v.
                University of Nevada at Las Vegas). Focus of cases was
                plaintiffs' contention that enforcement procedures of the
                NCAA violated plaintiffs' due process rights under the
                fourteenth amendment. Concludes with thoughts regarding
                the future of due process rights in relation to the NCAA.

0685.   Martin, Gordon A., Jr. "The NCAA and The Fourteenth
                Amendment." 11 New England Law Review 383-404. (Spring
                1976).
                    Surveys the litigation which challenges the regulations of
                the NCAA. Discusses Buckton v. NCAA and its implications.
                Reviews the nature of the NCAA and the issue of it being a
                voluntary association. Reviews the applicability of the state
                action concept to the NCAA.

0686.   Philpot, Kenneth J. and Mackall, John R. "Judicial Review of
                Disputes Between Athletes and The National Collegiate
                Athletic Association." 24 Stanford Law Review 903-929. (May
                1972).
                    Analyzes legal questions the enforcement of National
                Collegiate Athletic Association (NCAA) regulations presents
                and possible legal protections for those athlete's interest which
                have been adversely affected by the application of the
                regulations. Evaluates the substantive regulations and the
                present procedures used for their enforcement focusing on the
                "1.600 rule". (the prior academic performance of a college
                freshman must "predict" the ability to maintain this grade
                point average making the student eligible to compete in
                athletic events or to receive an athletic scholarship during the

first year of college.).   Analyzes limitations imposed on the NCAA under the common law doctrine of private associations and evaluates constitutional limitations on the NCAA's enforcement of its regulations.

0687.   Riegel, Robert G., Jr. and Hanley, Mark A.   "Judicial Review of NCAA Decisions: Does The College Athlete Have a Property Interest in Interscholastic Athletics?" 10 Stetson Law Review 483-505. (Spring 1981).

Examines a college athlete's property right in participating in interscholastic athletics and that right is entitled to due process of law when the athlete is disciplined by the NCAA. Explores NCAA decisions as state actions, the concept of constitutionally protected property rights, and the relationship between property interests and interscholastic collegiate athletics.

0688.   Shropshire, Kenneth L. "New Concepts of Contract Liabilities In College Sports: Member Institutions v. The National Collegiate Athletic Association." 11 Comm/Ent 1-33. (Fall 1988).

Analyzes role of NCAA in college sports, including historical background.   Reviews judicial intervention in disputes between NCAA and its member institutions. Explores possible application of a contractual framework to the NCAA and member institution relationship, and the breaching of such a contract as seen in Howard University v. NCAA. Concludes with discussion of awarding of damages in NCAA/member institution dispute.

0689.   Szwabowski, Russell W. "The Federal Courts Have Given The NCAA Back Its Home Court Advantage." 67 University of Detroit Law Review 29-94. (Fall 1989).

Explores the courts' use of the principle of self-restraint for the NCAA's advantage. Provides an overview of the NCAA and a discussion of the state action doctrine.

19
NEGLIGENCE

General

0690.   Brom, Thomas. "The Plaintiff Elects To Receive." 5 California Lawyer 11-12. (July 1985).

Reports on an insurance plan for interscholastic athletes that provides injured athletes an alternative to suing the school district for negligence.

0691.   Dias, R. W. M. "Negligence-Degree of Care Toward Spectators-Consent." 1962 Cambridge Law Journal (U.K.) 148. (November 1962).

Discusses Woolridge v. Sumner [1962] 3 W.L.R. 616 wherein plaintiff was injured by an horse ridden by an employee of the defendant. Questions the degree of care which a participant has to demonstrate toward a spectator. Examines the reasoning of the court which stated, in part, that an error in judgment is not negligence. Describes how a participant may be found negligent. Explores the test of volenti non fit injuria and how it applies to the spectators and participants in a sporting event.

0692.   "Duty of Proprietor of Place of Amusement To Provide For Safety of Patrons." 43 Chicago Legal Notes 112. (November 12, 1910).

Briefly discusses Roper v. Ulster County Agricultural Society (136 App. Div. 97,-Third Dept.). Examines other cases which support the rule that it is the duty of the proprietor to use reasonable care in providing for the safety of patrons. Reviews casework regarding questions of duty, reasonable care, and negligence when a proprietor permits an independent contractor to give exhibitions.

0693.   Fagan, John E.   "Avalanche Control: Negligence Over Strict
               Liability." 20 University of San Francisco Law Review 719-738.
               (Summer 1986).
                    Examines the application of strict liability for injuries
               sustained as a result of an avalanche that occurred after
               avalanche control procedures had been carried out. Discusses
               the development of strict liability, the danger involved in
               avalanche control and the application of negligence theories to
               those who conduct avalanche control.

0694.   Gerard, Robert J., Jr. "Surviving The Chubasco: Liability of
               California Beach Communities For Natural Conditions of
               Unimproved Public Property." 23 San Diego Law Review 723-
               740. (May-June 1986).
                    Examines Section 831.2 of California's Tort Claims Act
               which provides the government immunity from injury claims
               which were the result of natural conditions along unimproved
               public property.   Argues that said Section is being
               circumvented and calls for legislative action to reestablish the
               immunity of the Section.

0695.   Hander, Deborah Good.   "Negligence.   Shifting Risks:
               Washington Blocks Student Athlete Releases. A Public School
               District Cannot Require A Release Form Absolving The
               District of Future Negligence As A Condition of Student
               Participation In Recognized School-Related Activities.
               Wagenblast v. Odessa School District." 25 Gonzaga Law
               Review 359-372. (1989/1990).
                    Focuses on the Washington (State) Supreme Court decision
               and the Court's analysis of the relationship between
               exculpatory agreements and public policy. Presents rationale,
               background and analysis of the case.

0696.   Karns, Jack E.   "Negligence and Secondary School Sports
               Injuries in North Dakota: Who Bears The Legal Liability?" 62
               North Dakota Law Review 455-485. (1986).
                    Analyzes liability of North Dakota secondary school
               administrations. Shows what must be proved to recover
               damages and discusses possible claims. Places the issue in
               national perspective, and discusses respondent superior
               doctrine. Suggests ways to reduce negligence litigation.

0697.   Manby, C. Robert. "Assumption of Risk After Sunday v.
               Statton Corporation: The Vermont Sports Injury Liability
               Statute and Injured Skiers." 3 Vermont Law Review 129-146.
               (1978).
                    A note concerning the decision in Sunday (1978) which
               ruled that under Vermont's new comparative negligence
               statute, the defense of assumption of risk was no longer

available, and that on the facts in Sunday, the only defense would be contributory negligence. Discusses this decision with regard to ski injury liability in Vermont and various cases.

0698.   Mayrand A.   "Tentative de recuperer une partie deal jurisprudence occulte" (in French).   3 Revue de Droit Sherbrooke (Canada) 979-1006. (1972).

Review of thirty nonpublished decisions pertaining to the issue of responsibility while engaged in sporting activities. Includes gymnastics, baseball and softball, general ball-playing, motorboating, hunting, horseback riding, soccer, sledding, hockey, swimming, snowmobiling, and skiing.

0699.   "Negligence-Exculpatory Clauses-School Districts Cannot Contract Out of Negligence Liability in Interscholastic Athletics- Wagenblast v. Odessa School District, 110 Wash.2d 845, 758 P.2d 968 (1988).   102 Harvard Law Review 729-735. (January 1989).

Reviews decisions of Wagenblast and Vuillet in Washington State wherein parents and students were required to release the school districts from negligence before students would be permitted to take part in interscholastic athletics. Rulings went against the school districts.

0700.   Stewart, Brian S.   Atkins v. Glen Falls City School District: A Crack In The Wall of Comparative Negligence."   46 Albany Law Review 1533-1553. (Summer 1982).

Reviews duty of care and facts of case. Plaintiff was struck and injured by a foul ball while sitting in unprotected area. Trial court and appellate division ruled for plaintiff; court of appeals reversed. Analyzes rationale of court of appeals, the two-prong test, and the doctrine and varieties of assumption of risk.

Sports Facilities

0701.   Mandel, Bernard. "Negligent Design of Sports Facilities." 16 Cleveland-Marshall Law Review 275-283. (May 1967).

Note examining legal aspects surrounding the negligent design of a sport facility. Reviews the questions regarding what a sports participant is accountable for, what an owner or operator of a sports facility is accountable for, and what defenses are available to the owner or operator of a sports facility.   Discusses assumption of risk, negligence, and contributory negligence.

20

OLYMPICS

General

0702.   Baeumer, L.   "Vertag Von Nairobi Uber den Schutz Des
         Olympischen Symbols."   85 <u>Gewerblicher Rechtsschutz und
         Urheberrecht, Internationaler Teil</u> (West Germany) 466-470.
         (June-July 1983).
             Discusses the Treaty of Nairobi over the protection of the
         Olympic symbol.

0703.   Beckloff, Mitchell L.   "State Action In <u>San Francisco Arts &
         Athletics, Inc. v. United States Olympic Committee</u>: Let The
         Games Begin." 22 <u>Loyola of Los Angeles Law Review</u> 635-555.
         (January 1989).
             Reviews instant case within context of state action doctrine.
         Provides background on Olympics and USOC. Presents facts of
         case, reasoning of Ninth Circuit Court and analysis of the
         majority and dissenting opinions of Supreme Court. Reports
         previous state action tests of Supreme Court. Discusses the
         impact of <u>SFAA</u> and <u>West v. Atkins</u>.

0704.   Bradshaw, Alan C.   "Antitrust Policy and Olympic Athletes:
         The United States Ski Team Goes For The Gold." 1985 <u>Utah
         Law Review</u> 831-883. (1985).
             Reviews application of amateur athletic eligibility rules in
         relation to recent Supreme Court antitrust decisions regarding
         restraint of trade. Provides background on the structure and
         eligibility rules in amateur athletics. Discusses the basis and
         jurisprudence of Olympic athlete's antitrust cause of action.
         Presents policy options for consideration.

0705.   Edwards, Harry. "Perspective On Olympic Sportpolitics: 1968-1984." 9 Black Law Journal 38-50. (Spring 1984).
             Underscores the east-west use of sports for political ends. Reviews Olympic games of 1968, 1972, 1976, 1980 and 1984 and identifies how they were, and could be, used for political goals.

0706.   Galante, Mary Ann. "The Olympic Games: Legal Hurdles and Lawsuits," 4 Los Angeles Lawyer 19+. (June 1981).
             Analyzes the legal aspects of staging the Olympic Games. Surveys who is who in the legal hierarchy, the cost of advertising and television, and the legal problems that must be faced.

0707.   Hauff, Charles F., Jr. "San Francisco Arts & Athletics, Inc. v. United States Olympic Committee: USOC May Enforce Its Rights In Olympic Without Proof of Confusion." 22 Akron Law Review 93-106. (Summer 1988).
             Reviews Supreme Court case which held that USOC could enforce its right to the word "Olympic" in accordance with power granted to it by Amateur Sports Act. Presents facts of case, the holding and opinion, analysis of case and trademark and constitutional implications.

0708.   Lezin, Valerie. "Safety First: L.A.'s Gold Medal Image." 7 Los Angeles Lawyer 18(8). (April 1984).
             Points out the nature, extent and cooperation involved in the question of security at the 1984 Summer Olympics in Los Angeles.

0709.   Marks, Jeffrey M. "Political Abuse of Olympic Sport." 14 New York University Journal of International Law and Politics 155-185. (Fall 1981).
             Analyzes DeFrantz v. United States Olympic Committee and its place in modern political history of Olympic Games. Examines the phenomenon of the politicalization of the Olympic Games, the Olympic system, the International Olympic Committee (IOC) and the United States Olympic Committee (USOC). Also reviews consequences of DeFrantz decision.

0710.   Mertens, Pierre. "Le boycott des jeux olympiques" (in French). 18 Revue Belge de Droit International (Belgium) 195-201. (1984-1985).
             Discusses the boycott of the Olympic games. Examines the Olympics of 1976, 1980 and 1984, the boycotts involved and the consequent legal actions.

0711.   Nafziger, J. A. R. "Diplomatic Fun and The Games: A Commentary On The United States Boycott of The 1980

Summer Olympics."   17 Williamette Law Review 67-81. (Winter 1980).

Argues that President Carter's call for a boycott of the Summer Olympics was "...ineffective, costly, unjust, and unwise, and it may have been illegal." Questions the legality of the boycott with regard to both national and international law.

0712.   O'Neill, Barbara Ann and Nafziger, James A. R. "International Sports: Have States Succeeded Athletes As The Players?" 6 Dickinson Journal of International Law 403-436. (Spring 1988).

Reviews the organization of the International Olympic System, the use of sports in international politics and some attempts to minimize the degree to which sports is used as a tool of foreign policy.

0713.   Rich, Frederic C.   "The Legal Regime For A Permanent Olympic Site."   15 New York University Journal of International Law and Politics 1-53. (Fall 1982).

Examines possible legal regimes relating to the establishment of a permanent, neutral site for the Olympic games. Provides a brief background of issue, discusses the functional elements of autonomy and presents the legal devices for autonomy, the options and the precedents. Discusses the Greek offer of a permanent, neutral Olympic site and the problem of creating obligations that are binding, enforceable, and not subject to unilateral termination. Focuses on the issues of third party guarantors and the integration of financing arrangements.

0714.   Samuel, A. and Gearhart, R. Sporting Arbitration and The International Olympic Committee's Court of Arbitration For Sport." 6 Journal of International Arbitration 39-53. (December 1989).

0715.   "Would-Be Olympians Falter, But Press On." 7 Pennsylvania Law Journal-Reporter 1. (April 23, 1984).

International Olympic Committee

0716.   Goettel, James G. "Is The International Olympic Committee Amenable To Suit In A United States Court?" 7 Fordham International Law Journal 61-82. (1983/1984).

Raises the question, in relation to Martin v. International Olympic Committee, as to whether international organizations can be sued in United States courts. Reviews issues in Martin and the structure of the International Olympic Committee.

Examines the political question doctrine, policy considerations and the enforceability of each suits.

0717.   Mbaye, Keba. "Une nouvelle institution d'arbitrage: le tribunal arbitral de sport (T.A.S.)" (in French). 30 Annuaire Francais de Droit International (France) 409-424. (1985).

Examines a new phenomenon in arbitration, the sports arbitration tribunal, created by the International Olympic Committee. Reviews the tribunal's organization, functions and procedures.

0718.   Silance, L. "Regles du comite international olympique et le droit" (in French). 86 Journal des Tribunaux (Belgium) 694-696. (November 1971).

Examines the relationship between the rules of the International Olympic Committee and the law. Reviews the juridicial, civil, and sport-related governing body laws and rules pertaining to sports. Discusses the necessity of rules and laws in the activity of sports.

21

OTHER INDOOR SPORTS

Aerobics

0719.   Stahmer, Gregory M.   "The Aerobics Fitness Industry:
            Evolving Standards of Practice." 67 <u>Denver University Law
            Review</u> 341-355. (1990).
                Presents overview and history of the standard of practice,
            guidelines, the certification of instructors and legislation in the
            field.

Billiards

0720.   "Billiards As An Evil Amusement." 46 <u>American Law Review</u>
            910-913. (September 1912).
                Examines the reasoning and logic behind the Supreme
            Court decision <u>Murphy v. California</u> affirming an ordinance
            which prohibited any person from keeping billiard tables for
            hire or public use. Explores distinction between a nuisance and
            a nuisance <u>per se</u>, and questions the latitude and assumptions
            of Supreme Court in its interpretation of a nuisance <u>per se</u>.
            Concludes with examples wherein noted people and
            institutions view the game of billiards as healthful, innocent
            and proper.

Bowling

0721.   Koch, Matthew J.   "Bowling Alley Tort Liability."   16
            <u>Cleveland-Marshall Law Review</u> 284-290. (May 1967).
                Discusses the two principle grounds of negligence and
            nuisance upon which tort liability of the proprietor or owner

of a bowling alley may be predicated. Includes a discussion of the assumption of risks and contributory negligence. Concludes that the duty owed to the bowler is higher than to the non-bowler who is on the premises but specific standards of this duty have not been set in the cases concerning bowling.

Fencing

0722.   Vecchione, Renato. "La Questione Della Federscherman e il Rispetto Della Legge" (in Italian). 14 Rivista Trimestrale di Diritto e Procedura Civile" (Italy) 599-605. (June 1960).
          Discusses the problem of the fencing trade-unions and their following of the law.

Gymnastics

0723.   Cohen, Bernard S.   "Gymnastics Litigation: Meeting The Defenses." 16 Trial 34-36. (August 1980).
          Discusses ways of meeting two common defenses of contributory negligence and assumption of risk asserted in cases involving sporting events participants. Stresses the need for a keen analysis of the doctrines or proximate cause and venturousness in each jurisdiction and suggests the consideration of the applicability of the last clear chance doctrine. Uses a gymnastics case and Virginia law and court decision to illustrate the points.

0724.   Greenwald, Andrew E. "Gymnastics Litigation: The Standard of Care." 16 Trial 24-26. (August 1990).
          Deals with the basic considerations of the standard of care involved in sports injuries. While the emphasis is upon gymnastics, much of the material applies to other athletic events. Presents a list of source material for gymnastics litigation. Uses of technique which obtains necessary information from the defendant coach to prove what the standard of care is, that the coach is knowledgeable of it, and that he knowingly violated it, thus negligently causing the plaintiff's injuries.

22

OTHER OUTDOOR SPORTS

General

0725.   Alheritiere, D. "Reglementation du loisir, des activities de plein air et des sports au Canada; aspects constitutionnels" (in French). 14 Cahiers (Laval) (Canada) 33-80. (1973).

Reviews regulation, legislation, and constitutional foundation of outdoor sports and leisure-time activities in Canada. Includes a bibliography, a number of federal laws, and a list of applicable cases.

Autoracing

0726.   Reindle, Otto. "Probleme Ale Raspunderii Automobil Clubukui Roman Pentru Prejudicii Produse Cu Ocazia Unor Concursuri Sportive Automobilistice" (in Romanian). 33 Revista Romana de Drept (Romania) 42-45. (July 1977).

Provides legal justifications which argue that the Romanian Automobile Club did not have legal responsibility regarding the death of a spectator caused by a driver in a race organized by the Club. Reasons include the lack of a collective civil responsibility agreement between the Club, competitors and the spectators; legal conditions which stated that the competitors had total civil responsibility for their acts during the event. Compares the similarity between Romanian legislation and that of other Eastern European countries.

0727.   Render, Edwin R. "The Penalization of An Indy Race Driver." Annual Labor and Employment Law Institute 215-229. (1985).

Camping

0728.   Mabrouk, M. "Le regime juridique du camping" (in French).
             22 Actualite Juridique (France) 388-398. (August 1966).
                 Review of the system governing camping. Explores the
             policies, organization, administration and regulation of
             camping. Surveys jurisdictional control of camping, its being
             subject to the authority of the police, and the fact that camping
             is an activity with general interest.

Cricket

0729.   Buckley, R. A. "Cricket and The Law of Nuisance." 41 Modern
             Law Review (U.K.) 334-337. (May 1978).
                 Brief discussion of Miller v. Jackson [1977], Q. B. 966., an
             action against the local cricket club for negligence and
             nuisance. Courts of Appeals overruled court of first instance,
             awarding the plaintiff only damages, and not the injunction
             sought, and which were awarded by the lower court. Decision
             denied the defense that the plaintiff came to the event as a
             nuisance.

0730.   Newell, David. "Cricket's Winter Match." 94 Law Quarterly
             Review (U.K.) 340-344. (July 1978).
                 Discussion of Greig v. Insole [1978] 1 W.L.R. 302, (cricketers
             brought an action against the International Cricket Conference
             (I.C.C.) and the Test and County Cricket Broad (T.C.C.B.)
             alleging inter alia unlawful restraint of trade and denial of the
             right to work). Note examines the arguments of both parties,
             the reasoning and the court decision, which ruled in favor of
             the plaintiffs. Discusses the range and impact of the issues
             raised by this case.

0731.   "Not Quite Cricket." 6 Anglo-American Law Review (U.K.)
             133-137. (July-September 1977).
                 Brief editorial on the nature of cricket. Reports on Greig
             and Others v. Insole and Others, World Series Cricket Pty. Ltd.
             v. Insole and Others, and their implications for cricket.

Cycling

0732.   Blanplain, R. "Juridisch Statuut Van de Belgische
             Wielrenner" (in Dutch). 27 Rechtskundig Weekblad (Belgium)
             1729-1754. (May 1964).
                 Reviews the need for the comprehensive regulation of
             cycling throughout the sport. Examines the situation in
             Belgium.

0733.   Cuesta Cascajares, R. Ruiz de la. "Las Competiciones Ciclistas
             Ante el Derecho. (II)" (in Spanish). 60 Revista General de
             Lagislacion y Jurisprudencia (Spain) 696-745. (1970).
                  Second and final part of an article regarding cycling
             competitions, the incumbencies upon the various parties and
             the law.

0734.   Cuesta Cascajares, R. Ruiz de la. "Las Competiciones Ciclistas
             Ante el Derecho. (I)" (in Spanish). 60 Revista General de
             Legislacion y Jurisprudencia (Spain) 497-600. (1970).
                  Discusses the relationship between cycling competitions
             and the law.

0735.   Del, Ernest; Moss, Lawrence C; and Reicher, Thomas Z. A
             Handbook For Bicycle Activists. Stanford, California: Stanford
             Environmental Law Society, 1976.
                  Handbook discussing tactics for attempting to draw
             attention to benefits of bicycling. Describes planning and
             design of bicycle facilities. Provides perspective on the law as it
             applies to bicyclists. Reviews vehicle and equipment codes,
             insurance law, and compensation of injuries sustained while
             bicycling. Concludes with chapter on political tactics for
             bicyclists.

Dog Racing

0736.   Hochman, Marilyn. "The Flagler Dog Track Case." 7
             Computer-Law Journal 117-127. (Summer 1986).
                  Presents the facts, plan, operation and investigation of the
             "Flagler Dog Track Case" involving a computer scam on the
             trifecta. Discusses criminal and civil cases, and Florida's 1978
             Computer Crimes Act.

Horseracing

0737.   Bailey, Robert S.   "Administrative Law-Standing and
             Appealability." 8 Duquesne Law Review 161-169. (Winter 1969-
             1970).
                  Discusses Pennsylvania Supreme Court's decision in Man
             O'War Racing Association v. State Horse Racing Commission,
             433 Pa. 432, 250 A.2d 172 (1969). Examines issues involved, the
             scope of appealability, appealability by certiorari, Man O'War's
             standing to bring the appeal, the issues of procedural due
             process, and the abuse of administrative discretion.

0738.   Cernahan, A. Vernon and Versfelt, David S.   "Antitrust Boycott Analysis Applied To A Harness Racing Association." 70 The Kentucky Law Journal 915-940. (Fall 1981-1982).

0739.   Disney, Mitchell F. "The Right of Action For Lost Economic Advantage Is Recognized For Interference By One Equestrian Harness Race Drive." 14 Pepperdine Law Review 1095-1097. (May 1987).

0740.   Hawkins, James P. "Federal Court Jurisdiction Over LMRA Section 301 Cases Involving The Horseracing Industry." 29 Boston College Law Review 171-177. (December 1987).
          Review of Richards v. Local 134, International Brotherhood of Electrical Workers where the U.S. Seventh Circuit Court of Appeals ruled that a district court improperly declined jurisdiction in a labor dispute.

0741.   Holzberg, Brian. "Losing Her Equine-imity." 9 The National Law Journal 43. (January 12, 1987).

0742.   Mayer, H. "Commentaire du decret no. 83-878 du 4 Octobre 1983 relatif aux societies de courses de chevaux et au pari mutuel" (in French). 58 [I, II] La Semaine Juridique, Juris-Classeur Periodique (France) 3163. (1984).
          Discussion and review of the laws relating to parimutuel betting on horse racing. Surveys organizations relating to racing. Comments on decree number 83-878 of 4 October 1983.

0743.   Rooney, John Flynn. "$1 Million Settlement In Racehorse Death." 135 Chicago Daily Law Bulletin 1. (August 15, 1989).

0744.   Seebauer, Heidi J. "The Interstate Horseracing Act of 1978: An Evaluation." 12 Connecticut Law Review 883-919. (Summer 1980).
          Traces background of racing, parimutuel wagering and off-track betting (OTB) in the U.S. Analyzes Congressional response to OTB and to the Act itself.

0745.   Talley, Chuck. "Constitutional Law-Due Process-Horse Trainer Held Strictly Liable For The Condition of Horses." 8 Florida State University Law Review 365-375. (Spring 1980).
          A note which analyzes Division of Parimutuel Wagering v. Caple (Florida 1978) and demonstrates that strict liability imposed on horse trainers is appropriate give the activity involved and the procedural protections provided for the trainer. Examines State ex rel. Paoli v. Baldwin (Florida 1974), the Baldwin precedent, and compares it to other states' laws.

0746.   Telias, Bradley S. "Horse Racing and The Law: A Legislative Proposal To Harness Race-Fixing." 9 Fordham Urban Law Journal 253-277. (1980/1981).

Examines relevant court decisions concerning license suspensions in horse racing. Evaluates corruption in harness and thoroughbred racing. Proposes legislative amendments to the relative statutory provisions which should help restore the public's confidence in the sport by curtailing thoroughbred corruption.

0747.   Wesley-Smith, P. "Natural Justice." 13 Hong Kong Law Journal Limited (Hong Kong) 104-108. (1983).

Comments on the Court of Appeal in Peter James Miers v. Royal Hong Kong Jockey Club (1982), where appellant who had been jockey racing in Hong Kong since 1971 was denied his application for a license for the 1982-1983 season. Deals with whether applicant received a fair hearing and whether failure to disclose relevant evidence affect the decision might have affected the outcome. Two assumptions made by the court are explained with reference to cases leading to legal development in the area of racing from Hong Kong, South Australia, New South Wales, New Zealand and South Africa.

0748.   Wilson, Shelley A. "Employment Practices; Horseracing Employees-Working Hours and Compensation." 19 Pacific Law Journal 595-596. (January 1988).

California law stating that those involved in the care of racehorses must have the same standards applied to them as those who similarly take care of other livestock.

0749.   Wust, Herbert and Pelhak, Jurgen. "Staatsaufsicht und Vereinsautonomie im Deutschen Trabrennsport." 30 Offentliche Verwaltung (West Germany) 115. (January 1977).

Discusses the roles of state supervision of and club autonomy in German trotting sports.

Mountain Climbing

0750.   Blalock, Joyce. "The Sporting Suit." 53 American Bar Association Journal 58-62. (January 1967).

Reviews legal hazards associated with mountain climbing. Examines the extent of liability for injuries, the execution of releases, various theories of liability, product liability, defenses against liability and the issue of notification of death.

0751.   Poupart, J.-M. "A propos de l'alpinsme improvise qui expose autrui au danger" (in French). 41 Revue De Droit et de Criminologie (Belgium) 337. (Janaury 1960).

Focuses on impromptu mountain climbing, its practicality and its resultant exposure to danger to the climbers and others. Examines legal consequences involved. Surveys laws relating to the rights and duties of the individuals involved. Discusses the nature of various sporting activities and their margins of danger. Cites cases which involved impromptu climbing expeditions. Concludes by questioning the legal limits which have been imposed on impromptu climbing.

0752.   Sarraz-Bournet, Pierre. "Aspects juridiques du secours en Montagne" (in French). 43 La Semaine Juridique, Juris-Classeur Periodique (France) 2238. (April 1969).

Examines the legal aspects of rescue efforts of those use the mountains for recreation purposes. Focuses on mountain climbing. Reviews how rescue efforts are organized including the intervention of public services. Explores legal ramifications of organized rescue efforts for both those people in danger and those involved in the rescue effort.

Playgrounds

0753.   Farrell, Michael. "Playground Safety." 132 Solicitor's Journal (U.K.) 1168-1169. (August 19, 1988).

Review of research, safety guidelines and the Health and Safety at Work etc. Act 1974. Discusses essentials of playground safety.

Running

0754.   Carico, David D. "Wheelchair Participation In Road Racing: A Right Not A Privilege." 13 Pacific Law Journal 1117-1156. (July 1982).

Examines federal statutory guarantee of handicapped athlete to participate in wheelchair road race. Reviews definition of qualified handicapped person, program accessibility and remedies available for violation of Section 504 of rehabilitation Act of 1973. Examines federal equal protection and the right to participate. Discusses right to participate under California law.

0755.   Kozlowski, James C. "Fitness Factor In Fun Run Fatality." 24 Parks & Recreation 14. (August 1989).

Sailing/Windsurfing

0756.   Boisson, Phillippe. "La pratique de la planche a voile et la
             securite" (in French). 38 <u>Droit Maritime Francais</u> (France) 323-
             332. (1986).
                 Examines windsurfing safety in France. Discusses the
             prevention of accidents and the assistance and saving of those
             in windsurfing mishaps. Concludes with a discussion on
             questions of responsibility and insurance.

0757.   Gaeta, Dante. "Ordinamento Della Navigazione Da Diporto"
             (in Italian). 38 <u>Rivista Del Diritto Della Navigazione</u> (Italy) 21-
             60. (1972).
                 Discusses the regulations regarding the sport of sailing.

0758.   Grigoli, Michele. "Riflessi Sistematici Della Nuova Disciplina
             Della Navigazione Da Diporto" (in Italian). 37 <u>Rivista del
             Diritto Della Navigazione</u> (Italy) 288-299). (1971).
                 Systematic legal reflection on the new regulations of the
             sport of sailing.

Skiing

0759.   Antonioli, Pierre. "Quelques cas recents de responsabilite
             penale en matiere d'accidents de ski" (in French).   99
             <u>Schwizerische Zeitschrift fur Strafrecht</u> (Switzerland) 129-158.
             (1982).
                 Examines cases involving skiing accidents and legal
             responsibility plus liability. Discusses homicidal negligence,
             skiing accidents and care for injured skiers. Cites specific
             casework involving the legal liability of skiers.

0760.   Bernstein, Diane. "The Snowballing Cost of Skiing: Who
             Should Bear The Risk?" 7 <u>Cardozo Arts & Entertainment Law
             Journal</u> 153-183. (1988).
                 Reports on <u>Sunday</u> and its effects on the ski industry.
             Focuses on the states in which skiing is a major element of
             tourism. Reviews legislative and judicial approaches and the
             case law in ski injury instances. Proposes a model ski operator
             code which is designed for the interests of the skier and the ski
             resort industry.

0761.   Chalat, James H. "Ski Law in Michigan." 63 <u>Michigan Bar
             Journal</u> 355-361. (May 1984).
                 Provides history of ski law, categories of skiing cases, a
             bibliography and a list of resource materials on skiing in
             Michigan.

0762.   Chalat, James H. "Continuing Changes In Colorado Ski Law."
          13 Colorado Lawyer 407-410. (March 1984).
          Overviews ski law in Colorado. Briefly examines history of
          ski law in U.S., Colorado Ski Safety Act of 1979, case law on
          skiing in Colorado, a review of the Passenger Tramway Safety
          Act of 1965 and a brief analysis of the impact of skiing on the
          economy of Colorado.

0763.   Charpentier, J. and Peiser, G.   "Vers une reglementation
          Europeene de la pratique du ski?" (in French). Recuil Dalloz
          Sirey (France) 179-184. (December 1966).
          Explores the potential for the regulation of skiing practices
          in Europe. Acknowledges the fac that skiing by oneself often
          repercusses on others. Examines the multifaceted social and
          physical aspects and dangers of skiing. Discusses the nature
          and extent of the jurisdiction over skiing accidents.

0764.   Clawson, Carol. "Financing Community Impacts: Local
          Planning Issues In Ski Resort Development." 1985 Utah Law
          Review 783-811. (1985).
          Review and discussion of the impact of the development of
          a ski resort. Examines planning and zoning techniques and
          susequent devices used to lessen the impact of economic
          development. Analyzes the regulatory process as applied to ski
          resort development. Discusses the use of development fees,
          special use permits and negotiated conditions.   Reviews
          limitations on the use of fees and conditions.   Presents
          alternative view on the combining of zoning devices.

0765.   Collomb, Pierre. "Les activities sportives en montagne" (in
          French). 1 Revue Francais de Droit Administratif (France) 788-
          797. (1985).
          Overview of sporting activities in the mountain region of
          France. Reviews the utilization of mountain space and the
          nature of sporting activities. Focuses on the sport of skiing.
          Discusses specific legal ramifications of sporting activities.

0766.   Dutoit, Bernard. "Droit de la concurrence deloyale dans le
          domaine du ski" (in French).   102 (I) Zeitschrift fur
          Schwizerisches Recht (Switzerland) 293-307. (1983).
          Explores the sport of skiing and the successful and profitable
          marketing of skis. Presents relatively in-depth examination of
          certain select aspects and realities of buying skis.

0767.   Ferguson, Arthur B., Jr. "Allocation of The Risks of Skiing: A
          Call For The Reapplication of Fundamental Common Law
          Principles." 67 Denver University Law Review 165-192. (1990).
          Discusses common law development and the impact of
          state legislation on skiing.

0768. Kunnell, E. "Verkehrssicherungspflicht Auf Skipisten Und Tourenabfahrten Unter Berucksichtigung Der Neueren Rechtsprechung Des Bundesgerichtshofes" (in German). 38 Osterreichische Juristen-Zeitung (Austria) 10-13. (January 1983).

Discusses attempts to formulate rules for skiers and the extent of the applicability of those rules.

0769. Larguier, J. "Psychologie criminelle du skieur" (in French). 23 Revue de Science Criminelle et de Droit Penal Compare (France) 37-56. (January-March 1968).

Reports on criminal actions of skiers. Discusses the penal sanctions of behaviors and the need for enforcement through the use of ski patrols.

0770. Lockhart, Kim. "Legal Competition Takes To The Slopes: Canada's 'Skating Bar' Sharpens Its Skills for 1988 Post-Olympic Event." 11 Canadian Lawyer 41. (March 1987).

0771. Lovett, Richard A. "Dual Permits For Ski Resorts: An Analysis of The Forest Service Special Use Permit Policy." 1985 Utah Law Review 765-781. (1985).

Reviews the history of the Forest Service's procedure regarding the issuance of permits to downhill ski resorts. Examines that procedure in terms of its legality and legal history.

0772. Marilla, G.-D. "La responsabilite des communes et des autres collectivites publiques en matiere de ski: les 20 ans de l'arret lafont" (in French). 61 La Semaine Juridique, Juris-Classeur Periodique (France) 3285. (1987).

Examines the extent and responsibility of the communes, and other public groups regarding skiing accidents. Discusses and differentiates differences in types of skiing. Reviews the development of jurisprudential rules and their application to skiing.

0773. Mathys, Heinz Walter. "Rechtliche Probleme Des Skifahrens" (in German). 113 Zeitschrift der Bernischen Juristenvereins, Revue de al Societe des Juristes Bernois (Switzerland) 417-458. (October 1977).

Discusses problems of law as they apply to those who ski in Switzerland. Reviews the sport of skiing, its economic influence, accidents in skiing, liability and the responsibility regarding skiing accidents, and responsibility involving collision accidents.

0774. Murphy, Scott P. "Tort Law-Ski Area Operator's Liability Under The Massachusetts Ski Area Safety Act-Atkins v. Jiminy

Peak, Inc." 22 Suffolk University Law Review 909-917. (Fall 1988).

Reviews decision in instant case and statute of limitations found in Massachusetts Ski Safety Act. Discusses legislative attempts to balance interests of ski industry and individual person.

0775. Padrutt, Willy. "Grenzen Der Sicherungspflicht Fur Skipisten." 103 Schweizerische Zeischrift Fur Strafrecht (Switzerland) 384-408. (1986).

Skiing has existed ever since Thor first taught people how to ski. The few first questions of "responsibility" (in relation to skiing's dangers) were not asked until the 1930s and then after when a real skiing boom in Europe occurred. For approximately twenty years, no legal decisions were made, but since then, an enormous amount of activity has arisen between the responsibilities of skiers and ski resorts alike.

0776. Padrutt, Willy. "Verkehrssicherungspf fur Skipisten." 87 Schweizerische Zeitschrift fur Strafrecht, Penal Suisse (Switzerland) 63-77. (1971).

Discusses the extent to which there is an obligation to maintain a safe environment on the ski slopes and the surrounding area.

0777. Pichler, Josef. "Zum Problem Skischule-"Skiguide."" 42 Osterreichische Juristen-Zeitung (Austria) 684-686. (1987).

Skiing schools, which must conform to certain legal standards, are losing customers to "Ski Guides." "Ski Guides" are generally free-lance ski instructors who accompany guests, but in doing so provide no formal instruction. Examines the legal situation of the "Ski Guide" in relation to that of the skiing school.

0778. Pocar, Fausto. "Problemi di Diritto Internazionale Privato In Tema di Infortuni Sciatori e Prospettive di Una Regolamentazione Internazionale" (in Italian). 12 Rivista di Diritto Internazionale Privato e Processuale (Italy) 491-506. (July-September 1976).

Review of the problems of international private law regarding injured skiers and the possibility and potential of uniform international regulation.

0779. Richler, Josef. "Besteht Eine Rechspflicht Zur Sicherung Der Skipisten?" 64 Schweizerische Juristen-Zeitung, Revue Suisse de Jurisprudence (Switzerland) 281. (October 1968).

Discusses the question of legal obligations concerning the safety of ski slopes.

0780.   Siniscalchi, Vincenzo M. "Scontro Fra Sciator" (in Italian). 22 Diritto e Giurisprudenza (Italy) 715-718. (November-December 1966).
Discusses the regulation of and legal liabilities of accidents between skiers.

0781.   Sprung, R. and Konig, B.   "Pistenordnungen in Tirol" (in German). 102 Juristische Blatter (Austria) 133-140. (March 1980).
Pertains to rules and regulations governing the skier in the Austria province of Tirol.

0782.   Sprung, R. and Konig, B.   "Recht zur Mechanischen Schipistenpraparierung" (in German). 101 Juristische Blatter (Austria) 406-412. (August 1979).
Discusses the conflict between the receational ski needs of the public and the rights of property owners.

0783.   Sprung, R. and Konig, B.   "Umfang der Ersessenen Dienstbarkeit der Schiabfahrt" (in German). 34 Ostereichische Juristen-Zeitung (Austria) 209-212. (April 1979).
Discusses the process by which the value and commercial usefulness of a ski resort is determined. Examines the question of community involvement in the planning of a ski resort.

0784.   Stiffler, Hans-Kaspar.   "Verkehrssicherungspflicht fut Skipisten." 67 Schweizerische Juristen-Zeitung, Revue Suisse de Jurisprudence (Switzerland) 101. (April 1971).
Examines the duties and obligations of keeping the ski slopes and surrounding areas safe.

0785.   Strachan, Gordon and Boevers, James A.   "Antitrust Issues Facing The Ski Resort Industry: The Company Town Revisited." 1985 Utah Law Review 813-830. (1985).
Reviews antitrust issues facing ski resort industry. Discusses these issues from the context of Miami International Realty v. Town of Mt. Crested Butts, Gibson v. Greater Park City Co., and Aspen Skiing Co. v. Aspen Highlands Skiing Corp. Discusses economic domination and restraint of trade in the destination skier market and issues regarding monopolization and the destination skier.

Soccer

0786.   Grasselli, Sergio.   "Attivita Dei Calciatori Professionisti Nel Quadro Dell'ordinamento Sportivo" (in Italian).   126 Giurisprudenza Italiana (Italy) 44-59. (1974).

Reviews the activity of professional soccer players within the context of sports regulations.

0787.   Lyra Filho, J. "Autonomia e tipicidade do contrato desportivo" (in Portuguese). 237 Revista Forense (Brazil) 34-38. (January-March 1972).

Explores the nature and relationship of the contract between soccer clubs and their professional players. Reviews Brazilian legislation, customary law and international rules.

0788.   "Societa Calcistiche, Calciatori, Massificazione Contrattuale e Divaricazione Dei Poteri" (in Italian). 23 Rivista Delle Societa (Italy) 1387-1391. (September-October 1978).

Discussion on the nature of contracts which may be applied to professional soccer players.

0789.   Sotgia, Sergio. "Considerazioni su Azienda e Avviamento Della Impresa di Spettacoli di Calcio" (in Italian). 70 Rivista del Diritto Commericale e del Diritto Generale delle Obbligazione (Italy) 1-19. (January-February 1972).

Considers the initial and long-term organization pertaining to the enterprise of professional soccer.

0790.   Tomandl, T. and Schrammel, W.   "Rechsstellung Von Vertrages-und Lizenzfussballern I" (in German). 94 Juristische Blatter (Austria) 234-241. (May 1972).

Involves a discussion of the legal rights of professional soccer players. Examines the rules, regulations and penalties of sports clubs and organizations as they effect the players. Explores the issue of being a contractually bound athlete.

0791.   Veth, N.J.P. Giltay. "Uitsluiting Van Buitenlandse Voetballers: Mogelijk Binnen de EEG?" (in Dutch). 53 Nederlands Juristenbald (Netherlands) 504-413. (July 1978).

Discusses the possibility of excluding foreign soccer players, through the installation of regulations in the European Economic Community, and the possible contradictions with the Treaty of Rome.

Sports Aviation

0792.   Ariniaud, Max. "Problems de securite dans la pratique des sports aeriens" (in French). 18 Revue Francaise de Droit Aerien (France) 154-158. (April-June 1964).

Briefly discusses aspects of security problems at air shows and the activities involved with them. Presents data on accidents at airshows. Explores the causes of airshow accidents.

0793.   McCarthy, James J.   "Aerobatics, Sport Aviation and Student Instruction."   44 Journal of Air Law and Commerce 309-320. (1978).

Analysis of the factual and legal problems involved in aerobatics, sports aviation and student instruction.   Cites applicable regulations and casework.

0794.   McCarthy, James.   "Sports Aviation and The Student Flying." 14 Trial 24-27. (August 1978).

Examines aerobatics, hang-gliding and skydiving.   Reviews governmental regulation of activities and the relationship between a violation of regulations and the assignment of liability. Surveys student instruction.

Tennis

0795.   Levin, Chery Wyron and Bortz, Bruce L.   "Torts On The Courts." 14 Trial 25-27. (June 1978).

Explores tennis injuries.   Provides statistics on the number of injuries.   Discusses the growth of tennis, negligence, assumption of risk and the question of manufacturer's liability. Points out the problems which a plaintiff may encounter in a negligent or defective design case.

Watersports

0796.   Abbott, John W.   "Maine's Commercial Whitewater Outfitter Law: Maximizing Competition or Destroying It?" 11 Vermont Law Review 233-266. (Spring 1986).

Focuses on Maine's whitewater rafting laws, and the effects on competition.   Also offers suggestions on challenges to the law. Suggests alternatives to the present law.

0797.   Kloepfer, Michael and Brandner, Trier.   "Wassersport und Umweltzschutz." 7 Neue Zeitschrift fur Verwaltungsrecht (West Germany) 115-121. (1988).

Discusses the need for a limitation on watersports which adversely affect the environment.

Yachting

0798.   Angel, Carol. "Court May Decide America's Cup Winner." 102 The Los Angeles Daily Journal 1. (September 5, 1988).

0799.　　　　Giannini, Nadia A. "International Sports Competition: The America's Cup 1988-The Legal Battle." 30 Harvard International Law Journal 264-276. (Winter 1989).

Review of the proceedings between the Mercury Bay Boating Club of New Zealand and the San Diego Yacht Club starting with Mercury's challenge to the San Diego Y.C. for the America's Cup. Discusses the consolidation of the cases in 1987, the positions and arguments of both sides as well as the Court's reasoning and consequent decision.

0800.　　　　Gurney, Guy. "The Number of SORC Entries Is Well Up On Last Year's List, and Includes Several Hot New Prospects for Admiral's Cup Selection." 3 Health Law In Canada (Canada) 33. (Spring 1982).

0801.　　　　Johnson, Alex M., Jr. and Taylor, Ross D. "Revolutionizing Judicial Interpretation of Charitable Trusts: Applying Relational Contracts and Dynamic Interpretation to Cy Pres and America's Cup Litigation." 74 Iowa Law Review 545-591. (March 1989).

Examines New York State Supreme Court in Mercury Bay Boating Club v. San Diego Yacht Club and doctrine of cy pres modification. Provides historical overview and analysis of litigation involving the America's Cup. Calls for revolutionizing of judicial interpretation of charitable trusts and the application of the cy pres doctrine. Appendices include deed pertaining to America's Cup.

0802.　　　　Mairs, Patricia A. "Navigating Troubled Legal Waters: The America's Cup Fight Over The Winged Keel." 6 The National Law Journal 13. (September 26, 1983).

0803.　　　　Richter, Allan. "Their Cup Runneth To Thoughts of 1987." 6 The National Law Journal 43. (April 23, 1984).

0804.　　　　Sutterfield, James R. "Personal Injury and Death Aboard Racing Yachts." 12 Journal of Maritime Law and Commerce 233-242. (January 1981).

0805.　　　　Vogeler, William. "America's Cup Bound Back To San Diego Club." 102 The Los Angeles Daily Journal 1. (September 20, 1989).

23

PROFESSIONAL SPORTS

General

0806.   De Giorgi, Maria Vita. "Liberta e Organizzazione Nell'Attivita Sportiva" (in Italian). 127 <u>Giurisprudenza Italiana</u> (Italy) 122-127. (1975).
Explores whether sporting activities should be organized or not concerning amateur and professional athletes and sports.

0807.   Haserot, Phyllis Weiss. "Sports Team Models For Law Firm Management." 8 <u>Legal Management</u> 30-32. (May-June 1989).

0808.   Hochberg, Philip R. <u>Representing Professional and College Sports Teams and Leagues</u>. New York: Practising Law Institute, 1977.
Presents topics which include current developments in antitrust and labor, college sports and the law, television contracts, recent developments in tax law, trends in media rights, and general problems of representing teams.

0809.   Johnson, Arthur T. "Congress and Professional Sports: 1951-1978." 445 <u>The Annals of The American Academy of Political and Social Science</u> 102-115. (September 1979).
Discusses significant legislation introduced, conflicting Congressional perceptions of professional sports and political influence, on Congress, by owners of professional teams from 1951 to 1978.

0810.   Jones, Michael E., ed. <u>Current Issues In Professional Sports</u>. Durham, NH: University of New Hampshire, Whittemore School of Business and Economics, 1980.

Collection of articles from a symposium on professional sports. Topics include the contractual relationship between the representative and the athlete, the NCAA, agent and athlete, the role of the media in sports, revolutionizing professional sports telecasting, the use of athletic endorsements in consumer product advertising, protection and promotion of commercial value of professional athlete, recent developments in reserve clause, sports medicine and athletic injuries, tort aspects of sports injuries, and the relationship of Baseball Players Association, Team Management and League.

0811.   Lava, Leslie Michele. "Battle of The Superstars: Player Restraints In Professional Team Sports." 32 University of Florida Law Review 669-700. (Summer 1980).
          A note which examines federal antitrust and labor laws concerning their historical and analytical framework and which explains how the antitrust laws circumscribed the contractual restraints in professional baseball, basketball, football and soccer. Discusses athlete's ability to challenge restrictions. Recommends different word an analytical approach for courts concerning the controls on player mobility.

0812.   Leavell, Jerome F. and Millard, Howard L. "Trade Regulation and Professional Sports." 26 Mercer Law Review 603-616. (Winter 1975).
          Overview of unfair trade practices occurring in professional sports. Includes baseball, basketball, football and hockey. Reviews general antitrust policy, league structure, unfair trade practices and a discussion of the rationale for non-enforcement of the antitrust laws. Concludes with suggestions for alternatives to existing practices.

0813.   Reaves, Lynne. "Jersey Giants?" State Presses Teams On Names." 70 American Bar Association Journal 41. (February 1984).
          Brief discussion on a bill introduced in the New Jersey state legislature that would require the use of the name "New Jersey" for any professional team contracting to play in New Jersey sports arenas.

0814.   Rothenberg, Alan I. Representing Professional Sports Teams. New York: Practicing Law Institute, 1974.
          Discusses purchase and ownership of sports franchises; tax factors in buying, owning and selling professional sports teams; operation of a professional sports team and league; negotiations with players; and radio and television in professional sports.

0815.   Sobel, Lionel S. Professional Sports and The Law. New York: Law-Arts Publishers, Inc., 1976.

Discusses professional sport and the antitrust laws, the reserve and option clauses, player draft, professional sports and the labor laws, inter-league "wars", league mergers, discipline and eligibility, buying and moving team franchises, professional sports and tax laws, and professional sports broadcasting. Includes appendices which contain excerpts of various acts and laws, and examples of player contracts.

0816.   Uberstine, Gary A. Covering All The Bases: A Comprehensive Research Guide To Sports Law." Buffalo, NY: William S. Hein Company, 1985.

Provides strategy and materials for exploring sports law, chapters on books, symposia, A.L.R. Annotations, legislation, government publications, cases, periodicals, law review articles and bibliographies pertaining to sports law. Includes directory of leagues, organizations, associations, institutes, centers and prominent lawyers and glossary of terms related to sports law.

Antitrust

0817.   Allison, John R. "Professional Sports and The Antitrust Laws: Status of The Reserve System." 25 Baylor Law Review 1-25. (Winter 1973).

Examines six U.S. Supreme Court decisions (mentioning several others from the federal lower courts) and traces the history of the confrontation of professional sports and the antitrust laws. Includes an examination of legislative exemptions and the status of the reserve system in baseball, basketball, football and hockey. Details the confusing situation the courts have created and the need for Congress to act to clarify it. States that the reserve system as now employed in baseball and hockey should not be allowed to exist.

0818.   Atchinson, William K. "Modern Trend In Anti-Trust and Professional Sports." 22 Albany Law Review 272-286. (June 1958).

Reviews Federal Baseball Club v. National League, Hart v. Keith Vaudeville Exchange, Gardella v. Chandler, Martin v. National League Baseball Club, Mabee v. White Plains Publishing Company, Wickard v. Filburn, Toolson v. New York Yankees, United States v. International Boxing Club, and Radovich v. National Football League, examining how these cases are related to each other and to antitrust laws. Explores structure of professional sports-particularly baseball-including organization, territorial control, the farm system and the reserve clause.

0819.   Brown, Lori J. "The Battle: From The Playing Field To The
               Courtroom: United States Football League v. National Football
               League." 18 University of Toledo Law Review 871-918.
               (Summer 1987).
                   Presents thorough presentation and analysis of case from
               inception to decision. Overviews baseball, NFL and other
               professional sports antitrust litigation. Shows how NFL was
               ultimate victor.

0820.   Foley, James F. "Antitrust and Professional Sports: Does
               Anyone Play By the Rules of The Game?" 22 Catholic
               University Law Review 403-426. (Winter 1973).
                   Examines the problems of the bargaining ability of
               professional athlete and restraints on professional team
               operations from an antitrust perspective. Reviews antitrust
               policy and league structure. Discusses restrictive measures in
               baseball, football and basketball. Analyzes players drafts and
               blacklisting. Explores restraints on owners, potential owners,
               equal protection and the nonenforcement of the antitrust laws.

0821.   Freedman, Warren. Professional Sports and Antitrust. New
               York: Quorum Books, 1987.
                   Offers definitions and history of "sports law" and "sports
               business." Provides antitrust perspective on professional
               sports.   Discusses exemption and nonexemption of
               professional sports from antitrust laws. Focuses on issues such
               as monopolies, restraint of trade, other anti-competitive
               practices, state regulation, tort and contract liability, and first
               amendment expression as they relate to the professional
               athlete and/or professional sports.

0822.   Kabbes, David G. "Professional Sports' Eligibility Rules: Too
               Many Players On The Field." 1986 University of Illinois Law
               Review 1233-1253. (1986).
                   Focuses on eligibility rules of NFL and whether they violate
               antitrust laws. Discusses rule of reason and per se standards
               which courts use to determine possible violations. Argues rule
               of reason is most appropriate standard for NFL and Congress
               should enact legislation accordingly.

0823.   Keith, Maxwell.   "Developments In The Application of
               Antitrust Laws To Professional Team Sports." 10 Hastings Law
               Journal 119. (November 1958).
                   Analyzes Radovich v. National Football League. Begins
               with a brief, general review of antitrust laws plus antitrust laws
               and sports. Examines the cases of Federal Baseball Club of
               Baltimore v. National League of Professional Baseball Clubs,
               Gardella v. Chandler, Toolson v. New York Yankees and

United States v. International Boxing Club. Discusses the effects of Radovich. Points out that an antitrust analysis of professional sports would take the following factors into consideration: monopoly power, treatment of players (including reserve clause, players draft, ineligibility, blacklisting, banning, uniform players contracts), television and radio, powers of the commissioner or president, and the applicability of the antitrust laws. Reviews the role, issues, actions, reports and legislation introduced by the Congress after Radovich.

0824. Lock, Ethan. "The Scope of The Labor Exemption In Professional Sports." 1989 Duke Law Journal 339-419. (April 1989).

Concentrates analysis on labor exemption dispute in the NFL. Offers legal background of current disputes, discusses the Sherman Act's historical role in antitrust issues. Presents the non-statutory labor exemption, the current NFL dispute, and the nature and history of bargaining between the NFLMC and the NFLPA.

0825. Morris, John P. "Keeping The Game Fair and Square-Antitrust Laws and Professional Sports in America." 59 Australian Law Journal (Australia) 476-481. (August 1985).

Discusses the courts applying antitrust laws to the business operations of professional team sports, but with certain unique characteristics of these leagues are exempt. These include equal team playing strength, player selection, geographic restrict, and decisions to preserve public confidence. Uses case examples.

0826. Morris, John P. "Antitrust Laws and Professional Sports In America." 59 Law Institute Journal (Australia) 552-555. (June 1985).

Focuses on equalization of competitive playing strengths, selection and employment of players, the right to operate in specific geographical areas, and the importance and need to preserve public confidence in the honesty of professional sports.

0827. Morris, John P. "In The Wake of The Flood." 38 Law and Contemporary Problems 85-98. (Winter-Spring 1973).

Investigates the extent to which the unique attributes attendant to professional sports can be accommodated under traditional antitrust doctrine. Suggests the manner in which no radical change in the nature of sports can occur and where necessary changes in relationships within the industry can be effectuated.

0828.   Nelson, Paul L. "Professional Sports and The Non-Statutory Labor Exemption To Federal Antitrust Law. McCourt v. California Sports, Inc." 11 University of Toledo Law Review 633-653. (Spring 1980).

Consists of the origin of the labor exemption to the antitrust laws and the relationship between professional sports and the antitrust laws. Reviews McCourt within the context of the antitrust laws and the labor exemption.

0829.   O'Dea, John F. "Professional Sports and The Anti-Trust Laws." 9 Hastings Law Journal 18. (November 1957).

Examines relationship between professional sports and antitrust laws. Presents background and portions of opinions of Federal Baseball Club of Baltimore v. National League of Professional Baseball Clubs, Toolson v. New York Yankees, United States v. International Boxing Club of New York and Radovich v. National Football League. Discusses team sport argument of "monopoly for monopoly's sake" as well as the distinction which exists between baseball and other professional sports.

0830.   Roberts, Gary R. "The Evolving Confusion of Professional Sports Antitrust, The Rule of Reason, and The Doctrine of Ancillary Restraints." 61 Southern California Law Review 945-1016. (May 1988).

Stresses unique characteristics of professional sports leagues and consistent difficulties that courts have had when applying antitrust law. Presents caselaw, issues and determinations. Discusses internal league governance of antitrust and applicability of the ancillary restraints doctrine.

0831.   Roberts, Gary R. "Reconciling Federal Labor and Antitrust Policy: The Special Case of Sports League Labor Market Restraints." 75 Georgetown Law Journal 19-98. (October 1986).

Suggests restraints on labor market must be exempt from antitrust laws as stated in section 6 of Clayton Act. Analyzes section 6 in historical and political perspective, and relates it to particular sports cases.

0832.   Rosenbaum, Thane N. "The Antitrust Implications of Professional Sports Leagues Revisited: Emerging Trends In The Modern Era." 41 University of Miami Law Review 729-822. (March 1987).

Relates significance of USFL v. NFL antitrust challenge to Sherman Act. Presents historical perspective of antitrust litigation on the professional sports scene. Examines changes which have occurred in professional sports and evolving case law assumptions regarding antitrust laws. Suggests courts and commentators should update their thinking on the practices of professional leagues.

0833.   Rudkin, Sven C. "Implications of The Reserve Clause In Professional Sports." 3 <u>Glendale Law Review</u> 63-79. (1978-1979).

A comment which discusses some of the antitrust problems which have occurred in professional team sports from the inception of major league baseball in 1876 to the National and American Basketball Association merger in 1976. Presents the conflict and contradiction by the Congress and the Supreme Court in their regulatory roles.

0834.   "Solidarity For What?" 7 <u>Update</u> 22(6). (Spring 1983).

Explores the affect that labor law and antitrust law have both on each other and on professional sports.

0835.   "Super Bowl and The Sherman Act: Professional Team Sports and The Antitrust Laws." 81 <u>Harvard Law Review</u> 418-434. (December 1967).

Note presenting an antitrust analysis of the practices of professional sports leagues. Analyzes scheduling and playing rules, restriction of players, restraint of owners and potential owners, and the competition between the NFL and the AFL.

0836.   Terry, Robert B.   "Application of Antitrust Laws To Professional Sports' Eligibility and Draft Rules." 46 <u>Missouri Law Review</u> 797-828. (Fall 1981).

Examines the eligibility and draft rules of professional baseball, basketball and football. Argues that they violate the Sherman Antitrust Act which demands open competition.

0837.   Webb, Robert G. "Anti-Trust Laws-Sherman Anti-Trust Act-Professional Sports." 36 <u>North Carolina Law Review</u> 315. (April 1958).

Reports Supreme Court decision in <u>Radovich v. National Football League</u> which added football to sports now subject to Sherman Anti-Trust Act. Reviews history of sports and the applicability of antitrust laws. Informs of baseball exemption but due to court decisions, football, boxing and basketball are not exempt. Reports Congress making attempt to resolve this (states three categories of bills presented).

Arbitration

0838.   Abrams, Roger I. "Sports Labor Relations: The Arbitrator's Turn At Bat." 5 <u>Entertainment & Sports Law Journal</u> 1-12. (Fall 1988).

Explores, generally, labor relations in professional sports and, specifically, the role of arbitration in matters of salary.

Business of Professional Sports

0839.   Biddle, Steven G. "Less Restrictive Alternatives For Achieving and Maintaining Competitive Balance In Professional Sports." 30 Arizona Law Review 889-907. (1988).

Examines the draft, no-tampering rule, reserve and option rules, the compensation rule and other measures of restraint with regard to the antitrust laws. Presents the owners' and players' perspectives. Offers less restrictive alternatives. Lists other measures which influence competitive balance and player mobility.

0840.   Burr, Keith J. "Player Control Mechanisms In Professional Team Sports." 34 University of Pittsburgh Law Review 645-670. (Summer 1973).

Examines and reviews whether various player control mechanisms in professional sports are in violation of antitrust laws. Discusses control mechanisms of reserve and option clauses, player drafts and blacklisting.   Provides antitrust violation analysis of the question. Analyzes the Flood v. Kuhn and methods of alternative enforcement.

0841.   Carlson, Robert S. "The Business of Professional Sports: A Reexamination In Progress." 18 New York Law Forum 915-933. (Spring 1973).

Focuses on the reserve clause, player draft, four-year rule, and exclusive territory agreements in professional sports. Discusses the formation of the American Baseball Association and the merger agreement. Presents judicial and legislation examination of the above four concepts and analyzes what will maximize equality of competition.

0842.   Fleisher, Arthur A., III; Shughart, William F., II; and Tollison, Robert D. "Ownership Structure In Professional Sports." 12 Research In Law and Economics 71-75. (1989).

Argues that the concentration of ownership of a professional sports franchise is profit maximization rather than amenity production.

0843.   Goldstein, Seth M. "Out of Bounds Under The Sherman Act?: Player Restraints In Professional Team Sports." 4 Pepperdine Law Review 285-312. (Spring 1977).

Reviews player restraints in the professional sports of baseball, basketball, football and hockey: the draft, the option clause, and reserve system. Discusses the restraints from the

perspective of management and players.   Analyzes the labor
law aspects of the question.   Offers a number of alternatives

0844.   Lee, Brian E.   "Survey of Professional Team Sport Player-
Control Mechanisms Under Antitrust and Labor Law
Principles: Peace at Last." 11 <u>Valparaiso University Law
Review</u> 373-434. (Spring 1977).

Traces history of professional sports legal disputes through
the recent collective bargaining agreements. Examines major
player-control mechanisms that have been challenged by
athletes. Studies watershed case of <u>Denver Rockets v. All Pro
Management, Inc</u>. 325 F. Supp. 1049 (C.D. Cal. 1971). Analyzes
the draft, reserve and option systems and blacklists. Includes
changes made as a result of the player suits and the subsequent
collective bargaining agreements and a discussion of labor law
exemptions to the antitrust laws.

0845.   Lotter, Aline H.   "Keeping The Illusion Alive: The Public
Interest in Professional Sports." 12 <u>Suffolk University Law
Review</u> 48-96. (Winter 1978).

Points out that the lack of fan representation in the
operation of professional sports is a major deficiency of the
industry. Note describes the business mechanisms of
professional sports, external controls placed on the industry
and a proposed regulatory solution which would balance the
business interests of the sports industry with the interests of
the fans.

0846.   Macri, C.   "Problemi Della Nuova Disciplina Dello Sport
Professionistico" (in Italian).   27 (II) <u>Rivista di Diritto
Civile</u> (Italy) 483-503. (September-October 1981).

Review of the problems relating to the new field of
professional sports.

0847.   Penner, Gerald M.   "Syndication of A Sports Team."   3
<u>Entertainment and Sports Lawyer</u> 1(6). (Fall 1984).

Presents legal and practical matters which occur in the
process of the syndication of a professional sports team.
Surveys the concept and problems of syndication, and the type
of legal entity, securities law questions and league rules.

0848.   Ross, Stephen F.   "Monopoly Sports Leagues." 75 <u>Minnesota
Law Review</u> 643-761. (February 1989).

Comprehensive overview of professional sports leagues.
Argues the leagues are monopolies, that they are economically
harmful, that competition should take the place of regulation,
that neither baseball nor football are natural monopolies, that
the antitrust laws offer the structure for regulation and that
legislative means is preferable to judicial decree.

Collective Bargaining

0849.   Berry, Robert C. and Gould, William B. "Long Deep Drive To
           Collective Bargaining: Of Players, Owners, Brawls, and
           Strikes." 31 <u>Case Western Reserve Law Review</u> 685-813.
           (Summer 1981).
               Overviews development and growth of professional sports
           as an industry. Examines components of the industry, the
           league, clubs, players, agents, attorneys and player associations.
           Examines legal, labor and collective bargaining aspects of
           professional sports. Surveys role of contracts, antitrust and
           labor exemption. Reviews collective bargaining in baseball,
           football, hockey and soccer. Discusses unresolved issues for
           players and player associations.

0850.   Ensor, Richard J.   Comparison of Arbitration Decisions
           Involving Termination In Major League Baseball, The
           National Basketball Association and The National Football
           League." 32 <u>Saint Louis University Law Journal</u> 135-169. (Fall
           1987).
               Examines collective bargaining agreements, (in the
           professional sports of baseball, basketball and football), and
           their role in labor-management conflicts. Mentions uniform
           player contract as additional means of protection during
           termination of employment. Reviews termination issues in
           and out of sport settings. Discusses role and procedures of
           arbitration, and provides case examples.

0851.   Gerary, Bryan E. and Schlafly, Joseph. "Eighth Circuit Suggests
           A Labor Exemption From Antitrust Laws For Collectively
           Bargained Labor Agreements In Professional Sports." 21 <u>Saint
           Louis University Law Journal</u> 565-594. (1977).
               Examines <u>Mackey v. National Football League</u>. Reviews
           antitrust issues in <u>Mackey</u> and the labor exemption from
           antitrust laws including a discussion on antitrust labor
           legislation and judicial interpretation, professional sports
           antitrust case, the labor exemption for employers, and a
           guideline analysis of <u>Mackey</u>.

0852.   Gould, William G., IV. "Players & Owners Mix It Up." 8
           <u>California Lawyer</u> 56-59+. (August 1988).
               Discusses professional player/owner collective bargaining
           negotiations within the context of the labor exemption to
           antitrust laws.

0853.   Hobel, Michael S. "Application of The Labor Exemption After
           The Expiration of Collective Bargaining Agreements In

Professional Sports." 57 New York University Law Review 164-202. (April 1982).

Note discussing the development of the labor exemption in professional sports. Presents benefits of and argues for the availability of the labor exemption after the expiration of a collective bargaining agreement. Cites Mackety and McCourt.

0854.   Jones, Michael E.; Waters, Robert H.; and Sullivan, Kevin. "An Insider's View From The Stands: Collective Bargaining In Baseball, Football and Basketball." 25 New Hampshire Bar Journal 109-120. (January 1984).

Describes major legal developments between players and management in professional sports (baseball, football and basketball). Cites relevant statistics.

0855.   Lowell, Cym H. "Collective Bargaining and The Professional Team Sport Industry." 38 Law and Contemporary Problems 3-41. (Winter-Spring 1973).

Illustrates the types of problems which could arise from the full force application of the principles of collective bargaining on the professional team sport industry. Highlights the changes which could take place especially between owner and player.

0856.   McCormick, Robert A. "Labor Relations In Professional Sports-Lessons In Collective Bargaining." 14 Employee Relations Law Journal 501-512. (Spring 1989).

Discusses player restraint methods, their relationship to the collective bargaining process, the courts and antitrust laws. Argues the debate between owners and players could be resolved through the collective bargaining process.

0857.   Miller, David G. "Some Modest Proposals For Collective Bargaining In Professional Sports." 48 Los Angeles Bar Bulletin 155-160. (March 1973).

Brief comment on Flood v. Kuhn and whether the issue of the reserve clause should be collectively bargained or litigated. Presents certain terms and conditions of employment which could be bargained collectively. Explores the risks which would be involved if professional athletic unions went on strike in order to satisfy their demands.

0858.   Murphy, Betty Southard. "Keeping Owners and Players From Maiming Each Other: The NLRB As A Referee." 7 Update 30(7). (Spring 1983).

Discusses the role of the NLRB in the collective bargaining process of professional sports.

0859.   Shulman, Daniel S. and Baum, Bernard M.   "Collective
               Bargaining In Professional Athletics-The NFL Money Bowl."
               50 Chicago Bar Record 173-181. (January 1969).
                    Points out that, despite what may be an overly romanticized
               perception of professional athletics, there exists a number of
               very real economic and employment aspects.   Examines,
               historically, how, through labor organization and collective
               bargaining, professional football players were able to handle
               these economic and employment aspects.

0860.   Staudohar, Paul D.   The Sports Industry and Collective
               Bargaining. Ithaca, NY: ILR Press, 1986.
                    Reports on growth of collective bargaining in professional
               sports.   Provides overview of role and place of sports in
               American culture.   Presents model of the sports industry.
               Points out the basics of National Labor Relations Act, structure
               of bargaining and content of agreements.   Examines collective
               bargaining in baseball, football, basketball and hockey.

Commissioner, Professional Sports

0861.   "Professional Sports: Restraining The League Commissioner's
               Prerogatives In An Era of Player Mobility."   19 William and
               Mary Law Review 281-316. (Winter 1977).
                    Note examining the role and power of the professional
               sports commissioner over player mobility in light of the Finley
               and Atlanta National League decisions and the collective
               bargaining agreement. Examines the role which the owners of
               professional teams play in the player mobility equation.
               Provides a brief background on unincorporated associations
               and baseball's Major League Agreement.   Discusses antitrust
               issues in football, basketball and hockey.   Reviews collective
               bargaining agreements in the above sports plus baseball.

0862.   Rudkin, Sven.   "Affirming of A Sports Commissioner's
               Power." 3 Glendale Law Review 322-328. (1978/1979).
                    Demonstrates that the power of the baseball commissioner
               stems from the recognition of the right of disputing parties to
               waive access to the courts and from baseball's unique
               exemption from the antitrust laws.   Examines Milwaukee
               American Ass'n v. Landis (1931), the Atlanta Braves owner
               Ted Turner's court actions against Commissioner Kuhn (1977)
               and Oakland Athletics owner Charles Finley's court actions
               against Commissioner Kuhn (1977).

Compensation

0863.   Chafton, Steven M.   "Taking The Oakland Raiders: A
         Theoretical Reconsideration of The Concepts of Public Use
         And Just Compensation."   32 Emory Law Journal 857-899.
         (Summer 1983).
             Involves a definitive examination of the concepts of
         "taking for public use" and "just compensation" particularly
         within the context of the decision in City of Oakland v.
         Oakland Raiders, Ltd.

0864.   Closius, Phillip J. and Chapman, Douglas K.   "Below Market
         Loans: From Abuse To Misuse-A Sports Illustration."   37 Case
         Western Reserve Law Review 484-514. (Spring 1987).
             Focuses on the use of below market loans in professional
         sports. Surveys the tax treatment of said loans and taxation as
         a compensation substitute.

0865.   Scully, Gerald W.   "Economic Discrimination In Professional
         Sports."   38 Law and Contemporary Problems 67-84. (Winter-
         Spring 1973).
             Presents empirical evidence including tables and graphs
         which support the viewpoint that black athletes are underpaid
         and shunted into stereotyped positions. Concludes that race
         discrimination in professional team sports exists at least to the
         same degree as that found in the larger society.

Contracts

0866.   Alylvia, Kenneth.   "Professional Sports Contracts and The
         Players' Association."   5 Manitoba Law Journal (Canada) 359-
         385. (1972-1973).
             Analysis of the basis for and the future of players'
         associations in professional sports. Specifically examines the
         nature and contents of professional sports contracts, and the
         relationship between contracts and the players' association.
         Primary emphasis is on professional hockey (N.H.L., W.H.A.)
         and professional football (C.F.L.) in Canada. Comparative
         reference is made to professional baseball, basketball, football,
         and hockey in the United States.

0867.   Alylvia, Kenneth.   "Professional Sports Contracts and The
         Players' Association."   4 Canadian Communications Law
         Review (Canada) 170-196. (1972).
             Considers the reasons for, and the present and future roles
         of, player associations (National Hockey League, World Hockey
         Association, and Canadian Football League). Discusses
         professional baseball, basketball, and football in the U.S.

Reports through interviews with anonymous athletes, coaches and management in professional sports. Discusses monopoly and conspiracy in professional sports, the reserve clause in hockey, the option clause in football, the issues of fines and suspensions, blacklisting, and the proposed Competition Act. Examines the effect of the World Hockey Association on the professional hockey player. Describes the Players' Assocaition and its scope including monetary benefits, job security, salaries, league mergers, restrictive covenants, interleague trades, and miscellaneous problems.

0868.　　Bosch, Peter J. "Enforcement Problems of Personal Service Contracts In Professional Athletics." 6 Tulsa Law Journal 40-60. (March 1969).

　　Analyzes the personal service contract in professional athletics. Focuses on contract breaching and problems involved with specific performance enforcement of the contract. Examines the nature of personal service contracts and respective court opinions. Discusses issues of what constitutes "unique and extraordinary skill" and the issue of mutuality involving reserve and option clauses.

0869.　　Brennan, James T. "Injunction Against Professional Athletes Breaching Their Contracts." 34 Brooklyn Law Review 61-71. (Fall 1967).

　　Discusses the availability of specific performance to a professional sports team against an athlete who breaches his contract. Reviews case of Philadelphia Ball Club v. Lajoie; Central New York Basketball, Inc. v. Barnett; Winnipeg Rugby Football Club v. Freeman; and Dallas Cowboys Football Club, Inc. v. Harris.

0870.　　"Foundation Tax and Player Contract Bills Get Committee Nod." 10 Tax Notes 634. (April 28, 1980).

　　Brief review of H.R. 4103 pertaining to limiting the allocation of basis to player contracts. Provides limited analysis on the Bill and its progress through committee.

0871.　　Gallagher, Michael D. "Contractual Rights and Duties of The Professional Athlete-Playing The Game In A Bidding War." 77 Dickinson Law Review 352-400. (Winter 1973).

　　Discusses the bidding wars between the National Basketball Association (NBA) and the American Basketball Association (ABA) and the war between the World Hockey Association (WHA) and the National Hockey League (NHL). Examines the current state of contractual relations would be better protected by the adoption of a number of suggested changes. Reviews defenses available to players being sued for breach of contract for jumping leagues. Discusses the legal problems of college athletes who wish to turn professional and the changes in athletic contracts.

0872. Gessford, James B. "Arbitration of Professional Athletes' Contracts: An Effective System of Dispute Resolution In Professional Sports." 55 Nebraska Law Review 362-382. (1976).

Examines the most recent and far reaching decisions with regard to the new grievance arbitration mechanism. Presents historical overview. Discusses arbitration panel decisions (the facts and issues in Hunter, Messersmith, and McNally), the role and extent of arbitration and some suggested solutions. States the system of arbitration provides more advantages than disadvantages.

0873. Heiner, S. Phillip. "Post-Merger Blues: Intra-League Contract Jumping." 18 William and Mary Law Review 741-760. (Summer 1977).

Examines the phenomenon of intra-league contract jumping. Reviews factors which serve as would-be determinants of this phenomenon including the Uniform Player Contract. Explores common law contract principles which a "soon-to-be-jumped-from" team may employ in the course of its own strategy.

0874. Johnson, Alex M., Jr. "The Argument For Self-Help Specific Performance: Opportunistic Renegotiation of Player Contracts." 22 Connecticut Law Review 61-127. (Fall 1989).

Examines the contract, history and hypotheticals relating to relevant sports law cases, traditional remedies available to promisees and possible use of the self-help specific performance remedy.

0875. Kaplan, Fred. "Professional Athletic Contracts and The Injunctive Dilemma." 8 John Marshall Journal of Practice and Procedure 437-456. (Spring 1975).

Examines the use of an injunction as a relief for breach of contract. Reviews the basis of equity jurisdiction. Surveys Lumley v. Wagner, and analyzes elements set forth in Lumley. Discusses the post element inquiry of the court. Discusses the most frequently raised defenses of athletes who are breaching their contracts.

0876. Petrich, Ray. "Contract Matters and Disciplinary Procedures In Professional Sport." 39 Saskatchewan Law Review (Canada) 213-258. (1974-1975).

Discusses contractual and disciplinary circumstances which may interface with the modern athlete. Examines the player contract as both a restraint on movement and as an instrument

of discipline. Explores the issue of the protection of players'
rights. Concludes with suggestions for possible reforms.

0877.   "Reserve Clause In Athletic Contracts." 2 <u>Rutgers-Camden
Law Journal</u> 302-321. (Fall 1970).
A note explaining the reserve clause of players contracts, its
history, and problems concerning antitrust laws. Explains the
baseball exemption and one year clause of professional football,
and basketball decisions as interpreting the contract as an
option clause. Concludes this appears to be the most equitable
solution giving the player the right to terminate employment
with a team on a season's notice and gives the player more
bargaining power.

0878.   Scheffler, Mark D. "Injunctions In Professional Athletes'
Contracts-An Overused Remedy." 43 <u>Connecticut Bar Journal</u>
538-555. (September 1969).
Note discussing the use-and overuse-of the injunction as a
remedy for breach of contract. Extensive review of applicable
casework. Includes excerpts of the courts' opinions. Examines
the issue from an integrated legal-historical perspective.

0879.   Uberstine, Gary A. and Grad, Richard J. "The Enforceability of
Sports Contracts: A Practitioner's Playbook." 7 <u>Loyola
Entertainment Law Journal</u> 1-25. (1987).
Views the field of sports law as encompassing only a more
specialized area of fundamental legal principles. Focuses on
the sports contract and considers personal jurisdiction, judicial
relief, civil proceedings, remedies and defenses.

0880.   Whitehall, Bill. "Enforceability of Professional Sports
Contracts-What's The Harm In It?" 35 <u>Southwestern Law
Journal</u> 803-823. (September 1981).
Comments on contractual basis of professional sports,
athlete's breach of contract, the use of negative injunction and
requirements for obtaining a negative injunction. Explores
possibility of damages from player who breached contract.
Concludes with treatment of player defenses.

0881.   Yeam, Kevin W. "New Remedial Developments In The
Enforcement of Personal Service Contracts For The
Entertainment and Sports Industries: the Rise of Tortious Bad
Faith Breach of Contract and The Fall of The Speculative
Damage Defense." 7 <u>Loyola Entertainment Law Journal</u> 27-43.
(Winter 1987).
Surveys the employer options which are available against
the performer who breaches a personal service contract.

Disciplinary Action

0882.   Clancy, Christopher H. and Weiss, Jonathan A. "A Pine Tar
          Gloss On The Quasi-Legal Images." 5 Cardozo Law Review
          411-440. (Winter 1984).
              Argues for use of "judicial-type" decision making in the
          organizations of both sports and our daily lives. Elaborates on
          the nature of quasi-legal institutions. Applies decision making
          model within context of a number of baseball controversies.

0883.   "Discipline In Professional Sports: The Need For Player
          Protection." 60 Georgetown Law Journal 771-798. (February
          1972).
              Examines disciplinary abuses the regulatory systems
          governing professional sports have brought about and
          discusses the inability of existing remedies to cope with those
          abuses. Suggests judicial and legislative remedies capable of
          realizing a more equitable balance among the interests of
          sports, athletes, and the public.

0884.   Goore, Jeffrey. "Discriminatory Discharge In A Sports Context:
          A Reassessment of The Burden of Proof and Remedies Under
          The National Labor Relations Act." 53 Fordham Law Review
          615-638. (December 1984).
              Reviews burden of proof required-and its problems-in
          Section 8(a) of NLRA particularly as it relates to the area of
          sports and when a professional sports team dismisses an
          athlete who is involved in labor union activities. Discusses
          problems with traditional remedies for violation of section 8(a)
          (3) and proposes an alternative.

0885.   Hammer, Robert S. "Licensee Discipline and Due Process." 12
          Connecticut Law Review 870-882. (Summer 1980).
              Discusses governmental power to discipline licensees-
          especially in gambling industries-who engage in misconduct.
          Examines Barry v. Barchi which involved the suspension of
          horse trainer, without a presuspension hearing, because traces
          of Lasix were discovered in his horse's system during post-race
          analysis.   Presents the district court decision and the
          subsequent Supreme Court reversal on possible violations of
          due process and equal protection.

0886.   Heidt, Robert H. "'Don't Talk of Fairness': The Chicago
          School's Approach Toward Disciplining Professional
          Athletes." 61 Indiana Law Journal 53-64. (Winter 1985).
              Focuses on Chicago School's approach that antitrust laws
          will offer little remedy to player. Player must seek tort, contract
          or property remedies and rely more on player associations'
          collective bargaining units.

0887.   Weistart, John C.   "Player Discipline In Professional Sports:
               The Antitrust Issues." 18 William and Mary Law Review 703-
               739. (Summer 1977).
               Examines the power of professional sports teams and
               leagues to discipline players. Explores the extent to which
               antitrust laws could provide a framework for judicial review of
               cases relating to the disciplining of a professional athlete.
               Discusses the procedural and substantive aspects of
               team/league discipline in terms of expulsion, fines or
               suspension of the athlete.

Economics of Team Movement

0888.   Beisner, John.   "Sports Franchise Relocation: Competitive
               Markets and Taxpayer Protection." 6 Yale Law and Policy
               Review 429-448. (1988).
               Presents economic analysis of the lack of a competitive
               market for professional sports franchises. Notes the lack of
               judicial and legislative standards to protect taxpayers'
               investments in these franchises. Offers federal standards to
               reduce incentives to relocate.

0889.   Mead, Leon F., III.   "Raiders: $7.2 Million, City of Oakland:
               O...Was That The Final Gun? A Story of Intrigue, Suspense
               and Questionable Reasoning." 9 Loyola L.A. Entertainment
               Law Journal 401-424. (1989).
               Casenote providing background on Raiders case and
               discusses how the dormant commerce clause may not be a
               defense to sports franchise condemnation. Focuses the analysis
               on the power of eminent domain.

0890.   Newton, Carl K. and Slattery, Jeffrey D.   "The Changing Areas
               In Condemnation Law." 15 Urban Lawyer 791-803. (Fall 1983).
               Brief discussion on City of Oakland v. Oakland Raiders
               where the court held that, within the statutory context of the
               concept of property, a professional sports franchise could be
               condemned.

0891.   Quirk, James.   "An Economic Analysis of Team Movements In
               Professional Sports." 38 Law and Contemporary Problems 42-
               66. (Winter-Spring 1973).
               Outlines the economic structure of a professional sports
               league (one common to the four major team sports: baseball,
               football, basketball and hockey) and points out the implications
               of this rules structure for the distribution of playing strengths
               by teams within a league. Discusses the role played by
               franchise moves. Presents brief history and analysis of

franchise moves in organized baseball since 1953 and the public policy issues which are involved in franchise moves.

0892.   Schiano, Michael.   "Eminent Domain Exercised-Stare Decisis Or A Warning: City of Oakland v. Oakland Raiders." 4 Pace Law Review 169-193. (Fall 1983).

Analyzes facts and legal issues of the case. Concludes with analysis of the impact of case on business in America.

Expansion

0893.   McBurney, Christian.   "The Legality of Sports Leagues' Restrictive Admissions Practices." 60 New York University Law Review 925-955. (November 1985).

Examines policy of selective admissions in sports leagues in relation to section 1 of Sherman Act. Discusses courts product and geographic market tests which produce the relevant market to determine possible anticompetitive effects of new sports franchises.

Franchise Relocation

0894.   Amoroso, Richard.   "Controlling Professional Sports Teams Relocations: The Oakland Raiders' Antitrust Case and Beyond." 17 Rutgers Law Journal 283-319. (Winter 1986).

Questions whether a sports team has the right to abandon its home city and do business wherever it wishes. Provides background and case history of 1982 Raiders exodus from Oakland to Los Angeles. Discusses proposed Congressional legislation and NFL policies which would protect league and NFL cities from overzealous owners.

0895.   Barnett, Stephen R.   "High Court Rulings Show Contrasting Attitudes: Oakland Raiders Decision Differs In Approach From Recent Decision On A City's Right To Sue." 2 California Lawyer 58-61. (October 1982).

Comparison of City of Oakland v. Oakland Raiders and City of Long Beach v. Bozek.   Examines the workings of the California Supreme Court.

0896.   Brumback, Gordon J. and Heyman, Amy R.   "Eminent Domain: Condemnation of Professional Football Franchises and the Commerce Clause Defense." 28 Howard Law Journal 773-794. (1985).

Reviews eminent domain power and the Commerce Clause of the Constitution. Relates the issues in the Raiders' and Colts' cases to these defenses against franchise relocation.

Discusses the importance of the courts to balance legitimate state interests and interstate commerce interests.

0897.   Campbell, Thomas J. "Keeping Possession of The Ball: the Use of Eminent Domain To Prevent The Relocation of Professional Sports Franchises." 32 Washington University Journal of Urban and Contemporary Law 333-346. (Summer 1987).

Presents the basis for use of eminent domain to prevent a sports franchise from relocating. Reports attempts by the home cities of the NFL Raiders and Colts to block a relocation. Discusses legal issues and implications when a sports franchise is condemned, and suggests the eminent domain doctrine is inappropriate.

0898.   Davis, Robert N. "Congress To Tackle Legislation On Franchise Relocations." 3 Entertainment and Sports Lawyer 2(2). (Winter 1985).

Brief overview of S. 259, the Professional Sports Community Protection Act of 1985, regarding relocation, revenue and ownership of professional sports teams.

0899.   Franck, Richard L. and Bredesen, Karsten E. "Recent Developments In Condemnation Law." 17 Urban Lawyer 751-763. (Fall 1985).

Analyzes, in part, sports franchise condemnation, focusing on City of Oakland v. The Oakland Raiders (1982).

0900.   Gorton, Slade (Senator). "Professional Sports Franchise Relocation: Introductory Views From The Hill." 9 Seton Hall Legislative Journal 1-6. (1985).

Brief introduction on question of Congressional intervention in the relocation of professional sports teams. Discusses the problem, reasons for intervening and alternatives available to Congress.

0901.   Gray, Charles. "Keeping the Home Team At Home." 74 California Law Review 1329-1371. (July 1986).

Argues that the problem of sports franchise relocation is due to the lack of federal state legislation. Focuses on eminent domain law, the commerce clause and their relation to the Oakland Raiders decision. Mentions right to travel and antitrust liability.

0902.   Gray, John A. "Section 1 of The Sherman Act and Control Over NFL Franchise Locations: The Problem of Opportunistic Behavior." 25 American Business Law Journal 123-159. (Spring 1987).

Analyzes the relationship between the NFL to the member clubs and cities. Views the Ninth Circuit Raiders decision as potentially destructive to league stability. Critiques proposed legislation and solutions to the problem of franchise relocation. Offers suggestions to resolve this conflict.

0903.   Johnson, Arthur T.   "Municipal Administration and The Sports Franchise Relocation Issue." 43 Public Advertising Review 519-528. (November-December 1983).

0904.   Joyce, Thomas W. E., III.   "The Constitutionality of Taking A Sports Franchise By Eminent Domain and The Need For Federal Legislation To Restrict Franchise Relocation."   13 Fordham Urban Law Journal 553-596. (1984/1985).

          Argues that legislation is necessary to regulate sports franchise relocation.   Discusses Raiders case, eminent domain, just compensation and property rights, and the commerce clause.   Surveys proposals to restrict franchise relocations including Professional Football Stabilization Act and Professional Sports Team Community Protection Act.

0905.   Mitnick, Eric Alan.   "Anticipating An Instant Replay: City of Oakland v. Oakland Raiders." 17 University of California Davis Law Review 963-1007. (Spring 1984).

          Reviews Oakland's attempt to use eminent domain to acquire the Oakland Raiders.   Presents history of the case, overview of California's eminent domain law and analysis of the decisions relating to case.

0906.   Rubanowitz, Daniel B.   "Who Said "There's No Place Like Home?":   Franchise Relocation In Professional Sports."   10 Loyola Entertainment Law Journal 163-197. (1990).

          Provides brief history of antitrust law, its application to professional sports and franchise relocation rules with examples from professional basketball and baseball.

0907.   Shingler, Ronald J.   "Antitrust Law and The Sports League Relocation Rules." 18 Golden Gate University Law Review 35-55. (Spring 1988).

          Examines the Ninth Circuit's analysis and application of antitrust laws to professional sports leagues' franchise relocation rules, specifically NBA v. SDC Basketball Club, Inc. Presents facts of case, procedural background, the Court's analysis and a critique.   Cites other casework particularly the two antitrust case involving relocation of the Oakland Raiders football team.

0908.   Shropshire, Kenneth L.   "Opportunistic Sports Franchise Relocations: Can Punitive Damages In Actions Based Upon Contract Strike A Balance?"   22 Loyola of Los Angeles Law Review 569-602. (January 1989).

Reviews casework on franchise relocation, particularly Raiders I and II, and the effect of cases on the teams and the league. Analyzes the use of damages as a deterrent to relocating franchises.

0909. Staudohar, Paul D. "Team Relocation In Professional Sports." 36 Labor Law Journal 728-733. (September 1985).

Examination of franchise relocation in professional sports of baseball, football, basketball and hockey. Discusses the extent of relocation, court decisions, arguments for and against franchise relocation and legislative proposals regarding relocation.

0910. Tobin-Rubio, Lisa J. "Eminent Domain and The Commerce Clause Defense: City of Oakland v. Oakland Raiders." 41 University of Miami Law Review 1185-1222. (May 1987).

In-depth analysis of courts decision of the case. Discusses uniqueness of professional football as a business. Mentions different views as to the structure of the league and how the Court tied to balance competing interests through the application of the commerce clause and eminent domain.

0911. Wesker, Mark A. "Franchise Flight and The Forgotten Fan: An Analysis of The Application of Antitrust Laws To The Relocation of Professional Football Franchises." 15 University of Baltimore Law Review 567-590. (Spring 1986).

Examines feasibility of applications of antitrust law to NFL franchise relocation. Offers general antitrust principles. Discusses Raiders case with different analyses. Points out differences in applicability of antitrust to NFL, NHL and major league baseball. Argues against Congressional intervention. Stresses importance of sports fan as a consideration before relocation.

0912. Wong, Glenn M. "Of Franchise Relocation, Expansion and Competition In Professional Team Sports: The Ultimate Political Football?" 9 Seton Hall Legislative Journal 7-79. (1985).

Discusses political impact of pending Professional Sports Team Community Protection Act (S. 2505) of 1984. Includes the community losing a team, the league in question, the owner of the team and the players and their association. Presents historical perspective of franchise relocation, the financial impact of relocation and legislative options to relocation. Provides extensive and documentation.

0913. York, Daniel S. "The Professional Sports Community Protection Act: Congress' Best Response to Raiders?" 38 Hastings Law Journal 345-375. (January 1987).

Examines six Congressional proposals which attempt to solve the franchise relocation problem. Concludes this 1985 Protection Act offers the best solution. Provides additional suggestions.

Free Agency

0914.   Staudohar, Paul D. and McAtee, Jon. "Free Agency In Sports: Plum or Prune?" 40 Labor Law Journal 228-234. (April 1989).
              Surveys development of the free agency system in professional sports of baseball, football, basketball and hockey. Analyzes the operation of the reserve system, how free agency came about, its limits and whether it provides equal advantage across professional sports.

Labor Relations

0915.   Berry, Robert C.; Gould, William V., IV; and Staudohar, Paul D. Labor Relations In Professional Sports. Dover, Massachusetts: Auburn House Publishing Company, 1986.
              Provides models for understanding industrial environment. Also reviews sports industries and legal overlay. Specifically examines labor relations in baseball, football, basketball and hockey. Reports on 1982 football strike and unresolved issues facing sports unions.

0916.   Closius, Phillip J. "Not At The Behest of Nonlabor Groups: A Revised Prognosis For A Maturing Sports Industry." 24 Boston College Law Review 341-400. (March 1983).
              Examines maturation of professional sports within labor/management perspective.

0917.   Gilroy, Thomas P. and Madden, Patrick J. "Labor Relations In Professional Sports." 28 Labor Law Journal 768-776. (December 1977).
              Provides brief history of the employment relations system through the 1960s plus an overview of recent changes in employment relations in professional baseball, basketball, football and hockey. Examines the role of the NLRB. Discusses the direction that employment relations in professional sports may take in the future.

Liability

0918.   Turrow, Andrew J. "Tort Liability In Professional Sports." 44 Albany Law Review 696-718. (April 1980).

A note which examines and evaluates <u>Hackbart v. Cincinnati Bengals, Inc.</u> and <u>Tomjanovich v. California Sports, Inc.</u>, which extend into tort law by permitting recovery for injuries which had resulted from intentional and reckless conduct during professional sports events. Focuses on the assumption of risk/consent issue with regard to sports injury litigation with specific discussion of the "intentional and reckless conduct, solely by virtue of the specific forseeability of such conduct." Examines respondeat superior and negligent supervision (two theories of employer liability) and their property vis a vis modern professional sports.

Litigation

0919.   Brody, Burton F. "The Impact of Litigation on Professional Sports." 14 <u>Trial</u> 35-38. (June 1978).
Review of significant casework which has had the effect of restructuring specific professional sports. Examines casework in hockey, basketball, football and baseball.

Professional Athletes

0920.   "Balance of Power In Professional Sports." 22 <u>Maine Law Review</u> 459-480. (1970).
Focuses on problems which professional athletes face when dealing with what can be termed the "powers that be" in the world of sports. Contends the "balance of power" is not in favor of the athletes. Examines the restrictions placed on an athlete's bargaining power, and the contentions that the restrictions result in a monopoly in violation of antitrust laws. Offers suggestions for increasing the players' bargaining power.

0921.   Dewey, Addison E. "Professional Athletes-Affluent Elitists Or Victims of The Reserve System? An Emerging Paradox-Courts Protect Such Athletes From Antitrust Law Violations But Collective Bargaining Has Resulted In Antitrust Immunity For Leagues and Club Owners." 8 <u>Ohio Northern Law Review</u> 453-479. (July 1981).
Overviews relationship of professional sports and athletes with the antitrust laws. Explores baseball exemption, professional sports and National Labor Relations Act. Provides review of sports antitrust cases in football, basketball and hockey. Review <u>McCourt v. California Sports, Inc.</u> and the impact of collective bargaining on individual athlete and the Rozelle Rule.

0922.   Falk, Jonathan and Scheler, Brad Eric. "Professional Athlete
             and The Question of Judicial Intervention." 41 Hofstra Law
             Review 417-448. (Winter 1976).
                 General discussion of the gag-rule in professional sports
             with specific analysis of Kareem Abdul-Jabbar's 1975 attack on
             the gag-rule. Provides overview of athlete's route to court if
             athlete wishes to challenge the gag-rule. Analyzes the concept
             of state action. Discusses collective bargaining and the courts.
             Reviews the constitutional considerations, interests of
             management and rights of players as they relate to the question
             of freedom of speech.

0923.   "Freedom To Work Outside New Zealand." 5 Victoria
             University of Wellington Law Review (New Zealand) 237-246.
             (Fall 1969).
                 Reports on Blacker v. The New Zealand Rugby Football
             League (Blacker sought consent from his former league in New
             Zealand to allow him to play in Australia). Home league
             denied consent. Blacker argued that denial ruling was illegal,
             void, beyond the scope of the home league's power, and an
             unlawful restraint of his freedom and right to seek employ-
             ment. Examines the Court of Appeals and Supreme Court
             decisions.

0924.   Gordon, Kenneth I. "Home Court Advantage? Are U.S. Sports
             Franchises Negotiating With Soviet Athletes At Their Own
             Risk?" 13 Suffolk Transnational Law Journal 201-228. (Fall
             1989).
                 Focuses on Congressional and judicial treatment of Soviet
             athletes in the United States. Offers suggestions on how
             Congress can assist the athletes.

0925.   Hink, Barbara. "Compensating Injured Professional Athletes:
             The Mystique of Sport Versus Traditional Tort Principles." 55
             New York University Law Review 971-997. (November 1980).
                 Note focusing on the tortious nature of physical contact in
             professional sports. Argues that tortious conduct in
             professional sports should not be considered as being different
             from battery and recklessness as found in the community as a
             whole. Examines the concept of battery and the scope of
             consent from a general and from a sports perspective.
             Critiques the current approach of tortious conduct in sports.
             Analyzes recklessness and the proof of intent in sports.

0926.   Luntz, Harold. "Compensation For Injuries Due To Sports."
             54 Australian Law Journal (Australia) 588-601. (October 1980).
                 Examines the compensation of athletic participants,
             spectators and people/strangers outside the sport facility for
             sport injuries. Reviews the nuances involved in each of the

three categories. Explores the technicalities involved and the likelihood of recovery.

0927.   McAllister, Stephen R. "The Nonstatutory Labor Exemption and Players Restraints In Professional Sports: The Promised Land Or A Return To Bondage?" 4 Entertainment and Sports Law Journal 283-331. (Fall 1987).

Reviews the origin, development and some cases regarding the nonstatutory labor exemption. Offers legal analysis of the exemption including parties protected and the nonstatutory labor exemption test.

0928.   Nanscawen, Peter. "In RE Adamson: Ex Parte W.A. National Football League." 12 Melbourne University Law Review (Australia) 567-574. (December 1980).

Case note on a case where Brian Adamson attempted to enjoin the W.A. Football League, West Perth Football Club and the S.A. Football League, arguing the defendants were in restraint of trade as it applied to his soccer ability. Discusses facts of the case, the decision and whether the case falls within the Trade Practices Act.

0929.   Reaves, Lynne. "Cleaning Up Sports: Tough New Rules Draw Cheers-Most of The Time." 70 American Bar Association Journal 32. (January 1984).

Brief discussion on the reactions to stricter rules and regulations for professional athletes. Focuses on drugs and violence.

0930.   Schneiderman, Michael. "Professional Sport: Involuntary Servitude and The Popular Will." 7 Gonzaga Law Review 63-82. (Fall 1971).

Introduces the proposition that governmental regulation of business might be constitutionally required. Examines the freedom-denying practices in professional team sport and proposes that restraints upon the freedom of the athlete could not exist if there were actual business competition among teams. Sees the failure of antitrust enforcement as the cause of the denial of civil liberties in professional team sport. Indicts the government and the public by exploring America's broad cultural involvement in the professional sport enterprise. Given the extraordinary participation of black athletes in professional sports the question is raised whether or not the equal protection clause of the fourteenth amendment invites or requires governmental regulation.

0931.   Shapiro, Daniel I. "Professional Athlete: Liberty of Peonage?" 13 Alberta Law Review (Canada) 212-241. (1975).

Analyzes four basic restrictions used in baseball, football, basketball and hockey: the reserve system, the player draft, blacklisting, and the registration list. Discusses present and proposed antitrust legislation in Canada and the United States. States the restraints on players violate antitrust laws and that there appears to be little serious effect of legislation on these restraints. Suggests players challenge the restraints through negotiation and perhaps player strikes.

0932.   Sobel, Lionel S. "The Emancipation of Professional Athletes." 3 Western State University Law Review 185-222. (Spring 1976).
Presents history of the reserve clause and early cases (interleague and extraleague) allowing team owners control of players. Discusses the groundwork provided by the hockey cases in which American professional athletes convinced the courts that a reserve system was a restraint in trade and therefore illegal and unenforceable. Discusses the emancipation vis a vis football, basketball and baseball cases, and the legal issues still unresolved.

Strikes

0933.   Karch, Sargent. "Solidarity Forever." 7 Update 26(5). (Spring 1983).
Insights into the negotiations of the 1982 professional football strike.

0934.   Kovach, Kenneth A. "Professional Football Penalized For Delay of Game; The Coming Strike In The National Football League." 33 Labor Law Journal 306-310. (May 1982).
Examines the issues and potential for a strike in National Football League after contract expires in 1982. Discusses issues of free agency and player salaries.

0935.   Lock, Ethan. "Section 10(j) of The National Labor Relations Act and The 1982 National Football League Players Strike: Wave That Flag." 1985 Arizona State Law Journal 113-144. (1985).
Discusses 1982 NFL Strike which author contend Section 10(j) of NLRA should have been requested by NFLPA. Presents background on the strike, relief available, and appropriateness of section 10(j). Argues that 10(j) relief should be applied more liberally in the future.

Unionization

0936.   Jacobs, Michael S. and Winter, Ralph K., Jr.   "Antitrust
           Principles and Collective Bargaining By Athletes: Of
           Superstars In Peonage." 81 Yale Law Journal 1-29. (November
           1971).
               Discusses whether unions of professional athletes are
           entitled to special assistance from the courts and Congress in
           bargaining with their employers.   Examines the governing
           principles of labor law, the professional athlete and the
           bargaining representative, the reserve and option clauses and
           freedom of contract writing including the effect of Flood v.
           Kuhn (1970) and the basketball common draft and merger.
           Discusses the legality of reserve or option clauses. Concludes
           the clauses issue is miscast as an antitrust problem in sports
           where unions are recognized and where the players bring the
           challenge to court.   States that certioari was improvidently
           granted in Flood and proposes suggestions for the courts and
           Congress.

0937.   Krasnow, Erwin G. and Levy, Herman M.   "Unionization and
           Professional Sports." 51 Georgetown Law Journal 749-782.
           (Summer 1963).
               Discusses sports as an industry, how it is organized, and
           how the industry's enforcement of the reserve clause and
           player draft rules which govern athletes' futures illustrate the
           need for collective bargaining.   Presents history of player's
           association and attempts at unionization. Analyzes the defects
           of player associations and points out the benefits and problems
           of large scale unionization concerning professional athletes.

24

PROPERTY

General

0938. Chaves, Antonio. "Arena Rights: Legislative Problems Concerning Broadcasting of Large Shows." 23 Copyright (Switzerland) 310-319. (1987).

Reviews the social, economic, political and legal importance of sports. Examines the concept of legal nature of "arena rights." Discusses ownership of the right, the object of protection, an athlete's and football referee's participation in the profits, limitations involved, terms of protection, the collection and distribution of royalties, radio broadcasting of sports events and the extent of "arena rights."

0939. Coffey, Christopher W. "International Olympic Committee v. San Francisco Arts and Athletes: No Olympic Tourch For The Gay Olympics." 17 Golden Gate University Law Review 129-147. (Spring 1987).

Analyzes case which gave the IOC and USOC property rights of the word "Olympic." Presents background of Amateur Sports Act. Raises constitutional questions and offers the courts majority and minority opinions.

0940. Lee, Robert W. "The Taxation of Athletic Scholarships: An Uneasy Tension Between Benevolence and Consistency." 37 University of Florida Law Review 591-614. (Summer 1985).

Consists of an examination of the IRS's treatment of athletic scholarships, general provisions, tests of exclusion, current law, analyses under the various tests, the problem and suggestions for a solution.

0941.   Mufson, Ellen Z.   "Jurisdictional Limitations On Intangible
             Property In Eminent Domain: Focus On The Indianapolis
             Colts." 60 Indiana Law Journal 389-411. (Spring 1985).
                  Uses sports scene to review problems and lack of clarity in
             current eminent domain law regarding intangible property.
             Discusses condemnation, taxation, adjudication and escheat.
             Contends that mobilia sequuntur personam is the best
             standard for eminent domain.

0942.   Nadel, Paul J. "The Gold Stops Here." 7 Los Angeles Lawyer
             42(4). (July-August 1984).
                  Reviews the authority which Congress has given the USOC
             to control Olympic symbols. Examines both statutory power,
             appropriate casework and remedies available.

0943.   Nitti, Lois. "The Gay Olympics: San Francisco Arts & Athletics
             v. United States Olympic Committee." 8 Pace Law Review 373-
             425. (Spring 1988).
                  Reviews of the case where SFAA was enjoined from using
             the term "Olympic" in its promotion of the "Gay Olympic
             Games." Presents the facts and opinions of the case, and
             overviews of state action and first amendment issues.

0944.   "Property Assessment." 20 University of San Francisco Law
             Review 1053-1056. (Summer 1986).
                  Brief review of Los Angeles Country Club v. Pope where it
             was ruled that the property in question should be assessed
             according to its value in the 1975-1976 tax year and not the
             1982-1983 tax year.

Copyright

0945.   Chaves, Antonio.   "Cerecho de arena" (in French).   26-27
             Revue Internationale de Droit de'Auteur (France) 26-77.
             (January 1983).
                  Discusses the portion of the Brazilian Copyright Law of 13
             December 1973 that concerns "stadium rights." Examines the
             legal nature, whether the professional athlete is an artists or an
             employee, entitlement to the fee, collection and distribution of
             the fee, limitations, legislative divergences, case law, and
             whether soccer umpires should share in the fee.

0946.   Saxer, Shelley Ross.   "The Right of Publicity In Game
             Performances and Federal Copyright Preemption." 36 UCLA
             Law Review 861-888. (April 1989).
                  Discusses Baltimore Orioles, Inc. v. Major League Baseball
             Players, 805 F.2d 663 (7th Cir. 1986), and the ruling that

copyright law preempts state law right of publicity of an
athletes performance in an athletic contest.

0947.   Trechak, John. "The Seventh Circuit Beans Performer
           Publicity Rights In Baseball's Telecast Rights Rubarb." 8 Loyola
           Entertainment Law Journal 75-91. (Winter 1988).
                Analysis of the Seventh Circuit Court's decision in
           Baltimore Orioles, Inc. v. Major League Baseball Players
           Association regarding the relationship between state law and
           created publicity rights and federal copyright laws.

Property Interests and Rights

0948.   Browne, Kelly. "A Sad Time For The Gay Olympics: San
           Francisco Arts & Athletics, Inc. v. United States Olympic
           Committee." 56 University of Cincinnati Law Review 1487-
           1524. (1988).
                Focuses on Supreme Court's application of commercial
           speech and expressive speech standards and the relationship to
           trademark law.   Presents rationales for protection of
           trademarks. Reviews and discusses opinions of the Court.

0949.   Kolback, Kimberly D. "Property Rights: Athletes Await The
           Call From The Referee of The Courtroom." 2 Entertainment
           and Sports Law Journal 219-242. (Fall 1985).

0950.   Lehn, Kenneth. "Property Rights Risk Sharing and Player
           Disability In Major League Baseball." 25 Journal of Law and
           Economics 343-366. (October 1982).
                Examines effects of 1975 collective bargaining agreement on
           property rights and allocation of risk in professional baseball.
           Discusses property rights of baseball's labor market and effects
           of guaranteed multiyear contracts on player disability.

0951.   Menesini, Vittorio.   "Avvenimento Sportivo e Finzione
           Scenica Nel Dirritto D'autore" (in Italian). 53 Diritto di Autore
           (Italy) 15-29. (January-March 1982).
                Focuses on the property rights and legal ramifications of the
           broadcast of sporting events.

0952.   Porto, Brian L. "Balancing Due Process and Academic Integrity
           in Intercollegiate Athletics: The Scholarship Athlete's Limited
           Property Interest in Eligibility." 62 Indiana Law Journal 1151-
           1180. (1986/1987).
                Focuses on property and due process rights of student
           athletes who are declared ineligible for academic and
           misconduct reasons. Presents four rationales for property right
           issue.   Proposes that athletic scholarship is contractual in

nature. Denounces NCAA for unfair and improper procedures when a player's eligibility is at stake.

0953. Shipley, David E. "Three Strikes and They're Out At The Old Ball Game: Preemption of Performers' Right of Publicity Under The Copyright Act of 1976." 20 <u>Arizona State Law Journal</u> 369-421. (Summer 1988).

Provides analysis and critique of opinions in <u>Baltimore Orioles, Inc. v. Major League Baseball Players Association</u>, publicity rights of professional athletes and preemption of these rights when performances occur in copyrighted telecasts. Argues against preemption for professional athletes and other performers and entertainers.

0954. Solar, Keith Randall. "Collegiate Athletic Participation: A Property Or Liberty Interest?" 15 <u>Pacific Law Journal</u> 1203-1230. (July 1984).

Deals with issue that a college athlete has a property right in athletic participation. Discusses both NCAA disciplinary measures as state action, and issue of athlete's liberty interest. Cites casework including <u>Howard University Board of Regents v. Roth</u>, <u>Goss Bishop</u>, and <u>Paul</u>

Trademark Protection

0955. Cyrlin, Alan I. "Trademark Protection of Public Spectacles: <u>Boston Athletic</u> Changes The Rules." 10 <u>Loyola Entertainment Law Journal</u> 335-351. (1990).

Discussion of <u>Boston Athletic Association v. Sullivan</u> regarding the selling of products with registered names regardless of how the public may perceive the connection between the goods and the event. Reviews trademark law, facts, decisions and impact of the case.

0956. Hay, Steven B. "Guarding The Olympic Gold: Protecting The Marketability of Olympic Trademarks Through Section 110 of The Amateur Sports Act of 1978." 16 <u>Southwestern University Law Review</u> 461-503. (1986).

Focuses on how Congress and Courts have protected USOC trademarks and designations from exploitation. Provides background on the Act and analysis of section 110. Reviews cases involving interpretations of section 110. Describes Trademark Counterfeiting Act of 1984 and its inherent provisions to deter trademark violators.

0957. Jacoby, Jacob and Raskopf, Robert Lloyd. "Disclaimers In Trademark Infringement Litigation: More Trouble Than They

Are Worth?" 76 Trademark Reporter 35-58. (January-February 1986).

Review of the use of disclaimers in the area of sports licensing. Discusses disclaimers in general, sports licensing, surname decisions, recent decisions in the Second Circuit, and the Wichita study.

0958.   Kelly, David M. "Trademarks: Protection of Merchandising Properties In Professional Sports." 16 Intellectual Property Law Review 263-300. (1984).

Reviews casework on team insignias and symbols, analogous cases, the conflict between the two, uniforms and presents an argument for protection.

0959.   Kelly, David M. "Trademarks: Protection of Merchandising Properties In Professional Sports." 21 Duquesne Law Review 927-964. (Summer 1983).

Discusses the protection of merchandising properties in professional sports.

0960.   Kravitz, Robert N.   "Trademarks, Speech, and the Gay Olympics Case." 69 Boston University Law Review 131-184. (January 1989).

Analyzes trademark protection and first amendment rights particularly in this case. Argues Supreme Court decision was misapplication of trademark law creating an imbalance between protections under trademark law and first amendment rights.

0961.   Sidoti, Christopher A. "Service Mark Protection." 134 New Jersey Lawyer 28-31. (May/June 1990).

Examines trademark and service mark history and definitions, name ownership, service mark searches, and publicity and misappropriation.

0962.   Wong, Glenn M. "Recent Trademark Law Cases Involving Professional and Intercollegiate Sports." 1986 Detroit College of Law Review 87-119. (Spring 1986).

Discusses trademark law cases which have set precedent for sports trademark lawsuits. Analyzes secondary meaning and functionality defense.

25

RECREATION AND RECREATIONAL SPORTS

0963.   Abrams, Robert Haskell. "Governmental Expansion of Recreational Water Use Opportunities." 59 Oregon Law Review 159-199. (Summer-Fall 1980).
     Proposes a basis for increased governmental involvement and action on the issue of public rights to recreational water use on both public and private waters. Provides doctrinal base for said public right. Discusses governmental restraint, limits and enforcement.

0964.   Babij, Bruce J. "Water Slides: A Dangerous Amusement Ride." 20 Trial 60-61. (December 1984).
     Brief discussion on the number and kinds of water slide injuries. Explores the relationship between design, dangers and a lack of safety standards.

0965.   Butler, Jim. "Outdoor Sports and Torts: An Analysis of Utah's Recreational Use Act." 1988 Utah Law Review 47-111. (1988).
     Analyzes Act which limits liability of landowners who make their land and water available for general public use. Compares this statute to other states' approaches. Discusses classifications and uses of recreational lands. Questions the constitutionality of the statute.

0966.   "Fishing and Recreational Rights In Iowa Lakes and Streams." 53 Iowa Law Review 1322-1346. (June 1968).
     Note examining potential recognition of a public right of recreation in Iowa waters previously thought to be private. Reviews the nature of riparian rights and their constitutional protection. Explores the public v. riparian conflict as it relates to navigability, trust theories, custom and prior use, and the practical considerations doctrine. Discusses the right of access

to lakes and streams in Iowa. Concludes with suggestion for the best approach to the problem.

0967.   Hauver, Constance. "Water For Recreation: A Plea For Recognition." 44 Denver Law Journal 288-299. (Spring 1967).
Discusses a number of issues regarding water for recreation in Colorado. Examines the appropriation of water for recreational use and diversion. Examines the power of eminent domain and the police power to regulate the use of water for recreation. Concludes with a discussion of using a permit system to preserve water for a recreational use.

0968.   Herbert, David L.; Herbert, William G; and Berger, Susan M. Collins. "A Trial Lawyer's Guide To The Legal Implications of Recreational, Preventive and Rehabilitative Exercise Program Standards of Care." 11 American Journal of Trial Advocacy 433-452. (Spring 1988).
Discusses multiple standards of care and their legal ramifications. Reviews adult exercise programs and providers, program activities and staffing, equipment and facilities, and legal concerns plus the standards of various national groups.

0969.   James, L. D. "Economic Analysis of Recreational Reservoirs," 55 Kentucky Law Journal 822-843. (Summer 1967).
Consists of an example of a kind of study that might be carried out in order to justify large revenue requests for recreational reservoirs. Explores the nature of outdoor recreation, marginal cost curves, marginal benefit curves, optimum installed capacity, growth and recreation demand and the value of the visitor-day. Concludes with the limitations of the method of study.

0970.   Jolley, Dan M. "Recreation and The Local Economy." 13 Current Municipal Problems 72-76. (Summer 1986).
Reviews the tax revenue, health care and life style impact of recreation.

0971.   Lambert, Thomas F., Jr. "Where Subpermittee of Lessee of Landowner's Lakeside Cottages Was Fatally Injured Diving Into Lake's Shallow Water, The Third Circuit Held That The Landowner's Receipt of Rent From Lessee Defeated The Immunity Under New Jersey's Recreational Use Statute, Even Though The Payments Were Not Made by Decedent." 30 ATLA Law Reporter 5-7. (February 1987).
Reviews Hallacker v. National Bank of Trust Co., 806 F.2d 488 (3d Cir. 1986) pertaining to the construction of landowner immunity found in recreational use statutes.

0972.   Langavant, Emmanuel. "Responsibilities en navigation de plaisance: l'accident de la Rochelle" (in French). 34 Droit Maritime Francais (France) 259-274. (May 1982).

Discussion of maritime law and efforts to bring to light aspects of civil responsibility of those who use navigable waters for recreation and sport.

0973.   Mabrouk, M. "Le regime juridique du camping" (in French). 22 Actualite Juridique (France) 388-398. (August 1966).

Review of the system governing camping. Explores the policies, organization, administration and regulation of camping. Surveys jurisdictional control of camping, its being subject to the authority of the police, and the fact that camping is an activity with general interest.

0974.   Mauch, James C. "The Recreational Users Act: Effecting The Legislative Intent." 1 Cooley Law Review 311-325. (September 1982).

Focuses on Michigan's Recreational Users Act (1979), its intent and the problems the courts have had effecting said intent.

0975.   Myers, John. "Sporting Rights: Investment." 130 New Law Journal (U.K.) 843. (September 11, 1980).

Brief discussion on the arrangement and organization of sporting rights regarding hunting and fishing.

0976.   Romano, John F., and Taggart, Thomas. "Anatomy of A Recreational Tort Case." 5 American Journal of Trial Advocacy 457-484. (Spring 1982).

Presents basis of preparation for recreational tort case. Uses actual situation to review facts, make preliminary considerations, conduct investigation, initiating the complaint and filing suit, discovery, make requests for admissions, taking depositions, fulfilling interrogatories, conducting settlement negotiations, dealt with expert witnesses, conducting pretrial conference, constructing trial brief and motions in limine. Provides a final-product brief.

0977.   Smith, Arthur D., Jr. "Outfitting On Public Lands: A Study of Federal and State Regulation." 26 Idaho Law Review 9-83. (Winter 1990).

Examines the history, guidelines and regulations pertaining to outfitting in Idaho and on federal public lands.

0978.   Sweeney, Theodora Briggs. "Playground Injuries." 90 Case and Comment 3(3). (July-August 1985).

Reviews specific hazards and case law on playground injuries.

0979.   Whittingham, Ken. "Growth Market In Sport and Leisure Equipment." 6 <u>Middle East Executive Reports</u> 19-20. (March 1983).

Brief discussion of the present and future economic climate regarding sport and leisure equipment in Qatar.

26

RIGHTS

General

0980.   Conrad, A. F. "Privilege of Forcibly Ejecting An Amusement Patron." 90 University of Pennsylvania Law Review 809-823. (May 1942).
          Examines the right of an amusement proprietor to eject patrons arbitrarily and for cause. States this right is an illusion in that a jury may still find the proprietor liable for incivility and/or the excessive use of force. Reviews a number of cases involving the expulsion of patrons.

0981.   Green, John B. "The Rights of Amateur Sportsmen." 18 Case and Comment 243-247. (1911).
          Briefly traces rights of the hunger and fisherman which, no longer being inherent free rights, have become a privilege given by the legislature. Reports on the constitutionally of game laws as being repeatedly affirmed. Discusses several statutes (and whether courts allowed them or not) and the privileged a license to hunt gives to its owner and what rights are not granted.

0982.   "Rights of Person At Public Entertainment: Ticket Only A License." 44 American Law Review 768-769. (September-October 1910).
          Points out that a ticket for admission to a race course does not impose a duty upon the proprietor as to whom may be allowed or refused admission. That a ticket for admission is a license whose possible and potential revocation is completely in the control and power of the proprietor in question. Concludes that an aggrieved, turned away ticket holder has remedy in arguing breach of contract. That this argument

would entitle plaintiff to recover both the cost of the ticket and the expenses incurred as a function of attending the performance.

Athlete

0983.   Hofeld, Albert F.   "Athletes-Their Rights and Correlative Duties." 19 Trial Lawyer's Guide 383-405. (Winter 1976).

Asks what are the rights and duties of athletes with respect to one another? Analyzes Nabozny v. Barnhill (1975) in which the Illinois Appellate court ruled that a soccer goaltender had legal rights when an opposing player (who did not fulfill his correlative legal duty to avoid contact) inured him severely. The legal rights were ascertained because the goaltender, according to the rule of soccer, was well within the protected zone and where he should have been insulated from contact. Explains the Court espoused a workable doctrine which should curb deliberate or inexcusable violations of safety rules.

Referee

0984.   Narol, Mel. "Protecting The Rights of Sports Officials-Cases of Personal Injury and Damage To Reputation." 23 Trial 64-71. (January 1987).

Cites increase in civil and criminal complaints of officials against players, coaches, fans and others. Shows officials are not employees but independent contractors. Raises issues for claims under defamatory statements, invasion of privacy and emotional distress. Discusses liability for officials.

0985.   Narol, Melvin S. and Dedopoulous, Stuart.   "Guide To Referees' Rights: Potential Liability." 16 Trial 18-21. (March 1980).

Reviews cases where the referee is a defendant and presents theories of referee liability.   Advises that a thorough knowledge of general negligence theories and their application in sports injury litigation is a prerequisite to the trial attorney's undertaking a sports official negligence lawsuit.

0986.   Narol, Melvin S. and Dedopoulos, Stuart.   "Defamation: A Guide To Referees' Rights." 16 Trial 42-44. (January 1980).

Discusses and explains grounds for legal action of referees for defamation and the issue of "public figures" and some court decisions. Offers advice for evaluating cases and gives definitions of "public figure" and "private individual" as well as "limited public figure" to assist analysis of the facts.

0987.   Narol, Melvin S. and Dedopoulos, Stuart.   "Kill The Umpire:
            A Guide To Referees' Rights."   15 <u>Trial</u> 32-34. (March 1979).
                Reviews rights and liabilities of officials in athletic events
            specifically examines an official's right to recover from a player
            or coach from an injury and/or an accidental injury.   Explores
            official's possibility of successful recovery.

27

SEX DISCRIMINATION

General

0988.   Ingram, John D. "Sex Discrimination In Park District Athletic
          Programs." 64 Women Lawyers Journal 33-38. (Winter 1978).
              Overview of the legal ramifications of sex discrimination in
          park athletic programs. Includes a discussion on applicability
          of the equal protection clause of the fourteenth amendment,
          and the issues of equal opportunity, separate but equal,
          physiological differences, contact sports, and the Equal Rights
          Amendment and Title IX.

0989.   Kutner, Joan Ruth. "Sex Discrimination In Athletics." 21
          Villanova Law Review 876-903. (October 1976).
              Comment on Section 86.41 of Title IX which provides
          guidelines for the administration of athletic programs.
          Examines the constitutionality of Section 86.41. Reviews
          Supreme Court decisions in cases pertaining to sex-based laws.
          Surveys decisions of state and federal courts in cases on sex
          discrimination in athletics.

0990.   Norman, Ken. "The Charter Looks Different In The Land of
          Oz." 1 Canadian Human Rights Advocate (Canada) 6-7.
          (October 1985).
              Reports on the decision of Justice Steele of the Supreme
          Court of Ontario in Justine Blainey v. The Ontario Hockey
          Association and The Human Rights Commission (1985).
          Questions Justice Steele's reasoning and argues that leaving
          rights to be weighed in a simple balance with general welfare is
          wrong.

0991.   Postell, Claudia J. "Settlement Reached In Sports Sex-Bias
             Suit." 24 Trial 101-102. (September 1988).

0992.   Rusch, Carolyn. "Equality In Athletics: The Cheerleader v.
             The Athlete." 19 South Dakota Law Review 428-446. (Spring
             1974).
                 Discusses discrimination on the basis of sex in public and
             private school athletic programs. Analyzes the constitutional
             and statutory grounds available (the 14th amendment, Title IX
             of the 1972 Education Amendment, the South Dakota Human
             Rights Act) to challenge the unequal funding practices which
             result in deficient female sports programs in South Dakota.
             Presents alternative programs: opening exiting programs,
             separate but equal programs, and component-type approaches.
             Prefers the latter approach as being most viable of the
             alternatives and calls for evaluation of athletic programs to
             ensure that the opportunity for exercise and competition is
             provided on an equal basis for all.

0993.   "Sex Discrimination In Athletics: Conflicting Legislative and
             Judicial Approaches." 29 Alabama Law Review 390-425.
             (Winter 1978).
                 Comment observing that despite its intent, Title IX has
             relatively little impact on court deliberations of sex
             discrimination suits. Decisions in these cases are based on
             either the equal protection clause of the fourteenth
             amendment or state laws which prohibit sex discrimination.
             Surveys case and statutory law relating to this phenomenon.

0994.   Silas, Faye A. "Olympic Challenge: Women Sue for 5 and 10-K
             Races." 70 American Bar Association Journal 42. (March 1984).
                 Short comment on the sex discrimination case of Martin v.
             International Olympic Committee involving a failure to add 5
             and 10 kilometer races to the 1984 Summer Olympics.

Coaches

0995.   Dessem, R. Lawrence. "Sex Discrimination In Coaching." 3
             Harvard Women's Law Journal 97-117. (Spring 1980).
                 Surveys salary differentials for coaches of girls' and boys'
             athletic teams. Argues that a lower pay rate for girls' coaches is
             discriminatory and in violation of the fourteenth amendment
             to the Constitution. Examines this from Title IX, Title VII,
             Equal Pay Act and Constitutional perspectives.

Equality

0996. Berman, Martin. "Sex Discrimination: Another Hurdle On The Road to Equality." 7 Loyola Entertainment Law Journal 167-175. (1987).

Examines Martin v. International Olympic Committee (1984) decision where Ninth Circuit Court of Appeals held that Unruh Civil Rights Act of California does not compel the International Olympic Committee to add 5,000 meter and 10,000 meter running events for women in 1984 Los Angeles Summer Olympic Games. Reports Court's reluctance to apply state statute to an international event. States Martin has limited precedential value and will have relatively little impact on Unruh Civil Rights Act violations but will serve as useful model for analyzing future violations because of questions raised by Court. Points out contradictions in current state and federal law and that denying women the relief they asked for appears to be incorrect. Concludes that after Martin it remains unclear how far Unruh Civil Rights Act can go in protecting a class from arbitrary discrimination and as to what type of relief an injured party can be afforded.

0997. Berman, Martin P. "Sex Discrimination: Another Hurdle On The Road To Equality." 7 Loyola Entertainment Law Journal 167-175. (1987).

Discusses Martin v. International Olympic Committee whereby Ninth Circuit Court of Appeals held that middle distance running events for women did not have to be included in 1984 Summer Olympics Games (based on the interpretation and application of California Unruh Civil Rights Act).

0998. Carr, Stephen E. Austin. "Constitutional Law-Equal Protection-Sex Discrimination Against Males In Athletics-Physiological Differences Are Valid Reasons To Exclude Boys From Girls' Athletic Teams-Clark v. Arizona Interscholastic Association." 6 Whittier Law Review 151-175. (1984).

Discusses instant case which held that it was constitutionally justified to exclude boys from all-girl teams. Reviews fact of case, holding, analysis. Analysis includes an overview of precedent, intermediate scrutiny, objectives of the state and the question of overall or absolute equality.

0999. Croudace, Virginia P. and Desmarias, Steven A. "Where The Boys Are: Can Separate Be Equal In School Sports?" 58 Southern California Law Review 1425-1466. (September 1985).

Explores question surrounding the equal protection clause of the Constitution. Offers hypothetical to illustrate. Discusses need to separate based on inherent physiological differences.

Mentions challenges by males and females to participate on teams of opposite sex. Presents solutions to this problem.

1000.   "Female Athletes Denied Equality." 1 Canadian Human Rights Advocate (Canada) 11-13. (September 1985).

Points out that sex-based discrimination is permitted by law, Section 19(2) of the Ontario Human Rights Code. Reports on the case sponsored by the Women's Legal Education and Action Fund (LEAF) where a challenge under the equality section of the Charter (Section 15) by Justine Blainey to the Ontario Human Rights Code and to regulations of the Ontario Hockey Association which prevent her from playing in the Metro Toronto Hockey League because she is female.

1001.   Jacklin, Pamela L. "Sexual Equality In High School Athletics: The Approach of Darrin v. Gould." 12 Gonzaga Law Review 691-706. (Summer 1977).

Analyzes the decision where plaintiff sued to enjoin the enforcement of a rule which forbade qualified female athletes from playing on a high school football team. Court ruled sexual discrimination to be impermissible. Focuses on the constitutional issues and challenges of the case. Discusses the significance and impact of the case and the constitutional principles enunciated therein.

1002.   Johnson, Janet Junttila. "Half-Court Girl's Basketball Rules: An Application of The Equal Protection Clause and Title IX." 65 Iowa Law Review 766-798. (March 1980).

Focuses on whether the use of separate, half-court basketball rules for female high school players denies them the equal protection of the law by causing unequal treatment of female and male basketball players. Considers whether the provision of Title IX are applicable to high school athletic programs which enforce separate rules for male and female high school basketball players. Examines Dodson v. Arkansas Activities Association where a ninth grade girls basketball player sued her school district, the superintendent, and the Association for denying her equal protection and that the rules violated Title IX of the Education Amendments of 1972.

1003.   Maher, Fred. "Equality: Settlement Helps Women Athletes." 11 Pennsylvania Law Journal-Reporter 1. (June 20, 1988).

Legislation

1004.   Broder, Sherry, and Wee, Beverly. "Hawaii's Equal Rights Amendment: Its Impact On Athletic Opportunities and

Competition for Women." 2 <u>University of Hawaii Law Review</u> 97-143. (Winter 1979).

Discusses <u>Holdman v. Olim</u> as well as the impact of Hawaii's ERA on sex discrimination in athletics. Examines the treatment of contact sports, the nature of differences between males and females, and whether requirements of ERA can be met by separate-but-equal sex discrimination policy.

1005.   Seha, Ann M. "The Administrative Enforcement of Title IX In Intercollegiate Athletics." 2 <u>Law & Inequality</u> 121-326. (February 1984).

Discusses administrative enforcement of title IX in intercollegiate athletics for women. Reviews changes in the administration and coaching of female athletes since 1972, compliance standards and enforcement provisions, and the Office of Civil Right's compliance review of colleges and universities. Includes extensive and comprehensive appendices some of which pertain to compliance, violations, scholarships, scheduling, recruitment and medical provisions.

1006.   Tokarz, Karen L. "Separate But Unequal Educational Sports Programs: The Need For A New Theory of Equality." 1 <u>Berkeley Women's Law Journal</u> 201-245. (Fall 1985).

Reviews separate but equal, equal protection, the nature of sex discrimination, governmental interest and pertinent legislation in sports program.

1007.   Wong, Glenn M. and Ensor, Richard J. "Sex Discrimination In Athletics: Review of Two Decades of Accomplishments and Defeats." 21 <u>Gonzaga Law Review</u> 345-393. (1985-1986).

Reviews impact and changes which Title IX, equal protection and state equal rights amendments have made in women's athletics. Analyzes court decisions involving gender-based discrimination claims in the participation of and employment in sports.

Post-Secondary Schools

1008.   Kadzielski, Mark A. "Postsecondary Athletics In An Era of Equality: An Appraisal of The Effect of Title IX." 5 <u>Journal of College and University Law</u> 123-141. (1978-1979).

Examines the application, use and validity of the "separate but equal" construction of Title IX. Presents a general, brief overview of sex discrimination case law and the separate-but-equal concept. Discusses "separate-is-equal" concept used in sex discrimination in athletics. Reports on the continuity, controversy and extent of Title IX's regulations.

1009. Longo, Christina A. and Thoman, Elizabeth F. "Haffer v. Temple University: A Reawakening of Gender Discrimination In Intercollegiate Athletics." 16 Journal of College and University Law 137-150. (Summer 1989).

Discusses role of the District Court, the basis for the suit, defenses available in such a case and how Haffer was settled. Concludes with discussion of the impact of Haffer.

1010. "Sex Discrimination and Intercollegiate Athletics." 61 Iowa Law Review 420-496. (December 1975).

A note focusing on the nature and pervasiveness of sex-based inequalities in collegiate athletics and the permissibility of these inequalities in light of case law interpretation of Constitutional mandates, Title IX of the 1972 Education Amendments and the proposed Equal Rights Amendment. Illuminates legal and administrative problems which face the collegiate athletic program as more female athletes demand equal rights in collegiate sports. Discusses history of sexism in the United States and the legal system which developed and which frequently distinguishes among citizens on the basis of sex. Analyzes Title IX and serious problems or interpretation and application which have arisen, the HEW regulations and their evolution and intentions.

1011. "Sex Discrimination and Intercollegiate Athletics: Putting Some Muscle On Title IX." 88 Yale Law Journal 1254-1279. (May 1979).

Argues the regulations relating to Title IX need to be made more stringent. Reviews Title IX guidelines and existing regulations. Discusses relationship of the regulations to the statute in terms of the breath of the statute and social policy. Assesses the existing regulations and provides suggestions for alternative regulations.

1012. Willson, Sally and McCaffrey, Patrick. "Far Above Cayuga's Waters." 12 Perspectives 18-19. (Summer 1980).

Brief discussion of sex discrimination in sports at Cornell University.

Secondary Schools

1013. Austin, Katherine Ann. "Constitutional Law-Equal Protection-Sex Discrimination In Secondary School Athletics." 46 Tennessee Law Review 222-237. (Fall 1978).

Discusses Cape v. Tennessee Secondary School Athletic Association (1977) which challenged the different rules for girls basketball teams as violating the equal protection clause of the fourteenth amendment and where the court of appeals held, reversed, and remanded.   Traces development of a proper standard of review in sex discrimination cases at the Supreme Court level contrast in the struggle of the lower courts to apply the correct standard in high school athletics.   Criticizes the analysis of the appellate court as failing to deal with the issue of different rules and whether they can survive an equal protection challenge under the Craig (1976) standard: the decision in the case is not supported by U.S. Supreme Court opinions.   Mentions the relief that Title IX and an order from HEW's Office of Civil Rights would have afforded.

1014.   Hetzel, James V.   "Gender-Based Discrimination In High School Athletics."   10 Seton Hall Legislative Journal 275-297. (1987).

Examines issues presented in two New Jersey cases (Balsey 1985 and Carney 1986) involving gender-based discrimination in high school athletics.   Includes other related issues presented by cases in other jurisdictions.   Concludes these decisions are in accord with majority viewpoint as developed in other jurisdictions as recognizing that elimination of gender-based distinctions in this area would eliminate many female athletes from participating in high school athletics.

1015.   Jennings, Diane I.   "Petrie v. Illinois High School Association: Gender Classification and High School Athletes."   14 John Marshall Law Review 227-241.

Discusses the facts of the case, the standard of judicial review, a consideration of precedent and the court's reasoning in the case.

1016.   McNamara, Timothy K.   "Sex Discrimination In High School Athletics."   47 UMKC Law Review 109-120. (Fall 1978).

Analysis of Yellow Springs Exempted Village School District Board of Education v. Ohio High School Athletic Association.   Reviews the facts of the case, the irrebuttable presumption doctrine and a discussion of the traditional analysis of sex discrimination cases.   Raises the question of whether Title IX is discriminatory.

1017.   Pryor, Barbara L.   "Equal Protection Scrutiny of High School Athletics."   72 Kentucky Law Journal 936-950. (Winter 1984).

Review of Clark v. Arizona Interscholastic Association where males were prohibited from participating on a female volleyball team (where no male team was provided) even though females were permitted to participate on all-male teams.

1018.   Rubin, Richard Alan. "Sex Discrimination In Interscholastic High School Athletics." 25 Syracuse Law Review 535-574. (Spring 1974).

Identifies and comments on the key elements of each decision of cases in which females have claimed the right to participate in interscholastic high school athletics. Discusses contact and noncontact sports, physical distinctions, psychological effects, various programs for athletic participation (separate but equal, mixed competition, quota system, components approach). Answers stating that only "separate and mixed" programs are acceptable but that their viability is threatened by proposed federal regulations and the pending ERA.

1019.   "Sex Discrimination-Girls' High School Basketball Rules Held Unconstitutional." 16 Journal of Family Law 345-351. (February 1978).

Note and discussion on Cape v. Tennessee Secondary School Athletic Association, 424 F. Supp. 732 (E.d. Tenn. 1976), where the court ruled that rules designed specifically for girls' basketball were unconstitutional under the equal protection clause. Rules included, inter alia number of players, half-court, and certain player shooting restrictions.

1020.   "Sex Discrimination In High School Athletics: An Examination of Applicable Legal Doctrines." 66 Minnesota Law Review 1115-1140. (July 1982).

Analyzes legal doctrines available to female athlete who wants to compete for position on male high school team when there is an opportunity to participate on a female team. Doctrines examined are those raised under federal constitution, Title IX, state constitutional equal rights provisions and/or statutory provisions.

1021.   Sipkins, Thomas M. and Popovich, Peter S. "Sex Equity In The Public Schools." 12 Urban Lawyer 509-514. (Summer 1980).

Discusses athletic sex equity in the public schools from a Title IX perspective. Reviews the scope of Title IX, private causes of action under Title IX and the issue of equal access to public school athletic programs.

28

SPECTATORS

General

1022.   Coutts, J. A. "The Effect of Offering No Evidence." 51 Journal of Criminal Law (U.K.) 145-146. (May 1987).

1023.   "Extradition A Victory for Pragmatism." 137 New Law Journal (U.K.) 651. (July 17, 1987).

1024.   "Foul Ball-Indeed." 98 The Los Angles Daily Journal 4. (September 2, 1985).

1025.   Grayson, Edward. "Popplewell In Perspective." 135 New Law Journal (U.K.) 881-882. (September 6, 1985).

1026.   "The Police and The Tour." New Zealand Law Journal (New Zealand) 191-192. (May 21, 1981).

1027.   Redmond-Cooper, Ruth. "The Legal Aftermath of The Heysel Disaster." 135 New Law Journal (U.K.) 957-958. (September 27, 1985).

1028.   "Spectators Sue For Injuries." 23 Trial 84(2). February 1987.
         Discusses Grisim v. TapeMark Charity Pro-Am Golf Tournament 394 N.W.2d 261 (Main. Ct. App. 1986) and Vanchieri v. New Jersey Sports and Exposition Authority 514 A.2d (1323 (N.J. 1986) regarding injury suits of spectators against facilities and a security agency. Considers duty of care, assumption of risk and sovereign immunity.

Assumption of Risk

1029.   "Baseball Fan and The Duty To Protect Him." 54 <u>American Law Review</u> 433-436. (May 1920).

Provides portions of the opinion in <u>Crane v. Kansas City Baseball, Etc., Co.</u>, (168 Mo. App. 301, 153 S.W. 1076), wherein management is responsible to provide the choice of reasonably screened and open seating to protect spectators against the dangers of baseball. That when such a choice is provided, management cannot be held negligent; when a reasonably screened area is provided, the spectator assumes the risk of injury.

1030.   Collier, N.C. "Duty of Proprietors of Theatres, Amusement Gardens, etc., As To Safety of Patrons." 69 <u>Central Law Journal</u> 250-251. (October 1, 1909).

Discusses responsibility of the proprietor of grounds and grandstands to provide a safe viewing place for spectators including the physical integrity of the areas and the protection of guests and spectators from insults and physical attack. Questions the extent of the spectators' assumption of risk and the proprietors degree of reasonable care.

1031.   Dunlavey, James. "Heads Up!" The Defense of Assumption of Risk In Relation To Sports Spectator Injury Cases Is Alive and Well." 8 <u>Los Angeles Lawyer</u> 32 (5). (April 1985).

Reports on assumption of risk cases, in California, in the sports of baseball, hockey, sports-car racing and golf. Discovers that the assumption of risk defense is alive and well in California.

1032.   "In The Grand Stand." 24 <u>Law Notes</u> 5-7. (April 1920).

Discussion of the duties, responsibilities, rights, risks and assumptions involved in attending a baseball game. Presentation occurs and evolves as the result of what would have occurred if a lawyer brought his new bride to a baseball game at the Polo grounds. Explanation of the game-and the legal aspects involved with being a spectator-occur in the form of a monologue. This monologue, in turn, consists of a generous use of quotes from the decisions of various cases involving the spectators and a management at a baseball game.

1033.   Jeffers, Howard. "Amusements, Negligence." 11 <u>Notre Dame Lawyer</u> 93-100. (1935).

Reviews <u>Sutherland v. Onondaga Hockey Club</u> (281 NYS 505), and other cases pertaining to the responsibilities and risks incumbent upon the owner and the spectator. Points out cases where assumption of risk is clearly with the patron/spectator and that this assumption of risk precludes recovery by the patron/spectator.

1034.   "Theatres and Shows, Assumption of Risk, Spectators At A Baseball Game." 17 Michigan Law Review 594-596. (May 1919).

Focuses on the degree to which spectator at a baseball game assumes risk. Presents development of case history wherein a balance is struck between the responsibility of management to provide properly maintained, protected seating and unprotected seating at baseball games, and the spectator's assumption of risk in his choice of seating, knowing the nature of the game.

Liability

1035.   Grant, David and Wilson, Stephen R. "Nuisance Rules OK?-II." 129 Solicitor's Journal (U.K.) 163-165. (March 8, 1985).

Continuation discussing the prescription, remoteness of damage, acts of third parties and remedies available regarding nuisances at football contests.

Torts

1036.   Buxton, Joseph T., Jr. "Baseball and The Courts." 39 Law Notes 28-31. (September 1935).

Review of casework regarding whether a paying spectator can recover for injuries sustained as the result of being hit by a baseball. Indicates that recovery in such cases has generally been denied unless there are extenuating circumstances. Surveys the issues of assumption of risk, contributory negligence, duty and negligence.

1037.   Dickerson, Thomas A. "To All Frustrated (Boston) Sports Fans: Forget The Boos, Raspberries and Catcalls-Sue The Bums." 196 New York Law Journal 5. (November 14, 1986).

1038.   Hall, Frederick S. "Torts, Amusements, Assumptions of Risk." 17 Boston University Law Review 485-494. (April 1937).

Comments on 1936 Massachusetts Court decision (Shanney v. Madison Square Garden) which refused to follow doctrines previously followed concerning assumptions of risks taken by spectators. Maintains that the fact that a person who is a first time attendant at a performance should not change the rule of liability as far as the owner of the ball park, hockey rink or other place of amusement is concerned. Criticizes the court for stating that "every case must be decided by the application of general principles to the particular facts shown and not be arbitrary classification according to the names of various games." Contends that this will open up an unjustified field of litigation.

Violence

1039.   Appleson, Gail. "Spectator Violence: What They See Is What The Do?" 68 <u>American Bar Association Journal</u> 404. (April 1982).

1040.   Cowper, Francis.   "Violent Football Fans and The Justice System." 200 <u>New York Law Journal</u> 2. (July 1, 1988).

1041.   Dunand, Muriel A.   "Violence et panique dans le stade de football de Bruxelle en 1985:   approche psychosociale des envenements" (in French).   67 <u>Revue de Droit Penal et Criminologie</u> (Belgium) 403-400. (1987).
        A psycho-social examination of the 29 May 1985 violence and panic in a soccer stadium in Brussels which resulted in 39 deaths and 470 injured. Includes a bibliography.

1042.   "European Convention On Spectator Violence and Misbehavior At Sports Evens and In Particular At Football Matches."   24 <u>International Legal Materials</u> 1566-1572. (November 1985).

1043.   McFarland, Gavin. "The 'Hooligan' Trials: Problems For The System." 132 <u>Solicitors' Journal</u> (U.K.) 1138-1139. (August 12, 1988).
        Surveys problems that hooliganism creates for the legal system. Reviews causes and effects of hooliganism, why a number of trials have collapsed, and the effectiveness of the English jury system in these trials.

1044.   Salter, Michael. "Judicial Response To Football Hooliganism." 37 <u>Northern Ireland Legal Quarterly</u> (Northern Ireland) 280-292. (Spring 1986).
        Examines judges' interpretations of football hooliganism, kinds of behavior and type of person carrying out the behavior. Attempts to identify a common ground for all behaviors identified as hooliganism. Analyzes consequences of said typification process. Discusses meaning of a "public place" and "threatening behavior" in terms of Public Order Act 1936. Cites <u>Mail v. McDowell</u> and others. Concludes magistrates are not following deterrent sentencing directives.

1045.   Salter, Michael.   "The Judges v. The Football Fan: A Sporting
             Contest?"   36 Northern Ireland Legal Quarterly (Northern
             Ireland) 351-357. (Winter 1985.
                 Reviews cases through which football hooliganism is
             defined and characterized.   Analyzes type of person involved
             in "hooliganism" and need for appropriate and consistent
             application of existing statutes.

1046.   Samuels, Alec.   "Sporting Events Act."   129 Solicitor's Journal
             (U.K.) 581. (August 23, 1985).
                 Review of the 1985 Act and the control of alcohol at football
             matches in an attempt to decrease crowd violence.

1047.   Sims, P. N. and Tsitsoura, A.   "La convention Europeene sur la
             violence et les debordements des spectateurs lors des
             manifestations sportives et notamments les matches de
             football" (in French).   67 Revue de Droit Penal et
             Criminologies (Belgium) 393-401. (1987).
                 Overview of the Council of Europe's Convention on
             spectator violence in sports.   The Convention was made
             effective on 1 November 1985.

1048.   Taylor, Jefferson C.   "The War On Soccer Hooliganism: The
             European Convention On Spectator Violence and
             "Misbehavior" At Sports Events."   27 Virginia Journal of
             International Law 603-653. (Spring 1987).
                 Reviews the measures of the Convention from a members'
             domestic and international perspective.   Discusses the
             phenomenon of football hooliganism and provides an analysis
             of the Convention.

1049.   Trivizas, Eugene.   "Disturbances Associated With Football
             Matches: Types of Incidents and Selection of Charges."   24
             British Journal of Criminology (U.K.) 361-383. (October 1984).
                 Examines the kinds of disturbances which occur in a
             football crowd, the applicable legal provisions and the question
             of police discretion during such disturbances.

1050.   Trivizas, Eugene.   "Sentencing The Football Hooligan."   21
             British Journal of Criminology (U.K.) 342-349. (October 1981).
                 Examines the kinds of sentences given to those convicted
             during football games.   Analyzes how such football hooligans
             are treated in relation to those who are convicted of like
             offenses outside of the context of football games.

1051.   Trivizas, Eugene.   "Offences and Offenders In Football Crowd
             Disorders."   20 British Journal of Criminology (U.K.) 276-288.
             (July 1980).

Research project that attempts to achieve a greater understanding of "football hooliganism." Study examines the reasons for arrests and the nature of the offenders. Compares the football-related offences and the nature of the offenders with like offences which occur outside of a football environment.

1052.   Williams, John. "Football Hooliganism: Offences, Arrests and Violence-A Critical Note." 7 British Journal of Law and Society (U.K.) 104-111. (Summer 1980).

Attempts to clarify the phenomenon known as football hooliganism. Examines the relationship and use of section 5 of the 1936 Public Order Act to disorders and football fan violence. Argues there is a discrepancy between the law as it is written and the way it is implemented. Explores football arrests and violence, football related assaults, affray, and football hooliganism and violence.

1053.   Zimmerman, Manfred. "La violence dans les stades de football: le cas de l'Allemagne Federale" (in French). 67 Revue de Droit Penal et Criminologie (Begium) 441-463. (1987).

Reviews spectator violence and aggression in sports-particularly soccer. Discusses this from a socio-cultural research perspective. Reviews the role of the police and the possibility of prevention of such violence.

29

SPORT

General

1054.   Bernstein, Sandra. "Bernie Gluckstein Photographs Another
             Kind of Court. He Makes It Look Easy." 8 <u>Canadian Lawyer</u>
             (Canada) 36-37. (October 1984).
                 Reports on the legal and sports photography careers of
             Bernie Gluckstein.

1055.   Berti, Giorgio. "Premesse e Ipotesi Sui Compiti Della Rigione
             Nel Servizio Sociale Dello Sport" (in Italian). 24 <u>Rivista</u>
             <u>Trimestrale di Diritto Pubblico</u> (Italy) 600-624. (1974).
                 Reviews a number of premises and hypotheses regarding
             the role of local governments in relation to the social service of
             sports.

1056.   Bracquemond, J. "Sports et droit" (in French). 11 <u>Revue</u>
             <u>Generale de Droit</u> (Canada) 645-662. (1981).
                 Discusses the philosophical aspects of participating in
             sports. Considers the given, take, and challenge of sport.
             Specifically examines the sports of canoeing/kayaking from
             philosophical and legal perspectives.

1057.   Coma, M. Bassols. "Administracion Deportiva: Evolucion y
             Posible Configuracion" (in Spanish). 85 <u>Revista de</u>
             <u>Administracion Publica</u> (Spain) 375-390. (January-April 1978).
                 Review of the evolution, structure and administration of
             sports in Spain.

1058.   de Bianchetti, A. "Pena de Inhabilitacion en el Derecho
             Deportivo" (in Spanish). 98 <u>La Ley, Revista Juridica Argentina</u>
             (Argentina) 817-822. (May 10, 1960).

Focuses on the nature of sports, sports law and disciplinary measures in sports.

1059.   "Entertainers and Sportsmen."   117 Taxation (U.K.) 232(1). (June 20, 1986).

1060.   Fanning, J. "Sports and Entertainment; Panel." 1986 Canadian Bar Association Yearbook (Canada) 140-156. (1986).
Panel discussion of and with Jim Fanning, David Foster and Wayne Gretzky. Examines the nature, challenges, demands and complications of their lives, in sports and entertainment, legal and otherwise. Begins with a review of a typical week in each of their lives. Continues with panel discussion involving their lives, sports, entertainment, and the law.

1061.   Greenberg, Mannes F. "Rights of Ticketholders To Places of Amusements." 10 Maryland Law Review 169-185. (Spring 1949).
Discusses Greenfield v. Maryland Jockey Club of Baltimore. Examines plaintiff's right to acquire admission ticket and defendant's right, as a proprietor, to select those with whom he wishes to contract (including the selection of patrons). Examines common law rights and the extent of their statutory limitations. Presents discussion of state franchise creating authority not existing at common law. Touches on some states' civil rights law interpretations. Provides definition of license in terms of what a ticket of admission represents and opinions whether that license is revokable or not. Provides reference to English and American cases and court opinions of railroad and theatre tickets and their limitations and purpose. Discusses damages recoverable in an action of breach of contract as a result of a plaintiff's ejection from a place of amusement.

1062.   Gros, Manuel and Verkindt, P.-Y. "L'autonomie de droit du sport" (in French). 41 Actualite Juridique (Ser. Droit Administratif) (France) 699-711. (1985).
Examines whether the issue of autonomy in sports is a matter of fact or fiction. Posits that due to the ever-expanding nature of sports, and its involvement of the public, sport necessarily becomes less autonomous. Examines the judicial involvement in sports.

1063.   Johnson, Tony. "Natural Justice Before Sporting Tribunals." 59 Law Institute Journal(Australia) 538-540. (June 1985).
Discusses application of natural justice to sporting tribunals. Examines issues of the bases of jurisdiction, restraint of trade, domestic remedies, breach of rules, representation, onus and

standards of proof, the necessity of a decision, bias, the exclusion of natural justice and legislation.

1064.   Karaquillo, J.-P. "Activite sportive et salariat" (in French). Droit Social (France) 22-29. (January 1979).
Briefly discusses the parallels and relationship between sport and work. Explores the essence of the sporting milieu and its relationship to the nature and goals of business practices.

1065.   Kravchenko, V. V.   "Opyt Osushchestvleniia Gosudarstvennykh Funktsii Soiuznom Sportivnykh Obshchestv" (in Russian).   32 Sovetskoe Gosudarstvo i Pravo (USSR), No. 6, 48. (June 1962).
Discusses the experiences surrounding governmental organization and central administration of organized sports in the Soviet Union.

1066.   Lapeyre, Charles. "Les collectivites locales et le sport apres les lois de decentralisation" (in French).   103 Revue du Droit Public et de la Science Politique en France et a l'Etranger (France) 1603-1639. (1987).
Discusses the effects of the laws of decentralization on sports at the local level in France.

1067.   "Law and Customs of Sports." 134 Quarterly Review (London) 16-30. (January 1873).
Overview of the Law of Game in England, the English Colonies and in a number of foreign countries. Reviews the question of the Wild Bird Protection Act and its potential extension to other animals. Points out the differences in sport from the last generation to the present one. Also discusses changes in the law which have already taken place and changes which are expected to take place.

1068.   "Lener, A., et al. "Legge Per Lo Sport?" (in Italian). 104 Foro Italiano (Italy) 297-314. (November 1981).
Raises the question of whether there is a need to regulate sports.

1069.   Lineberry, William P., (ed). The Business of Sports. New York: H. W. Wilson Company, 1973.
Discusses sports as an investment, commercialism in sports, the dynamics of business, and promoters and players. Examines cost of college and professional sports. Concludes with chapter on regulation, reform and redemption in sports.

1070.   Mathews, Nancy N. "Sports News You Can Use." 7 Update 10(9). (Spring 1983).

Offers suggestions on how teachers can use sports as a means of teaching citizenship, values and the law to their students.

1071.   Nafziger, James A. R. and Strenk, Andrew. "The Political Uses and Abuses of Sports." 10 Connecticut Law Review 259-289. (Winter 1978).

Examination of the political use of sports and international sports competitions: diplomatic recognition and nonrecognition; protest; ideology and propaganda; official prestige; international cooperation; and conflict. Discussion of each includes references and examples to practices by specific countries. Analyzes the political uses and abuses of sports from a legal framework.

1072.   Noll, Roger G. (ed). Government and The Sports Business. Washington, D.C.: The Brookings Institution, 1974.

Edited volume containing essays which analyze economics of professional sports. Topics include introduction to U.S. team sports industry, economic theory of professional sports league, social benefits of restrictions on team quality, attendance and price setting, taxation and sports enterprises, labor relations in sports, baseball (a case study of discrimination), sports broadcasting, subsidies of stadiums and arenas, self-regulation in baseball, sports leagues and federal antitrust laws, and discussion of alternatives in sports policy.

1073.   Plouvin, J.-Y. "Relation de l'Etat et des groupments sportifs" (in French). 27 Revue Administrative (France) 237-244. (May-June 1974).

Explores the relationship of nations and sports. Calls for the need of a central sporting organization. Reviews requirements of being a number of said organization. Elaborates on the organization, role and administration of the organization and examines the nature of sport, and sportsmanship.

1074.   Saint-Jours, Y. "Sport au regard du droit du travail et de la securite social" (in French). 51 La Semaine Juridique, Juris-Classeur Periodique (France) 2848. (April 1977).

Discusses the principle right of the judicial officer to collect evidence without notifying the other interested parties involved. Reviews the role of sport as a professional, a business, and the existence of contracts and the nature of ethics in sports. Differentiates the role of amateurs and professionals in sports.

1075.   Sandrock, Otto, and Witte-Wegmann, Gertrud. "Wettbewerbsrechtlicher Schutz Von Sportveranstaltungs-

programmen." 80 <u>Gewerblicher Rechtsschutz und
Urheberrecht Internationaler Teil</u> (West Germany 335-345.
(June 1978).

Discusses the extent to which sports is and/or should be
legally commercialized.

1076.   Stillman, Grant. "The Sporting Life." 13 <u>Melbourne
University Law Review</u> (Australia) 264-265. (December 1981).

Brief discussion on sports boycotts and their use in today's
world.

1077.   Vatnikov, I.E. "Ruskovodstvo Mestnykh Sovetov Rasvitiem
Fizicheskoi Kul'tury i Sporta" (in Russian). 35 (1) <u>Vestnik
Moskovskogo Universiteta, Seriia Pravo</u> (USSR) 30-36.
(January-February 1980).

Focuses on the importance of physical education in the
Soviet Union and the local Soviets. Examines historical
codification of physical education and sport in the Soviet
Union. Reviews the impact of the XXII Olympiad on physical
education and sports.

1078.   Wilkinson, H.W. "Coping With Leisure-Leisure and
Amusement Centres and Leisure Parks." 136 <u>New Law Journal</u>
(U.K.) 1130(3). (November 28, 1986).

Associations/Clubs/Federations/Societies

1079.   Bianchi d'Urso, Fulvio. "Riflessioni Sulla Natura Giuredica
Del Vincolo Sportivo" (in Italian). 35 <u>Diritto e Giurisprudenza</u>
(Italy) 1-10. (January-March 1979).

Reflections on the legal nature of the relationship between
the players and the sponsoring sport societies.

1080.   Cirenci, Maria Teresa. "Associazioni Sportive Societa Per
Azioni" (in Italian). 68 (I) <u>Rivista del Diritto Commerciale e
del Diritto Generale delle Obbligazioni</u> (Italy) 467-498.
(November-December 1970).

Discusses the financial commitment of individuals and
joint-stock companies regarding the organization of sports
associations.

1081.   Huon, deKermadec, J.-M. "Le controle de la legalite des
decisions des federations sportives ayant le caractere d'acte
administratif" (in French). 101 <u>Revue de Droit Public et de la
Science Politique en France et a l'Etranger</u> (France) 407-441.
(1985).

Discusses the legality of decisions of an administrative
nature by sports federations.

1082.   Karaquillo, J.-P.   "Pouvoir disciplinaire dans l'association
             sportive' (in French).   Recuil Dalloz Sirey (France) 115-124.
             (April 1980).
                 Focuses on the disciplinary powers of sporting associations.
             Discusses the organization of the disciplinary process, looks at
             the disciplinary procedures and sanctions, and the legal aspects
             which empower organizations and their disciplinary activities.

1083.   Marasa, Giorgio.   "Societa Sportive e Societa Di Diritto
             Speciale" (in Italian).   27 Rivista Della Societa (Italy) 493-524.
             (May-June 1982).
                 Overview of the nature of sporting societies.

1084.   Mbaye, Keba.   "Une nouvelle institution d'arbitrage: le
             tribunal arbitral du sport (T.A.S.)" (in French).   30 Annuaire
             Francais de Droit International (France) 409-424. (1985).
                 Examines a new phenomenon in arbitration, the sports
             arbitration tribunal, created by the International Olympic
             Committee.   Reviews the tribunal's organization, functions
             and procedures.

1085.   Nordlinger, Angela. "Legal Obligations of Running A Sporting
             Club." 59 Law Institute Journal (Australia) 553-537. (June 1985).
                 Offers practical guidance to representing a sporting club.
             Points out structure of a sporting club as well as its rules,
             constitution and articles.   Also focuses on the application of
             both the Equal Opportunity Act of 1984 and the Liquor Control
             Act of sporting clubs.

1086.   Plouvin, J.-Y. "Associations sportives ou le sport a la recherche
             de son juge et de son droit" (in French). 36 Actualite Juridique
             (Ser. Droit Administratif) (France) 177-181. (March 1980).
                 Discusses sports associations and examines the extent of
             their rights in relation to their position in the hierarchical
             organization of sports.

1087.   Plouvin, J.-Y. "Reconnaissance par le juge administratif d'un
             service public administratif du sport" (in French).   49
             LaSemaine Juridique, Juris-Classeur Periodique (France) 2724.
             (July-August 1975).
                 Reviews the circumstances and legal recognition of the
             public administration of sports under the law of 22 November
             1974. Examines a number of cases relating to the intervention
             of the state on behalf of sports and the role played by the public
             administration of the sport.   Discusses the role of sporting
             federations and the extent to which the state retains power
             over sports.

1088.   Putzolu, G. Volpe. "Oggeto 'Sociale' ed Esercizio Dell'impressa Nelle Societa Sportive" (in Italian). 31 (I) <u>Rivista di Diritto Civile</u> (Italy) 333-348. (1985).

Examination of the social objectives and business practices of sporting societies.

1089.   Stoljar, Samuel J. "Sporting Clubs and Corporate Theory." 13 <u>Melbourne University Law Review</u> (Australia) 491-507. (October 1982).

Examines the relationship between unincorporated sporting clubs and the law, and the possibility of suing such an association and/or its members. Comments on the role of the judiciary in the clarification of the legal status of such associations.

1090.   Taupier, Michel. "Recherches sur la nature juridique des federations sportives et de leurs actes" (in French). 26 <u>Actualite Juridique</u> (Ser. Droit Administratif) (France) 75-89. (February 1970).

Examination of the research on the nature of sports federations and their acts. Reviews the origin, judicial nature, and mission of the federations.

1091.   Tetzlaff, Angelika. "Sport Unter Der Kartellupe." 38 <u>Wirtschaft and Wettbewerb</u> (West Germany) 93-100. (1988).

Shows concerns over new decision pertaining to cartels and which could lead to an "...abuse of a dominant position of [the] market..."

1092.   Verrucoli, Piero. "Le Societa e La Associazione Sportive Alla Luce Della Legge de Riforma" (in Italian). 1982 <u>Revista del Diritto Commerciale e del Diritto Generale Della Obbligazione</u> (Italy) 131-156. (1982).

Discussion of the law (n. 91) of 23 March 1981 and its relationship of sports associations and societies.

1093.   Vieweg, Laus. "Zur Einfuhrung: Sport und Recht." 23 <u>Juristische Schulung</u> (West Germany) 825-830. (November 1983).

Examines the relationship between the power of sports organizations and the normally established rules of justice.

Correlates of The Culture of Sport

1094.   Boyer, Allen. "The Great Gatsby', The Black Sox, High Finance, and American Law." 88 <u>Michigan Law Review</u> 328-342. (November 1989).

Relates F. Scott Fitzgerald's The Great Gatsby with the Black Sox scandal and trial of 1921.

1095.   Chemakin, I. M.   "Kul'turno-Sportivnye Kompleksy: Pravovoi Status" (in Russian). 56 Sovetskoe Gosudarstvo i Pravo (USSR) 20-27. (August 1986).

Discusses the status of sports-culture complexes in the Soviet Union. Focuses particularly on the legal aspects relating to the complexes.

1096.   Chemakin, I. M.   "Codification of Legislation on Physical Culture, Sports, and Tourism."   23 Soviet Law and Government 73-89. (Winter 1984-1985).

Discusses the goals and tasks of physical culture and sports in Soviet society. Reports that the USSR Constitution of 1977 spoke to the goals and tasks of development of physical culture, sports and tourism. Examines the vast body of current legislation being based on the USSR Constitution. Offers suggestions to improve the functioning of the soviet state's policy, organization, administration, and guidelines pertaining to physical culture, sports, and tourism.

1097.   Chemakin, I. M.   "Kodifikatsiia Zakonodatel'stva o Fizicheskoi Kul'ture Sporte i Turizme" (in Russian). 28 Pravovedenie (USSR) 20-30. (1984).

Discusses the codification of the law as it pertains to physical culture, sports and tourism.

1098.   Chemakin, I. M. and Kukushkin, M. I.   "Sootnoshenie Gosudarstvennykh i Obschestvennykh Nachal v Upravlenii fizicheskoi Kul'turoi i Sportom v SSSR" (in Russian). 46 Sovetskoe Gosudarstvo i Provo (USSR), No. 5, 130-134. (May 1976).

Discusses the cooperation between the governmental and public sectors regarding the administration of physical culture and sports in the Soviet Union.

1099.   Hiller, Jack.   "Language, Law, Sports and Culture: The Transferability or Nontransferability of Words, Lifestyles, and Attitudes Through Law."   12 Valparaiso University Law Review 433-465. (Spring 1978).

Explores the relationship between language, sports, law and culture. Presents cross-national examples which demonstrate that a nation's character is often reflected in attitudes toward language, sports and the law. Warns that legal systems cannot be transplanted wholesale, from one culture to another without acquiring what the author identifies as baggage.

1100.   Prusak, J. "Vztah Medzi Sportovym Pravidlom a Pravidlom
             Socialistikeho Spoluzitia a Kriticke Stanovisko k Tzv.
             Sportovemu Pravu" (in Slovak).   67 <u>Pravny   Obzor</u>
             (Czechoslovakia) 864-877. (November 1984).

             A critique of sports laws as regards its relationship between
             the rules of the game and the rule of socialist common life.
             States the immunity that often is applied to sportsmen is in
             conflict with the sovereignty of the state.   Argues that
             sportsmen who injure a fellow participant should not be free
             from liability if they are applying by the rules of the game: they
             should be judged in terms of whether the law was broken and
             whether any rules of the game were broken.

1101.   Uvarov, V. N. "State Administration of Physical Culture and
             Sports." 22 <u>Soviet Law and Government</u> 74-85. (Winter 1983-
             1984).

             Examines the organization and administration problems of
             physical education for Soviet society from a juridicial
             perspective.   Discusses development of physical culture and
             sports as one of the directions of state activity, the
             administration of physical culture and sports being an
             independent branch of state administration, and improving
             the competence of agencies that administer physical culture
             and sports.

1102.   Zhakaeva, L. S. "Mestnye Soveity i Organizatsiia Kul'turno-
             sportivnykh Kompleksov" (in Russian).   42 (3) <u>Vestnik
             Moskovskogo Universiteta, Seriia Pravo</u> (USSR) 71-77. (1987).

             Examines the role and involvement of the local Soviets in
             the organization of sports-culture complexes.

Environmental Impact

1103.   Birk, H.-J. "Umwelteinwirkungen Durch Sportanlagen" (in
             German). 4 <u>Neue Zeitschrift Fur Vewaltungsrecht</u> (West
             Germany) 689-697. (1985).

             Examines the environmental impact of sports facilities.
             Includes issues such as noise control, neighborhood location,
             and the planning of facilities.

1104.   Budavari, Rosemary. "Parramatta Park: Where Politics and
             Environment Don't Mix." 8 <u>Legal Services Bulletin</u> (Australia)
             25-28. (February 1983).

             Reviews   the   struggle   between   developers   and
             environmentalists over a proposed 30,000 seat stadium.

1105.   Uren, Tom. "Environmental Decision Making." 4 <u>University
             of New South Wales Law Journal</u> (Australia) 5-9. (June 1981).

Pertains to alleged improprieties in the New South Wales Government's decision to build a sports stadium in Sydney.

Financing of Sports

1106.   Bringewat, Peter. "Finanzmanipulation Im Ligafussball-ein Risikogeschaft?" 32 Juristenzeitung (West Germany) 667-672. (October 1977).
Discusses the manipulation of money in club soccer.

1107.   Dixon, D. M. "The Finance of Sport-A Talk To The British Academy of Forensic Sciences." 24 Medicine, Science and The Law (U.K.) 294-298. (October 1984).
Discusses the financing potential from the areas of government, lotteries, charity, T.V.-Fees and commercial sponsorship and advertising.

Gambling

1108.   "Football Betting Pools." 108 Justice of The Peace (U.K.) 218-219. (May 6, 1944).
Briefly reviews the impact of the 1934 Betting and Lotteries Act on football pools. Discusses cases where a distinction is made between ordinary pool betting and a prize competition.

1109.   "Football Pools." 200 Law Times (London) 148-149. (November 3, 1945).
Examines the conflict occurring between Elderton v. United Kingdom Totalisator Company, Limited, and Bretherton v. United Kingdom Totalisator Company, Limited, (173 L. T. Rep. 126).

1110.   "Football Pools." 200 Law Times (London) 20-21. (July 21, 1945).
Discussion of Elderton v. United Kingdom Totalisator Company Limited (152 L. T. Rep. 549; (1935) Ch. 373). Reviews Sec. 26(1) of the 1934 Betting and Lotteries Act and the facts of Elderton. Focuses particularly on Eve, J.'s decision in case and reactions to it. Reviews the issue of pool operations and prize competitions.

1111.   "Football Pool Clubs." 108 Justice of The Peace (U.K.) 123. (March 11, 1944).
Overview of a local summons involving the operational method of a football pool club. Discusses the preparation involved, contingencies planned for, remunerations derived and potential payoffs. Reports arguments and strategies of the

prosecution and the defence. Concludes with the opinion of the magistrate and the ultimate disposition of the case.

1112. Hardcastle, R. A. "The Examination of Films From Betting Shop Camera Recorders." 27 <u>Journal of The Forensic Science Society</u> (U.K.) 29-46. (February 1987).

1113. McIntire, Christopher. "RICO, Reporter's Privilege and The Boston College Point-Shaving Scandal." 5 <u>Loyola Entertainment Law Journal</u> 269-281. (1985).
Discusses the conspiracy to limit the scoring margin of Boston College's basketball team to increase gambling profits. Analyzes <u>U.S. v. Burke</u> which uncovered the RICO violations and protected a reporter's rights to not reveal his sources.

1114. Samuels, Howard J. "Legalization of Gambling On Sports Events." 18 <u>New York Law Forum</u> 897-914. (Spring 1973).
Presents background of U.S. legalized gambling. Reviews the innovative and pioneering New York State legalized gambling and results of the recent past. Illustrates how horse racing operates well within legal wagering and that it has taken a major part of the betting volume from illegal bookmakers. Examines betting in other sports and suggests that successful legalization of gambling can be duplicated there as well.

Lawful Sport

1115. Slusher, Howard S. "Sport: A Philosophical Perspective." 38 <u>Law and Contemporary Problems</u> 129-140. (Winter-Spring 1973).
Explains the function of the rules of sport contrasting those of basketball with those of football. Explores the institutional control of athletics, the reason for sport, and a right to expression in sport.

1116. Umana Soto, Manuel Francisco. "Contrato de Trabajo Deportivo" (in Spanish). <u>Revista de Ciencias Juridicas</u> (Costa Rica), No. 17, 201-225. (June 1971).
Examines the extent of the relationship between the law and the commerce of sports.

Municipal Play

1117. Laskowski, Gregory E. "An Improved Technique For The Visualization of Footprint Impressions In The Insoles of Athletes Shoes." 32 <u>Journal of Forensic Sciences</u> 1075-1078. (July 1978).

Analyzes advances in the identification of footprint/footwear castings.

1118.   Lockhart, Kim. "No Man An Island, In Premier's Home Riding." 10 Canadian Lawyer (Canada) 2(2). (December 1986).

Reviews the case in British Columbia involving Eddy Haymour's legal problems over his attempts to establish an amusement park.

1119.   "Right of Municipality To Amuse It's Citizens As A Function of Government." 27 Harvard Law Review 162-164. (December 1913).

Note on State ex rel. Toledo v. Lynch, 102 N.E. 670 (Ohio) where Supreme Court of Ohio denied the city of Toledo the right to establish a municipal picture show at public expense. Ponders the evolving purposes of government. Concludes that it is becoming increasingly difficult to determine strictly what the functions of government are but for an amusement to even being to seem governmental, the possibility of education, health and/or morality must be a function of the amusement.

1120.   Swift, Ray L. "Municipal Promotion of Play." 19 Case and Comment 184-188. (August 1912).

Explains necessity for play space and the importance of small parks in cities. Argues for equipping playgrounds for children to provide year-round safe places for play. Points out successful recreational programs of some cities (Philadelphia; Rochester, New York; Cincinnati, Ohio; St. Paul; Oakland, California; Chicago). Reports that his search for lawsuits revealed a dearth of cases involving the liability of cities for personal injuries growing out of playground activities.

Safety at Sports

1121.   Mikell, Melanie Floy. "Municipality Has Duty To Maintain Parks In Reasonably Safe Condition For Public Use." 15 Stetson Law Review 1007-1008. (Summer 1986).

Brief discussion of City of Miami v. Ameller, 472 So.2d 728 (Fla. 1985) where it was decided that a municipality has a duty to maintain its parks in a reasonably safe condition for public use.

1122.   "Safety At Sports." 130 Solicitor's Journal (U.K.) 114. (February 14, 1986).

Sports As A Nuisance

1123.   "When Equity Will Enjoin A Sport As A Private Nuisance."
            21 Yale Law Journal 414-417. (March 1912).
                Explores the power of equity courts to enjoin a sport as a
            private nuisance. Discusses aspects of sport and/or sporting
            events which may be part of the normal course, but when
            associated with activities which would offend public
            sensibilities or irreparably interfere with and contribute to the
            business loss of customers and/or profit, then the sport in
            question may be enjoined.

Stadia

1124.   Alfton, Robert J. and Jallo, Jerome R.   "Efforts To Prevent
            Minneapolis Sports Stadium By Charter Amendment
            Defeated." 23 Municipal Attorney 11-13. (July-August 1982).
                Brief discussion of Davies, et al. v. City of Minneapolis, et
            al. 316 N.W.2d 498 (1982) where a Minnesota Supreme Court
            decided that the Minneapolis City Council acted properly in
            not submitting an amendment to the city charter proposed by a
            citizens' petition to the voters.

1125.   Anderson, Cerisse.   "City Sale of Coliseum Passes Court Test:
            Judge Rules Against Realty Partnership's Challenge To Upset
            Award Given To A Low Bidder." 199 New York Law Journal 1.
            (June 22, 1988).

1126.   Brooks, David. "Bond Debt Size A Ballot Issue: Major Leagues
            For 'Triple A' State?" 120 New Jersey Law Journal 1. (October
            29, 1987).

1127.   Postel, Theodore. "Rosemont Horizon: Tort Immunity Act."
            135 Chicago Daily Law Bulletin 1. (July 25, 1989).

1128.   "Sweet-and-Sour Technology."   97 The Los Angeles Daily
            Journal 4. (January 19, 1984).

Unlawful Sports

1129.   Sibley, N. W. "Lawful and Unlawful Sports; and The Legality
            of A Sparring Match." 37 The Law Magazine and Review 137-
            161. (February 1912).
                Traces British common law of sport and criminal
            responsibility for death or injury occurring in the exercise of
            games or pastimes. Examines cases from 1643 and the views of
            legal writers including Dalton, Sir Michael Foster, Lord Hale,

and Sir James Stephen. Compares these analyses and judicial decisions. Comments on some recent cases and the issue of criminal responsibility of spectators of boxing or prize-fighting matches.

30

SPORTS AND THE LAW

General

1130.   Berry, Robert C. and Wong, Glenn M. Law and Business of
          The Sports Industries: Volume I: Professional Sports Leagues.
          Dover, MA: Auburn House Publishing Company, 1986.
              Provides discussions on development of professional
          sports, the legal structure of professional sports, matters
          representing the player, professional sports unions, and
          management perspectives on sports leagues and clubs.
          Provides statistics, references and citations.

1131.   Berry, Robert C. and Wong, Glenn M. Law and Business of
          The Sports Industries: Volume II: Common Issues In
          Amateur and Professional Sports. Dover, MA: Auburn House
          Publishing Company, 1986.
              Provides continued comprehensive examination of
          amateur athletic associations, the amateur athlete, sex
          discrimination in athletics, tort liability, criminal law and
          sports, and sports and the media.   Provides extensive
          discussion on applicable casework.

1132.   Berti, Giorgio. "Premesse e Ipotesi Sui Compiti Della Rigione
          Nel Servizio Sociale Dello Sport" (in Italian).   24 Rivista
          Trimestrale di Diritto Pubblico (Italy) 600-624. (1974).
              Reviews a number of premises and hypotheses regarding
          the role of local governments in relation to the social service of
          sports.

1133.   Cirell, Stephen and Bennett, John.   "Unsporting Activities
          Under The LGA 1988."   133 Solicitor's Journal 1210-1212.
          (September 29, 1989).

Discusses the problems which evolved from the government's attempt to privatize local services and the difficulties local authorities face in the sport and leisure field.

1134.   Clark, William D.   "1985 California Supreme Court and Courts of Appeal Survey: Entertainment Law."   8 Whittier Law Review 157-186. (Winter 1986).

Brief review of sports related cases before California Courts in 1985. Specifically examines Hulsey v. Elsinore Parachute Center and Noble v. Los Angeles Dodgers.

1135.   Consolo, Guiseppe. "Per Una Sociologia Del Diritto Sportivo: Premesse Giuridiche" (in Italian). 53 Rivista Internazionale di Filosofia del Diritto (Italy) 3-30. (January-March 1976).

In-depth study pertaining to the sociology of sport law.

1136.   Jay, C. B. and Grubb, M. J. "Defects In Polyurethane-Soled Athletic Shoes-Their Importance To The Shoeprint Examiner." 25 Journal of The Forensic Science Society 233-238. (May-June 1985).

Reviews voids in shoeprints and the care that must be taken in examination and association.

1137.   Joyal-Poupart, R. "Les sports et le droit: Tour d'horizon et commentaires" (in French). 23 Cahiers (Laval) (Canada) 479-485. (1982).

Brief overview discussing sports and the law. Discusses the dilemma between what may be desired and what can be achieved. Reviews the relationship between sports and penal responsibility, the Canadian criminal code, and the role of the jurist.

1138.   Koppett, Leonard. "Sports and The Law: An Overview." 18 New York Law Forum 815-839. (Spring 1973).

Discusses the current situation of sports and the law, the origins of the law explosion and three central issues: The player control policies (reserve clauses, one-year options and drafting arrangements), television policy and the movement of franchises from city to city. Presents ramifications of these issues and philosophical suggestions about the future.

1139.   Turnbull, J. A. "The Bradford Stadium Fire." 56 Medico-Legal Journal (U.K.) 54-73. (Spring 1988).

Review of the circumstances pertaining to the fire.

1140.   Umana Soto, Manuel Francisco.   "Contrato de Trabajo Deportivo" (in Spanish). Revista de Ciencias Juridicas (Costa Rica), No. 17, 201-225. (June 1971).

Examines the extent of the relationship between the law and the commerce of sports.

Bibliographies

1141.   Entertainment   and   Sports   Law   Bibliography: A Comprehensive Bibliography of Law-Related Materials on Sports, Motion Pictures, Music and The Right of Publicity. Chicago: American Bar Association, 1986.

Bibliography which includes entries on music and the law, sports and the law, theatrical motion pictures and the law, and the right of publicity.

1142.   Houdek, Frank G.   "Sports and The Law: A Comprehensive Bibliography of Law-Related Materials, Five Year Supplement (1979-1984)."   6 Comm/Ent Law Journal 921-949. (Summer 1984).

Includes sections on books, periodicals, Practising Law Institute   materials,   government   publications,   ALR Annotations, law review symposia, and law review articles. Law review articles are subdivided into amateur athletics, antitrust, broadcasting and sports, discrimination in athletics, labor relations, taxation, violence and injury in sports, agents and   attorneys,   sports   franchise   movements,   and miscellaneous.

1143.   "Legal Aspects of Sports." 24 Record 306-312. (May 1969).

Brief bibliography on the legal aspects of sports. Entries listed by author, subject and governmental agency. Includes references to hearings of the U.S. Congress.

Criminal Law

1144.   Padrutt, Willy.   "Strafrechtliche Aspekte Des Skilaufs und Des Lawinenunfalles In Schweizerischer Sicht." 63 Schweizerische Juristen-Zeitung, Revue Suisse de Jurisprudence (Switzerland) 333. (November 1967).

Modern sports technology has created not only new types of accidents and criminals but also uncharted areas of law and criminal justice. An influx of winter sports tourists gives rise to questions of jurisdiction and law-abiding conduct.

Defamation

1145.   Teague, Bernard. "Defamation Is Not Always Cricket." 59 Law Institute Journal (Australia) 541-544. (June 1985).

Focuses on case involving cricket player who alleged he was defamed by an article which speculated that the rules of World Series Cricket could influence the incentive to win and that it would be financially undesirable to win too soon. Presents overview of recent cricket legal history and the law of defamation in the U.S. Contains six steps for advising a sports figure who alleges to be defamed.

1146.   Wise, Richard M. "The Athlete As A Public Figure In Light of Gertz v. Robert Welch, Inc., or Torts In Sports: The Role of The Courts." 6 Comm/Ent Law Journal 325-368. (Winter 1984).

Presents history of defamation law and development of the public figure doctrine and how they apply to the athlete. Examines the defamed athlete pre- and post-Gertz perspectives. Examines athletes as limited and general public figures.

First Amendment and Sports Events

1147.   Ashman, Allan. "First Amendment...No Ban On Rugby." 67 American Bar Association Journal 1672(2). (December 1981).

Briefly discusses the first amendment considerations put forth in the U.S. District Court's ruling which did not ban a rugby match against a South African team.

1148.   Paterson, Nancy H. "Constitutional Law-Freedom of Speech-Since The Meadowlands Is Not A Public Forum, The Prohibition of All Literature Distribution and Fund Solicitation By Outside Organizations Does Not Violate The First Amendment." 28 Villanova Law Review 741-764. (March 1983).

Discussion of the case of International Society for Krishna Consciousness, Inc. v. New Jersey Sports & Exposition Authority (1982) where the U.S. District Court for the District of New Jersey ruled that defendant's ban on literature distribution and fund soliciting activities at the Meadowlands Sports Complex was not in violation of plaintiff's first amendment rights. Said determination was based on the fact that the complex was not a public forum.

1149.   Schachter, Charles I. "Selfridge v. Carey: The First Amendment's Applicability To Sporting Events." 46 Albany Law Review 937-979. (Spring 1982).

Examines question of whether sport is protected by the first amendment. Discusses rugby match in question as a political event, the issue of the foreign propaganda model and the hostile audience doctrine. Analyzes sport as a first amendment expression and its judicial and theoretical treatments.

Judicial Review

1150.   Narol, Melvin S. "Courts May Soon Be Asked To Be Monday-
             Morning Quarterbacks." 3 Entertainment and Sports Lawyer
             11-13. (Summer 1984).
             Discussion of the phenomenon and reasons for the
             increasing number of lawsuits involving the decisions of
             officials in athletic contests.

1151.   Steiner, Udo.   "Staat, Sport und Verfassung."   36 Die
             Offentliche Verwaltung (West Germany) 173-180. (March 1983).
             Sports and their relation to the state is not defined in the
             constitution and due to this, there exist many legal questions
             and problems between these three entities.

1152.   Winer, Kimberly G.   "Maintaining The Home Field
             Advantage: Rose v. Federal Court. 10 Loyola Entertainment
             Law Journal 695-713. (1990).
             Analysis of the facts and opinion of district court in Peter A.
             Rose v. A. Bartlett Giamatti. Argues that the court erred.

Judicial Review, Sports Courts

1153.   Beloff, Michael J. "Pitch, Pool, Rink, ... Court? Judicial Review
             In The Sporting World." 1989 Public Law (U.K.) 95-110.
             (Spring 1989).
             Discusses judicial review of actions of sports-governing
             bodies particularly disciplinary actions. Reviews problems and
             issues which arise as the result of judicial review.

1154.   Burmeister, Joachim.   "Sportverbandswesen Und
             Verfassungsrecht." 31 Die Offentliche Verwaltung (West
             Germany) 1-11. (January 1978).
             The area of organized sports operations is seen as being far
             outside the borders of legal jurisdiction.   Many sporting
             associations have their own laws (rules) and are rather
             autonomous; some even deny their members of set
             "constitutional" rights. This current condition calls for an
             immediate reorganization by the state's lawmakers.

1155.   Errera, Roger. "Judicial Review of Rules Made By Sporting
             Bodies-Treatment of Aliens of Basketball Players Naturalised
             For Less Than Three Years Ruled Unlawful." Public Law
             (U.K.) 497(2). (Autumn 1989).
             Judicial review includes scrutiny of sporting bodies
             involvement in disciplinary actions. Focuses on France and
             attempts by sporting federations to control and limit the

number of foreign basketball players through such rules was in conflict with article 80 of the Nationality Code.

1156.   Finkelstein, Jared Tobin. "In RE Brett: The Stickey Problem of Statutory Construction." 52 Fordham Law Review 430-440. (December 1983).
          Examines the rules, the issue of interpretation and question of spirit v. letter of law with regard to decision in George Brett pine tar dispute. Concludes decision followed rules of statutory interpretation.

1157.   Triffterer, Otto. "Vermogensdelikte Im Bundesligaskandal." 28 Neue Juristische Wochenschrift (West Germany) 612-617. (April 1975).
          Examines penalties relating to the German football league scandal during the 1970-71 season. Said scandal involved the awarding of compensation.

Labor Laws

1158.   Baron, Ronald L. "Sports Law: The Attorney's Role Expands." 49 Texas Bar Journal 832-834. (September 1986).
          Covers applications of antitrust, contract, labor and tort law in relation to sports. Highlights landmark cases and decisions in sports law. Points out trends in court decisions involving negligence and liability theory.

1159.   Buchner, Herbert. "Rechtsstellung Der Lizenzspieler."   29 Neue Juristische Wochenschrift (West Germany) 2242-2246. (December 1976).
          Discusses the legal positions of professional soccer players in relation to existing labor laws.

1160.   Goldman, Lee. "The Labor Exemption To The Antitrust Laws As Applied To Employers' Market Restraints In Sports and Non-Sports Markets." 1989 Utah Law Review 617- 686. (1989).
          Discusses the Sherman Act, the statutory labor exemption, non-statutory labor exemption and collective bargaining. Reviews the relationship between the antitrust laws and employers' labor market restraint and offers a theory on how to deal with such restraints.

1161.   Weistart, John C. "Judicial Review of Labor Agreements: Lessons From The Sports Industry." 44 Law and Contemporary Problems 109-146. (Autumn 1981).
          Surveys judicial review of labor agreements in professional sports. Examines labor exemption and issues in judicial

oversight of collective bargaining process.   Cites significant casework and their implications.

Law and Sports

1162.   Appenzeller, Herb and Appenzeller, Thomas. Sports and The Courts. Charlottesville, VA: The Michie Company, 1980.
Discusses case work on sports and sports related issues. Examines injuries to athletes, the handicapped athlete, and discrimination, and the athlete. Reviews cases involving the administrator, coach, official, spectator, team physician, athletic trainer, sports facilities, sports equipment and other athlete-related cases. Cites references to professional sports.

1163.   de Bianchetti, A. "El Contrato Deportivo" (in Spanish). 100 La Ley, Revista Juridica Argentina (Argentina) 895-904. (November 15, 1960).
General review on sports contracts and the growth of a specific legal area devoted to sports law.

1164.   Filho, A. Melo. "Direito desportivo: campo de atuacao e autonomia" (in Portuguese). 77 Revista Forense (Brazil) 303-309. (October-December 1981).
Focuses on sports law, its scope and self-sufficiency. Discusses the need for legal specialization in the area of sports.

1165.   Grayson, Edward. Sport and The Law. London: Butterworths, 1988.
Examines relationship of sport, the law and society. Speaks to amateur and professional players, officials, lawyers and administrators.   Discusses role of parents and clubs, international athletics, women, and sports medicine's relationship to law.

1166.   Hutchinson, Allan C. and Jones, Melinda. "Wheeler-Dealing: An Essay On Law, Politics, and Speech." 15 Journal of Law and Society (U.K.) 263-278. (Autumn 1988).
Examines the facts and judgment in Wheel and Others v. Leicester City Council regarding the Council's ban against the Leicester Rugby Football Club from using recreation grounds. Ban was the result of club's tour to South Africa.

1167.   "On The Law Relating To Sports." 9 Legal Observer (London) 65-68. (1834).
Discusses wagering and winning on activities associated with gaming, games of chance and sports. Includes court decisions on the nuances of the term "sport,." the nature of the winning purses and the extent to which wagering is legal or

illegal. Speaks to the legality of a game and whether a bet made on it was recoverable.

1168.   Plouvin, J.-Y. "Organisation et le developpement du sport et la loi du 29 Octobre 1975" (in French). 32 Actualite Juridique (ser. Droit Administratif) (France) 60-74. (February 1976).

Discusses the relationship between sports and the law of 29 October 1975. Examines the interrelationship between sports and culture. Reviews the law which grants each student the right to participate in athletics without charge. Discusses the organization of sports and the nature and purpose of the organization. Reviews the power of the government to disband athletic organizations which operate counter to the purpose of sports and the nation. Differentiates professional and nonprofessional sports. Overviews the development of the practice of sports. Includes support provided to "high quality" athletes. Concludes by addressing the issues of commercialization and state control of sports.

1169.   Prusak, J. "Vztah Medzi Sportovym Pravidlom a Pravidlom Socialistickeho Spoluzitia a Kriticke Stanovisko k Tzv. Sportovemu Pravu" (in Slovak).   67 Pravny Obzor (Czechoslovakia) 864-877. (November 1984).

A critique of sports law as regards its relationship between the rules of the game and the rule of socialist common life. States immunity that often is applied to sportsmen is in conflict with the sovereignty of the state. Argues that sportsmen who injure a fellow participant should not be free from liability if they are playing by the rules of the game, that they should be judged in terms of whether the law was broken and whether any rules of the game were broken.

1170.   Scanlan, John A., Jr. and Cleveland, Granville E. "The Past As Prelude: The Early Origins of Modern American Sports Law." 8 Ohio Northern Law Review 433-452. (1981).

Discusses origin of sports and development during Greek and Roman times. Elaborates on rules and law pertaining to athletes. Examines impact of Rome on European concept of sport. Traces attitudes toward sport over U.S. Concludes with overview of sport in modern America. Topics included are discrimination, tort liability and sport as a business.

1171.   Stern, Ralph D. "Legal Issues In Extracurricular Education." 9 NOLPE School Law Journal 142-163. (Winter 1981).

Legal issues examined are student liability, teacher obligation, eligibility, financing, aspects of discrimination and handicapped students.

1172.   Weistart, John C. and Lowell, Cym H. The Law of Sports. New York: The Bobbs-Merrill Company, Inc., 1979.

Comprehensive and in-depth examination of sports law. Covers regulation of Amateur athletics, public regulation of sports activities, legal relationships in professional sports, enforcement of professional sports contracts, antitrust aspects of sports activities, collective bargaining and professional sports, federal income taxation of sports activities, and liability for injuries in sports activities. Includes table of cases.

Litigation

1173.   Appenzeller, Herb. "Is The Law Ruining Sports?" 7 Update 42-45. (Fall 1983).

Argues that litigation is the only way for controlling and correcting the abuses found in sports.

1174.   Caporale, Robert L. "Litigation and Sports." 31 Boston Bar Journal 23(5). (July-August 1987).

Brief overview of the relationship between sports, litigation and arbitration.

1175.   Kotlowski, Bill. "PLS Fights Torts In Sports-Hardball Style." 30 For The Defense S1(3). (May 1988).

Reviews activities of PLS (Product Liability Sports) organization to protect the area of sports from litigation which threatens to damage it.

1176.   Silas, Faye A. "Tough To Tackle: Student Sports Suits Rising." 70 American Bar Association Journal 32-33. (May 1984).

Brief discussion on the rise of sports related lawsuits in interscholastic athletics.

Sports and Legal Controls

1177.   Alfton, Robert J. and Jallo, Jerome R. "Efforts To Prevent Minneapolis Sports Stadium By Charter Amendment Defeated." 23 Municipal Attorney 11-13. (July-August 1982).

Brief discussion of Davies, et al v. City of Minneapolis, et al 316 N.W.2d 198 (1982) where a Minnesota Supreme Court decided that the Minneapolis City Council acted properly in not submitting to the voters an amendment to the city charter proposed by a citizens' petition.

1178.   Ashman, Allan. "Courts...Saturday Afternoon Fever." 68 American Bar Association Journal 484-485. (April 1982).

Brief discussion of <u>Georgia High School Association v.</u> <u>Waddell</u> where the Supreme Court of Georgia rules that courts do not have the authority to review the referee's decisions in a football game.

1179.   de Ridder, E.   "Zelfkant Van de Sport" (in Dutch).   28 <u>Rechtskundig Weekblad</u> (Belgium) 1529-1554. (April 1965).
Discusses sports and sports law, and how expression of the phenomena needs to be regulated.

1180.   Gros, Manuel and Verkindt, P.-Y.   "L'autonomie du droit du sport" (in French).   41 <u>Actualite Juridique</u> (Ser. Droit Administratif) (France) 699-711. (1985).
Examines whether the issue of autonomy in sports is a matter of fact or fiction. Posits that due to the ever-expanding nature of sports and its involvement of the public, sport necessarily becomes less autonomous. Examines the judicial involvement in sports.

1181.   Hilf, Meinhard. "Die Freizugigkeit Des Berufsfussballspielers Innerhalb der Europaischen Gemeinschaft."   37 <u>Neue Juristische Wochenschrift</u> (West Germany) 517-523. (1984).
Discusses the freedom of movement of professional soccer players within the European community.

1182.   Kijowski, A.   "Legal Status of An Employee Engaged In Sporting Activities" (in Polish). 38 <u>Nowe Prawo</u> (Poland) 63-70. (September-October 1982).
Examines the legal status of a worker who is also an athlete. Explore the legal status of both those who serve in athletic support positions and those who are politically and/or economically associated with the athlete.

1183.   Lapeyre, Charles. "Les collectivites locales et le sport apres les lois de decentralisation" (In French).   103 <u>Revue du Droit Public et de la Science Politique en France et a l'Etranger</u> (France) 1603-1639. (1987).
Discusses the effects of the laws of decentralization on sports at the local level in France.

1184.   Lener, A., et al. "Legge Per Lo Sport?" (in Italian). 104 <u>Foro Italiano</u> (Italy) 297-314. (November 1981).
Raises the question of whether there is a need to regulate sports.

1185.   Nelson, Stephen. "Introduction: Bringing Sports Under Legal Control." 10 <u>Connecticut Law Review</u> 251-258. (Winter 1978).
Brief overview of the relationship of sports to the American legal system and other industries. Calls for the

regulation of sports in a manner common-and similar- to other commercial industries and enterprises.

1186.   Tomandl, T. and Schrammel, W.   "Rechtsstellung von Vertrages-und Lizenzfussballern."   94 Juristische Blatter (Austria) 289. (June 1972).
Discusses the situation of contracts and soccer licenses.

1187.   Veth, N. J. P. Giltay.   "Uitsluiting Van Buitenlandse Voetballers: Mogelijk Binnen de EEG?"   (in Dutch).   53 Nederlands Juristenblad (Netherlands) 504-513. (July 1978).
Discusses the possibility of excluding foreign soccer players, through the installation of regulations in the European Economic Community, and the possible contradictions with the Treaty of Rome.

1188.   Warburton, Jean.   "Sporting Decisions: Should The Courts Participate?"   131 Solicitor's Journal (U.K.) 368-369. (June 26, 1987).
Discusses involvement of courts in matters of sport. Proceeds from perspective of becoming involved in the internal affairs of a private sporting body.   Examines English law, the New Zealand approach, and use of interim injunctions.

Sunday Laws

1189.   "Baseball May Be Played On Sunday-Is Not "Labor.""   47 American Law Review 606-607. (July 1913).
Brief note referring to a New Mexico Supreme Count decision, Territory v. Davenport 124 P. 794, (decided that baseball was not in violation of the Sunday law and baseball could be legally played on Sunday).   Cites opinions from Supreme Courts of Kansas and Missouri which held that baseball was not held or classified as a game under the statutes of those states.   Analyzes Webster's definition of labor to demonstrate that playing baseball did not fall under the statutory prohibition of performing "labor" on Sunday.

1190.   Bronaugh, Minor. "Sunday Laws and Golf." 23 Law Notes 128-131. (October 1919).
Traces Sunday legislation from 321 to the first Sunday Law enacted in Virginia in 1617. Discusses further development of U.S. and British law to founding the validity of the so-called Sunday Laws on the valid exercise of the police power of the state rather than on any religious ground.   Discusses police power and its domain and argues it is difficult to see how a

game of golf comes within the scope of any reason for the state to be able to prohibit it.

1191.   Crafts, Reverend Wilbur F. "Why Are Sunday Amusements Prohibited?" 22 Case and Comment 553-557. (December 1915).
Quotes from speeches made in support of Sunday closing at national exhibitions to illustrate the acceptable and influential arguments in Congress concerning the proposed Sunday opening of the Columbian Fair in 1892.   Lists five governmental reasons for forbidding Sunday amusements presented not as being sinful but as being harmful.   Reports some attempted exceptions, and State Supreme Court actions on Sunday baseball. Sums up that all should rest on the Rest Day.

1192.   "Sunday Games Association."   146 Law Times (London) 427-428. (April 12, 1919).
Brief discussion of the formation of a Sunday Games Association (to promote the playing of games on Sunday and to press for the repeal of laws which prohibit the playing of games on Sunday).   Gives an overview of the historical development of more strict Sunday observances.

1193.   "Sunday Golf." 48 Law Journal 518. (September 6, 1913).
Discusses the proceedings taken under the Lord's Day Observance Act of 1625 concerning the chairman and two members of the Newport Golf Club who answered summonses for playing golf at a local club on the Sabbath Day, August 1913. Presents case, the Act and the outcome.   Deals with the question of whether the Act is obsolete. States that any future prosecutions under the statute ought to be dismissed. Offers explanation as to what ground to dismiss upon.

1194.   Wilder, L. Arthur.   "Sunday Amusements."   22 Case and Comment 571-574. (December 1915).
Briefly traces origins of the Sunday laws from biblical times through 17 century England and 18th century New England to the present.   Analyzes current status of Sunday amusement laws as they apply to motion picture houses, other forms of amusement and Sunday baseball. Cites casework for Sunday amusements including Sunday baseball.

1195.   Wilkinson, W. E.   "The English Law As To Acts Done On Sunday." 22 Case and Comment 585-587. (December 1915).
Cites origin of the Sunday Observance Act (1677), and states that many of the provisions have indeed become a dead letter. Examines chief statutory provisions, exceptions to the act and the penalty for violating it plus citing casework. Also discusses the application of the Act to the making of contracts, status of

bills of exchange, paying of rent, serving of process and writs, arrests, taking of sureties, commitment to and discharge from prison, corporate meetings, the running of carriages and railroads, and other acts.

1196.   Williams, G. W. "Christian Sabbath and The Law." 53 American Law Review 379-400. (June 1919).

Discusses the Sabbath becoming commercialized, and a day of amusement. Reviews Sunday Laws from their origins in Rome, their enactment in England, and the foundation these laws provided for enactment of Sunday Laws in the United States. Argues that Christianity is interrelated with the history, politics and social institutions of the United States. Cites casework supporting the interrelatedness and support for Sunday Laws.

Tort Law

1197.   Baley, James A. and Matthews, David L. "Sports and Torts." 15 Trial Lawyers Quarterly 26-29. (Summer 1983).

Brief overview of the increasing number of lawsuits in the area of sports. Discusses Tinker v. Des Moines Community School District (1969), Goss v. Lopez (1975) and Wood v. Strickland. Reviews the reasons for the increase in tort actions.

1198.   Narol, Mel. "Sports Torts: A Standard of Care Issue." 134 New Jersey Lawyer 41-44. (May/June 1990).

Focuses on the increase in sports tort cases. Reviews reckless disregard, recent trends, standards in New Jersey and the role of profit/non-profit organizations.

1199.   Yasser, Raymond L. Torts and Sports. Westport, CT: Quorum Books, 1985.

Presents seven chapters: Tort Liability of One Participant To Another; The Spectator As Plaintiff; Medical Malpratice in Athletics; Products Liability For Defective Athletic Equipment; Defamation and Invasion of Privacy; Worker's Compensation Laws and The Athlete; and International Interference With Contractual Relations. Outlines relevant substantive law. Includes landmark cases (either edited extracts from major cases or survey of case law), an in-depth look at important case or topic, raises pertinent issues and ends each Chapter with bibliography. Lists cases alphabetically in a table of contents.

31

SPORTS BROADCASTING
AND PROGRAMMING

General

1200.   Bellamy, Robert V., Jr. "Impact of The Television Marketplace On The Structure of Major League Baseball." 32 <u>Journal of Broadcasting and Electronic Media</u> 73-87. (Winter 1988).

1201.   Chaves, Antonio. "Arena Rights: Legislative Problems Concerning Broadcasting of Large Shows." 23 <u>Copyright</u> (Switzerland) 310-319. (1987).

        Reviews the social, economic, political and legal importance of sports. Examines the concept and legal nature of "arena rights." Discusses ownership of the right, the object of protection, an athlete's and football referee's participation in the profits, limitations involved, terms of protection, the collection and distribution of royalties, radio broadcasting of sports events and the extent of "arena rights."

1202.   Cryan, Thomas Joseph; Crane, James S.; and Marcil, Michael J. "The Future of Sports Broadcasting: An International Questions." 10 <u>Seton Hall Legislative Journal</u> 213-273. (1987).

        Discusses legal issues and questions which must be addressed due to the expansion of the global television market. Categorizes the different forms of distribution of T.V. signals via satellite. Presents historical perspective of the growth of the sports broadcasting market and barriers to the international marketplace. Offers solutions.

1203.   Garrett, Robert Alan and Hochberg, Philip R. "Sports Broadcasting and the Law." 59 <u>Indiana Law Journal</u> 155-193. (1983/1984).

Reviews multifaceted relationship between sports and television. Explores the establishment, identifying the beneficiaries and defining the scope of property right in sports. Considers the broadcasters, players and inter-club claims to the property right. Discusses royalty payments, FCC cable rules, superstations, piracy, home-taping, siphoning, pooling and blackouts.

1204.   Garubo, Philip A., Jr. "The Last Legal Monopoly: The NFL and Its Television Contracts." 4 Entertainment and Sports Law Journal 357-383. (Fall 1987).

Provides an historical background of the relationship between the NFL and television. Examines said relationship in light of the antitrust laws. Reviews antitrust case law and USFL v. NFL.

1205.   Gonzales, Ralph. "The Deregulation of Televised College Football." 2 Entertainment and Sports Law Journal 79-88. (Fall 1984).

Review of the effects of National Collegiate Athletic Association v. Board of Regents on the televising of college football.

1206.   Gregory, Byron L. and Busey, J. Craig. "Alternative Broadcasting Arrangements After NCAA." 61 Indiana Law Journal 65-84. (Winter 1985).

Analyzes Supreme Court decision over the disputed television plan. Offers alternative plans and outlines suggested guidelines.

1207.   Hochberg, Philip R. "Congress Tackles Sports and Broadcasting." 3 Western State University Law Review 223-249. (Spring 1976).

Focuses on two area of sports legislation particularly significant to professional sports and the public sector: restriction of home games blackouts and legislative activity concerning copyright legislation. Examines bills on which action was not taken but where the possibility remains that similar legislation may soon be enacted.

1208.   Hochberg, Philip R. "Congress Kicks A Field Goal: The Legislative Attack In The 93rd Congress On Sports Broadcasting Practices." 27 Federal Communications Bar Journal 27-79. (1974).

Reviews Congress with regard to broadcasting and sports. Analyzes the legislation introduced in the 93rd Congress: the Senate and House broadcasting bills, committee action and floor consideration of those bills.

1209.   Hochberg, Philip R. "Second and Goal To Go: The Legislative Attack In The Ninety-Second Congress On Sports Broadcasting Practices." 26 Federal Communications Bar Journal 118-182. (1973).

     Extensive examination of the Congressional attack on sports broadcasting practices. Provides brief background discussion on the matter. Analyzes legislation introduced in the House and Senate of the 92nd Congress.

1210.   Hochberg, Philip R. "Second and Goal To Go: The Legislative Attack In The Ninety-Second Congress On Sports Broadcasting Practices." 18 New York Law Forum 841-896. (Spring 1973).

     Analyzes the legislation introduced in the 92nd Congress which would have had some impact on sports broadcasting. Includes the Nixon administration's assault on sports broadcasting practices.

1211.   Ponsoldt, James. "The Unreasonableness of Coerced Cooperation: A Comment Upon The NCAA Decision's Rejection of The Chicago School." 31 Antitrust Bulletin 1003-1044. (Winter 1986).

     Explores television contract case which determined the NCAA had violated section 1 of Sherman Antitrust Act. Analyzes trial, appellate and Supreme Court holdings. Concentrates on relevant market, efficiency and market power arguments and determinations.

1212.   Reid, Cecelia. "First Right of Refusal Provision." 4 Loyola Entertainment Law Journal 103-108. (1984).

     Focuses on CBS v. French Tennis Federation and the issue of first right of refusal and exclusive negotiations on the broadcasting of a sports event.

1213.   Rudel, Michael I. "NBC Coverage of Olympics Showed How TV Industry Works." 200 New York Law Journal 3. (October 28, 1988).

Blackouts

1214.   Ching, Cori Jan. "A Critique of The National Football League's Blackout Exemption From The Antitrust Laws." 8 Journal of Legislation 104-120. (Winter 1981).

     Analysis of the nature and problems of and related to section 1292 regarding the blackouts of professional football games. Examines United States v. N.F.L. I and United States v. N.F.L. II Argues that the N.F.L. has misinterpreted section 1291. Provides an economic perspective on the continuation of blackouts.

1215.   DuBoff, Leonard D. "Picking Up Blacked-Out Sports Events
             Via Satellite Dish Antenna: First Down and Goal To Go." 11
             Columbia-VLA Journal of Law and the Arts 359-362. (Spring
             1987).
                 Brief introduction to a series of articles which address the
             scope of the Eighth Circuit Appellate Court's decision which
             enjoined bar owners from broadcasting blacked-out NFL
             games.

1216.   Griener, Paul. "NFL's Home Game Black-out Exemption." 4
             Loyola Entertainment Law Journal 209-213. (1984).
                 Surveys WTWV v. National Football League and the home
             game blackout exemption.

1217.   Peterson, Robert S. "'Blackouts' and The Public Interest: An
             Equitable Proposal." 4 Journal of Contemporary Law 143-168.
             (Spring 1978).
                 Explores issues of whether a "blackout" is in violation of
             the antitrust laws, whether a "blackout" ends up not being in
             the public interest, and thus is in violation of the
             Communications Act.   Analyzes jurisdiction, primary
             jurisdiction, standing and cause of action. Provides a proposal
             for an equitable solution to the issue of "blackouts."

1218.   Rice, David M.   "Calling Offensive Signals Against
             Unauthorized Showing of Blacked-Out Football Games: Can
             The Communications Act Carry The Ball?" 11 Columbia-VLA
             Journal of Law and the Arts 413-440. (Spring 1987).
                 Shows that section 705(a) of the 1934 Communications Act
             is a possible legal solution to the problem of unauthorized
             satellite signal piracy. Discusses the NFL blackout policy and
             historical perspective of acts and legislation to curtail improper
             satellite receptions.

1219.   Roberts, Gary R.   "Pirating Satellite Signals of Blacked-Out
             Sports Events: A Historical and Policy Perspective."   11
             Columbia-VLA Journal of Law and the Arts 363-386. (Spring
             1987).
                 Traces the history of NFL policy regarding blacked-out
             games of the major networks and cable television
             transmissions. Emphasizes consistency of federal position that
             sports leagues may restrict telecasts of their games which
             otherwise might negatively affect ticket sales and attendance.

1220.   Shooshan, H. M., III.   "Confrontation With Congress:
             Professional Sports and The Television Antiblackout Law." 25
             Syracuse Law Review 713-745. (Summer 1974).

Comprehensive review of Congressional antiblackout legislation (Public Law 93-107). Explores the legal background, legislative background and presents an overview of the antiblackout issue as it began to receive significantly greater amounts of attention. Chronicles the steps and actions of the Senate and the House up to the passage of Public Law 93-107.

1221.   Sobel, Lionel S. "Television Sports Blackouts: Private Rights vs. Public Policy." 48 Los Angeles Bar Bulletin 169+. (March 1973).

Reviews the private rights of professional sports leagues, public policy issues, federal antitrust law and the public ownership or other support of sports stadia.

1222.   Torrens, Thomas M. "Professional Football Telecasts and The Blackout Privilege." 57 Cornell Law Review 297-312. (January 1972).

Reviews the origin and current status of the blackout privilege in professional football in terms of its legislative history and its relationship with the public. Discusses the reform of the blackout exemption and the repeal of the blackout privilege.

1223.   Waldman, Ronald L. "Antitrust Law - Signal Penetration Or Station Location: The Scope of The National Football League's Television Blackout Antitrust Exemption - WTWV v. National Football League." 6 Western New England Law Review 877-895. (1984).

Provides background and analysis of the case and examination of the signal-penetration rule and the station-location rules and their relation to antitrust exemption.

Broadcast Rights

1224.   Clements, Robert S. "Constitutional Law-Sale of Radio and Television Broadcast Rights Makes Modern Organized Baseball Interstate Commerce In The Constitutional Sense." 37 Georgetown Law Journal 618-621. (May 1949).

Discusses aspects of Gardella. v. Chandler to it being remanded for trial. Reviews Sherman and Clayton Anti-trust Acts and appropriate casework. Explores Congressional intent and extent to regulate interstate commerce. Points out controlling influence of Federal Baseball Club v. National League in a number of decisions. Discusses casework relating to the question of the reserve clause. Briefly explore the relationship between interstate commerce and play-by-play in radio and television.

1225.   Goldberg, Victor P. "Television and The Quest For Gold: The Unofficial Paper of The 1984 Olympics." 79 <u>Northwestern University Law Review</u> 1172-1182. (December-February 1984).

Explores the exclusivity of the television rights to the 1984 Olympics. Discusses revenue in relation to audience size, revenues per viewer and cost per viewer.

1226.   Thompson, Larry R. and Young, J. Timothy. "Taxing The Sale of Broadcast Rights To College Athletics-An Unrelated Trade or Business." 8 <u>Journal of College and University Law</u> 33-345. (1981/1982).

Commentary on Internal Revenue rulings 80-295 and 80-296 and the impact they have on a university's sale of broadcast rights. Briefly reviews the statutory background of unrelated trade or business income.

Cable

1227.   Hochberg, Philip R. "The Four Horsemen Ride Again: Cable Communications and Collegiate Athletics." 5 <u>Journal of College and University Law</u> 43-54. (Fall 1977).

Overview of cable communications and the communications revolution of collegiate athletics. Discusses the impact and ramifications of pay-cable, local origination, copyright payments and protections, and distant signals.

1228.   Hochberg, Philip and Horowitz, Ira. "Broadcasting and CATV: The Beauty and The Bane of Major College Football." 38 <u>Law and Contemporary Problems</u> 112-128. (Winter-Spring 1973).

Discusses existing broadcast arrangements for major college football, historical forces which shaped the current pattern of this programming, and the economic implications of the broadcasting those games. Examines the potential impact of cable television (CATV) on major football telecasting and existing broadcasting arrangements which has become a concern to broadcasters, the National Collegiate Athletic Association, and the colleges involved.

1229.   Horowitz, Ira. "Implications of Home Box Office For Sports Broadcasts." 23 <u>Antitrust Bulletin</u> 743-768. (Winter 1978).

Discusses the regulation of pay TV sports. Briefly reviews <u>Home Box Office, Inc. et al. v. F.C.C.</u>, 567 F.2d 9. Explore economic and legal considerations of shifting some sports events from conventional television to pay television.

1230.   Rosen, James. "Super Stations-Local or National Broadcasters." 4 <u>Loyola Entertainment Law Journal</u> 129-139. (1984).

Reviews problems surrounding superstations. Specifically discusses <u>American Broadcasting Co. v. Atlanta National League Baseball Club, Inc.</u> and the difference between being a telecaster and a cablecaster.

1231. Ross, Stephen F. "An Antitrust Analysis of Sports League Contracts with Cable Networks." 39 <u>Emory Law Journal</u> 463-497. (Spring 1990).

Reviews antitrust law and its application to cable contracts, scrutiny under the rule of reason and objections to such scrutiny.

1232. Shooshan, Harry M. "Blessed By A Bandage of Cold Cash: Whatever The Legal Problems, The Marriage of Sports and Cable TV." 7 <u>Update</u> 38(5). (Spring 1983).

Examines the relationship between sports and cable television. Analyzes how pay TV works, how the dollars are divided and the selling of rights.

1233. Siedlecki, M. Agnes. "Sports Anti-Siphoning Rules For Pay Cable Television: A Public Right To Free T.V.?" 53 <u>Indiana Law Journal</u> 821-840. (Summer 1978).

Note examining whether anti-siphoning rules should be adopted and made applicable to sports programming. Discusses the siphoning effect, the first amendment limitations issue, the consequences of the deregulation of sports programs and whether a public right to free T.V. exists.

1234. Wilson, Darryl C. "The Pay Cable TV-Sports Broadcasting Nexus." 8 <u>Communication and The Law</u> 43-71. (February 1986).

Focuses on relationship between cable television and sports broadcasting. Describes regulatory power of F.C.C., the Congressional response to cable television and current areas of conflict. Reviews current regulations for sports broadcasting. Includes statistics on growth of cable television since 1950.

Copyright

1235. Ciaglo, Cathleen M. "Copyright Protection For Live Sports Telecasts." 29 <u>Baylor Law Review</u> 101-117. (Winter 1977).

Explores sources of protection for telecasts, state common law protection in telecasts, protection of telecasts under the copyright act and the threat of CATV.

1236. Kritzer, Paul E. "Copyright Protection For Sports Broadcasts and The Public's Right of Access." 15 <u>Idea</u> 385-404. (Fall 1971).

Examines the public's right of access to and the copyright protection of live sports broadcasts, especially cable television. Concludes with discussion of FCC plans for the regulation of cable television.

1237. McManis, Charles R. "Satellite Dish Antenna Reception: Copyright Protection of Live Broadcasts and the Doctrine of Anticipatory Infringement." 11 Columbia-VLA Journal of Law and the Arts 387-402. (Spring 1987).

Discusses copyright protections afforded to live sports broadcasts and the anticipatory infringement doctrine based upon the 1976 Copyright Act. Relates fundamental copyright law to sports broadcasts. Examines history and purpose of statutes 411 and 412 of the Act and fixation requirements and protections.

1238. Menesini, Vittorio. "Avvenimento Sportivo e Finzoine Scencia Nel Diritto D'autore" (in Italian). 53 Diritto di Autore (Italy) 15-29. (January-March 1982).

Focuses on the property rights and legal ramifications of the broadcast of sporting events.

1239. Nevins, Francis M., Jr. "Antenna Dilemma: The Exemption From Copyright Liability for Public Performance Using Technology Common In The Home." 11 Columbia-VLA Journal of Law and the Arts 403-411. (Spring 1987).

Criticizes court decision which determined that satellite dish receptions were not commonly found in private homes and therefore violated the 1976 Copyright Act exemption to copyright infringement.

1240. Yeldell, Eric. "Copyright Protection For Live Sports Broadcasts: New Statutory Weapons With Constitutional Problems." 31 Federal Communications Law Journal 277-301. (Spring 1979).

Comment examining the provisions of the new Copyright Act which specifically address the relationship between sports, cable television and the subsequent transmission of copyrightable live sports events. Discusses FCC regulations and broadcasting's "threat" to sports, live broadcasts and copyright protection, and a consideration of constitutional issues and potential problems.

Right Of Publicity

1241. Quinn, James W. and Warren, Irwin H. "Professional Team Sports New Legal Arena: Television and The Player's Right of Publicity." 16 Indiana Law Review 487-516. (Spring 1983).

Examines role of television and players' right of publicity; the right of publicity, and its application to professional sports and athletes.   Discusses first amendment considerations to right of publicity, and the interplay in publicity between contract and collective bargaining approach.

32

SWIMMING

1242.   Goldhaber, Gerald M. and deTurck, Mark A. "Effects of
          Consumers' Familiarity With A Product On Attention To and
          Compliance With Warnings." 11 Journal of Products Liability
          29-37. (Winter 1988).
              Studies the degree to which swimmers noticed and needed
          signs which warned against diving into above-ground
          swimming pools.

1243.   Lambert, Thomas F., Jr. "7.25 Million Settlement Achieved In
          Massachusetts For Quadriplegia Suffered By 19-Year-Old Star
          Swimmer and Student Contributed By Three Defendants-
          University, For Negligence of Swimming Coaches;
          Manufacturer of Diving Blocks; and Publisher of Swimming
          World, Bible of Competitive Swimming World-For
          Negligence Misinformation As To Safe Procedures For Doing
          Diving Drill." 31 ATLA Law Reporter 301-303. (September
          1988).
              Discusses Tricarico v. Northeastern University (1988).
          Reviews the facts, and the handling of the defendants' liability
          and solvency.

1244.   Lambert, Thomas F., Jr. "Products Liability-Above-Ground
          Swimming Pool." 26 ATLA Law Reporter 338-342. (October
          1983).
              Review of the facts and testimony in case of O'Brien v.
          Muskin Corp., 463 A.2d 298 (N.J., 1983) regarding the liability
          for injuries sustained when diving into an above-ground
          swimming pool.

1245.   Lambert, Thomas F., Jr. "Product Liability-Defective Above-
          Ground Swimming Pool-Quadriplegic Injuries Suffered By 15

Year-Old Boy When He Dove Into 4-Foot-Deep Above-Ground Pool Containing Three-and-a-Half Feet of Water."   26 ATLA Law Reporter 11-13. (February 1983).

Reviews Theodore Koenig v. Muskin Corporation and The W. T. Grant Co., (1982) regarding assumption of risk and manufacturer liability for a lack of safety devices and warnings.

1246.   Stern, James F.   "Swimming Pool Liability."   14 Trial 25-27. (June 1978).

Comment which identifies problem areas encountered in a case involving injury or death: the specialized terminology used by those who build or operate swimming pools, the relationship between boisterous behavior of those using the swimming pool and the number of supervisory personnel, and the notion of the "housekeeping" of the pool and the pool environment.

33

TAXATION

General

1247.   "Athletes' Professional Service Corps. Ignored For Income and Employment Tax Liability On Team Payments." 14 Tax Management Compensation Planning Journal 252-253. (September 5, 1986).

1248.   Meran, Harry B. "The Sale of Minor League Baseball Players During Liquidation-The Application of Corn Products To Depreciable Property." 45 Temple Law Quarterly 291-304. (Winter 1972).

          Discusses applicability of the Supreme Court holding 1955 Corn Products Refining Co. v. Commissioner, and the capital asset provisions of the Internal Revenue Code with regard to the sale of minor league baseball players' contracts. Follows Hollywood Baseball Assoc. v. Commissioner (1964-1970) through the courts to exemplify the uncertainties involved. Explains the Corn Products doctrine and suggests the application of Corn Products should be limited to transactions directly related to either inventory or property held primarily for sale to prevent giving capital gain treatment to items producing everyday profits and losses (thus protecting tax policies underlying Sections 337, 1221, and 1231).

1249.   Moot, Robert C., Jr. "Tax-Exempt Status of Amateur Sports Organizations." 40 Washington and Lee Law Review 1705-1728. (Fall 1983).

          Examines protection of merchandising properties in professional sports. Reviews both sports and analogous cases pertaining to protection of team insignias and symbols, uniforms and jerseys. Argues for the protection of sports merchandising properties.

1250.   Steuerle, Gene.   "Reducing Well-Being By Subsidizing Entertainment." 45 Tax Notes 1249-1250. (December 4, 1989).

1251.   "They Can't Do This To Me...Can They?" 59 Journal of Accountancy 107(3). (June 1985).

1252.   Warburton, Jean. "Football and The Recreation Charities Act 1958." 1980 Conveyancer and Property Lawyer (U.K.) 173-181. (May-June 1980).
         Review of I.R.C. v. McMullen [1979] 1 W.L.R. 130, which was an appeal of a ruling that the Football Association Youth Trust was not a charity. Discusses the decision of the court of appeals. Explores the greater issue of social welfare under the 1955 Rating and Valuation Act, the 1958 Recreational Charities Act and the case in question.

1253.   Zbacnik, Robert and Ellerhorst, Jim. "Entertainment Facility Takes On New Meaning." 19 The Tax Adviser 852(2). (December 1988).
         Reviews the impact of Ireland where the Tax Court disallowed all expenses associated with an entertainment facility.

Federal Income Tax-Amortization

1254.   Jones, John B.   "Amortization and Nonamortization of Intangibles In The Sports World." 53 Taxes-The Tax Magazine 777-788. (December 1975).
         Examines tax reform legislation as the House Ways and Means Committee considers the tax treatment accorded to owners of sports franchises.   Discusses the value of amortization to the purchaser of a going business (such as a manufacturing concern) and the availability of amortization. Explains sports contracts with regard to amortization.

1255.   Penick, S. Barksdale. "The Selig Case and Amortization of Player Contracts: Baseball Continues Its Winning Ways." 6 Comm/Ent Law Journal 423-446. (Winter 1984).
         Overviews use of sports teams as tax shelters in relation to Tax Reform Act of 1976 and the allocation to player contracts cases of Laird, First Northwest, and Selig. Presents comparison of cases. Concludes with, and supports, the argument that, on appeal Selig should be overturned.

Franchises, Taxes

1256.   Ambrose, James F.   "Recent Tax Developments Regarding
               Purchases of Sports Franchises-The Game Isn't Over Yet." 59
               Taxes 739-762. (November 1981).
                   Discusses taxing of professional sports teams.   Reviews
               evolution of the professional sports franchise into a promising
               tax shelter vehicle, Congressional intervention in taxation of
               professional sports franchises, court decisions on the subject
               and viability of the IRS's mass asset theory.   Examines
               shortcomings of current treatment and comments on new
               developments.

1257.   Beskin, Jay R.; Hanson, Douglas A.; and Nelson, John A.
               "Taxation: Substance v. Form and Other Esoterica."   62
               Chicago-Kent Law Review 657-685. (Winter 1986).
                   Discussion of Selig v. United States regarding the valuation
               of player contract in relation to the value of the franchise.

1258.   Jeffery, David. "A Thin Dividing Line." 119 Taxation (U.K.)
               196(2). (May 29, 1987).
                   Examines the pay-as-you-earn phenomenon of football
               clubs.

1259.   Klinger, Leslie S. "Tax Aspects of Buying, Selling and Owning
               Professional Sports Teams." 48 Los Angeles Bar Bulletin 162+.
               (March 1973).
                   Reports on the financial aspects of a hypothetical
               professional basketball team.   Examines the tax aspects of
               operations and the buyer's tax strategy plus the seller's tax
               strategy in professional sports.

1260.   Lewis, Michael L.   "Professional Sports Franchising and The
               IRS." 14 Washburn Law Journal 321-329. (Spring 1975).
                   Note examining the federal income tax and its treatment of
               asset sales and player contracts.   Reviews limitations of the
               applicable tax provisions.   Offers fair taxation suggestions for
               the stabilization of professional sports.

Tax Aspects

1261.   "Athletic Competition Supervisory Organization's Publication
               of Sports Program Treated As Unrelated Trade or Business." 26
               Tax Management Memorandum 296. (October 28, 1985).
                   Discussion of PLR 8538003 (May 21, 1985) where it was ruled
               that the advertising income earned by a tax exempt
               organization was unrelated business income.

1262.   "Exclusively Riding Abroad." 117 Taxation(U.K.) 53(1). (April 18, 1986).
             Discusses Robert Eddery Ltd. v. The Commissioners of Customs and Excise where an assessment was levied because certain "jockey services" were incorrectly zero-rated.

1263.   "Foundation Tax and Player Contract Bills Get Committee Nod." 10 Tax Notes 634. (April 28, 1980).
             Brief review of H.R. 4103 pertaining to limiting the allocation of basis to player contracts. Provides limited analysis on the bill and its progress through committee.

1264.   Halperin, Richard E. "Use of Loan-Out Corporations Has Been Limited, But Advantages Remain." 65 Journal of Taxation 74(8). (August 1986).
             Examines the advantages and unresolved issues of loan-out corporations. Reviews tax implications (specifically Section 269A) and use of loan-out corporations in foreign countries.

1265.   Hargreaves, Allan. "Charity Sponsorship: 'One Man's Meat...'" 122 Taxation (U.K.) 194(3). (December 1, 1988).
             Reviews the tax circumstances surrounding sponsorship. Examines the British Olympic appeal, whether sporting activities are charitable and the consequences of the value added tax.

1266.   Harmelink, Philip J. and Vignes, David W. "Tax Aspects of Baseball Player Contracts and Planning Opportunities." 59 Taxes 535-546. (August 1981).
             Discusses aspects of contracts of professional baseball players. Explores depreciation of player contracts and possibility of involuntary conversion upon player's death.

1267.   Jensen, Erik M.   "Taxation, The Student Athlete, and Professionalism of College Athletics." 1987 Utah Law Review 35-58. (Winter 1987).
             Discusses the possible tax liability issues that a tax-exempt college or university would face if it hired and payed its student-athletes. Reviews athletics and education, and open professionalism at the college level.

1268.   Murphy, Nina R. "Revenue Ruling 84-132: Sidelined But Not Forgotten." 19 University of Richmond Law Review 301-315. (Winter 1985).
             Focuses on the charitable contributions of alumni to colleges and universities. Specifically examines contributions to athletic programs, the history of the deducibility of charitable contributions, and Revenue Ruling 84-132 pertaining to

contributions and preferential seating.   Provides
recommendations for the revision of Rule 84-132.

1269.   Reed, Gregory J.   "Establishing Value-Is It Really Worth It?"   65
Michigan Bar Journal 1102-1107. (November 1986).
Analyzes value in baseball, boxing, football and basketball.
Discusses the setting, determination, distortion and factors
distorting value.

1270.   School District Amusement Tax Found Applicable To Ski
Facility."   10 Pennsylvania Law Journal-Reporter 9. (December
14, 1987).

1271.   Sheppard, Lee A.   "Charitable Contributions; IRS Punts On
College Athletic Ruling."   26 Tax Notes 116-117. (January 14,
1985).
Focuses on the 7 January 1984 hearing on Revenue Ruling
84-132 regarding the deducibility of payments to a college's
athletic scholarship fund.   Explores the meaning of
"contribution" or "gift."

1272.   "Sport As A Charitable Object."   99 Solicitor's Journal (U.K.)
463. (July 9, 1955).
Discusses whether it is possible for a gift or trust for the
furtherance of sport to be charitable.   Examines development
in law since the 5th (1929) edition of Tudor On The Law of
Charitable Trusts.   Concludes it remains obscure but, in the
writer's opinion, if there is public benefit, a gift for the
promotion of a sport should not be regarded as "necessarily
and essentially non-charitable" (based upon strength of earlier
cases or information in textbooks regarding those cases).

Tax Shelters

1273.   Gunn, Malcolm.   "Tax-Free Inducement: Footballer Escapes
Tax."   123 Taxation (U.K.) 352-353. (June 22, 1989).
Overview of Shilton v. Wilmhurst.

1274.   "IRS Rules On College Sports Contributions."   162 Journal of
Accountancy 18(1). (July 1986).

1275.   Koch, Richard A.   "Professional Sports Teams As A Tax
Shelter-A Case Study: The Utah Stars."   1974 Utah Law Review
556-573. (Fall 1974).
Surveys the economic history of the Utah Stars of the
American Basketball Association (A.B.A.). Reports on how the
tax shelter principles are applied to the business of professional
sports.   Reviews history of the team, amoritization of player

contracts, deferral of player compensation, team organization, sale of the team and the new owner's strategy.

1276.   Sargis, Kevin M. "Tax Planning For The Professional Athlete and The Impact of The Tax Reform Act of 1986." 5 Entertainment & Sports Law Journal 73-94. (Fall 1988).

Reports on effects of the Tax Reform Act of 1986 on professional athletes. Focuses on ways to reduce the athlete's tax burden. Explores the assignment of income doctrine, incorporation, tax shelters, alternative minimum tax, deferred compensation, income averaging, IRA's, investment tax credits and interest free loans.

1277.   Wiesner, Philip J. "Tax Shelters-A Survey of The Impact of The Tax Reform Act of 1976." 33 Tax Law Review 5-113. (Fall 1977).

Comprehensive examination focusing on the at risk limitation and minimum tax, an anti-tax shelter provisions. Examines specific provisions which Congress adopted to limit tax shelters in a number of areas including sports franchises.

Taxation of Professional Athletes

1278.   "Basketball Star's Corp. Caught In PHC Net." 13 Estate Planning 219-220. (July-August 1986).

1279.   Brown, Leonard G.   "Compensation Planning For The Professional Athlete." 7 Southern University Law Review 235-254. (Spring 1981).

Discusses compensation planning and strategies for the professional athlete. Reviews player-owner compensation arrangements, player deferral of income options and the incorporation of the athlete.

1280.   Connors, John.   "The Role of Self-Incorporation By Professional Athletes In Today's Tax Climate-After TEFRA and TRA '84." 2 Entertainment and Sports Law Journal 1-31. (Fall 1984).

Examines the effect of the TEFRA and the TRA of 1984 on self-incorporation of professional athletes.

1281.   Crum, J. V., III. "Issues In Income Tax Planning For The Team Sport Player." 3 Entertainment and Sports Law Journal 115-130. (Spring 1986).

Discusses tax considerations as they apply to team sports players. Focuses on gross income, exclusions from gross income, sport-related deductions, deferred compensation, income averaging and personal service corporations.

1282.   Del Rey, Alfred J.   "U.S. Immigration Procedures and The Employment of Alien Performers and Sports Personalities." 1 Journal of Copyright, Entertainment and Sports Law 119-133. (December 1982).

Overviews the problems and options for their solution regarding immigration. Discusses H-1 and third preference status.

1283.   Dicker, James W.   "Tax-Oriented Options For The Professional Athlete." 8 Review of The Taxation of Individuals 195-222. (Summer 1984).

Reviews choices available to the professional athlete's financial advisor/planner.   Examines the options of nonqualified deferred compensation, restricted property, incorporation and qualified deferred compensation plans, interest-free loans, income splitting, income averaging, and tax shelters. Draws the distinction, regarding financial options, for team-sport and individual athletes.

1284.   Fraade, Richard D.; Gardner, David B.; and Stewart, Allan. "The IRS, The INS and The Foreign Entertainer."   5 Comm/Ent Law Journal 191-224. (Winter 1983).

Focuses on the IRS and INS (Immigration & Naturalization Service) regulations as they apply to foreign entertainers and athletes. Examines and compares these regulations. Discusses types of visas and permanent resident applications. Explores the relationship between the IRS and INS.

1285.   Gombinski, Steven J. and Kaplan, Gary P.   "Demise of The Tax-Motivated Personal Service Corporation."   1 Journal of Copyright, Entertainment and Sports Law 74-118. (December 1982).

Examines the personal service corporations controlled by the performer.   Reviews tax benefits, factors against incorporation, means of challenging the PSC, legislative reforms, incorporation after TEFRA and the costs and benefits of incorporation.

1286.   Histrop, Lindsay Ann.   "The Taxation of Amateur Athlete 'Reserve Funds'."   33 Canadian Tax Journal (Canada) 1123-1153. (November/December 1985).

Discusses taxation of sponsored income earned by amateur Canadian athletes while competing. Offers some rules and the fundamental structure of these trust arrangements. Presents the tax effects depending upon the classification of the relationship between the athlete and the sports association. Examines accounting determinations. Recommends ways to help the athletes.

1287.   Histrop, Lindsay Ann.   "Taxation of Canadian Resident
               Athletes and Artists Performing In The United States."   32
               Canadian Tax Journal (Canada) 1060-1083. 32. (November-
               December 1984).
                    Review of the taxation of Canadian athletes and artists
               performing in the U.S. Discusses the special aspects of these
               performers including their status with the IRS and the
               Canadian-U.S. Tax Treaty.   Surveys definitions, allowable
               deductions, allocation and withholding tax.

1288.   Judge, William J. "Student-Athletes As Employees: Income
               Tax Consequences." 13 Journal of College and University Law
               285-309. (Winter 1986).
                    Suggests student-athletes in the near future may be
               considered employees and thus be taxed on income. Discusses
               section 117 of the Internal Revenue Code which provides
               exemptions for scholarships. Provides historical perspective of
               section 117 and the student-athlete model.

1289.   Lowell, Cym H.   "Planning Contractual Deferred
               Compensation Agreements for Professional Athletes." 10 Tax
               Adviser 68-75. (February 1979).
                    Discusses the planning and use of contractual deferred
               compensation arrangements for a professional athletes.
               Reviews problems involved in such planning in relation to
               the future, the terms of the individual contract, the Treasury's
               Department's Proposed Regulations and the Revenue Act of
               1978.

1290.   Maclean, D. M. "Prizemoney In Sports: Kelly's Case." 14
               Australian Tax Review (Australia) 156-161. (September 1985).
                    Analyzes decision in Kelly, (1985) 16 A.T.R. 478. [1985]
               A.T.C. 4283, regarding the assessability of sport prizemoney.
               Reviews related Australian and English casework.

1291.   "Players Deemed Employees of Teams Rather Than PSCs." 5
               Tax Management Financial Planning Journal 550(1). (December
               12, 1989).

1292.   Silbergleit, Kenneth R. "Linesman v. Commissioner: U.S.
               Avenges Olympic Team's Loss to Canadian Hockey Players."
               32 Canadian Tax Journal (Canada) 616-620. (May-June 1984).
                    Reviews the case.   Specifically examines the courts
               treatment of a sign-on bonus, item of income, which is not
               explicitly dealt with within the code and regulations of the
               I.R.S. Treats the greater issue of the allocation of income
               between sources within and outside the U.S.

1293.   Thomas, Henry I.   "Income Averaging and The Professional
         Athlete: A Re-Examination."   19 New England Law Review
         335-375. (1983/1984).
         Analyzes the income averaging provisions of the I.R.S.
         Code and the applicability to new professional athletes.
         Examines relationship between college athletes and
         institutions.   Discusses self-support requirement and major
         accomplishment rule.

1294.   Van De Ven, Martha A. and Kauffman, Steven A.   "Merits of
         Incorporating The Athlete."   9 Tax Adviser 478-482. (August
         1978).
         Examines the benefits of a qualified deferred compensation
         plan and other fringe benefits.   Reviews problems of
         incorporating the athlete.

1295.   Weis, Theodore Delaney.   "Tax Planning Issues Affecting
         International Entertainers and Athletes."   9 Fordham
         International Law Journal 97-133. (Winter 1986).
         Surveys issues of federal income taxation of foreign
         performers under the Internal Revenue Code, taxation of U.S.
         performers abroad and the impact of tax treaty provisions on
         the federal income taxation of international performers.

1296.   Weisman, Barry L.   "Taxes and The Professional Athlete."   26
         Boston Bar Journal 5-10. (October 1982).
         Reports on tax aspects and changes that should be
         considered when dealing with professional athletes.

1297.   Wietmarschen, Donald A.   "Planning For The Professional
         Athlete: Deferred Compensation Arrangements and Loans In
         Lieu of Compensation."   8 Ohio Northern Law Review 499-511.
         (July 1981).
         Focuses on professional athlete's use of deferred
         compensation.   Discusses methods of deferral and use of loans
         (interest free and low interest) as tax planning devices.
         Explores tax consequences for these planning arrangements.

1298.   Wray, Donald G. and Barnard, Scott R.   "Taxation On Non-
         resident Athletes and Entertainers Performing In Canada."   34
         Canadian Tax Journal(Canada) 1150-1163. (September-October
         1986).
         Discusses Canadian tax aspects pertaining to nonresident
         athletes and entertainers while performing in Canada.
         Specifically examines application to U.S. residents.   Includes
         self-employed individuals, corporate income, withholding tax
         and international tax treaties.

Taxation of Professional Sports Teams

1299.   "Athletes' Professional Service Corporations Ignored For
             Income and Employment Tax Liability On Team Payments."
             27 Tax Management Memorandum 210. (August 4, 1986).
                  Brief review involving the decision that the professional
             team employing the athlete (and not the professional service
             corporation which the athlete had established) was liable for
             income and employment tax.

1300.   Blum, Marc P. "Valuing Intangibles: What Are The Choices
             For Valuing Professional Sports Teams?" 45 Journal of
             Taxation 286-288. (November 1976).
                  Reviews decision and the court's reasoning in Laird, 391 F.
             Supp. 656 (DC Ga., 1975), and its approach to valuation.
             Focuses on the valuing of player contracts and television
             contract rights. Offers alternative methods of valuation which
             the author believes would be more fair to the IRS and the team
             in question.

1301.   Braun, Steven and Pusey, Michael. "Taxation of Professional
             Sports Teams." 7 Tax Advisor 196-206. (April 1976).
                  Examines Laird (391 F. Supp. 656 [DC, Ga., 1975]). Reviews
             the question of the intangible assets of sports teams. Discusses
             the player contracts, the TV rights and the college draft.
             Concludes with discussion of the applicability of state taxes and
             proposed legislation.

1302.   Harwood, Steven J. "Valuation of Player Contracts When
             Acquiring A Professional Baseball Team-An Analysis of Selig
             v. United States." 61 Taxes 670-677. (October 1983).
                  Examines the facts, decision of the district court and
             government's challenge regarding the valuation of
             professional baseball players' contracts. Discusses taxayer's
             allocations, broadcasting rights, Section 1056 and 50%
             presumption.

1303.   Horvitz, Jerome S. and Hoffman, Thomas E. "New Tax
             Developments In The Syndication of Sports Franchises." 54
             Taxes-The Tax Magazine 175-184. (March 1976).
                  Examines the influence of tax considerations on
             professional sports. Reviews franchise investment tax
             procedures and the composition of the sale of a franchise.
             Discusses tax objectives of the franchise seller and buyer.
             Presents a tax computation for hypothetical franchise owner.
             Reports on Laird, Jr. v. United States and its effects on player
             contract valuation. Discusses tax planning objectives for
             players. Surveys recent trends in the professional sports
             industry.

1304.   Katz, Robert Reiff.   "Federal Income Tax-Amortization and The Expansion Sports Franchise." 54 Washington Law Review 827-841. (October 1979).

A note which analyzes First Northwest Industries of America, Inc. v. Commissioner, 70 T.C. 817 (1978). Discusses past taxation practices of professional sports franchises and the "mass asset theory" as applied to tangible assets outside sports. Examines conflicting positions of the IRS and the Sonics concerning the theory's applicability to the expansion franchise. Presents the Tax Court's reasons for not applying the theory in First Northwest and suggests that the Ninth Circuit should also conclude that the theory is inappropriate in the context of expansion franchises.

1305.   Klinger, Leslie S.   "Professional Sports Teams: Tax Factors In Buying, Owning and Selling Them." 39 Journal of Taxation 276-280. (November 1973).

Analyzes tax factors involved with a professional sports team. Discusses the tax aspects of operations, the buyer's tax strategy, and the seller's tax strategy. Presents discussion within the context of a hypothetical professional basketball team.

1306.   Mona, Joseph.   "Amoritization and Valuation of Intangibles: The Tax Effect Upon Sports Franchises." 12 Loyola of Los Angeles Law Review 159-178. (December 1978).

Comment examining certain tax aspects of owning a franchise in professional sports. Analyzes the organizational structure of professional sports, tax aspects before 1976, the Tax Reform Act of 1976 and the change of position of the IRS as demonstrated in Laird v. United States.

1307.   Powers, Michael.   "It's Not Over Till It's Over."   3 Entertainment and Sports Lawyer 3-6 (Fall 1984).

Examines sports franchise depreciation allowances and the Tax Reform Act of 1976. Reviews Laird and First Northwest Industries. Specifically analyzes the decision in Selig v. IRS regarding the reasonability of the allocation between franchise value and the value of player contracts.

1308.   Raabe, William, Jr.   "Professional Sports Franchises and The Treatment of League Expansion Proceeds." 57 Taxes 427-430. (July 1979).

Discusses the tax treatment of the proceeds of league expansion entry fees. Reviews the case and pertinent facts of First Northwest Industries. Explores the majority opinion and dissenting opinion. Recommends the Commissioner of the

NBA reassess application of the mass asset theory particularly in the case of league expansion proceeds.

1309.   Strandell, Valerie Nelson.   "The Impact of The 1976 Tax Reform Act On The Owners of Professional Sports Teams." 4 Journal of Contemporary Law 219-232. (Spring 1978).

Discusses tax practices which, in part, caused a concerned Congress to pass the Tax Reform Act of 1976 to close a number of tax loopholes.   Examines, analyzes, and explains the results of this Tax Reform Act.

1310.   Weill, Jay R.   "Depreciation of Player Contracts-The Government Is Ahead At The Half."   53 Taxes-The Tax Magazine 581-591. (October 1975).

Reviews arguments of, and comments on, the district court decision E. Cody Laird, Jr. v. United States which deals with the issue of whether the owners of the Atlanta Falcons football team could claim amoritzation on the claimed value of the 42 player's contracts received in 1965 upon entry into the National Football League.   Weill represented the government as a trial attorney with the Tax Division of the Department of Justice.   States the area of player allocation is still in flux until the Court of Appeals in New Orleans decision or until some guidelines are issues by the Internal Revenue Service.

1311.   Zaritsky, Howard M.   "Amortizing A Sports Team's Player Contract: An Analysis of First Northwest Industries."   52 Journal of Taxation 88-91. (February 1980).

Points out that Tax Court's decision in First Northwest Industries of America, Inc., 70 TC No. 79 (1978). may function as a planning guideline for the sale of professional sports teams (Tax Court allowed for the amortization of players' contracts acquired as the result of the purchase of a professional sports team).   Discusses case in relation to Laird, 566 F2d 1244, and the Tax Reform Act of 1976.

1312.   Zaritsky, Howard.   "Amoritization of Intangibles: How The 1976 TRA and Laird Affect Sports Franchises."   48 Journal of Taxation 292-296. (May 1978).

Reviews effect of the Tax Reform Act of 1976, and Laird (556 F2d 1224) on intangible properties in professional sports. Examines the facts of Laird, the decisions of the district and Fifth Circuit courts, the impact of Laird, and the consistencies and inconsistencies between the Laird decision and the TRA of 1976.

1313.   Zaritsky, Howard.   "Taxation of Professional Sports Teams After 1976: A Whole New Ballgame." 18 William and Mary Law Review 679-702. (Summer 1977).

Discusses the change which must be made regarding the taxation of professional sports teams. Reviews the structure and operation of professional sports teams. Presents a general tax treatment of professional sports. Reports on the effects of judicial decisions, labor agreements on professional sports contracts, and how these changes, along with the Tax Reform Act of 1976, have changed the taxation of professional sports teams.

34

VIOLENCE AND SPORTS

General

1314.   Bertini, Christopher D.   "A Survey of Domestic and
         International Sanctions Against Spectator Violence at Sporting
         Events." 11 Houston Journal of International Law 415-438.
         (Spring 1989).
             Explains attempts to control spectator violence in U.S. and
         internationally.   Includes U.S., state and federal legislative
         attempts plus judicial and private efforts. Focuses on English
         control of hooliganism with context of Section 5, Public
         Disorder Act of 1936, the Sporting Events Act of 1985 and the
         Public Order Act of 1986. Offers recommendations.

1315.   de Doelder, H. and van Dorst, A. J. A. "Sport en Strafrecht" (in
         Dutch). 52 Nederlands Juristenblad (Netherlands) 164-170.
         (February 1977).
             Reviews player roughness in sports specifically soccer, the
         inability of sanctions to curtail such roughness and the
         problem of proving an intent to be rough except in the most
         flagrant instances.

1316.   de Francesco, Giovannangelo. "La Violenza Sportiva ed i Suoi
         Limiti Scriminanti" (in Italian). 26 Revista Italiana di Diritto e
         Procedura Penale (Italy) 588-610. (April-June 1983).
             Examination of the problems pertaining to violence in
         sports and the legal responsibilities which arise from such
         violence.

1317.   Engler, Terri. "Kill 'em!" Sports Violence and The Law." 7
         Update 2(7). (Spring 1983).

Discusses the phenomenon of violence in sports and its relationship to the law. Examines the importance of winning, the enforcement of civility and the assumption of risk.

1318.   Grayson, Edward. "The Taylor Report of Hillsborough." 140 New Law Journal (U.K.) 124(1). (February 2, 1990).

1319.   Grayson, Edward. "The Day Sport Dies." 138 New Law Journal (U.K.) 9(2). (January 8, 1988).
Brief discussion of violence on the playing fields of the U.K.

1320.   Igbinovia, Patrick Edobor. "Soccer Hooliganism In Black Africa." 29 International Journal of Offender Therapy and Comparative Criminology (U.K.) 135-146. (September 1985).
Reports on soccer violence in Black Africa. Offers theories on why the violence occurs as well as suggestions to prevent and control such hooliganism.

1321.   Letourneau, Gilles. "Problematique de la violence dans les loisirs et moyens d'action corrective et preventive: l'experience quebecoise et canadienne" (in French). 19 Revue Generale de Droit (Canada) 653-669. (September 1988).
Reports on violence in sports and the failure of traditional sport, civil and criminal law to control such violence. Discusses the province of Quebec's establishment of a Regie de al securite dans les sports. This Board attempts, through power and persuasion, to regulate and to heighten individual and collective awareness of the issues surrounding sports violence.

1322.   Letourneau, G. and Manganas, A. "La tolerance des droits penal et sportif, source de violence dans les sports" (in French). 17 Cahiers (Laval) (Canada) 741-776. (1976).
Review of the source of violence in sports. Examines the relationship between penal and sports law.

1323.   McEwan, V. G. "Playing The Game: Negligence In Sport." 130 Solicitor's Journal (U.K.) 581-582. (August 8, 1986).
Discusses duty of care, consent and negligence of players on the field.

1324.   Nielsen, Bradley C. "Controlling Sports Violence: Too Late For The Carrots-Bring On The Big Stick." 74 Iowa Law Review 681-712. (March 1989).
Examines sports violence and suggestions for its control in football, basketball, hockey and baseball. Considers societal implications of sports violence. Reviews legislative proposals, internal league controls and civil liability used to control sports violence. Suggests criminal prosecution as remedy.

1325.   Rains, Cameron Jay. "Sports Violence: A Matter of Societal Concern." 55 Notre Dame Lawyer 796-813. (June 1980).
Emphasizes the increase in violence in sports in the U.S. and Canada and calls for better means to control this behavior. Stresses that players must be responsible for their actions.

1326.   Sanders, Jane A. "Violence In The Stands: When Fans and Players Meet." 53 Insurance Counsel Journal 264-275. (April 1986).
Discusses theories on spectator violence and possible tort claims against players, owners and coaches. Offers possible solutions to curb the problem of violence in sports.

1327.   "Sporting Violence."   139 New Law Journal (U.K.) 1621(1). (December 1, 1989).

1328.   Stewart, J. B. "Crimes On The Football Field." 32 Journal of The Law Society of Scotland (Scotland) 420(3). (November 1987).

Criminal Law

1329.   Binder, Richard L. "Consent Defense: Sports, Violence, and The Criminal Law." 13 American Criminal Law Review 235-248. (Fall 1975).
Examines the reasonings of cases which have considered the consent defense in the context of sports activities. Applies principles and policies articulated in those cases to modern hockey. Presents criticisms of the traditional judicial approach in this area and offers suggestions for clarifying the law.

1330.   Carroll, Mary. "It's Not How You Play The Game, "It's Whether You Win or Lose: The Need For Criminal Sanctions To Curb Violence In Professional Sports." 12 Hamline Law Review 71-90. (Winter 1980).
Argues that violence in professional sports is in greater need of control. States that league sanctions and penalties and civil actions have failed. Calls for the imposition of criminal penalties on violent athletes. Reviews the effect of sports violence on society.

1331.   "Consent In Criminal Law: Violence In Sports." 75 Michigan Law Review 148-179. (November 1976).
Note examining the existence of the consent of an injured party in an incident of violence in sports. Reviews general theories of consent, the actual consent of sports participants, general theories of the effectiveness of consent and the effectiveness of consent in sports.

1332.   Eser, Albin. "Zur Strafrechtlichen Verantwortlichkeit des Sportlers, Insbesondere Des Fussballspielers." 33 Juristenzeitung (West Germany) 368-374. (June 1978).
Discusses the criminal responsibilities of athletes, especially soccer players, during sporting events.

1333.   Hallowell, Lyle and Meshbesher, Ronald I. "Sports Violence and The Criminal Law." 13 Trial 27-32. (January 1977).
Asks how violence in sports should be controlled. Explore problems and limitations involved in applying criminal law to actions and behaviors in sports. Analyzes offenses and defenses in a case of assault. Authors suggest the establishment of federal and/or state sports commissions.

1334.   Hechter, William. "Criminal Law and Violence in Sports." 19 Criminal Law Quarterly (Canada) 425-453. (September 1977).
Reviews the degree of violence, in hockey, football and baseball, and the relation of such violence to criminal law. Examines applicable casework for each sport. Discusses the principles of excuse used by players when players are found to be in violation of criminal statutes. The justifications reviews are consent, self-defense, and provocation.

1335.   Letourneau, Gilles. "Sports, Violence and Criminal Law in Canada." 22 Criminal Reports (Canada) 103-106. (October 15, 1981).
Overview of sport violence in Canada.

1336.   Letourneau, Gilles and Manganas, Antione. "Violence In Sports: Evidentiary Problems in Criminal Prosecutions." 16 Osgoode Hall Law Journal (Canada) 577-600. (November 1978).
Discusses the inadequacy of criminal law as it relates to violence in sports. Examines the weakness of testimony and the advantages and disadvantages of alternative forms of evidence such as videotape, the use of character and of similar fact evidence, and expert witness evidence.

1337.   Letourneau, Gilles and Manganas, Antoine. "Le Legalite Des Sports Violents et le Code Criminel." 55 Canadian Bar Review (Canada) 256-288. (1977).
Explores relationship between violence in sports and the criminal code. Reviews French and English law and problem of violence in sport. Discusses Article 81 or the Canadian Criminal Code as it relates to boxing and prizefighting. Explores social goals of sports.

Judicial Treatment

1338.   Baicker-McKee, Steven.   "Violence In Athletics: A Judicial
           Approach." 3 <u>Entertainment and Sports Law Journal</u> 223-242.
           (Fall 1986).
               Surveys violence in sports and the defenses to liability
           including   assumption   of   risk,   consent,   self-defense,
           provocation defense and involuntary reflex defense. Proposes
           a two-stage consent test.

1339.   Broadbent, G. P.   "Football Violence: The Courts' New Red
           Card." 131 <u>Solicitors' Journal</u> (U.K.) 1136-1138. (August 28,
           1987).
               Discusses Section 30-37 of Public Order Act 1986 regarding
           exclusion   order   designed   to   ban   and   control   football
           hooliganism.   Considers conditions which must be satisfied for
           the exclusion order, its effect and enforcement.   Examines the
           nature of the offence, its relation to violence and alcohol, the
           sentencing structure, and efficacy of the order in controlling
           violence and/or disorder.

1340.   Carlsen, Chris J. and Walker, Matthew S.   "Sports Court: A
           Private System To Deter Violence In Professional Sports."   55
           <u>Southern California Law Review</u> 399-440. (January, 1982).
               Examines extent of problem of violence in professional
           sports and suggests creation of a Sports Court.   Explore why
           violence exists and the systems for violence control.   Means of
           control include internal league sanctions, criminal sanctions,
           and   the   tort   suit.   Outlines   the   establishment,   staffing
           organization, financing, implementation, justification and
           purposes for a sports court.   Analyzes antitrust implications
           and application of labor exemption to sports court.

1341.   Carroll, John F.   "Tort In Sports-I'll See You In Court!"   16
           <u>Akron Law Review</u> 537-553. (Winter 1983).
               Examines violence in professional sports. Surveys football,
           hockey, basketball and baseball.   Reviews various sports
           leagues' systems of internal control and theories of recovery,
           applicable defenses, possibility of criminal recovery, and bills
           proposed in Congress to control such violence.

Legislation and Regulation

1342.   Langevin, Mark E.   "Proposed Legislative Solution To The
           Problem of Violent Acts By Participants During Professional
           Sporting   Events: The   Sports   Violence   Act   of   1980."   7
           <u>University of Dayton Law Review</u> 91-111. (Fall 1981).

Discusses H. R. 7903, The Sports Violence Act of 1980. Examines assault, battery, negligence, reckless misconduct, league internal controls and application of tort law to control violent acts. Reviews respondeat supervisor and negligent supervision as theories under which owners and coaches can be held liable for players' actions. Explores practicality of H. R. 7903.

1343.   Slonim, Scott. "Goal of Crime Bill To Curb Sports Violence." 66 American Bar Association Journal 1188-1189. (October 1980).

Discusses H. R. 7903, the Sports Violence Act of 1980. Focuses on the reasons for, and the particulars of, the bill. Provides perspectives of both the bill's supporters and detractors.

1344.   Sprotzer, Ira. "Violence In Professional Sports: A Need For Federal Regulation." 86 Case and Comment 3(7). (May-June 1981).

Note the different approach to violence in athletics versus everyday society. Discusses the attempt to regulate this violence, federally, through the Sports Violence Act of 1980. Believes that the Act would benefit society.

Violence in Professional Sports

1345.   DiNicola, Ronald A. and Mendeloff, Scott. "Controlling Violence In Professional Sports: Rule Reform and The Federal Professional Sports Violence Commission." 21 Duquesne Law Review 843-916. (Summer 1983).

Provides overview of violence in sports, causes of violence and issue of the limits of control of player conduct. Offers model for analyzing competitive conduct. Reviews traditional criminal and tort remedies for injury resulting from sports violence and factors restricting recovery. Examines provisions of proposed Sports Violence Arbitration Act of 1981. Argues against independent arbitration to control sports violence. Discusses hypothetical establishment of Federal Professional Sports Violence Commission.

1346.   Gibson, Don Eugene-Nolan. "Violence In Professional Sports: A Proposal For Self Regulation." 3 Journal of Communications and Entertainment Law 425-453. (Spring 1981).

Reports on attempts at deterrence and control of violence in professional football, basketball and baseball through internal discipline and introduction of criminal law. Discusses limitations of application of criminal sanctions to professional athletes. Explores defenses of consent, involuntary reflex and self-defense. Analyzes Sports Violence Act of 1980. Points out self-regulation of violence is needed.

1347. Gulotta, Stephen J., Jr. "Torts In Sports-Deterring Violence In Professional Athletics." 48 Fordham Law Review 764-793. (April 1980).

Questions whether civil actions will have an impact on the problem of violence escalating violence in professional sports. Examines the civil forum and its potential for deterrence and compensation, considering the historic effect of league-administered sanctions and criminal prosecutions. Concludes that at the present time both internal control and judicial intervention are needed to quell the violence and that civile action should be taken when necessary.

1348. Harrow, Richard B. Sports Violence. Arlington: VA: Carrollton Press, Inc., 1980.

Studies criminal violence in professional sports in-depth. Provides overview of violence in hockey, football, basketball, and baseball. Discusses pressure in professional sports to suppress the litigating of potential criminal law violations which occurred during the game. Reviews internal league disciplinary measures. Explores factors which contribute to a prosecutor's decision to use the judicial system when criminal law violations occur. Provides analysis of legal elements of assault and battery, and relevant defenses used in sports violence cases. Includes surveys, bibliography, cases, interviews, and appendices.

1349. Harrow, Richard B. "Violence In Professional Sports: Is It Part of The Game?" 9 Journal of Legislation 1-15. (Winter 1982).

Focuses on the problem and causes of violence in professional sports. Reports the sports industry is unable to handle the problem. Examines the elements of battery and defenses to it. Reviews possible legislative and judicial solutions to the phenomenon.

1350. Kuhlmann, Walter. "Violence In Professional Sports," 1975 Wisconsin Law Review 771-790. (1975).

Explores applicability of criminal and civil law to violent incidents in sports. Reviews Forbes in professional hockey. Discusses the general probability of successful prosecution of such incidents, the problem of prosecutorial discretion, the range of conduct in sports, and the pros and cons of internal league control.

1351. Testan, Steven. "Controlling Violence In Professional Sports." 2 Glendale Law Review 323-325. (1978).

A comment using professional ice hockey as an example. Reviews civil actions with battery as cause of action and concludes this would probably not solve the problem of violence. States criminal prosecution is constitutionally vague as a recourse but was suggested which would make use of criminal prosecutions of professional athletes possible (for acts committed during the game) without violating the constitutional rights of the player in question.

35

WOMEN IN SPORTS

General

1352.   Dessem R. Lawrence. "Sex Discrimination In Coaching." 3 Harvard Women's Law Journal 97-117. (Spring 1980).
Surveys salary differentials for coaches of girls' and boys' athletic teams. Argues that a lower pay rate for girls' coaches is discriminatory and in violation of the fourteenth amendment to the Constitution. Examines this from Title IX, Title VII, Equal Pay Act and Constitutional perspectives.

1353.   Henley, Elizabeth J. "Irrebutable Presumption Doctrine: Applied To State and Federal Regulations Excluding Females From Contact Sports." 4 University of Dayton Law Review 197-210. (Winter 1979).
Note examining the findings in Yellow Springs Exempted Village School District Board of Education v. Ohio High School Athletic Association, 443 F. Supp. 753 (S.D. Ohio 1978). Discusses the court's findings that a rule which results in an irrebutable presumption of female nonqualification violates the due process clause of the fourteenth amendment. Examines the court's finding that the due process clause of the fifth amendment of the Constitution was violated by 45 C.F.R. section 86.41(b).

1354.   Hitchens, Donna J. "Litigation Strategy On Behalf of The Outstanding High School Female Athlete." 8 Golden Gate University Law Review 423-442. (Spring 1979).
Discusses the existence and quality of athletic programs for female athletes. Examines the organization of interscholastic high school athletics in California, the public policy considerations which must be spoken to when formulating a

strategy, the legal theories available for said strategy, and a discussion of the practical considerations of the strategy.

1355.   McDonald, Barbara A. "Equal Pay For Coaches of Female Teams: Finding A Cause of Action Under Federal Law." 55 Notre Dame Lawyer 751-776. (June 1980).

A note which examines and evaluates federal causes of action available to coaches of female teams that have been subjected to compensation discrimination: the Equal Pay Act, Title VI, Title IX of the Education Amendments of 1972, and the fourteenth amendment of the United States Constitution.

1356.   Nelson, Kevin Alfred. "Women's Collegiate Athletics in Limbo." 40 Washington and Lee Law Review 297-312. (Winter 1983).

Discusses Title IX's impact on programs and continuing growth in intercollegiate sports for women. Reviews program-specific approach, benefit theory and institutional interpretation of Title IX.

1357.   Thomas, Ann Victoria and Sheldon-Wildgen, Jan. "Women In Athletics: Winning The Game But Losing The Support." 8 Journal of College and University Law 295-230. (1981/1982).

Overview of the growth and development of women's athletics. Surveys legal developments of the last decade. Reviews the challenges to a sex-based classification in athletics, the Title IX regulation and the conflict between the organizational regulations of the NCAA and the AIAW.

Equal Rights Amendments (ERA)

1358.   Beck, Phyllis W. "Equal Rights Amendment: The Pennsylvania Experience." 81 Dickinson Law Review 395-416. (Spring 1977).

Discusses problems which the lack of guidelines for judicial construction and the broad and sweeping language of the Pennsylvania ERA has caused resulting in the court's general adoption of an absolutist point of view in interpreting cases in the light of the ERA. This position ignores social nuances, lacks flexibility and precludes anticipating problems. Examines sex as a suspect classification requiring strict scrutiny analysis to permit gender-based classifications which have compelling social value.   Briefly touches on Commonwealth v. Pennsylvania Interscholastic Athletic Association (PIAA) (1975) where the latter analysis may have been appropriate and where in interscholastic athletics certain classifications may be both desirable and reasonable.

1359.   Graff, Doralice McEven; Meyers, Kathleen M.; and Tyler, John
          E. "Blair v. Washington State University: Making State ERA's
          A Potent Remedy For Sex Discrimination In Athletics."   14
          Journal of College and University Law 575-589. (Spring 1988).
          Presents the facts of Blair, outlines the traditional avenues
          used to combat sex discrimination in intercollegiate athletics
          (the equal protection clause of the fourteenth amendment to
          the Constitution, the federal statutes, Title VII, the Equal Pay
          Act, and Title IX), examines judicial development of
          Washington's ERA which culminated in Blair. Analyzes the
          effect of Blair and state ERA's as tools for combating college
          and university sex-based discrimination. Concludes that a state
          ERA is a viable and powerful clause of action to combat sex
          discrimination where traditional remedies proved ineffective.

1360.   Mikula, Jacqueline. "Pennsylvania Constitution-Equal Rights
          Amendment-Sex Discimination-Interscholastic Sports."   14
          Duquesne Law Review 101-110. (Fall 1975).
          Analyzes Commonwealth of Pennsylvania v. Pennsylvania
          Interscholastic Athletic Association (1975) (a state-wide high
          school athletic association by-law which prohibited female
          students from competing against males violated on its face the
          ERA to the Constitution of Pennsylvania). Reviews reasoning
          of the court and arguments of the defense, Pennsylvania ERA
          and federal ERA intent, and the resulting ambiguity
          concerning the standard the court used. States decision can be
          read as support for either an absolute or less than absolute
          standard for the validity of a classification under the
          Amendment (which can also be said of prior ERA cases).
          Presents another analysis the court could have used and
          suggests it might have reached a different result in which the
          classification might have been upheld and where the ERA
          would have had a certain flexibility.

1361.   Richardson, Kristin V. "Touchdown, But A Flag On The Play:
          Antidiscrimination In Colleges Athletics and Recovery of
          Public Interest Attorney Fees Under Blair v. Washington State
          University." 24 Williamette Law Review 525-538. (Spring
          1988).
          Explores court's use of Washington State's ERA and Law
          Against Discrimination (and paucity of case law dealing with
          discriminatory athletic funding distribution), decision's effect
          on college program, and likelihood of similar suits (taking
          court's determination of who should finance such claims into
          consideration). Concludes women at Washington State
          University have greater opportunity for participation, financial
          support, and general equity, under the remedies State Supreme
          Court fashioned in Blair.

Female Athletes

1362.   Branchfield, Edward and Grier, Melinda. "Aiken v. Lieuallen and Peterson v. Oregon State University: Defining Equity In Athletics." 8 Journal of College and University Law 369-398. (1981/1982).

Analyzes and compares the cases regarding women's athletic programs. Discusses the effects of Oregon's antidiscrimination law.

1363.   Fabri, Candace J. and Fox, Elaine S. "The Female High School Athlete and Interscholastic Sports." 4 Journal of Law and Education 285-300. (April 1975).

Analyzes the effect the legally protectable interest of female high school athletes may have on existing athletic programs (in the benefits of an interscholastic sports program where one is provided for male athletes). Examines the legal consequences of four possible positions that could be taken regarding interscholastic athletic programs: to provide no program for males or females, to provide a program for male and female students only, to provide a program for male and female students as separate and unequal or to provide a program for male and female students as separate and equal. Concludes the latter program appears to be the most equitable and the most practical for female high school athletes as far as benefiting from interscholastic competition, given budgetary considerations. However, the ideal program would require three teams; one all female, one all male, and the other based on ability without regard to sex.

1364.   Hawley, Donna Lea. "Legal Problems of Sex Discrimination." 15 Alberta Law Review (Canada) 122-141. (1977).

Brief discussion of sex testing of women athletes within the greater context of the issue in question. Examines the nature of the tests and the legality of the test.

1365.   Lemaire, Lyn. "Women and Athletics: Toward A Physicality Perspective." 5 Harvard Women's Law Journal 121-142. (Spring 1982).

Examines traditional model of sports based on winning. Posits the physicality model based on participation for its own sake. Considers limitations, assumptions and planning in athletics.

1366.   Skilton, Robert H. "Emergent Law of Women and Amateur Sports: Recent Developments." 28 Wayne Law Review 1701-1757. (Summer 1982).

Traces development and growth and law regarding women and amateur sports. Examines Title IX and the authority of

HEW, application of the 14th amendment equal protection clause, state law on sex discrimination in sports and other recent developments.

1367.   Wien, Sandra. "Case For Equality In Athletics." 22 Cleveland State Law Review 570-584. (Fall 1973).
Explores the questions of a women's right and opportunity to participate as a member of all-male teams.   Examines casework where female high school athletes have attempted to gain access to all-male athletic teams. Reviews the applicability of state action and the denial of equal protection under the fourteenth amendment.

AUTHOR INDEX

The author index includes authors and joint authors. Since the bibliography is numbered consecutively throughout the chapters, the numbers refer to individual entry numbers.

Abbott, John W., 0796
Abrams, Bobby, 0296
Abrams, Robert, 0342
Abrams, Robert Haskell, 0963
Abrams, Roger I., 0838
Adams, Frank, 0076
Ahern, Terrance, 0322
Alessandro, Christopher J., 0455
Alfton, Robert J., 1124, 1177
Allen, Richard B., 0127
Allen, William B., 0277
Allison, John R., 0817
Alylvia, Kenneth, 0866-0867
Amador, M. Dennis, 0355
Ambrose, James F., 1256
Amoroso, Richard, 0894
Anderson, Cerisse, 1125
Anderson, Mark F., 0287
Angel, Carol, 0798
Antonioli, Pierre, 0582, 0759
Appenzeller, Herb, 1162, 1173
Appenzeller, Thomas, 1162
Appleson, Gail, 1039
Arico, James S., 0644
Ariniaud, Max, 0792
Arkfield, JoAnn M., 0241
Ashman, Allan, 0053, 0119, 0458, 0645, 1147, 1178

Ashworth, John P., 0550
Atchinson, William K., 0818
Atkinson, Mark Alan, 0447
Austin, Arthur D., 0442
Austin, Katherine Ann, 1013
Ayers, Deanne L., 0247

Babij, Bruce J., 0964
Baeumer, L., 0702
Bagley, Martha, 0547
Baicker-McKee, Steven, 1338
Bailey, Robert S., 0737
Balbi, Lonny L., 0616-0618
Baley, James A., 1197
Baragwanath, David, 0518
Barklage, Daniel K., 0396
Barnard, Scott R., 1298
Barnes, John, 0054, 0508
Barnett, Stephen R., 0895
Baron, Ronald L., 1158
Barrett, John C., 0556
Bartolini, Anthony L., 0297
Barton, B.J., 0298
Bashinsky, Major, 0646
Baum, Bernard M., 0859
Beavers, Timothy P., 0203
Beck, Phyllis W., 1358

Beckloff, Mitchell L., 0703
Beisner, John, 0888
Bellamy, Robert V., Jr., 1200
Bellas, Peter W., 0647
Beloff, Michael J., 1153
Benitez, Miriam, 0017
Bennett, John, 1133
Berger, Robert G., 0161
Berger, Susan M. Collins, 0968
Berman, Martin, 0996
Berman, Martin P., 0997
Berry, Robert C., 0849, 0915, 1130-
    1131
Bernstein, Diane, 0760
Bernstein, Sandra, 1054
Berti, Giorgio, 1055, 1132
Bertini, Christopher D., 1314
Beskin, Jay R., 1257
Beumler, Candyce, 0565
Bhirdo, Kelly W., 0648
Bianchi d'Urso, Fulvio, 1079
Biddle, Steven G., 0839
Bieker, Neal, 0503
Binder, Richard L., 1329
Birk, H.-J., 1103
Blackwell, Richard B., 0212
Blalock, Joyce, 0750
Blanplain, R., 0732
Blaxland, Michael, 0583
Blecher, Maxwell M., 0093
Blodgett, Nancy, 0546
Blum, Marc P., 1300
Bluver, Howard C., 0420
Boevers, James A., 0785
Bognanno, Michael L., 0339
Boisson, Phillippe, 0756
Bortz, Bruce L., 0795
Boswell, Thomas M., 0213
Bojarski, Marek, 0521, 0536
Bosch, Peter J., 0868
Bourque, Stephen, 0649
Boyer, Allen, 1094
Bracuemond, J., 1056
Bradshaw, Alan C., 0704
Branchfield, Edward, 1362
Brandner, Trier, 0797
Braun, Steven, 1301
Bredesen, Karsten E., 0899
Brennan, James T., 0869

Brennan, Mary Lynn, 0278
Brent, Audrey S., 0347
Briggs, William B., 0356
Briggs, William Buckley, 0443
Bringewat, Peter, 1106
Broadbent, G. P., 1339
Brock, James L., Jr., 0120
Brock, Stephen F., 0248
Broder, Sherry, 1004
Brody, Burton F., 0323, 0623, 0919
Brom, Thomas, 0690
Bronaugh, Minor, 1190
Brookfield, F.M., 0519
Brooks, David, 1126
Brower, Edith S., 0242
Brown, Charles C., 0299
Brown, Fred R., 0295
Brown, Lori J., 0819
Browne, Kelly 0948
Brumback, Gordon J., 0896
Brumbaugh, John C., 0300
Bryce, Philip R., 0301
Buchner, Herbert, 1159
Buckley, R. A., 0729
Budavari, Rosemary, 1104
Buoniconti, Nicholas A., 0459
Burger, John Edward, 0229
Burkow, Steven H., 0055
Burmeister, Joachim, 0357, 1154
Burr, Keith J., 0840
Busey, J. Craig, 1206
Buskus, Michael L., 0557
Busto, Mercedes C., 0529
Butler, Jim, 0965
Buxton, Joseph T., Jr., 1036
Byrne, J. Peter, 0655

Caliendo, Nat S., 0467, 0474
Campbell, Dana Mark, 0094
Campbell, Thomas J., 0897
Capetta, John, 0397
Caporale, Robert L., 1174
Capper, James E., 0398
Carico, David D., 0754
Carlesen, Chris J., 0358, 1340
Carlson, Robert S., 0841
Carr, Stephen E. Austin, 0998
Carrafiello, Vincent A., 0056

Carroll, John F., 1341
Carroll, Mary, 1330
Carter, P.B., 0491
Cavrich, Joseph W., 0374
Cernahan, A. Vernon, 0738
Chafton, Steven M., 0863
Chalat, James H., 0584, 0588, 0761-0762
Chamberlain, John D., 0558
Chambers, Marcia, 0039
Chamblis, Samuel M., III., 0288
Champion, Walter T., Jr., 0359
Chapman, Douglas K., 0864
Chapman, Mayer, 0624
Charpentier, J., 0763
Chaves, Antonio, 0938, 0945, 1201
Chelius, James R., 0131
Chemakin, I. M., 1095-1098
Ching, Cori Jan, 1214
Chorlton, M.D., 0393
Ciaglo, Cathleen M., 1235
Cirell, Stephen, 1133
Cirenci, Maria Teresa, 1080
Clancy, Christopher H., 0882
Clark, Alan W., 0081
Clark, Ronald J., 0550
Clark, William D., 1134
Classen, H. Ward, 0162
Clawson, Carol, 0764
Clear, Delbert K., 0547
Clements, Robert S., 1224
Clendenon, Donn A., 0302
Cleveland, Granville E., 1170
Closius, Phillip J., 0864, 0916
Coben, Larry E., 0549
Cochran, J. Otis, 0249
Coffey, Christopher W., 0939
Cohen, Bernard S., 0723
Colapietro, Bruno, 0361
Coleman, Edward G., 0163
Collier, N. C., 1030
Collomb, Pierre, 0765
Coma, M. Bassols, 0523, 1057
Conners, John, 1280
Conrad, A. F., 0980
Consolo, Guiseppe, 1135
Constant, Jean, 0272-0273
Conway, Ellen Sue, 0088
Coutts, J. A., 1022

Covell, Kerrie S., 0250
Cowper, Francis, 1040
Cox, Thomas A., 0468
Cozzillio, M.J., 0428
Crafts, Reverend Wilbur F., 1191
Crandell, Jeffrey P., 0010
Crane, James S., 1202
Cromley, Charles, 0164
Cross, Harry M., 0448
Croudace, Virginia P., 0999
Crum, J. V., III., 1281
Cryan, Thomas Joseph, 1202
Cuesta Cascajares, R. Ruiz de la, 0733-0734
Cullum, Philip R. A., 0527
Cummings, William Leamon, 0095
Curle, David, 0133
Cypher, Elspeth B., 0089
Cyrlin, Alan I., 0955

Daniels, Eric D., 0650
Daniels, Howard F., 0093
Daspin, D. Albert, 0224
David, Ernest L., 0537
Davies, D. K., 0509
Davis, James H., 0619
Davis, Melonie L., 0082
Davis, Robert N., 0898
Davis, Victoria J., 0578
de Bianchetti, A., 1058, 1163
deCrow, Karen, 0469
de Doelder, H., 1315
Dedopoulous, Stuart, 0985-0987
de Francesco, Giovannangelo, 1316
DeGiorgi, Maria Vita, 0057, 0806
Dell, Ernest, 0735
Del Rey, Alfred J., 1282
Demoff, Marvin A., 0289, 0324
de Ridder, E., 1179
De Santis, Kathleen, 0460
DeSerpa, Allan, 0187
Desmarias, Steven A., 0999
Dessem, R. Lawrence, 0995, 1352
deTurck, Mark A., 1242
DeVine, Stephen W., 0470
Dewey, Addison E., 0921
Dias, R. W. M., 0691
Dicker, James W., 1283

Dickerson, Jaffe D., 0624
Dickerson, Thomas A., 1037
DiLisi, Richard A., 0651
DiLorenzo, Louis P., 0471-0472
DiNardo, Annemarie, 0435
DiNicola, Ronald A., 1345
Disney, Mitchell F., 0739
Dixon, D. M., 1107
Dixon, Thomas M., 0436
Dobberstein, Eric, 0251
Dobray, Debra, 0492
Dokovska, D., 0364
Doll, P.-J., 0274
Dolling, D., 0399
Donnelly, Joseph C., 0559
Dow, T. Andrew, 0018
Dragonetti, Gerald C., 0219
DuBoff, Leonard D., 1215
Duckworth, Roy D., III., 0449
Dunand, Muriel A., 1041
Dunlavey, James, 1031
Dunn, David Lawrence, 0019
Dunn, Scott A., 0165
Dutoit, Bernard, 0766
Dworkin, Gerald, 0421
Dworkin, James B., 0131, 0134,   0183

Eagles, Ian, 0520
Eckler, John, 0206
Econn, Douglass Andrew, 0352
Edmonds, Edmund P., 0446
Edwards, Harry, 0705
Eglinski, Georgann Hansen, 0303
Ehrhardt, Charles W., 0011
Eisen, David Spencer, 0015
Eisen, Jeffrey M., 0135
Elie, Steven J., 0136
Ellerhorst, Jim, 1253
Elliott, Jeffrey M., 0304
Elmore, Len, 0012
Engler, Terri, 1317
Enrenberg, Ronald G., 0339
Ensor, Richard J., 0231, 0276,
    0681, 0850, 1007
Enten, Harold N., 0214
Eppel, J.P., 0166
Epstein, Robert K., 0363
Errera, Roger, 1155

Eser, Albin, 1332
Etter, William F., 0047
Evans, A., 0528
Evans, Thomas S., 0472
Eves, Roderick D., 0538

Faber, Wendy A., 0585
Fabian, David M., 0653
Fabri, Candace J., 1363
Faccenda, Philip J., 0456
Fagan, John E., 0693
Fagen, John E., 0586
Falk, Jonathan, 0922
Fanning, J., 1060
Farnsworth, A. Randall, 0325
Farrell, Michael, 0753
Farrow, Michael J., 0587
Faverhelm, Kent, 0588
Ferguson, Arthur B., Jr., 0767
Fidel, Noel, 0372
Filho, A. Melo, 1164
Finkelstein, Jared Tobin, 1156
Fischman, Joel, 0184
Fleisher, Arthur A., III., 0842
Fletcher, Shirley, 0625
Foley, James F., 0820
Fonti, Joseph F., 0243
Foraker, Scott J., 0225
Forbes, Frank S., 0579
Ford, James B., 0252
Forlati Picchio, Laura, 0279
Fox, Dana Alden, 0020
Fox, Elaine S., 1363
Fraade, Richard D., 1284
Fraley, Robert E., 0032, 0052
Franck, Richard L., 0899
Frank, Janice R., 0092
Freedman, Warren, 0821
Freundenberger, Tim, 0275
Friedrich, Paul M., 0566

Gaal, John, 0471-0472
Gaeta, Dante, 0757
Galante, Mary Ann, 0706
Gallagher, Michael D., 0871
Gaona, David F., 0626
Gardner, David B., 1284

Garland, Jeffrey, 0226
Garrett, Robert Alan, 1203
Garubo, Philip A., Jr., 1204
Garvey, Ed, 0013, 0326
Gerard, Robert J., Jr., 0694
Gerary, Bryan E., 0851
Gessford, James B., 0872
Giannini, Nadia A., 0799
Gibbs, Annette, 0250
Gibson, Don Eugene-Nolan, 1346
Gignoux, C., 0607
Gilroy, Thomas P., 0917
Girard, Timothy H., 0264
Girginov, A., 0364
Giulietti, James J., 0014
Goettel, James G., 0716
Goldberg, Victor P., 1225
Goldhaber, Gerald M., 1242
Goldman, Lee, 0096, 1160
Goldsmith, Arthur H., 0604
Goldstein, Lynn A., 0567
Goldstein, Mark L., 0185
Goldstein, Seth M., 0843
Gombinski, Steven J., 1285
Gonzales, Grimaldo, Mariano-
   Carmelo, 0524
Gonzales, Ralph, 1205
Goodman, Mark C., 0034
Goodman, Stephen S., IV., 0090
Goore, Jeffrey, 0884
Gorla, Gino, 0365
Gordon, Kenneth I., 0924
Gorton, Slade (Senator), 0900
Gould, William B., 0849
Gould, William G., IV., 0852,
Gould, William V., IV., 0915
Grad, Richard J., 0879
Graf, Richard M., 0473
Graff, Doralice McEwen, 1359
Grant, David, 0539, 1035
Grasselli, Sergio, 0786
Graver, Myron C., 0121
Grauer, Myron C., 0305
Graves, Judson, 0083
Gray, Charles, 0901
Gray, John A., 0327, 0902
Grayson, Edward, 0366-0367, 1025,
   1165, 1318-1319
Grebey, C. Raymond, Jr., 0186

Green, John B., 0981
Greenberg, Mannes F., 1061
Greene, Linda S., 0457
Greenblatt, David J., 0253
Greenspan, David, 0654
Greenwald, Andrew E., 0724
Gregory, Byron L., 1206
Gregory, I. Francis, II., 0604
Griener, Paul, 1216
Grier, Melinda, 1362
Grigoli, Michele, 0758
Gros, Manuel, 1062, 1180
Grubb, M. J., 1136
Grunsky, Wolfgang, 0400
Gulland, Eugene D., 0655
Gulotta, Stephen J., Jr., 1347
Gunn, Malcolm, 1273
Gurney, Guy, 0800
Guthrie, R. Claire, 0474

Hagglund, Clarence E., 0590
Hainline, Jon S., 0035
Hall, Frederick S., 1038
Halligan, T.F., 0137
Hallowell, Lyle, 1333
Halperin, Richard E., 1264
Hames, Eugene S., 0591
Hamilton, Jackson D., 0048
Hammer, Robert S., 0885
Hander, Deborah Good, 0695
Hanley, Mark A., 0687
Hanson, Douglas A., 1257
Haray, Richard J. 0227
Hardcastle, R. A., 1112
Hargreaves, Allan, 1265
Harmelink, Philip J., 1266
Harrow, Richard B., 1349
Harty, James D., 0580
Harwell, F. Russell, 0033, 0052
Harwood, Steven J., 1302
Haserot, Phyllis Weiss, 0807
Hastings, Leslie, 0568
Hauff, Charles F., Jr., 0707
Hauver, Constance, 0967
Haviland, Linda A., 0648
Hawkins, Deborah H., 0021
Hawkins, James P., 0740
Hawley, Donna Lea, 1364

Hay, Steven B., 0956
Hayes, Jacquelyn K., 0401
Hazelwood, Mark F., 0138
Hechter, William, 1334
Heidt, Robert H., 0886
Heiner, S. Phillip, 0873
Helal, Basil, 0402
Henley, Elizabeth J., 1353
Hepp, Camill, 0592
Herbert, David L., 0968
Herbert, William G., 0968
Herman, Anne Marie Canali,   0461
Herrmann, H., 0532
Hetzel, James V., 1014
Heydon, J.D., 0117
Heyman, Amy R., 0896
Hickman, William, 0656
Hilf, Meinhard, 1181
Hill, James Richard, 0139, 0210
Hiller, Jack, 1099
Hink, Barbara, 0925
Histrop, Lindsay Ann, 1286-1287
Hitchens, Donna J., 1354
Hobel, Michael S., 0853
Hochberg, Philip R., 0808, 1203,
    1207-1210, 1227-1228
Hochman, Marilyn, 0736
Hofeld, Albert F., 0983
Hoffman, Robert B., 0204
Hoffman, Scott Lee, 0167
Hoffman, Thomas E., 1303
Hogrogian, John, 0321
Holahan, William L., 0140
Holford, Elizabeth J., 0306
Holzberg, Brian, 0741
Honorat, J., 0368
Horn, Stephen, 0429
Horowitz, Ira, 1228-1229
Horvitz, David S., 0369
Horvitz, Jerome S., 1303
Houdek, Frank G., 1142
Houser, Douglas G., 0550
Howard, James J., 0437
Hudson, A.H., 0403
Huff, Michele Iris, 0657
Huon, deKermadec, J.-M., 1081
Hutchinson, Allan C., 1166

Igbinovia, Patrick Edobor, 1320
Ingram, John D., 0988

Jacklin, Pamela L., 1001
Jackstadt, Robert L., 0658
Jacobs, Donald P., 0404
Jacobs, Francis G., 0494
Jacobs, Michael S., 0936
Jacobson, Charles, 0141
Jacoby, Jacob, 0957
Jahn, Gary Norman, 0569
Jallo, Jerome R., 1124, 1177
James, L. D., 0969
Jarriel, Judith E., 0058
Jay, C. B., 1136
Jedruch, Stanislaw, 0514, 0540
Jeffers, Howard, 1033
Jeffery, David, 1258
Jenkins, John A., 0001
Jennings, Diane I., 1015
Jennings, Marianne, 0002, 0257
Jennings, Marianne M., 0659
Jensen, Erik M., 1267
Jensen, June E., 0476
Johnson, Alex M., Jr., 0801, 0874
Johnson, Arthur T., 0809, 0903
Johnson, Christina, 0477
Johnson, David V., 0022
Johnson, Derek Quinn, 0462
Johnson, Frederic A., 0097, 0142,
    0168
Johnson, Janet Junttila, 1002
Johnson, Tony, 1063
Joiner, W. Joseph, 0059
Jolley, Dan M., 0970
Jones, J.C.H., 0349, 0509
Jones, John B., 1254
Jones, Melinda, 1166
Jones, Michael E., 0810, 0854
Joseph, Kenneth, 0405
Joyal-Poupart, Renee, 0370, 1137
Joyce, Thomas W. E., III., 0904
Judge, Wiiliam J., 1288

Kabbes, David G., 0822
Kadzielski, Mark A., 0478, 1008
Kaplan, David A., 0003
Kaplan, Fred, 0875

Kaplan, Gary P., 1285
Kaplan, Richard L., 0431
Kaplin, William A., 0463
Karaquillo, J.-P., 1064, 1082
Karch, Sargent, 0933
Karns, Jack E., 0696
Katz, Robert Reiff, 1304
Kauffman, Steven A., 1294
Keating, Kenneth B., 0098
Keenan, Robert M., III., 0254
Keith, Maxwell, 0823
Kelly, David M., 0958-0959
Kelly, G.M., 0343, 0608
Kemp, Deborah A., 0660
Kempf, Donald G., Jr., 0099
Kessler, Remy, 0169
Keyes, G. Preston, 0627
Khan, A. N., 0541
Kiersh, Edward, 0045
Kijowski, A., 1182
King, Joseph H., Jr., 0609
Kirby, James, 0146
Kirby, Robert J., 0661
Kirby, Wendy T., 0079
Kirkwood, Genevieve, 0371
Klammer, Steven R., 0662
Klein, Deborah E., 0443
Kleppe, Peter, 0593
Kligman, R.D., 0394
Klinger, Leslie S., 1259, 1305
Kloepfer, Michael, 0797
Koch, James V., 0060, 0479, 0628
Koch, Matthew J., 0721
Koch, Richard A., 1275
Koester, Anne Y., 0077
Kohn, Alan, 0004
Kohn, Gary P., 0036
Kolback, Kimberly D., 0949
Konig, B., 0781-0783
Koppett, Leonard, 1138
Korn, Peter L., 0005
Kornmehl, Bernard B., 0307
Kosin, Phil, 0147
Kotlowski, Bill, 1175
Kovach, K.A., 0328
Kovach, Kenneth A., 0934
Kozik, Susan Marie, 0663
Kozlowski, James C., 0755
Krakora, Joseph E., 0480

Krasnow, Erwin G., 0937
Kravchenko, V. V., 1065
Kravitz, Robert N., 0960
Kritzer, Paul E., 1236
Kroll, Lea, 0584
Kruger, Daniel H., 0337
Krzywicki, Clausen J., 0570
Kuhlmann, Walter, 1350
Kuhn, Janet Lammersen, 0481
Kukushkin, M. I., 1098
Kunnell, E., 0768
Kunz, Marco B., 0588
Kurlantzick, Lewis S., 0308
Kutner, Joan Ruth, 0989
Kyer, Clifford Ian, 0351

Lambert, Dale J., 0406
Lambert, Thomas F., Jr., 0344, 0971,
    1243-1245
Langavant, Emmanuel, 0972
Langerman, Samuel, 0372
Langevin, Mark E., 1342
Lapchick, Richard E., 0280
Lapeyre, Charles, 1066, 1183
Larguier, J., 0769
Laskowski, Gregory E., 1117
Laufer, Laurence, 0238
Lava, Leslie Michele, 0811
Lazaroff, Daniel E., 0100-0101
Leavell, Jerome F., 0812
Leduc, Benoit, 0391
Lee, Brian E., 0844
Lee, Robert W., 0940
Leeson, Todd A., 0244
Lefferts, Lori J., 0023
Lehn, Kenneth, 0950
Lemaire, Lyn, 1365
Lempinen, Edward W., 0220
Lener, A., 1068, 1184
Letourneau, Gilles, 0510, 1321-1322,
    1336-1337
Levick, Marsha, 0115
Levin, Chery Wyron, 0795
Levy, Herman M., 0937
Lewis, Darryll M., 0579
Lewis, Frank B., 0170
Lewis, Michael L., 1260
Leyendecker, R. Socini, 0495

Lezin, Valerie, 0708
Lindgren, Penny P., 0407
Lineberry, William P., 1069
Lisman, Carol H., 0594
Lock, Ethan, 0187, 0255-0257, 0329-0330, 0824, 0935
Lockhart, Kim, 0770
Lockman, John S., 0207
Longo, Christina A., 1009
Lotter, Aline H., 0845
Lovett, Ricahrd A., 0771
Lowell, Cym H., 0062, 0086, 0855, 1172, 1289
Lubell, Adele, 0620
Lubinsky, Theodore A., 0422
Lund, John, 0588
Luntz, Harold, 0926
Lyra Filho, J., 0507, 0787

Mabrouk, M., 0728, 0973
Maclean, D. M., 1290
MacDonald, Alistair, 0542
Macdonald, J. Ross, 0350
Mackall, John R., 0686
Macri, C., 0846
Madden, Patrick J., 0917
Maher, Fred, 1003
Mairs, Patricia A., 0802
Manby, C. Robert, 0697
Mandel, Bernard, 0701
Manganas, A., 1322
Manganas, Antione, 1336-1337
Manisco, Joseph Michael, 0046
Marasa, Giorgio, 1083
Marcil, Michael J., 1202
Marcus, Richard M., 0373
Marencik, Karen A., 0331
Marilla, G.-D., 0595, 0772
Markham, Jesse W., 0171
Marks, Jeffrey M., 0709
Martha, Paul J., 0374
Martin, Gordon A., Jr., 0258, 0684-0685
Martin, James P., 0482
Martin, Philip L., 0172-0173
Massey, Craig, 0024
Mathews, Nancy N., 1070
Mathys, Heinz Walter, 0773

Matthews, David L., 1197
Mauch, James C., 0974
Mayer, H., 0742
Mayrand, A., 0698
Mbaye, Keba, 0717, 1084
McAllister, Stephen R., 0927
McAtee, Jon, 0914
McBride, Deborah Holmes, 0259
McBroom, Douglas D., 0581
McBurney, Christian, 0893
McCaffrey, Patrick, 1012
McCarthy, James, 0794
McCarthy James J., 0793
McClelland, Robert W., 0102
McCormick, Robert A., 0197, 0309, 0856
McCormick, Robert E., 0223, 0281
McDonald, Barbara A., 1355
McDonald, Eugene J., 0474
McEwan, V. G., 1323
McFarland, Gavin, 1043
Mcfarlane, Neil, 0610
McGahey, Robert L., Jr., 0087
McIntire, Christopher, 1113
McKenna, Kevin M., 0248, 0282, 0629
McKenney, Samuel S., 0174
McKenzie, Richard B., 0630
McKeown, Richard B., 0213
McKinney-Browning, Mabel C., 0408
McKinnon, Matthew C., 0309
McLain, William T., 0664
McLeese, Don, 0006
McManis, Charles R., 1237
McManus, Bill, 0665
McNamara, Timothy K., 1016
McQuaide, John J., 0215
Mead, Leon F., III., 0889
Meiners, Roger E., 0281
Meissner, Nancy Jean, 0216
Mellowitz, Jim, 0063
Meloch, Sally L., 0260
Meltzer, Bernard, 0148
Mendeloff, Scott, 1345
Menesini, Vittorio, 0951, 1238
Menitove, Barton J., 0175
Meran, Harry B., 1248
Meredith, Robert J., 0261

Merritt, William C., 0551
Mertens, Pierre, 0710
Meshbesher, Ronald I., 1333
Meyers, Kathleen M., 1359
Mikell, Melanie Floy, 1121
Mikula, Jacqueline, 1360
Millard, Howard L., 0812
Miller, David G., 0857
Miller, David K., 0631
Miller, Mark S., 0348
Miller, Marvin J., 0188
Miller, Michael J., 0239
Mills, Michael R., 0041, 0044
Mitnick, Eric Alan, 0905
Mona, Joseph, 1306
Moore, Charles C., 0375
Moot, Robert C., Jr., 1249
Moriarty, Dick, 0496
Morris, John P., 0825-0827
Morris, Timothy P., 0409
Moss, Lawrence C., 0735
Moynihan, David S., 0122
Mufson, Ellen Z., 0941
Muller, P., 0596
Mullins, Charles E., 0064
Munic, Martin D., 0157
Murphy, Betty Southard, 0858
Murphy, Nina R., 1268
Murphy, Scott P., 0774
Musuals, Kevin G., 0543
Myers, John, 0975

Nachin, G., 0597
Nadel, Peter, 0392
Nadel, Peter J., 0942
Nafziger, James A. R., 0065, 0497-
    0499, 0530, 0711-0712, 1071
Nanscawen, Peter, 0504, 0928
Narol, Mel, 0410, 0984-0987, 1198
Narol, Melvin S., 1150
Nelson, John A., 1257
Nelson, Kevin Alfred, 1356
Nelson, Paul L., 0103, 0828
Nelson, Stephen, 1185
Neville, John W., 0104, 0177
Nevins, Francis M., Jr., 1239
Newell, David, 0730
Newman, Pamela J., 0007

Newton, Carl K., 0890
Newton, Jon P., 0228
Nicolau, G., 0189
Nielsen, Bradley C., 1324
Nimoy, Adam B., 0048
Nirk, Rudolf, 0598
Nitti, Lois, 0943
Nogay, Arlie R., 0085
Noll, Roger G., 1072
Nordlinger, Angela, 1085
Norman, Ken, 0990
Norton, Clark, 0464
Novick, Donald, 0333

O'Connor, Christine, 0667
O'Dea, John F., 0829
O'Kane, H. J., 0346
Oliphant, Judith Lee, 0483
Oliver, Eugene, Jr., 0284
O'Neill, Barbara Ann, 0712
Opie, Hayden, 0572
Ostroff, Ron, 0067

Padrutt, Willy, 0775-0776, 1144
Paonessa, Joseph P., 0178
Paragano, Vincent D., 0025
Parker, Jonny Clyde, 0285
Parmanand, Suryia K., 0411
Pate, Steve, 0008
Patino, Jose Luis, 0668
Patterson, Nancy H., 1148
Partin, Matt, 0573
Pauly, Judith Anne, 0450
Peiser, G., 0763
Pelhak, Jurgen, 0749
Pemstein, Jason Michael, 0634
Penick, S. Barksdale, 1255
Penner, Gerald M., 0847
Pernell, LeRoy, 0262
Peterson, Robert S., 1217
Peterson, Terri L., 0376
Petr, Todd A., 0286
Petri, John T., 0290
Petrich, Ray, 0876
Pfeifer, Robert M., 0669
Philippart, M., 0234
Philo, Harry M., 0544

Philpot, Kenneth J., 0686
Pichler, J., 0552-0553, 0599-0600, 0777
Pierce, Samuel R., Jr., 0106
Pitt, Morley Ben, 0621
Plouvin, J.-Y., 0068, 1073, 1086- 1087, 1168
Pocar, Fausto, 0500, 0778
Podgers, James, 0484
Pogge-Strubing, Marianne, 0485
Ponsoldt, James, 1211
Pooler, Sanford, 0422
Popovich, Peter S., 1021
Porto, Brian L., 0952
Poskanzer, Steven G., 0084
Postel, Theodore, 0377, 0423, 1127
Postell, Claudia J., 0378, 0991
Potter, Dirk D., 0184
Poupart, J.-M., 0751
Power, Vincent J. G., 0515
Powers, Brian A., 0109
Powers, Michael, 1307
Prescott, Allie J., III., 0179
Preston, F. S., 0611
Prettyman, Keith A., 0334
Prusak, J., 0379, 0513, 1100, 1169
Pryor, Barbara L., 1017
Psarakis, Emanual N., 0422
Purdue, Michael, 0371
Pusey, Michael, 1301
Putzolu, G. Volpe, 1088

Quade, Vicki, 0554
Quinn, James W., 1241
Quinn, Terence R., 0412
Quinn, Thomas F., 0486
Quirk, James, 0891

Raabe, William, Jr., 1308
Rafferty, Robert C., 0465
Rains, Cameron Jay, 1325
Ramphal, Shridath S., 0501
Rand, Suzanne E., 0670
Randolph, Robert D., Jr., 0671
Rapson, Donald J., 0150
Raskopf, Robert Lloyd, 0957
Rathie, D. S., 0380

Ream, Davidson, 0407
Reaves, Lynne, 0190, 0813, 0929
Redmond-Cooper, Ruth, 1027
Reed, Gregory J., 1269
Reicher, Thomas Z., 0735
Reid, Cecelia, 1212
Reindle, Otto, 0726
Remick, Lloyd Zane, 0015
Remington, Frank J., 0635
Render, Edwin R., 0727
Ribette, J., 0607
Rice, David M., 1218
Rich, Frederic C., 0713
Richard, Andrea Leah, 0636
Richardson, Kristin V., 1361
Richler, Josef, 0779
Richter, Allan, 0803
Riegel, Robert G., Jr., 0687
Riffer, Jeffrey K., 0091
Riga, Peter J., 0311
Riguera, Jose R., 0672
Ring, Bart Ivan, 0026
Rings, Kevin A., 0191
Rivera, Rhonda R., 0092
Roberts, Barry S., 0109
Roberts, Gary R., 0110, 0124-0126, 0830-0831, 1219
Rochefort, Lawrence P., 0413
Rodgers, J. Mark, 0011, 0027
Rogers, C. Paul, III., 0180
Roman, Neil K., 0312
Romano, John F., 0976
Rooney, John Flynn, 0743
Rose, Allison, 0263
Rose, Laurence H., 0264
Roseberg, Normal L., 0151
Rosen, James, 1230
Rosenbaum, Thane N., 0832
Rosenblatt, Albert M., 0564, 0601
Ross, C. Thomas, 0451
Ross, Gail, 0487
Ross, Stephen F., 0848, 1231
Roth, Norma, 0245
Rothenberg, Alan I., 0291, 0814
Rothernberg, Alan I., 0335
Rowe, Kaeol K., 0673
Rubanowitz, Daniel B., 0906
Rubin, Richard Alan, 1018
Rudel, Michael I., 1213

Rudkin, Sven C., 0833, 0862
Rueter, Dieter, 0382
Rusch, Carolyn, 0992
Ruschmann, Paul A., 0028
Rush, Sharon Elizabeth, 0452
Russell, Charles V., 0612
Ruxin, Robert H., 0037
Ryan, Allan J., 0613

Safian, Robert, 0049, 0432
Sahl, J. P., 0637
Saint-Jours, Y., 1074
Salter, Michael, 1044-1045
Samuel, A., 0714
Samuels, Alec, 0383, 1046
Samuels, Howard J., 1114
Sanbar, S. S., 0614
Sandefer, Larry, 0574
Sanders, Jane A., 1326
Sandrock, Otto, 1075
Sargis, Kevin M., 1276
Sarraz-Bournet, Pierre, 0752
Saunders, O. O. R., 0502
Saxer, Shelley Ross, 0946
Scanlan, John A., Jr., 0080, 0265, 1170
Schachter, Charles I., 1149
Schaller, W. L., 0346
Schambeck, H., 0506
Scheffler, Mark D., 0878
Scheler, Brad Eric, 0922
Schiano, Michael, 0892
Schlafly, Joseph, 0851
Schneiderman, Michael, 0930
Schrammel, W., 0790, 1186
Schuck, Donald L., Jr., 0069
Schuett, Patricia K., 0575
Schwartz, J. M., 0674
Scott, Mary L., 0266
Scully, Gerald W., 0865
Scully, Thomas, 0675
Scutti, Thomas A., 0424
Seebauer, Heidi J., 0744
Seha, Ann M., 1005
Seib, Jonathan E., 0676
Seitz, Peter, 0192-0193
Seki, James H., 0414
Seymour, Harold, 0152

Shafer, Nathaniel, 0615
Shannon, David J., 0078
Shapiro, Daniel I., 0931
Shapiro, Paul W., 0153
Shea, Michael Charles, 0313
Sheldon-Wildgen, Jan, 1357
Sheppard, Lee A., 1271
Shimoyama, E., 0516
Shingler, Ronald J., 0907
Shipley, David E., 0953
Shooshan, H. M., III., 1220
Shooshan, Harry M., 1232
Shropshire, K. L., 0029, 0688
Shorpshire, Kenneth L., 0531, 0908
Shulman, Daniel S., 0859
Shulman, Leonard M., 0453
Shulruff, Lawrence, 0050
Sibley, N. W., 1129
Sidoti, Christopher A., 0961
Siedlecki, M. Agnes, 1233
Silance, L., 0718
Silas, Faye A., 0070, 0994, 1176
Silbergleit, Kenneth R., 1292
Simmons, Sheryl L., 0488
Simon, Richard K., 0230
Sims, P. N., 1047
Sims, William, 0677
Singman, Bruce H., 0336
Sinischalchi, Vincenzo M., 0602, 0780
Sipkins, Thomas M., 1021
Siskind, Gary E., 0425, 0606
Skilton, Robert H., 1366
Slattery, Jeffrey D., 0890
Slaughter, Fred L., 0055
Sloane, Arthur A., 0202
Slonim, Scott, 1343
Slusher, Howard S., 1115
Smith, Arthur D., Jr., 0977
Smith, Rodney K., 0438, 0638-0639
Smith, Scott A., 0376
Smith, Frederick F., Jr., 0030
Smith, Walt, 0489
Snider, Jim, 0387
Sobel, Lionel S., 0031, 0154, 0815, 0932, 1221
Solar, Keith Randall, 0953
Sopinka, J., 0320
Sosniak, Mieczyslaw, 0415

Sotgia, Sergio, 0789
Spellman, William, 0139, 0210
Spevacek, Charles E., 0384
Spicer, Robert E., Jr., 0268
Springer, Felix J., 0454
Sprotzer, Ira, 1344
Sprung, R., 0781-0783
Spurgin, Gerald, 0387
St. John, Mary C., 0221
Stahmer, Gregory M., 0719
Stanley, James R., 0314
Staton, Richard, 0433
Staudohar, Paul D., 0198, 0860, 0909, 0914-0915
Steele, Robert T., 0385
Steinbach, Sheldon Elliot, 0071
Steinback, Sheldon E., 0655
Steinberg, David, 0155
Steinberg, David L., 0353
Steiner, Udo, 1151
Stern, James F., 1246
Stern, Ralph D., 0072, 1171
Steuerle, Gene, 1250
Stewart, Allan, 1284
Stewart, Brian S., 0700
Stewart, J. B., 1328
Stifler, Hans-Kaspar, 0603, 0784
Stillman, Grant, 1076
Stine, Gregory, 0544
Stokes, Jerome W. D., 0439
Stoljar, Samuel J., 1089
Stoner, Edward N., II., 0085
Strachan, Gordon, 0785
Strandell, Valerie Nelson, 1309
Strauss, Steven M., 0315
Strenk, Andrew, 1071
Sullivan, E. Thomas, 0630
Sullivan, Kevin, 0854
Sullivan, Michael J., 0038
Sutterfield, James R., 0804
Sweeney, Theodora Briggs, 0978
Swift, Ray L., 1120
Swygert, H. Patrick, 0359
Symington, James W., 0116
Szwabowski, Russell W., 0689
Szwarc, A. J., 0522

Taggart, Thomas, 0976
Tagliabue, Paul J., 0111

Talley, Chuck, 0745
Tanaka, Y., 0517
Tanick, Marshall H., 0157
Taplitz, Paul V., 0171
Tapp, Mara, 0269
Tarone, Gregory J., 0292-0293
Tashjian-Brown, Eva S., 0490
Taupier, Michel, 1090
Taylor, Jefferson C., 1048
Taylor, Ross D., 0801
Teague, Bernard, 1145
Telias, Bradley S., 0746
Tellem, Arn H., 0291, 0335
Terry, Robert B., 0836
Testan, Steven, 1351
Tetzlaff, Angelika, 1091
Thaler, Craig H., 0270
Thoman, Elizabeth F., 1009
Thomas, Ann Victoria, 1357
Thomas, Henry I., 1293
Thompson, Larry R., 1226
Thornley, Arthur, 0337
Thorpe, James A., 0181
Tobin-Rubio, Lisa J., 0910
Todaro, Gerald J., 0386, 0622
Tokarz, Karen L., 1006
Tollison, Robert D., 0223
Tomandl, T., 0790, 1186
Topkis, Jay H., 0182
Torbert, Dixie, 0387
Torrens, Thomas M., 1222
Trechak, John, 0947
Triffterer, Otto, 1157
Trossman, J., 0511
Trossman, Jeff, 0271
Trivizas, Eugene, 1049-1051
Troy, F. E., 0388
Tsitsoura, A., 1047
Tucker, Neil R., 0418
Turnbull, J. A., 1139
Turow, Stuart, 0678
Turrow, Andrew J., 0918
Tyler, John E., 1359

Uberstine, Gary A., 0816, 0879
Uerling, Donald F., 0294
Umana Soto, Manuel Francisco, 1116, 1140
Underhill, David S., 0316

Uren, Tom, 0505, 1105
Uvarov, V. N., 1101

VanCamp, Stephen R., 0679
Van De Ven, Martha A., 1294
van Dorst, A. J. A., 1315
Vatnikov, I. E., 1077
Vecchione, Renato, 0722
Vera, Jose Bermejo, 0525
Verkindt, P.-Y., 1180
Verrucoli, Piero, 1092
Versfelt, David S., 0738
Veth, N.J.P. Giltay, 0791, 1187
Vieweg, Laus, 1093
Vignes, David W., 1266
Vogeler, William, 0805
von Nessen, Paul, 0503

Wacke, Andreas, 0389
Waicukauski, Ron, 0440
Waldman, Ronald L., 1223
Walker, Matthew S., 1340
Walsh, William D., 0349
Walters, Stephen J. K., 0327
Warburton, Jean, 1188, 1252
Ward, Brian, 0118
Warren, Irwin H., 1241
Warth, Thomas J., 0648
Waters, Robert H., 0854
Watson, John H., 0341
Waugh, Katherine, 0009
Webb, Robert G., 0837
Wee, Beverly, 1004
Weiland, Bernd H., 0533
Weill, Jay R., 1310
Weis, Theodore Delaney, 1295
Weisman, Barry L., 1296
Weiss, Allan J., 0318
Weiss, Jonathan A., 0882
Weistart, John C., 0112, 0445, 0466,
    0642, 0887, 1161, 1172
Wesker, Mark A., 0911
Wesley-Smith, P., 0747
Wessels, Hubert, 0534
Westover, Susan, 0680
Weymouth, T. Clark, 0079
White, Diane, 0512

Whitehall, Bill, 0880
Whiting, John T., 0319
Whittingham, Ken, 0979
Wien, Sandra, 1367
Wiesner, Philip J., 1277
Wietmarschen, Donald A., 1297
Wilder, L. A., 0158
Wilder, L. Arthur, 1194
Wilkinson, H. W., 1078
Wilkinson, W. E., 1195
Williams, G. W., 1196
Williams, John, 1052
Williams, Weldon C., III., 0016
Willson, Sally, 1012
Wilkinson, Allen P., 0545
Wilson, Darryl C., 1234
Wilson, Ryan S., 0640
Wilson, Shelley A., 0748
Wilson, Stephen R., 0539, 1035
Winer, Kimberly G., 1152
Winter, Bill, 0051
Winter, Ralph K., Jr., 0936
Wise, Richard M., 1146
Witte-Wegmann, Gertrud, 1075
Wolff, Maria Tai, 0246
Wolfgarten, A., 0541
Wong, Glenn M., 0073-0074,
    0194-0196, 0276, 0643, 0681,
    0912, 0962, 1007, 1130-1131
Woods, Richard P., 0041, 0044
Wray, Donald G., 1298
Wright, Charles Alan, 0641
Wulsin, Richard, 0354
Wust, Herbert, 0749

Yasser, Ray, 0434, 0441
Yasser, Raymond L., 1199
Yeam, Kevin W., 0881
Yeldell, Eric, 1240
York, Daniel S., 0913
Young, J. Timothy, 1226
Young, Rowland L., 0682

Zaritsky, Howard M., 1311-1313
Zbacnik, Robert, 1253
Zhakaeva, L. S., 1102

Zimmerman, Manfred, 1053
Zioiko, Lynn, 0002
Zollers, Frances E., 0338
Zollman, C., 0427
Zuckman, Harvey L., 0390

SUBJECT INDEX

The numbers in the subject index refer to page numbers in the text.

A.A.U., 14-15
Academic Standards, 102-103
Academics and the Student
  Athlete, 15
Accountability, 146-147
Aerobics, 165
Agent-Athlete Relationship,
  2-3
Agents, 1-10
Agents, Ethics and Abuses, 6-7
Agents, Litigation, 7
AIAW, 300
Amateur Athletics and
  Sports, 11-18, 181
Amortization, 278
Antitrust, 15, 19-25, 33-38,
  49-50, 69-74, 81, 104, 147-
  153, 183-187
Arbitration, 38-41, 187-188
Arena Rights, 209
Arkansas, 5
Association of Representa-
  tives of Professional
  Athletes, 3, 6
Assumption of Risk, 232-233
Athlete Rights, 220
Australia, 115, 117, 245
Austria, 117-118, 177
Autoracing, 167

Baseball, 27-47, 120, 159, 182-184,
  187-193, 196-198, 201-204, 207,
  232-233, 292, 294-297
Basketball, 49-51, 182-184,
  187-188, 191-194, 196,
  198, 201-204, 207-208,
  226, 292, 295-297
Belgium, 62, 168, 234
Betting, 54
Bibliographies, 104, 253
Billiards, 165
Black Athletes, 3
Blackouts, 267-269
Blair v. Washington State
  University, 301
Bowling, 165-166
Boxing, 53-55, 294
Brazil, 118, 178, 210
British Columbia, 134, 248
Broadcast Rights, 269-270
Buoniconti v. The Citadel
  et al., 132
Business of Professional
  Sports, 188-189

Cable, 270-271
California, 4, 5, 8, 14, 17, 57, 60,
  126, 131, 158, 171-172, 232,
  299
Camping, 168

Canada, 62, 74-75, 98, 115-
    116, 118-119, 138, 167,
    175, 193, 252, 283-285,
    293-294
Canoeing, 237
Cape v. Tennessee
    Secondary School Atheletic
    Association , 228, 230
Certification of Agents, 3-6
Albert Chandler, 27, 31
Chemical Substances, 57-63
City of Oakland v. Oakland
    Raiders, Ltd., 193, 198-
    202
Civil Liability, 91-92
Civil Rights, 65-66
Coaches and Discrimination,
    224
Coaches Liability, 127
Coaching of Amateur
    Athletics, 15-16
Collective Bargaining, 34, 41,
    50, 190-192, 204-205,
    208, 211
College Athletes, 105-106
Colorado, 14, 101, 134, 174,
    216
Commissioner, Professional
    Sports, 192
Commonwealth v.
    Pennsylvania
    Interscholastic Athletic
    Association, 300-301
Compensation, 81-82, 193
Condon v. Basi, 87, 94, 131
Contracts, 41-42, 75, 82, 193-196
Copyright, 210-211, 271-272
Corn Products Refining Co.
    v. Commissioner, 277
Correlates of the Culture of
    Sport, 243-245
Cricket, 168, 253
Criminal Law, 253, 293-294
Criminal Liability, 92
Cross-Ownership, 19, 24-25
Cycling, 168-169
Czechoslovakia, 89, 119

Defamation, 253-254
Denver Rockets v. All-Pro
    Management, Inc., 50, 189
Disciplinary Action, 197- 198
Discrimination in Sports, 65-66
Dog Racing, 169
Drug Testing, 58-62

Economics of Team
    Movement, 198-199
Edling v. Kansas City Baseball
    & Exhibition Company, 30
Eligibility Rules, 67-68
Entertainment 3, 22, 238
    252-253, 278
Environmental Impact, 245-246
Equal Rights Amendment,
    300-301
Equality, 225-226
Europe, 140, 167, 174, 235
European Economic
    Community, 65, 178
Expansion, 199

Federal Baseball Club of
    Baltimore v. National
    League of Professional
    Baseball, 21-22, 33-34, 36-38,
    43, 70, 72-73, 183-184, 186, 269
Federal Control of Sports, 42
Federal Income Tax, 278
Federal Intervention in
    Amateur Athletics, 16-17
Female Athletes, 302-303
Fencing, 166
Financing of Sports, 246
First Amendment and   Sports
    Events,   254
First Northwest Industries of
    America, Inc. v.
    Commissioner, 278, 287-288
Flood v. Kuhn, 21, 38, 33, 36-37,
    44-45, 188, 191, 208
Florida, 2, 95, 169
Football, 69-78, 182-184, 187-193,
    196, 198, 202-204, 207, 292,
    294-297

France, 119, 173-174, 239,
    255, 294
Franchise Relocation, 183,
    198, 199-203
Franchises, Taxes, 279
Free Agency, 203

Gambling, 246-247
Game Law, 239
Gardella v. Chandler, 21, 36, 43,
    45, 47, 70, 184, 269
Georgia, 2, 103
Golf, 79-80
Grove City College v. Bell,   113
Gymnastics, 159, 166

Hackbart v. Cincinnati
    Bengals, 88, 91-93, 95-96,
    132-133, 204
Handicapped Students, 107
Hawaii, 226
Higher Education, 106
Hockey, 68, 72, 81-83, 159,
    183, 188, 190, 192-194, 198,
    202-204, 207, 232-233, 292, 294-
    295, 297
Horseracing, 169-171, 197
Hunting, 159

Idaho, 217
Indiana, 2
Indoor Sports, 165-166
Injuries, 85-99
Insurance, 2
Intercollegiate Athletics,
    101-113
International Olympic
    Committee, 163-164, 242
International Sports Law,
    115-123
Interscholastic Sports, 11-12, 14-
    17, 127, 134, 157, 226, 228-230,
    259
Interstate Commerce, 43-44
Iowa, 215
Ireland, 119

Japan, 120
Judicial Review, 154-155, 255
Judicial Review, Sports
    Courts, 255-256
Judicial Treatment of Violence,
    295

Kansas, 28
Kapp v. NFL, 72, 77
Kayaking, 237
Kentucky, 12
Kuhn Bowie, 27, 31

Labor Laws, 256-257
Labor Relations, 203
Laird v. United States, 278,
    286-288
Judge Kenesaw Mountain
    Landis, 20, 27, 31, 41
Law and Sports, 257-259
Lawful Sport, 247
Legislation and Regulation
    of Violence, 295-296
Liability, 54-55, 125-138,
    203-204, 233
Litigation, 204, 259
Los Angeles Memorial
    Coliseum Commission v.
    NFL, 23, 29, 71

Mackey v. NFL, 49, 70-71, 74, 90
Maine, 179
Manufacturer Liability, 127-128
Martin v. International
    Olympic Committee, 224-
    225
Massachusetts, 175
Massachusetts Ski Act of 1978,
    13, 176
McCourt v. California
    Sports, Inc., 21, 81-83, 186, 204
Medical Care, 139-141
Medical Malpractice, 140-141
Mercury Bay Boating Club v.
    San Diego Yacht Club, 180
Michigan, 18, 173, 217

Minnesota, 2, 33, 249
Minority Athletes, 107
Minor League Baseball, 32-33,
    36, 183
Model University
    Coaching Contract, 16
Montana, 15
Motion Pictures, 55
Motorboating, 159
Mountain Climbing, 171-172
Municipal Play, 247-248

Nabozny v. Barnhill, 91-92,
    131-132, 220
National Basketball
    Association, 50-51
NCAA, 3, 6-8, 11-12, 14-15, 57-62,
    65, 101-107, 111, 211-212, 267,
    270, 300
National Collegiate Athletic
    Association (NCAA), 143-155
NCAA v. Board of Regents of
    The University of
    Oklahoma, 147-153
NCAA v. Tarkanian, 148,
    150-154
National Football League, 75-78
Negligence, 44, 80, 157-159
Nevada, 5
New Jersey, 53, 127, 182, 229, 254,
    263
New Mexico, 261
New York State, 53, 54, 122,
    137, 247
New Zealand, 120-121, 180, 261
NFL Collective Bargaining
    Agreement, 5, 22, 190- 191
NFL Draft, 69
NFLPA, 4-5, 59, 72-73, 76-78, 184
North American Soccer
    League v. NFL, 19, 24, 71
North Dakota, 158

Ohio, 2, 14, 60, 229, 248
Olympics, 116, 161-164
Ontario, 226
Oregon, 128, 302

Outdoor Sports, 167-180
Owner Liability, 128-130

Pan Am Games, 12
Participant Liability, 130-133
Participants, 92-97
Pennsylvania, 86, 94,
    127, 169, 300-301
Personal Manager, 3-4
Peter A. Rose v. A. Bartlett
    Giamatti, 255
Philadelphia Ball Club, Ltd. v.
    Lajoie, 30, 194
Playgrounds, 172, 217
Poland, 96, 121
Polo, 131
Post-Secondary Athletes   and
    the Law, 107-108
Post-Secondary Schools   and
    Discrimination, 227-228
PreSeason/Season Tickets, 23
Professional Athletes, 204-207
Professional Sports, 181-208
Professional Sports
    Community Protection
    Act of 1985, 200-202
Property, 209-213
Property Interests and
    Rights, 211-212
Proposition 48, 102

Qatar, 218
Quebec, 292

Radovich v. National
    Football League, 21, 25, 32,
    69-70, 72-73, 183-184, 186-187
Recreation and Recreational
    Sports, 215-218
Referee Liability, 133
Referee Rights, 220-221
Release Clauses, 44
Representational Contracts,
    8
Reserve Clause, 44-46
Reserve System, 82-83

Restraint of Trade, 23-24
Rhode Island, 17
RICO, 247
Right of Publicity, 272-273
Rights, 219-221
Role of Lawyer and Sports, 8-9
Romania, 167
Rozelle Rule, 75, 77-78, 204
Running, 172
Rutter v. Northeastern
    Beaver County School
    District, 86

Safety at Sports, 248
Sailing, 173
Salary Cap, 49-50
School Liability, 133-134
Secondary Schools and
    Discrimination, 228-230
Selig v. United States, 278-
    279, 286-287
Sex Discrimination, 17-18,
    223-230
Sex Discrimination
    Legislation, 226-227
SFAA v. USOC, 61, 209-120
Sherman Act, 24-25
Skiing, 130, 134-138, 159,
    173-177
Smith v. Pro-Football, 71, 75
Soccer, 159, 177-178, 182, 190,
    220, 261, 292, 294
Solicitation, 9
South Africa, 117
Southeastern Underwriters
    Association et al. v.
    United States, 21, 34
Soviet Olympic Committee, 58
Soviet Union, 205, 239, 241, 244
Spain, 121, 237
Spectator Liability, 138
Spectators, 97-99, 231-236
Sport, 237-250
Sports and Legal Controls,
    259-261
Sports and the Law, 251-263
Sports as a Nuisance, 249
Sports Associations, 241-243

Sports Aviation, 178-179
Sports Broadcasting and
    Programming, 265-273
Sports Clubs, 241-243
Sports Facilities, 159
Sports Federations, 241-243
Sports Lawyers, 1-2, 5-6, 8-9,
    27, 89
Sports Societies, 241-243
Sports Violence Act of 1980, 295-
    296
Stadia, 249
Strikes, 207
Substance Abuse, 62-63
Sunday Laws, 261-263
Sunday v. Stratton Corp.,
    134-135, 158, 173
Swimming, 159, 275-276
Switzerland, 175

Taiwan, 115, 122
Tax Aspects, 279-281
Tax Reform Act of 1976, 282,
    287-288
Taxation, 277-289
Taxation of Professional
Taxation of Professional
Tax Shelters, 281-282
Tennessee, 2
Tennis, 179
Texas, 4, 17
Title IX, 109-113
Trade Regulations, 47
Tomjanovich v. California
    Sports, Inc., 96, 204
Toolson v. New York
    Yankees, 34-35, 45, 69-70, 72-
    73, 183-184, 186
Tort Law, 263
Torts, 46, 233-234
Trademark Protection, 212- 213
Treaty of Nairobi, 161

Unionization, 208
United Kingdom, 98, 115,
    121-122, 138, 238, 249, 262-
    263, 292, 294

United States, 98, 122-123,
      138, 140, 238, 258, 260, 262-
      263, 291, 293
United States v.
      International Boxing Club,
      25, 69, 72-73, 183-184, 186
United States Olympic
      Committee, 58, 209-210, 212
USFL v. NFL, 74, 76, 186, 266-
      267
Unlawful Sports, 249-250
Utah, 134, 215

Vermont, 158
Violence, 234-236, 291-298
Violence in Professional
      Sports, 296-298
Virginia, 261

Washington, 128, 158-159
Watersports, 179
West Germany, 123, 171, 256
Windsurfing, 173
Women in Sports, 299-303
Workman's Compensation, 14-
      15, 105
WTWV v. National Football
      League, 268-269

Yachting, 179-180
Yellow Springs Exempted
      Village School District
      Board of Education v.
      Ohio High School Athletic
      Association, 299

About the Compilers

JOHN HLADCZUK is President of X/L Management and director of the Center for Interdisciplinary Studies in Knoxville, Tennessee and East Amherst, New York. He is the author of *International Handbook of Reading Education* (forthcoming, 1992) with William Eller and a compiler with Sharon Hladczuk and others of the academically acclaimed *General Issues in Illiteracy: A Bibliography* (1990), among other works.

SHARON HLADCZUK is an associate with the Center for Interdisciplinary Studies in Knoxville, Tennessee and East Amherst, New York.

CRAIG SLATER is a department chairman for Saperston & Day, P.C., law firm in Buffalo, New York concentrating in litigation and corporation law.

ADAM EPSTEIN is a current JD/MBA student at the University of Tennessee.